WOBBLIES OF THE WORLD

Wildcat: Workers' Movements and Global Capitalism

Series Editors:
Peter Alexander (University of Johannesburg)
Immanuel Ness (City University of New York)
Tim Pringle (SOAS, University of London)
Malehoko Tshoaedi (University of Pretoria)

Workers' movements are a common and recurring feature in contemporary capitalism. The same militancy that inspired the mass labour movements of the twentieth century continues to define worker struggles that proliferate throughout the world today.

For more than a century labour unions have mobilised to represent the political-economic interests of workers by uncovering the abuses of capitalism, establishing wage standards, improving oppressive working conditions, and bargaining with employers and the state. Since the 1970s, organised labour has declined in size and influence as the global power and influence of capital has expanded dramatically. The world over, existing unions are in a condition of fracture and turbulence in response to neoliberalism, financialisation, and the reappearance of rapacious forms of imperialism. New and modernised unions are adapting to conditions and creating class-conscious workers' movement rooted in militancy and solidarity. Ironically, while the power of organised labour contracts, working-class militancy and resistance persists and is growing in the Global South.

Wildcat publishes ambitious and innovative works on the history and political economy of workers' movements and is a forum for debate on pivotal movements and labour struggles. The series applies a broad definition of the labour movement to include workers in and out of unions, and seeks works that examine proletarianisation and class formation; mass production; gender, affective and reproductive labour; imperialism and workers; syndicalism and independent unions, and labour and Leftist social and political movements.

Also available:

Just Work? Migrant Workers' Struggles Today
Edited by Aziz Choudry and Mondli Hlatshwayo

Southern Insurgency: The Coming of the Global Working Class
Immanuel Ness

The Spirit of Marikana: The Rise of Insurgent Trade Unionism in South Africa
Luke Sinwell with Siphiwe Mbatha

Working the Phones: Control and Resistance in Call Centres
Jamie Woodcock

Wobblies of the World

A Global History of the IWW

Edited by Peter Cole, David Struthers,
and Kenyon Zimmer

PLUTO  PRESS

First published 2017 by Pluto Press
345 Archway Road, London N6 5AA

www.plutobooks.com

British Library Cataloguing in Publication Data
A catalogue record for this book is available from the British Library

ISBN 978 0 7453 9960 7 Hardback
ISBN 978 0 7453 9959 1 Paperback
ISBN 978 1 7868 0151 7 PDF eBook
ISBN 978 1 7868 0153 1 Kindle eBook
ISBN 978 1 7868 0152 4 EPUB eBook

This book is printed on paper suitable for recycling and made from fully managed and sustained forest sources. Logging, pulping and manufacturing processes are expected to conform to the environmental standards of the country of origin.

Typeset by Curran Publishing Services, Norwich, England

Simultaneously printed in the United Kingdom and United States of America

Contents

Acknowledgments   *vii*

Introduction   1

Part I: Transnational Influences on the IWW   27

1   "A Cosmopolitan Crowd": Transnational Anarchists, the IWW, and the American Radical Press   29
Kenyon Zimmer

2   Sabotage, the IWW, and Repression: How the American Reinterpretation of a French Concept Gave Rise to a New International Conception of Sabotage   44
Dominique Pinsolle

3   Living Social Dynamite: Early Twentieth-Century IWW–South Asia Connections   59
Tariq Khan

4   IWW Internationalism and Interracial Organizing in the Southwestern United States   74
David M. Struthers

5   Spanish Anarchists and Maritime Workers in the IWW   89
Bieito Alonso

Part II: The IWW in the Wider World   103

6   The IWW and the Dilemmas of Labor Internationalism   105
Wayne Thorpe

7   The IWW in Tampico: Anarchism, Internationalism, and Solidarity Unionism in a Mexican Port   124
Kevan Antonio Aguilar

8   The Wobblies of the North Woods: Finnish Labor Radicalism and the IWW in Northern Ontario   140
Saku Pinta

9   "We Must Do Away with Racial Prejudice and Imaginary Boundary Lines": British Columbia's Wobblies before the First World War   156
Mark Leier

10 Wobblies Down Under: The IWW in Australia   168
   Verity Burgmann

11 Ki Nga Kaimahi Maori ("To All Maori Workers"): The
New Zealand IWW and the Maori   186
   Mark Derby

12 Patrick Hodgens Hickey and the IWW: A Transnational
Relationship   204
   Peter Clayworth

13 "The Cause of the Workers Who Are Fighting in Spain Is
Yours": The Marine Transport Workers and the Spanish
Civil War   212
   Matthew White

14 Edith Frenette: A Transnational Radical Life   228
   Heather Mayer

Part III: Beyond the Union: The IWW's Influence and Legacies   237

15 Jim Larkin, James Connolly, and the Dublin Lockout of
1913: The Transnational Path of Global Syndicalism   239
   Marjorie Murphy

16 Tom Barker and Revolutionary Europe   253
   Paula de Angelis

17 P. J. Welinder and "American Syndicalism" in Interwar
Sweden   262
   Johan Pries

18 "All Workers Regardless Of Craft, Race Or Color": The First
Wave of IWW Activity and Influence in South Africa   271
   Lucien van der Walt

19 Tramp, Tramp, Tramp: The Songs of Joe Hill Around the
World   288
   Bucky Halker

Index   *301*

Acknowledgments

Like many great ideas, this book was born while drinking beers with friends. The three of us were presenting papers on our different research projects during the 2008 conference of the Pacific Northwest Labor History Association. Dave and Kenyon already were friends and met Peter, for the first time, that rainy weekend in Vancouver. We vaguely discussed putting together a book on the history of the Wobblies around the world, but promptly forgot about our idea—like many such grand alcohol-fueled notions. Over the next few years, we emailed each other intermittently, and even organized a panel on the topic at the 2012 meeting of the American Historical Association, but all of us were busy with various other work and life commitments. Eventually, in 2015, our lives converged, windows opened, the sun shone, and we finally undertook this project. From there, it moved surprisingly fast. We already knew many other folks, around the world, who shared our interest in—or rather, fascination with—the Wobblies. We reached out to many of them and put out a "call for papers" to make sure we reached a wider network of scholars, both in the academy and outside of it, who studied the IWW.

We would like to thank every contributor to the book who (for the most part) submitted drafts on time, and all of whom were passionate about the project. We are proud of this book and trust everyone else involved is, too. We also thank one of the Wildcat series editors, Manny Ness, for his steadfast and enthusiastic support from the get-go, as well as the six anonymous reviewers who commented on the project. Thanks, also, to David Shulman at Pluto Press and the incredible team of committed, skilled workers who help this global publishing house spread the word about the Wobs and so many other important subjects, past and present.

Peter Cole thanks his partner, Wendy Pearlman, who listened to countless tales about the Wobblies (some of them even true), and provided moral and intellectual support; he also thanks his co-conspirators (um, co-editors) for their friendship and thoughtfulness. Dave Struthers thanks his wife Irina Shklovski for listening to him talk about the past, his daughter Freya for taking him to the skatepark, Devra Weber for first introducing him to the IWW in a labor history seminar, his co-plotters for making this collaboration a pleasure, and the contributors for keeping him excited every time he sat down to read drafts. Kenyon Zimmer thanks his wife Rafia Mirza for her support throughout, Salvatore Salerno for first introducing him to the hidden anarchist connections to the IWW, Robert Helms for taking time out of a visit to the International Institute of Social History in Amsterdam to scan rare documents for him, and his co-editors for their hard work, patience, and humor.

Finally, we would like to thank all of those, dead and alive, who keep the Wobbly flames burning. We know that Wobblies and fellow travelers are committed to a more just and equitable world. So are we—that's why we imagined and, now, helped create this book. Thanks for reading!

Introduction

Peter Cole,
David Struthers, and Kenyon Zimmer

This book proudly proclaims itself the first-ever global history of the Industrial Workers of the World (IWW, or Wobblies). In this collection of essays, 20 scholars from around the world begin a long-overdue conversation about the IWW as a global phenomenon. Although the union's official membership never was numerically as large as mainstream unions, its influence during its early years—1905 into the 1920s—was enormous in the United States, where it was founded, and worldwide. The IWW was part of a global upsurge of anarchism and syndicalism, which in the early twentieth century, before the Russian Revolution and birth of the Soviet Union, arguably occupied the central positions among the global Left as the dominant anti-capitalist ideologies. Subsequent scholarship focusing on western Europe and those leftist currents that fed into social democratic state structures has obscured the influence and vibrancy of anarchism and syndicalism around the world. Syndicalism envisioned replacing capitalism with a socialist economy, but simultaneously, maintained great suspicion of state power and centrally planned systems, and viewed the labor movement as the primary vehicle for revolutionary change. In every industrial and industrializing nation in the world, varieties of syndicalism emerged by the early twentieth century, but few were better known or more globally influential than the IWW's "revolutionary industrial unionism."

Wobbly ideals, Wobbly branches, and Wobbly members traveled far and wide, gaining adherents and fellow-travelers across the proverbial seven seas, with sailors and shipping being central, then as now, to the global economy. However, nearly all scholars who have examined the IWW focus narrowly on the IWW experience in a single nation, usually the United States, and neglect the rich archive of non-English-language sources.[1]

Fortunately, in 2017, the world and even academic scholarship are changing. In recent years, global and world history have become major academic fields, dramatically remaking how many historians research, write, and teach about the past. Hence, assessing the history of the IWW on a global scale—considering its worldwide reach and influence—screams for attention. Similarly, historians and other scholars increasingly employ comparative and transnational frameworks. Again, considering the global nature of the organization and its ideals, assessing the IWW using these methods seems practically mandatory. The Wobblies themselves understood these matters more than a century ago. They founded their organization as a self-consciously global union; indeed, its very name suggested that, since capitalism was (and remains) global, so must be a revolutionary movement of the working class. In recent years some writers have begun to pay greater attention to how Wobblies, like other syndicalists and radicals, routinely crossed and transgressed borders, bringing their ideas and tactical strategies with them and adapting them to new circumstances. The contributors to this volume are among those scholars who utilize these new methods to analyze the Wobbly phenomenon.

This book assembles a selection of essays on the IWW as a worldwide movement. At its peak, the organization enrolled members and established branches in literally dozens of countries, and its organizers and sympathizers traveled to many more to work, agitate, educate, and organize. Although founded in the United States and with far more members there than in any other nation, Wobblies dreamed of overthrowing capitalism worldwide and far too many scholars have chosen to ignore "the World" in the organization's title. This book, then, outlines a global history of the Wobblies and deploys comparative and transnational methods to widen our gaze. It is a collaborative and international effort, as the linguistic skills and far-flung archival digging needed to research the global dimensions of the IWW limit the ability of any single scholar to write this history alone. Thus, an edited volume more effectively pulls together the talents of a diverse group of researchers to uncover the transnational and multilingual organizing of the IWW. In the twenty-first century, interest in the Wobblies, who still organize in countries around the globe, remains high. This book does not intend to—and cannot—be a comprehensive history of the IWW, but the following section provides a brief introduction and history for readers unfamiliar with the organization.

Who Were the Wobblies?

The IWW captured the imagination of a generation of workers and rebels, in the United States and around the globe, with its fiery rhetoric, daring tactics, and program of revolutionary industrial unionism. Pledging to replace the narrow craft unionism of the American Federal of Labor (AFL) with massive industrial unions strong enough to overthrow capitalism, the organization grew in numbers and reputation in the years before the First World War by organizing workers neglected by the AFL, notably immigrants in the Northeast, migratory farmworkers in the Great Plains, and multiethnic mine, timber, and harvest workers in the West. Simultaneously, Wobbly ideas, members, and publications began to spread beyond the borders of the United States—to Mexico and Canada, into the Caribbean and Latin America, to Europe, Africa, Asia, and Australasia in rapid succession. The expansion of the IWW and its ideals across the world within a single decade is a testament to their power, as well as the passionate commitment of many members and supporters. However, the IWW's revolutionary program and class-war rhetoric yielded more enemies than allies.

The IWW was born in 1905, the same year as the first, albeit failed, Russian Revolution. On January 2, 1905, several dozen people identifying as "industrial unionists" met in Chicago and issued a call to form a new labor union. They declared that "The great facts of present industry are the displacement of human skill by machines and the increase of capitalist power through concentration in the possession of the tools with which wealth is produced and distributed." Accordingly, that June several hundred people belonging to more than 40 unions and radical organizations returned to Chicago, where they founded the Industrial Workers of the World. The largest union represented was the Western Federation of Miners (WFM). Eugene V. Debs and other members of the Socialist Party of America (SPA) along with Daniel De Leon of the Socialist Labor Party (SLP) attended. So did Lucy Parsons, a prominent anarchist and widow of Albert Parsons, one of Chicago's Haymarket Martyrs, and Mary Harris "Mother" Jones, a freethinking socialist and union organizer most closely associated with the United Mine Workers. Numerous less famous radicals and organizers also took part in the proceedings as informal delegates, including Spanish anarchists Pedro Esteve and Florencio Bazora. William D. "Big Bill" Haywood, a WFM leader, presided over the gathering, which he called the "Continental Congress of the Working Class," a reference to the body formed in 1775 that declared and helped lead the American Revolution. Haywood hoped the IWW would lead a new revolution to emancipate workers from "the slave bondage of capitalism."[2]

On July 8, attendees adopted the now-legendary Preamble to the IWW's Constitution, which boldly and famously declared:

The working class and the employing class have nothing in common. There can be no peace so long as hunger and want are found among millions of the working people and the few, who make up the employing class, have all the good things in life. Between these two classes a struggle must go on until all the toilers come together ... and take and hold that which they produce by their labor.

Clearly, the IWW believed in class struggle and the need for a proletarian revolution to bring socialism to the world. However, unlike most socialists, and later communists, be they in the Soviet Union or elsewhere, the IWW did not privilege political means (or armed struggle) for achieving socialist ends. Rather, the IWW and other syndicalist organizations saw industrial unions, direct action on the job, and the climactic general strike as the logical and best ways to enact revolutionary change. Already in 1905, and even more so after 1908, this ideological distinction mattered a great deal.

The IWW, from its inception, committed itself to organizing all workers regardless of their ethnic, national, racial, or gender identities. Article 1, Section 1 of the Constitution's By-Laws declared, "No workingman or woman shall be excluded from membership in local unions because of creed or color." The founders made this point clear because of the noted racism, sexism, and xenophobia of many unionists in the AFL, as well as in organizations claiming to be socialist. For instance, the Socialist Party compromised its principles of class struggle by supporting Asian exclusion, and in some cases racial segregation, in order to recruit and maintain the membership of racist white members.[3] In 1906 and 1907, the IWW helped organize striking factory workers in Paterson, New Jersey and Bridgeport, Connecticut, many of whom were Italian immigrants in Paterson and Hungarian immigrants in Bridgeport. The IWW continued to organize unskilled and immigrant factory workers across the industrial cities of the United States, and soon other nations.

The IWW, while mighty in imagination, started off small. Its first big victory occurred among gold miners in Goldfield, Nevada, where lengthy boycotts and strikes won the eight-hour day. Despite this collaboration with the IWW, the WFM soon withdrew from the organization, highlighting the tensions that the IWW and other radical unions continued—and continue—to grapple with, namely how to agitate for and win short-term gains while also fighting for socialist revolution.

Similarly, those committed to political parties as an important means of struggle, led by Daniel De Leon, left the IWW in 1908. This group, primarily connected to the SLP, abandoned the IWW but refused to go quietly into the night. Instead they formed an alternative IWW, nicknamed the "Detroit IWW" for its new headquarters location. Another such split later occurred with the SPA, as individuals had to choose between the more radical IWW or more moderate SPA, which supported an electoral path towards socialism, also called evolutionary or democratic socialism. Haywood, for instance, had been elected to the SPA National Executive Committee in 1912, but was recalled the following year as part of a campaign against "direct actionists" within the party; thousands of other Wobblies who also belonged to the SPA joined Haywood in abandoning it. The splits inside the American IWW were replicated, time and again, in other countries where socialists (and later, communists) broke with syndicalists and anarchists over the proper path to socialism.

The IWW also faced challenges from employers and city, state, and national governments that opposed the Wobblies for both pragmatic and ideological reasons. Among the earliest attempts to quash the IWW was an elaborate, multi-state, corporate-backed effort to frame Haywood and two other WFM leaders for the murder of a former Idaho governor in the first so-called "trial of the century." Although Haywood and the others were found not guilty in 1908, anti-IWW repression had only just begun.[4]

The IWW's "free speech fights" proved among the most noteworthy chapters in its US history. The first broke out in 1909 in Spokane, Washington, an important employment center in the Pacific Northwest for migratory workers in timber, agriculture, and construction. Many laborers wintered in Spokane until work picked up in the spring, but employment "sharks" preyed on these workers by collaborating with employers by charging "fees" for jobs. In response, Wobbly street speakers in Spokane urged workers to boycott the sharks and force employers to hire workers directly, without fees. When employment agencies convinced the city council to ban street speakers, the IWW announced its first "free speech fight." The *Industrial Worker* announced: "Wanted—men to fill the jails of Spokane." Sure enough, footloose Wobblies traveled to Spokane and deliberately broke this law, and the city arrested them—500 in the first month. After four months of beatings and arrests, with the jails overflowing, the IWW won: all its members were released from prison, the ordinance was overturned, and licenses of "sharks" revoked. Despite this victory, other cities copied Spokane's repressive efforts, and some of these cities beat back the IWW's organizing efforts.[5]

Another signature chapter in Wobbly history was the "Bread and Roses" textile strike in Lawrence, Massachusetts in 1912. In the nineteenth century the New England-based textile industry had been the domain of native-born workers, but technological changes led to deskilling and the rise of immigrant labor. By the 1900s, workers hailed from over 20 nations and spoke 50 languages, with the majority of workers female and many children. Their situation was atrocious: poverty wages, long hours, and tyrannical, racist, sexist managers. Thirty-six percent of mill workers died by age 25! Their strike began when employers cut wages. Though some already belonged to unions, tens of thousands walked out—led by Italian women who claimed it was "better to starve fighting than starve working." Predictably, the local police and state militia soon arrived to assist the employers. Also typically, the AFL refused to assist because the strikers were "unskilled," female, and immigrant. The IWW entered the picture, dispatching Italians Joe Ettor and Arturo Giovannitti who helped establish strike and relief committees in which each nationality had representatives, with literature and speeches distributed in many languages. In the dead of winter, pickets marched 24 hours a day, constantly moving to avoid city injunctions. Women strikers were arrested en masse, and one Italian woman was murdered; although strikers testified that a soldier killed her, Ettor and Giovannitti were arrested. After two months and national publicity, 20,000 voted unanimously to accept a 25 percent increase in wages for the lowest-paid workers with lower raises for the higher-paid, new overtime rates, along with no discrimination against strikers.[6] A strike by nearly 25,000 silk workers in Paterson, New Jersey in 1913, where Italian anarchists had established an IWW local in 1906, shared much in common with Lawrence—a largely immigrant, heavily female workforce which the AFL had shunned proved themselves quite interested in the militant, leftist IWW.[7]

Similarly, the IWW organized in the supposedly impossible American South, where black and white workers managed to overcome pervasive racism to form the Brotherhood of Timber Workers (BTW). Despite laws and customs that prevented interracial or biracial unionism, the BTW, which emerged independently but quickly affiliated with the IWW, lined up tens of thousands of black and white men in Louisiana and Texas. From 1910 to 1913, employers used lockouts, strikebreakers, private police forces (including Pinkertons), and racism to prevent workers from organizing. This campaign gave lie to the notion that the IWW could not organize in the South, among rural workers, or across racial lines. The IWW successfully organized timber workers, primarily in the Northwest, for many years to come. Only the concerted, repressive effort of the US government, including the deployment of Army troops to break strikes and replace Wobblies, prevented the IWW from dominating this industry into the 1920s.[8]

The other major IWW effort to organize African Americans occurred on the Philadelphia waterfront where, for almost a decade, the IWW's Marine Transport Workers Local 8 dominated one of the nation's largest ports. As in Louisiana's piney woods and Massachusetts' textile mills, on Philadelphia's docks employers of longshoremen—those who load and unload cargo—had built a diverse workforce that was roughly one-third African American, one-third European immigrant, and one-third Irish American. Such heterogeneity often prevented workers from organizing effectively, but the IWW directly challenged this issue. Born out of a successful strike in 1913, Local 8 represented upwards of 5,000 dockworkers, among them the Wobblies' most well-known African American, Ben Fletcher. A brilliant speaker and organizer, Fletcher, together with other Wobbly organizers—black and white, native-born and immigrant—forced employers to hire Local 8 members exclusively for nearly a decade. As in the Northwest's woods, the government collaborated with employers (as well as the AFL's longshore union) to undermine the Wobblies. Unlike most other places, Local 8 held onto power until nearly 1923 before succumbing to ferocious pressures and repression, and it remains the Wobblies' most impressive example of interracial unionism—perhaps the most integrated union in the United States in its time.[9]

In the mid-1910s, the IWW also organized among migratory farmworkers in the nation's many agricultural regions, especially the Great Plains and California. Despite the need of employers for seasonal workers, massive labor surpluses translated into poverty wage rates, long days, and horrible working conditions. The AFL considered migratory farmworkers unorganizable but the IWW proved that such workers were ready and willing to unionize. In 1913, for example, Wobblies agitated among thousands of laborers who showed up in Wheatland, California to harvest hops. Notably, the workers spoke several dozen languages, and it was one of the first times the IWW organized Asian immigrants—another taboo for the AFL, which openly vilified Asian workers. The awful living and working conditions proved a good base for protest and organizing. Local police helped the management by trying to arrest Wobbly organizers, resulting in a violent clash. Several people were killed, and two IWW organizers were later charged with murder, in what came to be known as the Wheatland hop riots. Soon thereafter, in 1915, the Wobblies launched the Agricultural Workers Organization (AWO), which eventually lined up 20,000 workers in the Midwest and Plains, most of whom traveled by train and followed the agricultural season from planting to harvest, south to north, and back again. The tremendous success of the AWO helped revitalize the entire IWW in the mid-1910s.[10]

The economies and workforces of North America always have been intertwined, and the IWW was present in Canada and Mexico almost from the start. Semi-autonomous "national administrations" of the IWW were created in both countries. As Wobbly influence expanded globally, other national administrations formed in England, Australia, New Zealand, South Africa, Chile, and briefly Sweden. The Chilean IWW alone enrolled at least 9–10,000 members by 1920, and was a powerful national union until repressed by Chile's government in 1927. In addition, IWW locals also formed in Argentina, Cuba, Ecuador, Germany, Japan, Peru, Russia, and Uruguay, as well as in the US territories of Guam and Puerto Rico. De Leon's breakaway "Detroit IWW" (renamed the Workers' International Industrial Union in 1915) likewise established locals in Canada, Britain, Australia, and South Africa before dissolving in 1924.[11] True to its name, the IWW reached almost every corner of the globe.

Everywhere, Wobblies faced severe resistance. Frequently jailed or beaten when they tried to organize, American Wobblies faced even graver consequences after the United States mobilized for war in 1917. One such example, even before the war, was the Everett Massacre; in 1916, hundreds of Seattle Wobblies aboard a ferry traveling to nearby Everett were fired upon from shore by local law enforcement, resulting in seven killed, and the Wobblies being charged for the troubles. Once the US formally declared war, federal and state governments moved to suppress the organization, imprisoning hundreds of Wobblies, deporting others, and passing criminal syndicalism laws that made membership in the union a crime. Vigilantes also targeted Wobblies with extralegal, sometimes lethal violence. Inside the IWW, the question of what stand to take on the war proved quite divisive. When the conflict originally broke out in Europe, US Wobblies condemned it in typically socialist fashion: the "real" war, they claimed, was the class war, whereas wars between nations simply resulted in working-class people killing each other on behalf of the ruling class. However, Wobblies were quite mindful that, once the United States officially declared war in April 1917, the situation could be used to attack the union. Hence the IWW officially took no stand for or against the war, although many Wobblies were openly and loudly anti-war—most famously Frank Little, a legendary organizer brutally murdered in Butte, Montana in August 1917.[12]

Ultimately, the Espionage and Sedition Acts of 1917–18 were used as battering rams which drastically weakened the IWW. Only a few months after formally declaring war in 1917, President Woodrow Wilson's administration targeted the IWW for destruction. Two thousand local and state law enforcement officers rounded up about 1,200 striking copper miners

"M.T.A. Offensiv I Europa (M.T.W. Offensive in Europe)," *Marinarbetaren* (Stockholm), February 1, 1921. This cartoon from the Swedish affiliate of the ɪww's Marine Transport Worker's Industrial Union shows the ᴍᴛᴡ spreading throughout Europe, while businessmen cry, "Oh God help us poor ship owners," and "Help! The ɪ.w.w. is coming."

and family members in Bisbee, Arizona, and illegally dumped them in the New Mexico desert; they remained confined at a US Army camp for several months while the federal government did nothing. In September 1917, federal agents raided ɪww offices across the nation and arrested hundreds of ɪww leaders in this and subsequent raids. Multiple federal and state courts put these Wobblies on trial in 1917 and 1918. The largest and most important trial took place in Chicago, where 101 Wobblies were charged with violating the Espionage and Sedition Acts. After more than four months, in the largest and longest federal trial in US history to that time, a jury found every defendant guilty after spending less than an hour deliberating. The Wobblies were sentenced to federal prison for terms ranging from one to 20 years and given crushingly large fines.[13]

The ɪww continued to operate after the war, in some places quite effectively, despite being greatly weakened. In Philadelphia, Local 8 pulled off its largest strike ever in 1920 to push for raises and the eighthour day, and Wobbly dockworkers and sailors organized out of dozens of ports in the United States and throughout the Atlantic. In the woods of the Pacific Northwest, timber workers continued to follow the ɪww. So, too, did workers tenaciously carry its red card in copper mines in the

Mountain West, the iron mines of Michigan and Minnesota, wheat fields of the Plains, and industrial cities across the nation. As Fred Thompson, the first historian of the IWW who was also a Wobbly, noted, US membership in the IWW actually peaked in 1923. Of course, numbers do not tell the entire story, but the event that finally rent the organization asunder was the 1924 schism over what was referred to as the Emergency Program. This was a confusing episode involving rifts over how much power the central administration should possess over locals, the union's stance on post-war commutations and pardons of Wobbly prisoners, as well as relations with the Communist Party and Communist International, all of which the federal government manipulated toward a destructive climax.[14] Of course, the IWW survived, with pockets of real influence persisting locally and internationally into the 1930s, and it remains active today, but it never regained the momentum of its early years.[15]

Wobbly Historiography

In 2003, longtime Wobbly Franklin Rosemont complained, "Amazingly, after all these years, there is nothing even faintly resembling a comprehensive and reliable history of the union."[16] During its heyday in the 1910s rivers of ink were spilled writing about the IWW, but much was sensationalistic and outright hostile. Sympathetic sociologists Paul F. Brissenden and Louis Levine wrote the best contemporary studies and recognized the union's syndicalist character, but both authors emphasized the American roots of the IWW in response to accusations that the Wobblies were mere imitators of the French syndicalists. Brissenden did note, "The activities of the I.W.W. are by no means confined to the United States and Canada," but he failed to explore its international reach "because of the difficulty of getting at the facts of the situation." The only contemporary treatment of the IWW as both part of the transnational rise of syndicalism and an international organization came, instead, in *The New Unionism* (1913), a popular study of syndicalism by André Tridon, the American correspondent for the French syndicalist paper *La Bataille syndicaliste*. For decades thereafter little scholarly writing on the IWW occurred, partially owing to the limited popularity of labor history more generally. The only significant study of the interwar years was John S. Gambs's narrowly conceived *The Decline of the I.W.W.* (1932), which dedicated just four paragraphs to the union's activities abroad and concluded, "The organization itself does not lay claim to having done much by way of international organization."[17]

Interest in the IWW by scholars and the general public exploded in the

1960s, when social upheavals rocked nations around the globe. Many people looked to the organization as one of the most dramatic, passionate, and thoughtful examples of a radical past with lessons for those seeking for answers in the present. The most important historical surveys of the IWW—regarded as the standard works to this day—were written in the 1960s by Melvyn Dubofsky and Philip Foner, accompanied by a popular treatment by British journalist Patrick Renshaw. Dubofsky and Foner made little mention of the IWW outside the United States, and although Renshaw included an 18-page "Postscript" surveying IWW activities abroad, it was treated separately from the rest of his narrative. Moreover, all three authors relied exclusively on English-language sources. Even the wonderfully creative *Rebel Voices*, edited by Joyce Kornbluh in 1964, fell into the same trap of focusing exclusively on the United States and English-language sources. When Dubofsky revised his book in the late 1980s and Joseph McCartin abridged it in 2000, the focus on the United States remained, and Renshaw's 1999 updated edition expanded his coverage of neither foreign-language nor international aspects of Wobbly history. The most prominent recent history and analysis of the IWW in the United States, by Eric Chester, falls into the same limited historiographical mold.[18]

Another problem of these works is their dated methodologies. These major surveys, now more than half a century old, are institutional histories that largely ignore gender, race, and culture, aside from Dubofsky's employment of a now-discarded "culture of poverty" theory in his original edition. Meanwhile, Foner was a strict Marxist who interpreted the IWW as a precursor to the Communist Party which suffered from ideological "errors." This generation of literature also minimized transnational influences on the IWW and its connections to the global syndicalist movement, at times arguing against using the "syndicalist" label at all, a position most stridently made by historian Joseph R. Conlin.[19] Most subsequent histories of the IWW—many of them quite excellent—continued to focus on a particular location, industry, individual, or strike within the United States, and to rely on English sources.[20] Thus, as Devra Weber noted:

> Many studies have viewed the IWW through a paradigmatic lens of what it was not: a geographically rooted union, bounded by the U.S. nation-state, and composed of Anglo-Americans or immigrants in the process of "becoming American." Understandably, this lens has yielded an IWW that failed: failed to develop as a permanent union, failed to understand the nature of U.S. workers' "job consciousness," and failed to lastingly change the United States.[21]

These earlier historians might be excused for writing surveys and mono-graphs of the IWW that exclusively examined the Wobbly experience in the United States, though perhaps not for their neglect of the rich and well-archived store of multilingual IWW periodicals and other documents.

Beginning in the 1970s and 1980s, however, a handful of scholars—some of them contributors to this volume—began studying the IWW in other countries, such as Australia, New Zealand, Canada, Chile, and Mexico. Yet for many years, one of the only studies of the IWW in Latin America was an unpublished 1974 manuscript by Peter DeShazo and Robert J. Halsted, read by and circulated among a handful of specialists.[22] This research spawned several comparative studies of the IWW in the Anglophone world, but sur-prisingly little work has otherwise been done to connect these disparate narratives or to incorporate their findings into new surveys of the IWW.[23] For example, when the IWW published a revised and expanded version of Wobbly Fred Thompson's 1955 history of the union in 2006, it included only a two-page addendum briefly summarizing IWW activities outside of the United States—less coverage than Renshaw's book had included three decades earlier.[24] Meanwhile, autonomist Marxists in Germany and Italy looked to the IWW to inform their theories of worker self-activity, class recomposition, and the "mass worker" of industrial capitalism, but this materialist approach, although breaking from an institutional and Leninist framework, also paid scant attention to transnationalism or non-English sources.[25] Little of this work, in turn, was translated into English and, accordingly, it has been widely ignored by American historians.

In the 1970s and 1980s, scholars in the growing fields of ethnic history[26] and gender history[27] also began looking to the IWW, producing a plethora of important case studies. However, gender and women's historians still tended to rely on English-language sources, whereas ethnic historians inevitably limited their scope to a single immigrant or linguistic group. Nevertheless, these works did expand comparative and transnational frameworks for studying the IWW. Since the 1980s, a number of international scholars also charted the interconnected rise of syndicalist movements throughout the world in the late nineteenth and early twentieth centuries, and finally, placed the IWW firmly within this global phenomenon.[28]

Salvatore Salerno's *Red November, Black November: Culture and Community in the Industrial Workers of the World* (1989) was a ground-breaking attempt to integrate many of these disparate threads into a new understanding of the Wobblies. Departing from earlier historians like Dubofsky, Salerno framed the IWW as more of a social movement, rather than a formal organization, and focused on the interplay between "indigenous" American and transatlantic factors in the development of the IWW, with a particular focus on the ideological and cultural influence of European syndicalism and anarchism. The preceding scholarship, he rightly argued, was "seriously flawed for its lack of analysis and underestimation of the role played by immigrant rank-and-file activists who carried European traditions of revolutionary unionism into the American labor movement." Although *Red November, Black November* was hampered by Salerno's own linguistic limitations at the time, his subsequent research in Italian-language sources confirmed and expanded the arguments he first put forth in the book.[29] Franklin Rosemont's less academic, if more ambitious, *Joe Hill: The IWW and the Making of a Revolutionary Workingclass Counterculture* (2003) similarly brought together new historical approaches and recent research in areas like gender, race, and culture, but was limited in its international scope to Joe Hill's Swedish origins and the Wobbly songwriter's brief forays into Mexico and Canada.[30]

Just as the rise of the New Left in the 1960s sparked interest in the Wobblies so, too, have recent social movements (anti-globalization, Occupy Wall Street, the Arab Spring, and so on) revived interest in the IWW. Dozens of articles, dissertations, and books about the union have appeared since the 1990s, as well as new editions of classic texts by and about the Wobblies, and even a graphic history.[31] Furthermore, a number of recent works on a variety of transnational topics include significant material on the IWW both in the United States and abroad.[32] As historian Paul Buhle noted on the 2005 centenary of the IWW's formation:

> The globalism that had been the very heart of the Wob understanding has become increasingly real in daily life. Workers of many countries now have no choice. They are being forced into solidarity with each other for dignity and survival, even if the official labor leaders maintain an outdated and conservative approach to the rapidly changing world economy. Antiglobalization demonstrations from Seattle to Manhattan to Latin America, Europe, and Asia, often brought out Wobbly signs for the best possible reasons. Perhaps, after a century, the organic basis for IWW-envisioned success had finally arrived. At any rate, given the accelerating attack of corporations upon the planet and all living creatures, it is getting close to now or never.[33]

Once more, activists and historians alike are looking to the example of the IWW for strategies to confront global capitalism.[34] This anthology intends to contribute to this effort.

Overview and Contributions to This Volume

Wobblies of the World is both a culmination and new beginning for studies of the IWW. It brings together some of the best and most cutting-edge scholarship on the union and, we hope, also lays out parameters for future research. The histories told in these chapters highlight several fundamental, but often ignored, characteristics of the Wobblies. Subsequent scholarship must, we believe, take these factors into account, and the historiography practically cries out for a new, synthetic overview that incorporates them.

First, the IWW emerged as part of a global syndicalist movement, simultaneously influencing and influenced by syndicalist movements in other countries. This fact is self-evident, especially today, after the "transnational turn" in historical studies. Even Dubofsky eventually conceded:

> The emergence and growth of revolutionary syndicalism in the United States between 1900 and 1919 was inextricably linked to the rise of labour movements and socialism internationally in the era of the Second International. Although each national syndicalist movement bore its own characteristic cultural traits, syndicalism emerged and grew at a time when capital, people, and ideas moved freely across borders and oceans.[35]

Historians like Salerno and Michael Miller Topp have studied how French and Italian syndicalism and anarchism shaped the Wobblies, and Dominique Pinsolle and Kenyon Zimmer's chapters here elaborate on these connections.[36] There are also scattered historical references to the IWW's influence on the ideology and tactics of radicals in China, Japan, Germany, India, Norway, Spain, and Sweden, and the chapters here by Marjorie Murphy, Paula de Angelis, Tariq Khan, Johan Pries, Peter Clayworth, Lucien van der Walt, and Matthew White explore further dimensions of Wobbly influence on non-Wobbly organizations and movements abroad.[37] However, the precise scope and nature of the IWW's reciprocal, transnational influences remains largely unexplored.

Second, the IWW was an international organization, with national administrations, local branches, and mobile members spread out across the globe. In 1921, the *Industrial Pioneer* noted, "before the war broke out, some semblance of organization on a world-scale did exist. Administrations of the I.W.W. were functioning in Australia, Mexico, Chile, South Africa, England, Sweden and elsewhere," including New Zealand and Canada, and IWW locals formed in many more countries. In recent decades, small IWW branches have reappeared in many of these places, as well as new locations such as Austria, Germany, Greece, Iceland, Lithuania, Switzerland, Sierra Leone, Taiwan, and Turkey. Although some of these foreign IWW organizations were ephemeral, others grew into significant labor movements in their own right.[38] But all were outgrowths of the American organization, with most founded by and including migrant laborers or maritime workers who first joined the union in the United States. The chapters by Kevan Antonio Aguilar, Verity Burgmann, Paula de Angelis, Mark Derby, Mark Leier, Heather Mayer, Marjorie Murphy, Saku Pinta, Johan Pries, Wayne Thorpe, and Lucien van der Walt explore some of these international branches, but many others remain historiographical black holes.

Third, the IWW was neither monolithic nor independent of other political movements; instead, its ideology, tactics, and goals varied enormously between different local and national contexts. Thus, attempts to define the ideology of the union are exercises in futility, especially if they are based— as so many have been—exclusively on writings in English. For example, after abandoning his earlier efforts to define the IWW as a non-syndicalist movement, Joseph R. Conlin concluded there were in fact "many I.W.W.'s." whose differences were "confusing and irreconcilable." Paul Brissenden more generously noted the "many-sided intellectual character" of the IWW and ventured, "Perhaps the least indefinite term which would give them all standing-room would be 'revolutionary socialism'."[39] The organization's openness and the relative autonomy of its locals and foreign administrations allowed militants of different political hues to find what Michael Löwy calls "elective affinity" with its somewhat vague radical program.[40] Those who identified their own ideologies with the Wobblies included the doctrinaire Marxists of the SLP (before breaking away in 1908), "Industrial Socialists" from the left wing of the SPA, European syndicalists of many stripes (including both Marxists and anarcho-syndicalists), class-struggle-oriented anarchists from around the world, and the Mexican revolutionaries of the Partido Liberal Mexicano, itself a multi-tendency movement containing anarchist, socialist, and nationalist elements. The IWW was many things to many people, depending on place and language, as the chapters by Kevan Antonio Aguilar, Bieito Alonso, Verity Burgmann, Peter Clayworth, Tariq Khan, Saku Pinta, Johan Pries, David Struthers, Matthew White, and Kenyon Zimmer illustrate.

Next, the history of the IWW is a multilingual one. In addition to the union's presence in non-Anglophone countries, a large percentage of its US membership was foreign-born. Even in the American West during the union's heyday, 42 percent of its dues-paying members were immigrants.[41] Moreover, the majority of American IWW periodicals were not printed in

English. Of the 14 weekly and biweekly Wobbly newspapers appearing in 1917, only three were for English readers. Before the Second World War, the union published newspapers in at least 18 other languages, including the IWW's only daily, the Finnish *Industrialisti*. And even English papers circulated internationally within non-English-speaking countries; A. S. Edwards, editor of the *Industrial Union Bulletin*, reported that that his paper "literally circulates around the world. It goes to England, Scotland, Ireland, Germany, France, Sweden, Roumania [sic], Hungary and Australia." Furthermore, the union's international branches published a number of newspapers. These included, in addition to many publications in the Anglophone world, Sweden's *Marinarbetaren* (1924–25), Germany's *Der Marine-Arbeiter* (1930–32), and at least ten Spanish-language IWW periodicals produced in Latin America. The New Zealand IWW paper *Industrial Unionist* even carried articles in the Maori language, as explored in Mark Derby's chapter. Clearly, therefore, the Wobblies cannot be adequately researched utilizing English-only sources. Based on his examination of its Latin American press, for example, Anton Rosenthal convincingly argues that "the i.w.w. is a missing chapter in Latin American labor history and the i.w.w. in Latin America is a missing chapter in the global history of the Wobblies."[42] Several contributors to this volume have similarly unearthed previously unknown dimensions of IWW activity by mining untapped foreign-language sources, such as Bieito Alonso, Mark Derby, Saku Pinta, Johan Pries, David Struthers, and Kenyon Zimmer.

Fifth, the chronology of IWW history is highly variable, depending on local and national context. It no longer is tenable, therefore, simply to date the union's decline to government repression during the First World War, or even to the IWW's disastrous 1924 split. Among many American immigrant groups, and within many countries, the organization's size and influence did not peak (or in some cases, did not even begin) until the 1920s or 1930s. Some elements of the Wobblies continued to exercise significant power or influence in these decades (and beyond), as seen in the chapters by Bieito Alonso, Bucky Halker, Johan Pries, and Matthew White. Moreover, the IWW—like the Joe Hill of Alfred Hayes's and Earl Robinson's song—never really died; it lives on to this day as both a source of inspiration and, in some locales, a functioning labor union willing to take on corporate giants like Starbucks and Jimmy John's.[43] So too must the historiography of the IWW evolve and expand in chronological scope over the coming years.

This book's contributions to these topics are organized in three thematic sections. The first section includes chapters examining the transnational influences on the IWW in the United States. These influences included French syndicalism, the anarchism of Italians, Spaniards, and Mexicans, and South Asian anti-colonialism. Wobbly ideals and practices germinated in these interconnected transnational movements, which in turn helped to further their own global growth. The second section shifts outward, with chapters providing case studies of the expansion and transmission of the IWW at the institutional and individual levels to locations outside of the United States. Here contributors explore Wobblies in Australia, Canada, Mexico, New Zealand, and Spain. The final section moves further toward expanding our understanding of the IWW's legacy by examining the many softer forms of diffusion that carried its influence worldwide, with a focus upon the cultural transmission and reinterpretation of Wobbly ideals beyond the organization and the country of its initial formation.

Just as the Wobblies were quite heterodox, so too is this anthology. Each essay stands alone and can be read independently, though many of the chapters interconnect and they have been arranged in a logical sequence. In addition, we wished to make this book accessible to non-academics. Thus some of the essays are relatively short biographical accounts, and none are overly long. This choice also allowed us to include more contributions, and therefore better sketch the incredible breadth of the IWW's global history.

Conclusion

As economic inequality in the United States, Europe, and across the world has increased, the national and global narrative of economic fairness has expanded drastically. In recent years, the domination and inequality fostered by neoliberalism has pushed some people rightward and others leftward. The Brexit vote, election of Donald Trump, and growing popularity of right-wing and fascist parties across Europe all exemplify the former. The Occupy Wall Street movement, and the popularity of Bernie Sanders in the United States, Podemos, Syriza, and other growing left parties represent the latter. Not surprisingly, both left and right populists imagine themselves as fighting the 1 percent on behalf of the 99 percent. Yet what has been missing from nearly all of the left responses has been organized labor. That is because neoliberalism—along with its handmaidens, corporate-driven globalization and automation—has decimated unions and other working-class organizations.

Nevertheless, many aspects of the current moment reveal a growing interest in and influence of Wobbly tendencies, with the roots going back to the union's heyday a century ago. This is no accident. As Buhle noted:

The world of the Wobs was made up of immigrant workers (like ours now), without steady employment, health plans, social security, or drug benefits (like the future that Republicans and many a Democrat envision), without any responsibility on the part of the filthy rich for the growing class of poor—so much like the society around us. The world of the Wobblies was one realized in its best moments by solidarity across race, ethnic, gender, and nationality lines …. What the Wobs did was to hold up an alternative vision of labor and social solidarity against capital, the alternative we need now more than ever. Lacking this, we confront a continuing collapse of organized labor.[44]

The general public, of course, does not know of the IWW, even when they invoke its ideas and tactics. This book attempts to correct the scholarly record and educate those beyond the academy by showing a more sophisticated historical treatment of the Wobblies using global and transnational methods of scholarship.

Given the current weaknesses of unions and decline of welfare state capitalism around the world, we believe that alternative forms of unionism and political praxis must be explored, now more than ever. In the words of the editors of the Wildcat series, "New and modernized unions are adapting to conditions and creating class-conscious workers' movement rooted in militancy and solidarity." The IWW defined, in a very real way, the ideal of solidarity when it coined the legendary motto, "An Injury to One is an Injury to All." That slogan, like the Wobblies themselves, spread globally. For example, it was introduced by Wobbly sailors to South Africa in the First World War era, and today remains the motto of South Africa's largest labor federation, the Congress of South African Trade Unions. The struggles of a century ago still resonate throughout the industrializing Global South as well as the deindustrializing Global North. Only when workers around the world embrace the spirit and internationalism of the Wobblies will they be strong enough to challenge global capitalism, which might as well formally adopt as its own motto, "divide and conquer."

Notes

1 Eric J. Hobsbawm, *Revolutionaries: Contemporary Essays* (New York: New American Library, 1973), 61; Larry Peterson, 'The One Big Union in international perspective: revolutionary industrial unionism 1900–1925,' *Labour/Le Travail* 7 (1981): 41–66; Marcel van der Linden and Wayne Thorpe (eds.), *Revolutionary Syndicalism: An International Perspective* (Aldershot, UK: Scholars' Press, 1990); Steven Hirsch and Lucien van der Walt (eds.), *Anarchism and Syndicalism in the Colonial and Postcolonial World, 1870–1940: The Praxis of National Liberation, In-*

ternationalism, and Social Revolution (Boston, Mass.: Brill, 2010). For an example of the minimization of syndicalism's importance, see Geoff Eley, *Forging Democracy: The History of the Left in Europe, 1850–2000* (Oxford: Oxford University Press, 2002), pp. 96–8. On the role of sailors see Jon Bekken, "Marine Transport Workers IU 510 (IWW): direct action unionism," *Libertarian Labor Review* 18 (1995): 12–25; Peter Cole, *Wobblies on the Waterfront: Interracial Unionism in Progressive-Era Philadelphia* (Urbana, Ill.: University of Illinois Press, 2007).

2 *The Founding Convention of the IWW: Proceedings* (1905; reprint, New York: Merit, 1969); Salvatore Salerno, *Red November, Black November: Culture and Community in the Industrial Workers of the World* (New York: State University of New York Press, 1989), ch. 3.

3 Mark Pittenger, *American Socialists and Evolutionary Thought, 1870–1920* (Madison, Wisc.: University of Wisconsin Press, 1993); Sally M. Miller, "For white men only: the Socialist Party of America and issues of gender, ethnicity and race," *Journal of the Gilded Age and Progressive Era* 2:3 (2003): 283–302.

4 J. Anthony Lukas, *Big Trouble: A Murder in a Small Western Town Sets Off a Struggle for the Soul of America* (New York: Simon & Schuster, 1997).

5 *Industrial Worker*, October 28, 1909; Philip S. Foner (ed.), *Fellow Workers and Friends: I.W.W. Free-Speech Fights as Told by Participants* (Westport, Conn.: Greenwood Press, 1981); Matthew S. May, *Soapbox Rebellion: The Hobo Orator Union and the Free Speech Fights of the Industrial Workers of the World, 1909–1916* (Tuscaloosa, Ala.: University of Alabama Press, 2013).

6 Ardis Cameron, *Radicals of the Worst Sort: Laboring Women in Lawrence, Massachusetts, 1860–1912* (Urbana, Ill.: University of Illinois Press, 1995); Bruce Watson, *Bread and Roses: Mills, Migrants, and the Struggle for the American Dream* (New York: Viking, 2005).

7 Steve Golin, *The Fragile Bridge: Paterson Silk Strike, 1913* (Philadelphia, Pa.: Temple University Press, 1988); Kenyon Zimmer, *Immigrants against the State: Yiddish and Italian Anarchism in America* (Urbana, Ill.: University of Illinois Press, 2015), ch. 2.

8 James R. Green, "The Brotherhood of Timber Workers 1910–1913: a radical response to industrial capitalism in the Southern U.S.A.," *Past & Present* 60 (1973): 161–200; Robert L. Tyler, *Rebels of the Woods: The I.W.W. in the Pacific Northwest* (Portland, Ore.: University of Oregon Books, 1967).

9 Cole, *Wobblies on the Waterfront.*

10 Nigel Anthony Sellars, *Oil, Wheat, and Wobblies: The Industrial Workers of the World in Oklahoma, 1905–1930* (Norman, Okla.: University of Oklahoma Press, 1998); Greg Hall, *Harvest Wobblies: The Industrial Workers of the World and Agricultural Laborers in the American West, 1905–1930* (Corvallis, Ore.: Oregon State University Press, 2001).

11 F. N. Brill, "A brief history of the IWW outside the US (1905–1999)," Industrial Workers of the World, January 1999, https://iww.org/history/library/misc/FNBrill1999 (accessed January 7, 2017); Peter DeShazo, *Urban Workers and Labor Unions in Chile, 1902–1927* (Madison, Wisc.: University of Wisconsin Press, 1983); Kirk Shaffer, "Tropical libertarians: anarchist movements and networks in the Caribbean, Southern United States, and Mexico, 1890s–1920s," in Hirsch and Van der Walt (eds.), *Anarchism and Syndicalism in the Colonial and Postcolonial World,*

p. 292; Steven Hirsch, "Peruvian anarcho-syndicalism: adapting transnational influences and forging counterhegemonic practices, 1905–1930," in Hirsch and Van
der Walt (eds.), *Anarchism and Syndicalism in the Colonial and Postcolonial World*,
pp. 255–56; Kirwin R. Shaffer, *Black Flag Boricuas: Anarchism, Antiauthoritari-
anism, and the Left in Puerto Rico, 1897–1921* (Chicago, Ill.: University of Illinois
Press, 2013), pp. 137, 146–47; Peter M. Wilcox, "These we will not compromise:
the 'Detroit' Industrial Workers of the World, 1908–1927," MA thesis, San Diego
State University, 1995, pp. 78 n27, 129. Further works on foreign branches are cited
below.

12 William Preston, Jr., *Aliens and Dissenters: Federal Suppression of Radicals, 1903–
1933* (New York: Harper & Row, 1963); Eric Thomas Chester, *The Wobblies in
Their Heyday: The Rise and Destruction of the Industrial Workers of the World during
the World War I Era* (Santa Barbara, Calif.: Praeger, 2014); Michael Cohen, "'The
Ku Klux government': vigilantism, lynching, and the repression of the IWW,"
Journal for the Study of Radicalism 1:1 (2006): 31–56.

13 Chester, *The Wobblies in their Heyday.*

14 Fred Thompson, "They didn't suppress the Wobblies," *Radical America* 1:2 (1967):
3–5; Kenyon Zimmer, "Premature anti-communists? American anarchism, the
Russian Revolution, and left-wing libertarian anti-communism, 1917–1939,"
Labor: Studies in Working-Class History of the Americas 6:2 (2009): 60–61; Chester,
The Wobblies in their Heyday.

15 For IWW activity up into the twenty-first century see Fred Thompson and
Jon Bekken, *The Industrial Workers of the World: Its First One Hundred Years*
(Cincinnati, Ohio: IWW, 2006).

16 Franklin Rosemont, *Joe Hill: The IWW and The Making Of A Revolutionary Workingclass Counterculture* (Chicago, Ill.: Charles H. Kerr, 2003), p. 13.

17 Paul Frederick Brissenden, *The I.W.W.: A Study of American Syndicalism* (New
York: Columbia University Press, 1919), quote on pp. 339–40; Louis Levine, "The
development of syndicalism in America," *Political Science Quarterly* 28 (September
1913): 451–79; André Tridon, *The New Unionism* (New York: B. W. Huebsch,
1913); John S. Gambs, *The Decline of the I.W.W.* (New York: Columbia University Press, 1932), 92–94. The prototypical negative treatment of the union is John
Graham Brooks, *American Syndicalism: The I.W.W.* (New York: Macmillan, 1913).

18 *Melvyn Dubofsky, We Shall Be All: A History of the Industrial Workers of the World*
(Chicago, Ill.: Quadrangle, 1969); Philip S. Foner, *History of the Labor Movement
in the United States, Vol. 4: The Industrial Workers of the World, 1905–1917* (New
York: International Publishers, 1965); Patrick Renshaw, *The Wobblies: The Story
of Syndicalism in the United States* (Garden City, N.Y.: Doubleday, 1967); Joyce L.
Kornbluh (ed.), *Rebel Voices: An I.W.W. Anthology* (Ann Arbor, Mich.: University
of Michigan Press, 1964); Melvyn Dubofsky, *We Shall Be All: A History of the Industrial Workers of the World*, 2nd edn. (Urbana, Ill.: University of Illinois Press,
1988); Melvyn Dubofsky, *We Shall Be All: A History of the Industrial Workers of the
World*, abridged, ed. Joseph McCartin (Urbana, Ill.: University of Illinois Press,
2000); Patrick Renshaw, *The Wobblies: The Story of the IWW and Syndicalism in the
United States* (Chicago, Ill.: Ivan R. Dee, 1999); Chester, *The Wobblies in Their
Heyday.*

19 Joseph R. Conlin, *Bread and Roses Too: Studies of the Wobblies* (Westport, Conn.: Greenwood, 1969).

20 The best of these works, not otherwise cited, include Joseph R. Conlin (ed.), *At the Point of Production: The Local History of the I.W.W.* (Westport, Conn.: Greenwood Press, 1981); Peter Carlson, *Roughneck: The Life and Times of Big Bill Haywood* (New York : W.W. Norton, 1983); Anne Huber Tripp, *The I.W.W. and the Paterson Silk Strike of 1913* (Chicago, Ill.: University of Chicago Press, 1987); Dorothy Gallagher, *All the Right Enemies: The Life and Murder of Carlo Tresca* (New Brunswick: Rutgers University Press, 1988); Howard Kimeldorf, *Battling for American Labor: Wobblies, Craft Workers, and the Making of the Union Movement* (Berkeley, Calif.: University of California Press, 1990); Helen C. Camp, *Iron in Her Soul: Elizabeth Gurley Flynn and the American Left* (Pullman, Wash.: Washington State University Press, 1995); Frank Tobias Higbie, *Indispensable Outcasts: Hobo Workers and Community in the American Midwest, 1880–1930* (Urbana, Ill.: University of Illinois Press, 2003); Charles H. McCormick, *Seeing Reds: Federal Surveillance of Radicals in the Pittsburgh Mill District, 1917–1921* (Pittsburgh, Pa.: University of Pittsburgh Press, 2003); William M. Adler, *The Man Who Never Died: The Life, Times, and Legacy of Joe Hill, American Labor Icon* (New York: Bloomsbury, 2011).

21 Devra Weber, "Keeping community, challenging boundaries: indigenous migrants, internationalist workers, and Mexican revolutionaries, 1900–1920," in John Tutino (ed.), *Mexico and Mexicans in the Making of the United States* (Austin, Tex.: University of Texas Press, 2012), p. 218.

22 Bob Holton, *British Syndicalism, 1900–1914: Myths and Realities* (London: Pluto Press, 1976); Erik Olssen, *The Red Feds: Revolutionary Industrial Unionism and the New Zealand Federation of Labor 1908–14* (Auckland, New Zealand: Oxford University Press, 1988); Mark Leier, *Where the Fraser River Flows: The Industrial Workers of the World in British Columbia* (Vancouver, BC: New Star Books, 1990); A. Ross McCormack, *Reformers, Rebels, and Revolutionaries: The Western Canadian Radical Movement 1899–1919* (Toronto, Ont.: University of Toronto Press, 1991); Frank Cain, *The Wobblies at War: A History of the IWW and the Great War in Australia* (Melbourne, NSW: Spectrum, 1993); Verity Burgmann, *Revolutionary Industrial Unionism: The Industrial Workers of the World in Australia* (Cambridge: Cambridge University Press, 1995); Norman Caulfield, *Mexican Workers and the State: From the Porfiriato to NAFTA* (Fort Worth, Tex.: Texas Christian University Press, 1998); Lucien van der Walt, "Bakunin's heirs in South Africa: race and revolutionary syndicalism from the IWW to the International Socialist League, 1910–21," *Politikon* 31:1 (2004): 67–89; Lucien van der Walt, "The first globalisation and transnational labour activism in southern Africa: white labourism, the IWW, and the ICU, 1904–1934," *African Studies* 66:2–3 (2007): 223–51; Lucien van der Walt, "Anarchism and syndicalism in an African port city: the revolutionary traditions of Cape Town's multiracial working class, 1904–1931," *Labor History* 52:2 (2011): 137–71; Raymond B. Craib, *The Cry of the Renegade: Politics and Poetry in Interwar Chile* (Oxford: Oxford University Press, 2016); Peter DeShazo and Robert J. Halstead, "Los Wobblies del Sur: the Industrial Workers of the World in Chile and Mexico," unpublished manuscript, University of Wisconsin, Madison, 1974.

23 Verity Burgmann, "Antipodean peculiarities: comparing the Australian IWW with

the American," *Labor History* 40:3 (1999): 371–92; Francis Shor, "'Virile Syndicalism' in comparative perspective: a gender analysis of the IWW in the United States and Australia," *International Labor and working-class history* 56 (1999): 65–77; Francis Shor, "Left labor agitators in the Pacific rim of the early twentieth century," *International Labor and Working-Class History* 67 (2005): 148–63; Francis Shor, "Gender and labour/working class history in comparative perspective: the syndicalist and Wobbly experience in the USA, Australia, and New Zealand," *Left History* 11:2 (2006): 118–36; Verity Burgmann, "The IWW in international perspective: comparing the North American and Australasian Wobblies," in Julie Kimber, Peter Love, and Phillip Deery (eds.), *Labour Traditions: Papers from the Tenth National Labour History Conference, University of Melbourne, 4–6 July 2007* (Melbourne, Vic.: Australian Society for the Study of Labour History, 2007), pp. 36–43; Peter Cole and Lucien van der Walt, "Crossing color lines, crossing the continents: comparing the racial politics of the IWW in South Africa and the United States, 1905–1925," *Safundi* 12:1 (2011): 69–96.

24 Thompson and Bekken, *The Industrial Workers of the World*, pp. 242–3.

25 Steve Wright, *Storming Heaven: Class Composition and Struggle in Italian Autonomist Marxism* (London: Pluto Press, 2002), pp. 190–6. Much of this literature was first published in the journal *Primo Maggio* (Milan, 1973–89); see also Gisela Bock, *Die "andere" Arbeiterbewegung in den USA von 1905–1922: Die Industrial Workers of the World* (Munich: Trikont, 1976); Bruno Ramirez, *When Workers Fight: The Politics of Industrial Relations in the Progressive Era, 1898–1916* (Westport, Conn.: Greenwood Press, 1978). More recently, see Bruno Cartosio (ed.), *Wobbly! L'Industrial Workers of the World e il suo tempo* (Milan: ShaKe, 2007).

26 Douglas Ollila, Jr., "From socialism to industrial unionism (IWW): social factors in the emergence of left-labor radicalism among Finnish workers on the Mesabi, 1911–19," in Michel G. Karini, Matti E. Kaups, and Douglas J. Ollila, Jr. (eds.), *The Finnish Experience in the Western Great Lakes Region: New Perspectives* (Turku, Finland: Institute for Migration Studies, 1975), pp. 156–71; Paul Buhle, "Italian-American radicals and Rhode Island labor, 1905–1930," *Radical History Review* 17 (1978): 121–51; Auvo Kostiainen, *The Forging of Finnish-American Communism, 1917–1924: A Study in Ethnic Radicalism* (Turku, Finland: Turin Yliopisto, 1978); Bruno Cartosio, "Gli emigrati italiani e l'Industrial Workers of the World," in Bruno Bezza (ed.), *Gli italiani fuori d'Italia: gli emigrati italiani nei movimenti operai dei paesi d'adozione 1880–1940* (Milan, Italy: Franco Angeli, 1983), pp. 359–95; Norman Caulfield, "Wobblies and Mexican workers in mining and petroleum, 1905–1924," *International Review of Social History* 40 (1995): 51–76; Michael Miller Topp, *Those Without a Country: The Political Culture of Italian American Syndicalists* (Minneapolis, Minn.: University of Minnesota Press, 2001); Nunzio Pernicone, *Carlo Tresca: Portrait of a Rebel,* revised edn. (Oakland, Calif.: AK Press, 2010); Janelle Bourgeois, "'Believe comrades … the day is coming when those at the end of their rope will require struggle. It will be, perhaps, tomorrow.' Franco-Belgian immigrants and the 1912 strike," in Robert Forrant and Jürg K. Siegenthaler (eds.), *The Great Lawrence Textile Strike of 1912: New Scholarship on the Bread and Roses Strike* (Amityville, N.Y.: Baywood, 2014), pp. 15–35; Devra Anne Weber, "Wobblies of the Partido Liberal Mexicano: reenvisioning internationalist and

transnational movements through Mexican lenses," *Pacific Historical Review* 85:2 (2016): 188–226.

27 Meredith Tax, *The Rising of the Women: Feminist Solidarity and Class Conflict, 1880–1917* (New York: Monthly Review Press, 1980); Ann Schofield, "Rebel girls and union maids: the woman question in the journals of the AFL and IWW, 1905–1920," *Feminist Studies* 9:2 (1983): 335–58; Francis Shor, "Masculine power and virile syndicalism: a gendered analysis of the IWW in Australia," *Labour History* 63 (1992): 83–99; Cameron, *Radicals of the Worst Sort*; Shor, "'Virile syndicalism' in comparative perspective"; Shor, "Gender and labour/working class history in comparative perspective."

28 In addition to the works cited in note 1, see Bruno Cartosio, "L'IWW nel sindacalismo rivoluzionario internazionale, 1900–1914," *Ricerche storiche* 11:1 (1981): 167–89; Wayne Thorpe, *"The Workers Themselves": Revolutionary Syndicalism and International Labour, 1913–1923* (Boston, Mass.: Kluwer Academic, 1989); Ralph Darlington, *Syndicalism and the Transition to Communism: An International Comparative Analysis* (Burlington, Vt.: Ashgate, 2008); Marcel van der Linden, "Second thoughts on revolutionary syndicalism," *Labour History Review* 63:3 (1998): 182–96; David Berry and Constance Bantman (eds.), *New Perspectives on Anarchism, Labour and Syndicalism: The Individual, the National and the Transnational* (Newcastle upon Tyne, UK: Cambridge Scholars, 2010); Constance Bantman and Bert Altena (eds.), *Reassessing the Transnational Turn: Scales of Analysis in Anarchist and Syndicalist Studies* (New York: Routledge, 2014).

29 Salerno, *Red November, Black November*, quote on p. 2; Salvatore Salerno, "I Delitti Della Razza Bianca (crimes of the white race): Italian anarchists' racial discourse as crime," in Jennifer Guglielmo and Salvatore Salerno (eds.), *Are Italians White? How Race Is Made in America* (New York: Routledge, 2003), pp. 111–23; Salvatore Salerno, "No god, no master: Italian anarchists and the Industrial Workers of the World," in Philip V. Cannistraro and Gerald Meyer (eds.), *The Lost World of Italian American Radicalism: Politics, Labor, and Culture* (Westport, Conn.: Praeger, 2003), pp. 171–87.

30 Rosemont, *Joe Hill*. Adler's *The Man Who Never Died*, though less epic in scope, actually covers these international episodes of Hill's life in greater detail.

31 Paul Buhle and Nicole Schulman (eds.), *Wobblies! A Graphic History of the Industrial Workers of the World* (New York: Verso, 2005). The number of articles, dissertations, and reprints dealing with the IWW published in the past 25 years is too large to enumerate. For a partial list see Steve Kellerman, *A Century of Writing on the IWW 1905–2005: An Annotated Bibliography of Books on the Industrial Workers of the World* (Cambridge, Mass.: IWW, Boston General Membership Branch, 2007).

32 Javier Torres Parés, *La Revolución sin frontera: El Partido Liberal Mexicano y las relaciones entre el movimiento obrero de México y el de Estados Unidos, 1900–1923* (Mexico City: Universidad Autonoma de Mexico, 1990); Dan La Botz, "American 'slackers' in the Mexican revolution: international proletarian politics in the midst of a national revolution," *The Americas* 62:4 (2006): 563–90; Gregor Benton, *Chinese Migrants and Internationalism: Forgotten Histories, 1917–1945* (New York: Routledge, 2007); Katherine Benton-Cohen, *Borderline Americans: Racial Division and Labor War in the Arizona Borderlands* (Cambridge, Mass.: Harvard University Press, 2009); Phylis Cancilla Martinelli, *Undermining Race: Ethnic Identities*

in Arizona Copper Camps, 1880–1920 (Tucson, Ariz.: University of Arizona Press, 2009); Jennifer Guglielmo, *Living the Revolution: Italian Women's Resistance and Radicalism in New York City, 1880–1945* (Chapel Hill, N.C.: University of North Carolina Press, 2010); Dave Struthers, "The world in a city: transnational and inter-racial organizing in Los Angeles, 1900–1930," PhD diss., Carnegie Mellon University, Pittsburgh, Pa., 2010; Maia Ramnath, *Haj to Utopia: How the Ghadar Movement Charted Global Radicalism and Attempted to Overthrow the British Empire* (Berkeley, Calif.: University of California Press, 2011); Kornel Chang, *Pacific Connections: The Making of the U.S.-Canadian Borderlands* (Berkeley, Calif.: University of California Press, 2012); Zimmer, *Immigrants against the State.*

33 Paul Buhle, "The legacy of the IWW," *Monthly Review* 57:2 (2005): 26–7.

34 See also Staughton Lynd and Andrej Grubacic, *Wobblies and Zapatistas: Conversations on Anarchism, Marxism and Radical History* (Oakland, Calif.: PM Press, 2008); Immanuel Ness (ed.), *New Forms of Worker Organization: The Syndicalist and Autonomist Restoration of Class-Struggle Unionism* (Oakland, Calif.: PM Press, 2014).

35 Melvyn Dubofsky, "The rise and fall of revolutionary syndicalism in the United States," in Van der Linden and Thorpe (eds.), *Revolutionary Syndicalism*, p. 203.

36 Salerno, *Red November, Black November*, quote on p. 2; Salerno, "I Delitti Della Razza Bianca"; Salerno, "No god, no master"; Topp, *Those without a Country*; Zimmer, *Immigrants against the State.*

37 Benton, *Chinese Migrants and Internationalism*, pp. 13, 123 (n68); John Crump, *The Origins of Socialist Thought in Japan* (New York: St. Martin's Press, 1983), p. 197; Hans Manfred Bock, *Syndikalismus und Linkskommunismus von 1918–1923: zur Geschichte und Soziologie der Freien Arbeiter-Union Deutschlands (Syndikalisten), der Allgemeinen Arbeiter-Union Deutschlands und der Kommunistischen Arbeiter-Partei Deutschlands* (Meisenheim am Glan, Germany: Anton Hain, 1969), pp. 124–6; Hartmut Rübner, *Freiheit und Brot: die Freie Arbeiter-Union Deutschlands: eine Studie zur Geschichte des Anarchosyndikalismus* (Berlin: Libertad, 1994), ch. 7; Walter Galenson, *Labor in Norway* (Cambridge, Mass.: Harvard University Press, 1949), pp. 21–2, 59, 61; Renshaw, *The Wobblies*, pp. 236–8; Robert J. Alexander, *The Anarchists in the Spanish Civil War* (London: Janus, 1998), p. 1:30; Lennart K. Persson, "Revolutionary syndicalism in Sweden before the Second World War," in Van der Linden and Thorpe (eds.), *Revolutionary Syndicalism*, p. 90.

38 G. C., "The international relations of the I.W.W.," *Industrial Pioneer* (July 1921): 24; "International Directory," *Industrial Workers of the World*, www.iww.org/cs/branches (accessed January 7, 2017). Although the Chilean branch of the IWW is not represented in this volume, it has received significant scholarly treatment elsewhere; see Peter DeShazo, "The Industrial Workers of the World in Chile: 1917–1927," MA thesis, University of Wisconsin, 1973; DeShazo and Halstead, "Los Wobblies del Sur"; DeShazo, *Urban Workers*; Mario Araya, "Los wobblies criollos. Fundación e ideología en la región chilena de la Industrial Workers of the World–Iww (1919–1927)," BA thesis, Universidad ARCIS, Santiago, 2008; Anton Rosenthal, "Radical border crossers: the Industrial Workers of the World and their press in Latin America," *Estudios Interdisciplinarios de América Latina y el Caribe* 22:2 (2011): 39–70; Craib, *The Cry of the Renegade.*

39 Joseph R. Conlin, "Introduction," in *At the Point of Production*, p. 24; Brissenden, *The I.W.W.*, p. 76.

40 Michael Löwy, *Redemption and Utopia: Jewish Libertarian Thought in Central Europe; A Study in Elective Affinity*, trans. Hope Heaney (Stanford, Calif.: Stanford University Press, 1992), ch. 1.

41 Salerno, *Red November, Black November*, p. 10.

42 Vincent St. John, *The I.W.W.: Its History, Structure and Methods*, rev. edn. (Chicago, Ill.: IWW Publishing Bureau, 1917), pp. 16–17; IWW History Project, "IWW newspapers," *Mapping American Social Movements through the 20th Century*, http://depts.washington.edu/iww/newspapers.shtml (accessed January 6, 2017); "Proceedings of Third Annual Convention Industrial Workers of the World Held at Chicago, Ill., 1907: Official Report," *Socialist Labor Party of America*, 2011, p. 274, www.slp.org/pdf/slphist/iww_conv_1907.pdf (accessed January 7, 2017); Rosenthal, "Radical border crossers," p. 40.

43 Daniel Gross and Staughton Lynd, *Solidarity Unionism at Starbucks*, PM Press Pamphlet Series 9 (Oakland, Calif.: PM Press, 2011); Erik Forman, "Revolt in fast food nation: the Wobblies take on Jimmy John's," in Ness (ed.), *New Forms of Worker Organization*, pp. 205–32.

44 Buhle, "The legacy of the IWW," 27.

Part I

Transnational Influences on the IWW

I

"A Cosmopolitan Crowd:" Transnational Anarchists, the IWW, and the American Radical Press

Kenyon Zimmer

It is no coincidence that Salvatore Salerno's groundbreaking study of transnational influences on the Industrial Workers of the World, *Red November, Black November*, devoted much space to the role of anarchists. Within the constellation of late-nineteenth and early-twentieth-century radical movements that gave rise to the IWW, anarchism was the most transnational in its activities and internationalist in its commitments. Anarchists, Jose Moya notes, "formed the world's first and most widespread transnational movement organized from below and without formal political parties," and both anarchism and syndicalism spread across the globe through the same international migrations of workers, exiles, activists, and students. Many transnational anarchists were therefore instrumental in shaping the IWW and its ideology, at both the institutional and local levels. To a great extent, globetrotting anarchists were responsible for forging the IWW into "a diverse, multilingual, transnational organization."[1]

This aspect of the IWW's history, however, remains largely unknown. Most scholarship on the Wobblies in the United States relies on English-language sources, whereas the vast majority of anarchists—and a great number of Wobblies—were immigrants. In particular, Mexican, Italian, Spanish, Finnish, and Russian immigrants were over-represented in the union, and anarchism ran strong within each of these ethnic groups. Moreover, as Davide Turcato observes, "a key reason for ... the inherent difficulty in studying anarchist organization, is that anarchism is often an opaque movement," and deliberately so. Anarchist involvement in the IWW is no exception.[2]

For example, the Paterson silk strike of 1913 is typically portrayed as beginning with a spontaneous work stoppage, after which IWW organizers were invited to the city to aid the strikers. Even Steve Golin's excellent study of the strike, which emphasizes Paterson's strong IWW presence leading up to the conflict, concedes that the union's local leaders "remain largely unknown."[3] English-language IWW sources are, in fact, conspicuously evasive on this topic. Organizer Elizabeth Gurley Flynn noted, "the preparation and declaration as well as the stimulation of the strike was all done by the I.W.W., by the militant minority among the silk workers," but gave no specifics, and when a Paterson rabbi asked William D. Haywood who belonged to the strike committee, the IWW co-founder replied, "I don't know; and if I did I wouldn't tell." There was a simple reason for this obfuscation, as organizer Adolf Lessig told the Commission on Industrial Relations: "I should not care to mention anybody's name outside of those that to-day are free from losing their position" in Paterson's silk mills.[4]

But in 1914 Margaret Sanger, who had aided the strike, described in an anarchist publication how "the Italian anarchists had been working among the silk workers for years, sowing the seeds of dissatisfaction and rebellion against their slavery, and when the strike was called this small minority formed the backbone of the strike." Italian-language sources confirm this claim, and show that Paterson's immigrant anarchists had been organizing their fellow silk workers into militant, revolutionary unions since the 1880s, and expounded syndicalist ideas and tactics years before the formation of the IWW. In 1906 Paterson's anarchists founded one of the first stable IWW locals in the country and proceeded to lead a series of strikes under its auspices. They also emblazoned the masthead and storefront offices of their newspaper, *La Questione Sociale*, with the union's logo, and spent more than a year quietly laying the groundwork for the general strike that broke out in 1913—a task that included forming shop committees in most of the city's mills.[5] During the struggle, Flynn lodged with Firmino Gallo and Ninfa Baronio, weavers who had belonged to an anarchist circle in Italy, were founding members of Paterson's anarchist Gruppo Diritto all'Esistenza, and ran the local radical bookstore in their off hours. Likewise, Haywood stayed with Paolo Guabello, another Italian anarchist weaver, who was arrested for picketing during the strike. Paolo's brother Alberto was also a veteran anarchist as well as the IWW's leading local organizer, and one of the strike committee members whom Haywood refused to name.[6] In 1919, former *La Questione Sociale* editor and Wobbly organizer Ludovico Caminita boasted,

Offices of *La Questione Sociale*, Paterson, New Jersey, 1908. Note the ɪww logo on the windows. Courtesy of the Newark Public Library.

"damn modesty, the ɪ.w.w. enjoys the glory which to a great extent is due to us."[7]

The same year of Caminita's outburst, *One Big Union Monthly* editor John (Johan) Sandgren penned an article on "The importation of ideas in the labor movement." He declared social democracy, anarchism, syndicalism, craft unionism, and communism to be European creeds unfit for "purely American conditions," whereas the indigenous ɪww was "the correct expression of the form needed here in America." Sandgren neglected to mention that he was himself a Swedish immigrant and "self-admitted anarchist" who, after helping to organize the founding convention of the ɪww, had argued in favor of removing all references to "political action" from the union's constitution. He also wrote for Swedish anarchist and syndicalist newspapers, and authored two Swedish-language books that "became important for political development of the Swedish syndicalists during the 1920s."[8] In other words, Sandgren concealed—even disparaged—the very strands of transnational radicalism that animated his participation in the ɪww. The contributions of Sandgren and the Paterson anarchists are emblematic of two overlapping spheres in which immigrant anarchist influence was simultaneously pervasive and opaque: the ɪww's formation and doctrinal evolution, and its multilingual press. Anarchist members pushed the organization in a more decentralized direction, disseminated libertarian socialist ideas among its membership, and connected the union to international anarchist currents and struggles.

Anarchists in the Making of the IWW

Vincent St John listed anarchists as one of four major factions at the union's founding convention, in addition to socialists, industrial unionists, and opportunistic "labor union fakirs." At least 14 anarchist delegates participated—fewer than 7 percent of the representatives present, but wielding more than 14 percent of the convention's total votes. At least seven of these anarchists were foreign-born, out of only "thirty emigrants" among the delegates, making anarchists substantially over-represented among the union's immigrant founders.[9] At this and subsequent conventions, they rallied to infuse the new union with anarcho-syndicalist values.

Several delegates were local Chicago anarchists: veteran anarchist agitator and Haymarket widow Lucy Parsons; Haymarket riot survivor and editor Jay Fox; Julia Mechanic, a former editorial board member (along with Fox) of the anarchist newspaper *Free Society*; Jean E. Spielman, a Romanian bookbinder who immigrated in 1902; and one A. Wrink or Wermich, about whom few details are known.[10] Spanish-born anarchist Florencio Bazora attended from St Louis, and Italian anarchists Joseph Corna and Antonio Andrà came from Spring Valley, Illinois, where they organized for the United Mine Workers and Corna later formed a small IWW local. This pair reported on the proceedings (and the anarchists present) for Paterson's *La Questione Sociale*.[11]

Josef Peukert, once a leader of the extreme "autonomist" faction of German-speaking anarchists, represented the Chicago Debaters Club, an organization "composed of socialists and anarchists." However, he voted against affiliation with the new union. By contrast, Slovene anarchist Andrew ("Al") Klemencic played a major role in the proceedings and voted to install the Pueblo, Colorado local of the Journeymen Tailors' Union that he represented in the IWW. Born near Trieste in 1860, Klemencic was an experienced, multilingual radical organizer whose activism had taken him across most of Europe as well as to San Francisco and Hawai'i, and he regularly contributed to anarchist publications in both the United States and Europe.[12] The largest anarchist-controlled bloc of votes, however, belonged to three delegates from the Western Federation of Miners (WFM) and American Labor Union (ALU) whom Corna and Andrà identified as fellow anarchists: ALU Executive Board member M. E. White, Arizona mine organizer Albert Ryan, and WFM member John Riordan of Phoenix, British Columbia (also discussed by Leier in Chapter 9). Thomas J. Hagerty, another ALU member, had been involved in Chicago anarchist circles in the 1880s, but then entered a seminary and became a priest, only to be suspended for using the pulpit to champion socialism. Although now affiliated with the Socialist Party, he invoked French and Spanish anarcho-syndicalism and opposed electoral activity in favor of direct action and the general strike.[13] Hagerty belonged to the delegation of the Industrial Workers Club of Chicago, an organization composed of antiparliamentary socialists like himself and anarchists like Robert C. Goodwin, the final individual named in Corna and Andrà's report. Several other anarchists attended as observers, including Spaniard Pedro Esteve (see Alonso, Chapter 5).

During the convention M. E. White nominated Riordan to the union's General Executive Board, to which he was elected by a wide margin. The convention also adopted a resolution by Klemencic and Corna condemning militarism, and Riordan and Hagerty helped draft the organization's constitution, including its famous Preamble. Even the union's name bore an anarchist imprint; when some delegates proposed "The Industrial Union of America," Riordan and Klemencic passionately appealed for the global "Industrial Workers of the World." In Klemencic's words:

> we are a cosmopolitan crowd. Now, then, as it is, all lines that were ever established have always been established by men who were a bunch of robbers, thieves and exploiters, and we want to combine ourselves as humanity, as one lot of people, those that are producing the wealth of our oppressors, and we want to have under that banner our brothers and sisters of the world.[14]

This cosmopolitan internationalism reflected Klemencic's anarchist beliefs, as well as his own experiences as a transnational labor radical.

When the IWW's second convention met in 1906, Albert Ryan and John Riordan again attended, joined by anarchist Michel Dumas, a representative of Paterson's silk workers, who had published that city's French anarchist paper *Germinal* from 1899 to 1902. Ryan and Riordan played major roles in the tumultuous proceedings, which saw the removal of sitting president Charles O. Sherman and the abolition of that office altogether. Dumas also cosponsored a failed motion to strike the words promoting action "on the political field" from the Preamble.[15] At the following year's convention *La Questione Sociale* editor Ludovico Caminita was the only known anarchist delegate. He spoke against a proposal to reinstate the office of president, and in support of yet another motion to remove the "political clause" from the union's preamble. This provoked a heated exchange with Socialist Labor Party leader Daniel De Leon, whose defense of the existing document carried the day.[16] However, the 1908 convention finally removed the "political clause" and ejected De Leon from the organization.

Nevertheless, not all anarchist members approved of the degree of centralization that remained in the IWW's structure or its version of syndicalism. Several, including Jay Fox and Lucy Parsons, broke away from the union in 1912 to join William Z. Foster's Syndicalist League of North America, which, influenced by the French model of anarcho-syndicalism, aimed to "bore from within" the mainstream unions of the American Federation of Labor (AFL). Foster, a future leader of the Communist Party, also drew heavily on anarchism, championing anti-statism and arguing, "Syndicalism has placed the Anarchist movement upon a practical, effective basis."[17] In 1924, anarchists participated in a more consequential clash between IWW "centralists" and the "decentralists," with many supporting the latter's "Emergency Program" for union reorganization. This conflict overlapped with struggles between and pro- and anti-Communist members, as well as disagreements over clemency campaigns for IWW prisoners. The result was a violent annual convention and disastrous organizational split that left the union in a shambles.[18] Throughout the union's institutional development, then, anarchist influence was significant, if not always self-evident or successful.

Paper Politics

The depth and breadth of anarchists' role in the organization was even greater within the multiethnic, multilingual web of IWW-affiliated publications. In 1913, sociologist Louis Levine noted "the numerous anarchists who have joined the organization during the past few years. In the Far West and in the East many of the i.w.w. locals are dominated by anarchistic elements, who have come to regard the i.w.w. as the most promising agency for revolutionary propaganda and action." These local efforts were linked—and made visible to historians—through anarchists' informal networks, within which "radical newspapers were the major connective tissue linking the scattered nodes ... facilitating the exchange of resources, the movement of people, the creation of identity, and the spread of tactics."[19] Anarchists edited at least 19 IWW periodicals in the United States before the Second World War—over 20 percent of all Wobbly titles published—and in 1919–20, anarchist-edited IWW publications had a combined circulation of over 47,000 copies, more than four times that of the union's English-language *Industrial Worker*.[20] These editors' transnational anarchist politics manifested themselves in ways both implicit and explicit.

John Sandgren was one such Wobbly who wove anarchism into his editorial duties. Fluent in both Swedish and English, he began editing the *One Big Union Monthly* and the IWW's Swedish-language *Nya Världen* in 1919. Although Sandgren did not explicitly voice his anarchism in these publications, he was removed from the *One Big Union Monthly* in 1920 after publishing anti-Bolshevik editorials and translations of anti-communist articles from Swedish anarchist and syndicalist papers, at a time when friendly feelings toward Soviet communism still persisted among many Wobblies. Sandgren also opposed IWW affiliation with the communists' Red International of Labor Unions (the Profintern), and supported affiliation with the Berlin-based anarcho-syndicalist International Working Men's Association (see Thorpe in Chapter 6). Nor was Sandgren the union's only Swedish anarchist newspaperman; Gustav Bergman, an "active anarchist in Sweden" before coming to America, edited Seattle's bilingual Swedish-Norwegian *Industri-Arbetaren* in 1924–25.[21]

William Risto, a Swedish-born Finn who led an anarcho-syndicalist faction in the Midwest's Finnish Socialist Federation before his expulsion, served as a contributing editor of the popular IWW-affiliated daily *Industrialisti*, beginning in 1916.[22] Risto's close comrades, Carl Paivio and Gust (or Gus) Alonen, belonged to a Finnish IWW group in the Bronx composed of anarchists, and co-edited its paper, *Luokkataistelu*. Some members of this organization hoped to turn the paper into an explicitly anarchist organ, and in 1919, New York State convicted Paivio and Alonen under its criminal anarchy statute. Following their 1923 release from prison, Alonen, a carpenter by trade, moved to the anarchist community in Mohegan, New York, where he built homes and the schoolhouse. Paivio, by contrast, joined the Communist Party and died in 1952 while awaiting deportation as a communist alien.[23]

Finnish radicals featured prominently in the IWW's 1916 mining strike on the Mesabi Iron Range, which also propelled Bulgarian IWW organizer George Andreytchine to national prominence. Andreytchine's Macedonian parents reared him on the Christian anarchist teachings of Leo Tolstoy, and in high school he read the works of Peter Kropotkin and joined a radical Tolstoyan group. Traveling to France and Germany, he also absorbed syndicalist ideas. In 1913 Andreytchine came to the United States, where he found work at a Minnesota iron mine, read Alexander Berkman's paper *The Blast*, met Emma Goldman, joined the IWW, and became secretary of his local branch. Ralph Chaplin, in his autobiography, described Andreytchine as "a fiery young Bulgarian intellectual turned anarchist who had joined forces with the I.W.W. because of its ideological kinship

with European syndicalism."[24] Andreytchine also founded and edited the
iww's first Bulgarian newspaper, *Rabotnicheska Misul*, and contributed to
the Parisian syndicalist paper *La Vie Ouvrière*. Postal authorities banned
Rabotnicheska Misul in the summer of 1917, but Andreytchine immediately
launched a new publication, *Rabotnik*.

After helping lead the Mesabi strike and narrowly avoiding deportation,
Andreytchine attended the iww's tenth convention, in 1916, and drafted the
anti-militarist resolution adopted there, which declared the Wobblies to be
"the determined opponents of all nationalistic sectionalism, or patriotism,
and the militarism preached and supported by our one enemy, the capitalist
class."[25] A revised version of this statement was used as a key piece of evidence in the 1918 conviction of 93 iww leaders, including Andreytchine,
for violating the wartime Espionage Act. The Bulgarian was among those
to receive the maximum sentence of 20 years in prison and a $30,000 fine.[26]

Meanwhile, new editor Georgi Zafirov replaced *Rabotnik* with *Probuda*
(later changed to *Rabotnicheska Probuda*), which was subsequently
banned by authorities in 1920 for anarchist content. Zafirov then revived
Rabotnicheska Misul and Andreytchine, out on bail while appealing against
his conviction, took over as editor once again while also assuming editorship of the iww's flagship publication *Solidarity* (briefly published
as *New Solidarity*) and writing for Sandgren's *One Big Union Monthly*.
Andreytchine, however, clashed with Sandgren over the Bolsheviks, whom
he strongly supported. After Sandgren's removal, the Bulgarian briefly
edited the *One Big Union Monthly*, and wrote in favor of affiliation with
the Profintern.[27] In April 1921, after losing their appeal, Andreytchine,
William D. Haywood, and seven others jumped bail and fled to the Soviet
Union.

In 1915, the founders of the iww's first Russian newspaper, *Rabochaia
Rech'*, included anarchist Anatolii Gorelik, a veteran of the failed 1905
Russian Revolution who spent time as a labor organizer in France before
coming to the United States in 1913 and joining the Wobblies. Postal authorities banned the publication in 1916, so in 1918 the union launched a
new paper, *Golos Truzhenika*, edited by anarchist Yakov Sanzhur (who in
1921 wrote a Russian-language history of the iww).[28] Lithuanian anarchist Juozas Laukys, meanwhile, published a string of radical newspapers
in Chicago before editing *Darbiniku Balsas*, organ of a Lithuanian iww
garment worker local in Baltimore, and then the national organization's
official Lithuanian paper, *Proletaras*, from 1919 to 1923.[29] The iww also
worked closely with the Union of Russian Workers of the United States
and Canada (uorw), formed in New York in 1908 by anarchist refugees.

In 1912, the UORW adopted an anarcho-syndicalist program profoundly influenced by the IWW, and at its 1918 convention the organization resolved that its members should, wherever possible, also join the IWW. Several Russian anarchists were organizers for both organizations, and some UORW branches functioned as de facto Russian IWW locals. By the end of 1919, the UORW reached a membership of more than 9,000.[30]

This growth occurred in spite of the departure of hundreds of UORW members for Russia following the 1917 February Revolution, including experienced Wobblies like Vladimir ("Bill") Shatoff, Anatolii Gorelik, and Aron and Fanya Baron. These returned radicals led a resurgent Russian anarchist movement. In Ukraine, 25–30,000 miners joined newly created IWW locals, although "the subsequent civil war destroyed those beginnings," and returned Wobblies in Vladivostok requested American aid for "starting a Russian i.w.w. paper there."[31] But Soviet Russia did not long remain a haven for either anarchists or Wobblies. Communist authorities shot Fanya Baron in 1921, and repeatedly arrested and imprisoned her husband Aron, before executing him in 1937. Bill Shatoff, after two decades of service to the Soviet regime (despite never renouncing anarchism or joining the Communist Party), was arrested in 1937 and shot in 1941, a victim of Stalin's purges. Expatriate George Andreytchine did join the party, but his newfound allegiance to Leon Trotsky led to his expulsion in 1927 and a series of arrests, culminating in his execution in 1950.[32] Gorelik was more fortunate: he was expelled from Russia in 1921 and went to live in exile in Argentina. Deported with him was prominent anarcho-syndicalist G. P. Maximoff, who made his way to the United States in 1924, where he immediately joined the IWW and became editor of *Golos Truzhenika*, continuing the close association between Russian anarchism and the IWW.[33]

On the West Coast, anarchists spearheaded efforts to enroll Asian workers into the IWW. In 1906 Japanese socialist-turned-anarchist Kotoku Denjiro (aka Shusui Kotoku) visited San Francisco, where he frequented IWW events and incorporated Wobbly ideas into the program of the Social Revolutionary Party he founded in Berkeley, which consisted of dozens of Japanese radicals. They helped translate IWW literature into Japanese and founded the short-lived bilingual newspaper *Kakumei* (*Revolution*), which promoted the IWW. Members of this group then founded the paper *Rodo* in 1907 as the organ of the anarchist-led Japanese Workers' Union, which the following year became the IWW-affiliated Fresno Labor League and went on to organize a majority of the region's Japanese grape pickers. In 1909 the Chicago-based Japanese IWW Propaganda League published the bilingual paper *Proletarian*, which denounced anti-Japanese sentiment among American workers and socialists in English, and propagated IWW ideas in Japanese. Emma Goldman described its editor, T. Takahashi, as an "energetic comrade" who "strives to acquaint his readers with the modern ideas of Anarchism and to free them from jingoism." Through such connections, IWW literature was sent "by all manner of routes" to Japan, where it influenced the developing socialist and anarchist movements.[34] Similarly, during his stay in California anarchist Har Dayal adapted and disseminated the IWW's version of syndicalism among his fellow Indian revolutionaries within the Ghadr movement (see Khan, Chapter 3).

Nowhere, however, was anarchism as pronounced among IWW members as among Spanish-speaking Wobblies (see also Chapters 4, 5, and 7, by Struthers, Alonso, and Aguilar). In the Southwest, most Mexican IWW members also belonged to the anarchist-led Partido Liberal Mexicano (PLM), whose official newspaper, *Regeneración*, carried so much Wobbly news that in 1913 a well-informed observer mistakenly labeled it a "Spanish I.W.W. weekly."[35] This mutual support worked both ways: during the opening phase of the Mexican Revolution a few hundred American Wobblies and Italian anarchists joined the ranks of the PLM's armed insurgency in Baja California to fight for "Land and Liberty." Paterson anarchist and IWW organizer Ludovico Caminita helped direct the invasion, and briefly edited a special Italian section of *Regeneración*. Furthermore, as Nicolás Kanellos notes, "The Hispanic affiliates of the Industrial Workers of the World ... produced numerous labor newspapers that promoted anarchism."[36]

In fact, PLM members edited nearly every Spanish-language IWW periodical.[37] The remainder were directed by Spanish-born anarchists like Herminio González, who edited *El Obrero Industrial* in Tampa, Florida, on behalf of a local of Cuban and Spanish cigar workers, "inclined to be anarchists if anything." José Castilla Morales, a Spaniard who organized maritime workers and collaborated on several anarchist newspapers in Cuba before migrating to Brooklyn, likewise edited the IWW's *Solidaridad*.[38] New York's anarchist *Cultura Obrera* also became an official IWW publication. These Spanish-language newspapers—like all IWW periodicals—circulated widely both within and outside of the United States, joining other papers produced by Wobblies in Latin America, where the union's connections to anarchism were even "stronger than they were in the United States."[39]

English-language anarchist periodicals sustained interethnic links between these networks. Lucy Parsons founded *The Liberator* three months after the IWW's formation, and placed the union's logo prominently on its masthead. During its short run, the paper served as a voice for the IWW's anarchist faction, and included Albert Ryan, Andrew Klemencic, and

Joseph Corna among its contributors. That same year, Jay Fox took over editorship of the *Demonstrator*, published out of the anarchist community of Home, Washington, and added an ɪᴡᴡ section edited by Klemencic. Fox also carried frequent articles on the ɪᴡᴡ in its successor, the *Agitator*, which he edited from 1910 until he left the organization in 1912.[40]

Jean E. Spielman, the Romanian anarchist who attended the founding convention, wrote occasional pieces for the *Liberator*, the *Agitator*, and the *Industrial Worker*. In 1907, he defended the ɪᴡᴡ from criticisms in Emma Goldman's *Mother Earth*, arguing, "though the i.w.w. organization is not imbued with Anarchist views, it is, nevertheless, revolutionary."[41] Spielman, a Wobbly organizer active in Minneapolis and Connecticut, also participated in the 1912 Lawrence strike. However, he was expelled in 1913 "as a result of internal politics"—probably linked to his sympathy for Foster's strategy of "boring from within." He became an ᴀғʟ organizer and in 1916 co-edited the short-lived anarchist paper *Free Lance*.[42]

In November 1906, the first issue of San Francisco's *Emancipator* announced, "This Paper has no right to call itself an organ of 'The Industrial Workers of the World,' but it stands as an advocate of industrial unionism." Its editor was the miner and anarcho-syndicalist Laurent Casas, who spent six years in a French penal colony for attacking a foreman before moving, in 1902, to the United States, where he contributed to both the *Liberator* and the Parisian anarchist paper *Les Temps Nouveaux*. When the failing *Emancipator* was absorbed by *The Demonstrator* in 1907, Casas temporarily replaced Fox as editor. Casas later joined the Latin Branch of San Francisco's ɪᴡᴡ Local 173, a pan-ethnic organization encompassing Italian, French, and Spanish-speaking workers led by anarchists like Casas (who later became a socialist) and Italian organizer Luigi Parenti, convicted in the federal ɪᴡᴡ trial in 1918 and subsequently deported.[43] As this and many of the examples above illustrate, anarchist-edited ɪᴡᴡ publications were intimately linked to practical organizing—as well as revolutionary undertakings—at the local and transnational levels. They also proved instrumental in mobilizing anarchist support for ɪᴡᴡ initiatives, and recruiting radicalized workers for anarchist projects like the invasion of Baja California.

Conclusion

Contrary to the old shibboleth, anarchists in the ɪᴡᴡ organized not only themselves but also tens of thousands of their fellow workers into a militant minority dedicated to building a libertarian socialist world within the shell of the old. Decades of their "opaque" activism profoundly shaped the union, and their influence only increased over time. Their contributions ranged from constructive and organizational—even, at times, remarkably procedural—to disruptive, factional, and insurgent. They did their best to push against bureaucracy and centralization within the union, and to support workers' initiative and rebellion wherever they could. They also used the IWW as a vehicle for anarchist ideology and forms of organization—though not always by that name—and in doing so blurred the lines between Wobblies and anarchists, as well as between local, national, and international struggles. Non-anarchist IWW leaders and organizers, in turn, usually were more than happy to accept the aid of anarchist activists and tap into the pre-existing networks that connected them to anarchist and syndicalist movements abroad. And quite often, it was through these anarchist intermediaries that the IWW and its influence spread outside the United States.

Notes

1 Salvatore Salerno, *Red November, Black November: Culture and Community in the Industrial Workers of the World* (New York: State University of New York Press, 1989); Jose C. Moya, "Anarchism," in Akira Iriye and Pierre-Yves Saunier (eds.), *The Palgrave Dictionary of Transnational History* (New York: Palgrave Macmillan, 2009), pp. 39–41; Devra Anne Weber, "Wobblies of the Partido Liberal Mexicano: reenvisioning internationalist and transnational movements through Mexican lenses," *Pacific Historical Review* 85:2 (2016): 226.

2 Davide Turcato, "Collective action, opacity, and the 'problem of irrationality': anarchism and the first of May, 1890–1892," *Journal for the Study of Radicalism* 5:1 (2011): 3.

3 Steve Golin, *The Fragile Bridge: Paterson Silk Strike, 1913* (Philadelphia, Pa.: Temple University Press, 1988), p. 41.

4 Elizabeth Gurley Flynn, "The truth about the Paterson strike," in Joyce L. Kornbluh (ed.), *Rebel Voices: An I.W.W. Anthology* (Ann Arbor, Mich.: University of Michigan Press, 1968), p. 216; *Solidarity*, April 19, 1913; *Final Report and Testimony Submitted to Congress by the Commission on Industrial Relations* (Washington DC: Government Printing Office, 1916), p. 2455. See also Elizabeth Gurley Flynn, *The Rebel Girl: An Autobiography* (New York: International Publishers, 1973), pp. 155, 166–7.

5 Margaret R. Sanger, "The Paterson strike," in Hippolyte Havel (ed.), *The Revolutionary Almanac: 1914* (New York: Rabelais Press, 1914), p. 47; Salvatore Salerno, "No god, no master: Italian anarchists and the Industrial Workers of the World," in Philip V. Cannistraro and Gerald Meyer (eds.), *The Lost World of Italian American Radicalism: Politics, Labor, and Culture* (Westport, Conn.: Praeger, 2003), pp. 171–87; Kenyon Zimmer, *Immigrants Against the State: Yiddish and Italian Anarchism in America* (Urbana, Ill.: University of Illinois Press, 2015), ch. 2.

6 Paul Avrich, *Anarchist Voices: An Oral History of Anarchism in America* (Princeton, N.J.: Princeton University Press, 1995), p. 155; Francesco Rigazio, "Alberto Guabello, Firmino Gallo e altri anarchici di Mongrando nella catena migratori dal biellese a Paterson N.J.," *Archivi e storia* 23/24 (2004): 143–258; Jennifer Guglielmo, *Living the Revolution: Italian Women's Resistance and Radicalism in New York City, 1880–1945* (Chapel Hill, N.C.: University of North Carolina Press, 2010), pp. 154, 193–5; Zimmer, *Immigrants against the State*, pp. 79–80, 83–85.

7 Translation of *La Jacquerie*, May 21, 1919, in file 61-4185, Old German Files, Records of the Federal Bureau of Investigation, Record Group 65, National Archives and Records Administration, College Park, Maryland (hereafter FBI).

8 *One Big Union Monthly*, November 1919; Nels Hokanson, "Swedes in the I.W.W.," *Swedish Pioneer Historical Quarterly* 23:1 (1972): 25, 32; Daniel De Leon, *As to Politics: A Discussion upon the Relative Importance of Political Action and of Class-Conscious Economic Action, and the Urgent Necessity of Both* (New York: Labor News Press, 1907); Johan Sandgren, *Samhällsproblemet och dess lösning* (Stockholm: Ugsocialistska partiets förlag, 1912); Johan Sandgren, *Från primitiv till industriell kommunism, eller Syndikalismen från samhällshistorisk synpunkt* (Malmö, Sweden: Accidens- & Reklamtryckeriet, 1915); Per Nordahl, *Weaving the Ethnic Fabric: Social Networks Among Swedish-American Radicals in Chicago, 1890–1940* (Stockholm: Almqvist & Wiksell, 1994), p. 41.

9 Vincent St John, *The I.W.W.: Its History, Structure and Methods*, rev. edn. (Chicago, Ill.: IWW Publishing Bureau, 1917), p. 6; *La Questione Sociale*, July 15, 1905; Salerno, *Red November, Black November*, ch. 3; *Les Temps Nouveaux*, August 26, 1905.

10 *La Questione Sociale* lists "A. Wermich," which appears to be a misspelling of the name "A. Wrink" that appears in the official proceedings.

11 Gianna S. Panofsky, "A view of two major centers of Italian anarchism in the United States: Spring Valley and Chicago, Illinois," in Dominic Candeloro, Fred L. Gardaphe, and Paolo A. Giordano (eds.), *Italian Ethnics: Their Languages, Literature and Lives* (Staten Island, N.Y.: American Italian Historical Association, 1990), p. 278; *La Questione Sociale*, July 15, 1905.

12 Josef Peukert, *Erinnerungen eines Proletariers aus der Revolutionären Arbeiterbewegung* (Berlin: Sozialistischen Bundes, 1913), p. 301; *The Founding Convention of the IWW: Proceedings* (1905; reprint, New York: Merit Publishers, 1969), p. 615; Michel Cordillot (ed.), *La sociale en Amérique: dictionnaire biographique du mouvement social francophone aux États-Unis (1848–1922)* (Paris: les Éditions de l'Atelier, 2002), entry for Klemencic A.; Zimmer, *Immigrants against the State*, pp. 91, 122.

13 Salerno, *Red November, Black November*, pp. 73–7; Robert E. Doherty, "Thomas J. Hagerty, the church, and socialism," *Labor History* 3:1 (1962): 39–56.

14 *Founding Convention*, pp. 546, 269, 113–14, 297–9.

15 *Proceedings of the Second Annual Convention of the Industrial Workers of the World* (Chicago, Ill.: IWW, 1906), p. 190.

16 "Proceedings of Third Annual Convention Industrial Workers of the World held at Chicago, Ill., 1907: Official Report," *Socialist Labor Party of America*, 2011, pp. 459, 109–10, 134–7, 140–9, www.slp.org/pdf/slphist/iww_conv_1907.pdf

17 Earl C. Ford and William Z. Foster, *Syndicalism* (Chicago, Ill.: William Z. Foster [1912]), pp. 5, 31.

18 Eric Thomas Chester, *The Wobblies in Their Heyday: The Rise and Destruction*

of the Industrial Workers of the World during the World War I Era (Santa Barbara, Calif.: Praeger, 2014), pp. 223–4; Kenyon Zimmer, "Premature anti-communists? American anarchism, the Russian Revolution, and left-wing libertarian anticommunism, 1917–1939," *Labor* 6:2 (2009): 59–61.

19 Louis Levine, "The development of syndicalism in America," *Political Science Quarterly* 28 (September 1913): 475; Andrew Hoyt, "Methods for tracing radical networks: mapping the print culture and propagandists of the Sovversivi," in Jorell A. Melendez Badillo and J. Nathan Jun (eds.), *Without Borders Or Limits: An Interdisciplinary Approach to Anarchist Studies* (Newcastle upon Tyne, UK: Cambridge Scholars, 2013), p. 85. On the functions of both the anarchist and IWW press, see also Linda J. Lumsden, *Black, White, and Red All Over: A Cultural History of the Radical Press in Its Heyday, 1900–1917* (Kent, Ohio: Kent State University Press, 2014).

20 New York State Senate, Joint Legislative Committee Investigating Seditious Activities, *Revolutionary Radicalism: Its History, Purpose and Tactics with an Exposition and Discussion of the Steps Being Taken and Required to Curb It*, vol. 2 (Albany, N.Y.: J. B. Lyon, 1920), pp. 2004–06; Louis Loebl, "i.w.w. publications," April 21, 1920, File 340162, Bureau Section Files, FBI; Philip S. Foner, *History of the Labor Movement in the United States*, vol. 4 (New York: International Publishers, 1965), p. 150.

21 *One Big Union Monthly*, December 1920, January 1921; Dirk Hoerder (ed.), *The Immigrant Labor Press in North America, 1840s–1970s: An Annotated Bibliography*, vol. 1 (New York: Greenwood Press, 1987), p. 96.

22 Marcus C. Robyns, Katelyn Weber, and Laura Lipp, "Reluctant revolutionaries: Finnish iron miners and the failure of radical labor and socialism on the Marquette Iron Range, 1900–1914," in Robert Archibald (ed.), *Northern Border: Essays on Michigan's Upper Peninsula and Beyond* (Marquette, Mich.: Northern Michigan University Press, 2014), pp. 212–43; Auvo Kostiainen, "A dissenting voice of Finnish radicals in America: the formative years of *Sosialisti-Industrialisti* in the 1910s," *American Studies in Scandinavia* 23:2 (1991): 83–94.

23 New York State Senate, *Revolutionary Radicalism*, pp. 865–9; Thomas Hyder, "An American journey: the 'activist' lives of Gust Alonen and Carl Paivio," *Siirtolaisuus-Migration* 38:2 (2011): 21–30.

24 Ralph Chaplin, *Wobbly: The Rough-and-Tumble Story of an American Radical* (Chicago, Ill.: University of Chicago Press, 1948), p. 211.

25 Jordan Baev and Kostadin Grozev, *An Odyssey across Two Worlds: George the Bulgarian and Soviet-American Relations During the First Half of the 20th Century*, trans. Greta Keremidchieva, rev. edn. (Sofia: n.p., 2014), n.p., https://www.academia.edu/5891252/Andreytchine_Eng2014.

26 Baev and Grozev, *Odyssey across Two Worlds*.

27 Hoerder, *Immigrant Labor Press*, vol. 2, p. 457; Baev and Grozev, *Odyssey across Two Worlds*; *One Big Union Monthly*, February 1920; File 154434, Bureau Section Files, FBI; *Industrial Pioneer*, February 1921.

28 Frank Mintz (ed.), *Anatol Gorelik: el anarquismo en la revolucion rusa* (La Plata, Argentina: Terramar, 2007), p. 21; *Proceedings of the Tenth Convention of the Industrial Workers of the World* (Chicago, Ill.: IWW, 1917), p. 95; Avrich, *Anarchist Voices*, p. 368; Yakov Sanzhur, *Istoriia industrial'nykh rabochikh mira* (Chicago, Ill.: Izd. Ispolnitelnago komiteta russkikh otdelov I.R.M.), 1921.

29 Jon Everett Bekken, "Working-class newspapers, community and consciousness

in Chicago, 1880–1930", PHD diss., University of Illinois at Urbana-Champaign (1992), p. 224.

30 Sanzhur, *Istoriia industrial'nykh rabochikh mira*, pp. 183–4; New York State Senate, *Revolutionary Radicalism*, p. 861.

31 Paul Avrich, *The Russian Anarchists* (Princeton, N.J.: Princeton University Press, 1967), pp. 125, 205–6, 137–51; G. P. Maximoff, *The Guillotine at Work: Twenty Years of Terror in Russia (Data and Documents)* (Chicago, Ill.: Alexander Berkman Aid Fund, 1940), p. 366; "Synopsis of minutes of meeting of General Executive Board, held June 29th–July 6th, 1917," p. 3, folder 3, box 7, Industrial Workers of the World Collection, Wayne State.

32 Avrich, *Russian Anarchists*, pp. 232–3, 245; Matthew J. Payne, *Stalin's Railroad: Turksib and the Building of Socialism* (Pittsburgh, Pa.: University of Pittsburgh Press, 2001), p. 309 n.53; Baev and Grozev, *Odyssey across Two Worlds*.

33 Mintz, *Anatol Gorelik*, pp. 22–5; Sam Dolgoff, *Fragments: A Memoir* (Cambridge, Mass.: Refract, 1986), pp. 47–8.

34 "Third Annual Convention," p. 274; Yuji Ichioka, *The Issei: The World of the First Generation Japanese Immigrants, 1885–1924* (New York: Free Press, 1988), pp. 50–5; *Proletarian*, August 25, 1909; *Mother Earth*, July 1910; John Crump, *The Origins of Socialist Thought in Japan* (New York: St Martin's Press, 1983), p. 197.

35 Paul F. Brissenden, *The Launching of the Industrial Workers of the World* (Berkeley, Calif.: University of California Press, 1913), p. 82.

36 William M. Adler, *The Man Who Never Died: The Life, Times, and Legacy of Joe Hill, American Labor Icon* (New York: Bloomsbury, 2011), ch. 8; Zimmer, *Immigrants against the State*, pp. 125–8; Nicolás Kanellos, "Spanish-language Anarchist Periodicals in early twentieth-century United States," in James L. Baughman, Jennifer Ratner-Rosenhagen, and James P. Danky (eds.), *Protest on the Page: Essays on Print and the Culture of Dissent* (Madison, Wis.: University of Wisconsin Press, 2015), p. 74.

37 Weber, "Wobblies of the Partido Liberal Mexicano," p. 209 n.47.

38 Hoerder, *Immigrant Labor Press*, vol. 3, p. 180; Gary Ross Mormino and George E. Pozzetta, *The Immigrant World of Ybor City: Italians and Their Latin Neighbors in Tampa, 1885–1985* (Chicago, Ill.: University of Illinois Press, 1987), p. 126; Montse Feu, "José Castilla Morales y *España Libre* (1939–1977): sátira contra la dictadura de Francisco Franco desde Henry Street, Brooklyn," *Migraciones y Exilios* 14 (2014): 89–91.

39 Anton Rosenthal, "Radical border crossers: the Industrial Workers of the World and their press in Latin America," *Estudios Interdisciplinarios de América Latina y el Caribe* 22:2 (2011): 39–70 (quote on 63).

40 Greg Hall, "Jay Fox: a journey from anarchism to communism," *Left History* 16:1 (2012): 19–23.

41 *Mother Earth*, December 1907; *Syndicalist*, April 1, 1913; "Biographical sketch," *Jean E. Spielman: An Inventory of His Papers at the Minnesota Historical Society*, p. 4, www2.mnhs.org/library/findaids/mo535.pdf

42 Ernesto A. Longa, *Anarchist Periodicals in English Published in the United States (1833–1955): An Annotated Guide* (Lanham, Md.: Scarecrow Press, 2009), p. 79.

43 *Emancipator*, November 1906; Cordillot, *La sociale en Amérique*, entry on Casas Laurent; Zimmer, *Immigrants against the State*, chs. 3, 5.

2

Sabotage, the IWW, and Repression: How the American Reinterpretation of a French Concept Gave Rise to a New International Conception of Sabotage

Dominique Pinsolle
(translated by Jesse Cohn)

Symbolized by the famous black cat drawn by Ralph Chaplin, sabotage is closely associated with the Industrial Workers of the World (IWW). However, France was where this practice was theorized (though not invented) in the middle of the 1890s, particularly by the revolutionary syndicalist Emile Pouget.[1] The Confédération Générale du Travail (General Confederation of Labour, or CGT) officially adopted sabotage as a means of struggle at the Toulouse Congress of 1897, although the term's etymology is obscure. The IWW generally endorsed the legend of wooden shoes (*sabots*) being thrown into machines by workers,[2] which explains the recurrence of the symbol of the wooden shoe in its iconography. However it seems rather that the term derives from the verb *saboter*, which, in the French slang of the early nineteenth century, indicates the act of working badly on purpose, "as if by sabot blows."[3]

At the beginning, certain French revolutionary syndicalists conceived of sabotage as a voluntary and clandestine degradation of the quality of work, of materials, or of the product itself, in order to harm the interests of the employer alone.[4] The IWW enthusiastically embraced the concept of sabotage, including using the French term, and routinely advocated this tactic from at least 1912 until the great Chicago trial of 1918.[5] Many historians have studied the defense of this means of action, its real or ostensible influence on the practices of the Wobblies, as well as its use by local and federal authorities to repress the organization.[6] However, few have studied the very definition of the concept of sabotage and its evolution during this period. The extreme malleability of this concept raises another question: was sabotage, such as it was propounded and denounced in the United States during the period when the IWW considered it a legitimate means of struggle, merely the prolongation of the tactic adopted by certain French syndicalists and revolutionaries since the mid-1890s? This chapter contends that, far from being reduced to a French influence, IWW defenders of sabotage actually reinterpreted this concept, which, while used by the Wobblies' enemies to justify attacks on the organization, ended up acquiring characteristics peculiar to the United States, the likes of which did not appear in France.

William D. "Big Bill" Haywood, for one, delivered a speech on March 16, 1911 in New York, in which he used the strike of the French railway workers and the methods of the "sabotagers" as an example.[7] This speech launched the process of reinterpreting the concept of sabotage first developed within the CGT. Then, between 1912 and 1913, this tactic became the object of intense debates and discussions that led to a particular American conception of sabotage. Lastly, this chapter will examine the way in which the repression directed at the IWW during the First World War helped broaden the definition of sabotage by associating it with subversive and clandestine acts ostensibly in the service of a foreign power.

The Partial Importation of a French Concept

In the United States, as elsewhere, the practices associated with the term "sabotage" predate its adoption.[8] The word first appeared in the English-language US press to account for the new methods used by French syndicalists.[9] However, only during the French railroad strike of October 1910 did American newspapers take a more specific interest in sabotage, presented as a French peculiarity and very strongly related to the anti-militarist agitation which, up to that point, had been absent from the United States.[10] In the *International Socialist Review*, Austin Lewis, a lawyer specializing in trade union questions, noted, "[s]o far nothing of the sort has been reported in this country," but he predicted the inevitable use of such practices in the United States.[11] The term appears for the first time in the IWW paper *Solidarity* on June 4, 1910, in connection with a garment workers' strike in Chicago.[12] However, it was William D. Haywood's visit to Europe that proved decisive in the concept's adoption by the IWW. Haywood attended the Copenhagen congress of the Second International (August 28 to September 3, 1910) as a delegate of the Socialist Party of America (SPA), but extended his stay in Europe beyond Denmark.[13] Haywood arrived in France that October, with the railroad strike in full swing. Following a visit to Italy, he returned to France, and met with the revolutionary socialist Gustave Hervé, then incarcerated in the prison of La Santé, where he also met Miguel Almereyda and Eugène Merle.[14] All three belonged to the editorial board of *La Guerre Sociale*, a revolutionary journal founded by Hervé in 1906 that had consistently advocated sabotage since the postal strike of 1909.

Haywood's time in France left a strong impression on him. On his return to the United States, he cited the French railway workers' strike as proof of the effectiveness of revolutionary syndicalism. In his speech of March 16, 1911, he even exaggerated the movement's effectiveness. The striking workers' demands, far from having been met after three days, as Haywood claimed,[15] only resulted in concrete measures several months later.[16] As for the dismissed workers, less than half of them had been reinstated by the end of 1915, for reasons having little to do with continued disruptions caused by militants.[17]

The October 1910 strike, however, remained an exceptional event, as much for its scope as for the methods used by the railway workers.[18] Haywood's interest is understandable, insofar as the IWW, which he helped found, was in a delicate situation.

Weakened by the schism of 1908, the organization scarcely averaged 12,800 members during 1911,[19] whereas the American Federation of Labor represented 80 percent of the country's approximately 2 million unionized workers.[20] Similarly, at the beginning of the twentieth century, the CGT was isolated, numbering approximately 108,000 members in 1902. The French revolutionary syndicalists considered sabotage to be a tactic well suited to their theory of the general strike and the action of conscious minorities.[21] Sabotage, thus, likely also appealed to Haywood as an effective tactic both fully compatible with the direct action tactics celebrated by the IWW and ready to be put into practice by a small number of militants. While speaking to workers in New York, he emphasized this point: "I tell it to you in hopes that you will spread the good news to your fellow-workers and apply it yourselves whenever occasion demands."[22]

However, the IWW leader only mentioned part of what those he referred to as "sabotagers" had done.[23] In his speech, it is only a matter of the "*grève perlée*"; he used the French term, which he translated as "drop strike," that is, the intentionally poor performance of tasks. In focusing on this aspect of the French railway workers' resistance, Haywood omitted the more destructive dimension, as manifested in the cutting of an unprecedented number of telephone and telegraph lines, along with other sorts of damage inflicted upon the rail network.[24] Haywood could not have been unaware of these events because line cuts were a daily occurrence while he was in France and he talked with sabotage's principal theorists.[25]

In other words, he only discussed the least violent aspect of the French railway workers' mobilization on his return to the United States, and for good reason. First, Haywood delivered his speech in New York in March 1911, less than six months after the bombing of the *Los Angeles Times* building which, in October 1910, took 21 lives. The McNamara brothers, accused of that crime, remained fugitives and were not caught until April 1911, while the United States remained in a state of shock. In this context, Haywood's cautious celebration of sabotage—only citing non-destructive methods as examples—glossed over the rest. His choice also can be understood given the bloody repression visited upon past mobilizations involving US transportation, particularly the Great Railroad Strike of 1877 and Pullman strike of 1894. These examples likely dissuaded Haywood from praising the merits of sabotage directed against the telephone and telegraph lines with the intent of disrupting or even preventing the normal operation of France's transportation systems. As a former leader of the Western Federation of Miners, he knew full well of the violence of the "Colorado labor wars" a few years before, which quite possibly led him to remain very moderate about sabotage. Finally, his own two-year travail, when he was prosecuted and eventually acquitted for hiring someone to blow up the former governor of Idaho, could not have been far from his mind.[26]

The other explanatory factor probably lies in the question of anti-militarism, which had much greater weight in France than in the United States at that time. Since 1909, Gustave Hervé and his friends had theorized sabotage from an anti-militarist perspective. In their eyes, workers had the power to paralyze the country and to prevent the mobilization of soldiers in case of war by sabotaging the telecommunications network.[27] Haywood and the editors of *La Guerre Sociale* had talked a great deal about opposition to militarism and war when he visited the prison of La Santé.[28] Even though the French anarchists scarcely had begun working out their plans for "mobilisation sabotage" by March 1911, when Haywood delivered his New York speech,[29] advocates of sabotage in France already widely embraced the idea that attacks targeting certain points of the transportation and telecommunications systems could block an entry into war. Many increasingly advocated anti-militarism, especially as concern over a new conflict with Germany increased following the First Moroccan Crisis of 1905, during which Wilhelm II challenged French domination over Morocco by going to Tangier. By contrast, no compulsory military service existed in the United States and war did not seem to be on the agenda after the ending of the US–Philippines war in 1902. Therefore Haywood retained only the strictly labor aspect of sabotage, at the same time that the French increasingly integrated this tactic into large-scale anti-militarist projects.

The French influence on the IWW is thus undeniable with regard to the promotion of sabotage, but it remained limited. In the end, Haywood did not entirely import the concept first developed by the CGT and then *La Guerre Sociale*, and as put into practice during the railway workers' mobilization he witnessed in 1910: instead, it inspired him to praise the merits of a non-destructive form of direct action adapted to the American context. While perhaps not the first to speak of this means of struggle, Haywood nonetheless set out the bases of a conception specific to the IWW, clearly distinguished from the methods then adopted by certain French anarchists and syndicalists.

The IWW's Specific Conception of Sabotage

Only amidst the legendary "Bread and Roses" textile workers' strike in Lawrence, Massachusetts did the word "sabotage" become truly "Americanized."[30] When the strike erupted in January 1912, Joseph Ettor and Arturo Giovannitti, important figures in the IWW, helped lead the strike but they suffered imprisonment after being brought up on bogus murder charges. Into the breech came Elizabeth Gurley Flynn and Haywood, who became deeply involved in the strike, "preaching [like Ettor] 'solidarity', 'passive resistance', 'direct action', and 'sabotage' as means to victory."[31] The especially violent conflict also elicited a wave of solidarity across the country, and in early March, ended in an impressive victory for the workers, including wage increases and the subsequent release of Ettor and Giovannitti.[32]

Due to this strike, the IWW became more widely known by the general public, but the Wobblies' advocacy of sabotage posed a problem for the SPA. Then enjoying increasing electoral success, the SPA leadership feared the loss of potential voters scared off by overly radical methods.[33] The question of violence thus took a central place in its Indianapolis convention of May 1912.[34] Although it was not explicitly mentioned at the beginning,[35] the call to endorse the use of sabotage was condemned, after a sharp debate, by the vast majority of the socialist delegates—191 to 90 votes.[36] This amendment seemed to be aimed at the IWW militants, including Haywood, who was forced off the party's executive committee in 1913. Even though this split was owing to a broader conflict between the ballot and direct action, the sabotage issue crystallized the debates and "[t]he discussion centered on [this] motion to insert a new clause in the constitution of the Socialist Party."[37]

For their part, the Wobblies continued to develop their own concept of sabotage. In 1912, IWW secretary-treasurer William Trautmann published a booklet entitled *Direct Action and Sabotage*.[38] Active in Russia and Germany before emigrating to the United States in 1890, Trautmann was one of the first promoters of European-style "syndicalism" in the United States, first in the Brewery Workers Union, then in the IWW.[39] After reviewing the various forms of direct and indirect action available to workers, Trautmann, just like the first French advocates of sabotage, affirmed that capitalists were the real saboteurs, as proven by their willingness to sacrifice the quality of the products they sell to increase profits. He used the example of bakeries to support the same argument made at the time of the Parisian bakers' strike of 1906.[40] Trautmann's definition of the method—the withdrawal of efficiency from work—strongly recalled the first forms of sabotage theorized in France before 1909, which were in turn strongly influenced by the practice of "ca'canny," a Scottish slang expression indicating the act of working at less than full effort, or in other words "going slow." Glasgow dock workers used this method in 1889 and, in spite of their strike's failure, then achieved their goals by working as poorly as did the strikebreakers employed during the conflict.[41] However, Trautmann also recalled the example of the French railway workers' strike of 1910 (without referring to it explicitly), relying on Haywood's account.[42] Here, still, Trautmann said nothing about the cutting of telephone or telegraph lines.

Unlike Trautmann, Walker C. Smith, a Colorado militant, was directly inspired by Emile Pouget's book, *Le Sabotage*.[43] Starting in January 1913, Smith published 13 articles on the subject of sabotage in the *Industrial Worker*, which were collected in the form of a booklet later that year.[44] In these, Smith reproduced extracts from Pouget, adapting Pouget's propositions to the US context. After describing various forms of sabotage, including the destructive ones, the author took care to specify, from the outset, that he opposed any action endangering human life or harming consumers. However, his defense of sabotage went farther than Haywood's and Trautmann's insofar as, according to Smith, this tactic also constituted a means of resisting war. The examples he gave, however, remained the same, again defined in terms of the "withdrawal of efficiency," the slow-down, the *grève perlée*, obstructionism (excessive application of the rules), and the "open mouth" technique (informing consumers about an employer's fraudulent practices).[45]

During his imprisonment after the Lawrence strike, Arturo Giovannitti translated Pouget's book into English, and it was published in Chicago in 1913. In the introduction, Giovannitti denounced the adoption of the anti-sabotage amendment by the Socialist Party, but he proved more cautious than Smith in his defense of sabotage: whether it entailed reducing productivity or putting machines out of service, he assured readers, "[i]t is not destructive. It has nothing to do with violence, neither to life nor to property."[46]

Writings devoted to sabotage multiplied after 1912, discussing tactics as well as theoretical questions. In February 1913, the great silk workers' strike of Paterson, New Jersey, broke out. During the conflict, Frederick Sumner Boyd, an IWW militant, delivered a speech in which he advised strikers, as a last resort, to sabotage the spinning and dyeing operations. On September 30, he was tried and convicted of having advocated the destruction of private property. This sentence was the first in the country involving the advocacy of sabotage. The IWW quickly published a booklet in New York denouncing Boyd's punishment and highlighting that sabotage did not necessarily mean destruction of property.[47] Boyd was nevertheless imprisoned. Elizabeth Gurley Flynn took up his defense, and in a famous speech made to the Francisco Ferrer School in New York on December 21, explained the principles of sabotage.[48] This text, published in April 1915 and again in 1917 (without the permission of its author[49]), synthesized the imported European principles and their American interpretation.[50]

While acknowledging the significance of the CGT congress of 1897, Flynn immediately emphasized that this tactic already existed in the form of the "withdrawal of efficiency." Her description otherwise generally tracks closely to Pouget in *Sabotage*, except for the passages devoted to Boyd's case. As in the writings previously quoted, she made no allusion to the French workers' severing of telecommunication lines in 1909–11. "Sabotage is not physical violence," explained the orator, who assured readers that this tactic "is an internal, industrial process. It is something that is fought out within the four walls of the shop."[51] This rather willfully restrictive definition demonstrates the reinterpretation of the concept in the American context. Ralph Chaplin emphasized this key point in his memoirs: "Gurley Flynn's pamphlet ... was a brief restatement of the type of sabotage advocated by European anarchists and syndicalists from which the IWW had adopted only a few features applicable to conditions in the USA."[52]

Cartoon by Ralph Chaplin ["Bingo"], 1910s

Setting aside Smith's remarks suggesting the usefulness of this tactic for anti-militarist ends and presenting some destructive acts as legitimate, the promotion of sabotage by IWW leaders remained generally much more limited than in France, where anarchists and anti-militarists had hoped, since 1911, to paralyze the country in the event of war.[53] The discrepancy between the two countries was so great that the Scottish influence at times seemed predominant in America. After the war, returning to the Wobblies' use of the term "sabotage," Austin Lewis rightly noted: "IWW literature has used it in many ways and frequently in the mere sense of passivity, what is called ca'canny."[54] However, in spite of its overall moderated character, the defense of sabotage by the IWW (which only officially endorsed this mode of action after its ninth convention, in 1914)[55] served as a pretext for the authorities to criminalize the organization. Beginning in 1915, a campaign of repression, initially conducted on the local level, then on the federal level after 1917, helped to associate the figure of the saboteur with that of the criminal, and then the traitor.

How the Saboteur Became a Traitor

In the West, where the IWW managed to rebuild itself following the failure of the Paterson strike,[56] the question of sabotage took on a new dimension. Following the August 1913 Wheatland hop riot in the northern part of California's Central Valley, two IWW militants, Dick Ford and Herman Suhr, were arrested. The California IWW immediately demanded their release, threatening to launch a campaign of sabotage in the agricultural industries, and, in the summer of 1915, hinted that fields might be set on fire. These threats, approved by the leaders of the organization (including Haywood),[57] were taken all the more seriously by the Government of California when suspicious fires multiplied that summer. The California Commission of Immigration and Housing, soon assisted by the Pinkerton National Detective Agency, investigated, hoping to prove the culpability of the Wobblies. In spite of the absence of credible evidence linking the fires to the rhetoric of the IWW, the governors of several Western states requested federal intervention, in vain. Simultaneously, the IWW abandoned its strategy of threats in the autumn of 1915, yet left behind the image of a dangerous, extremist trade union—and without having obtained the release of Ford and Suhr. Although the organization's responsibility for these fires was never proven, local authorities believed the IWW was behind a vast plot across the West. This theory failed to convince the federal government, for the moment, but the enemies of the IWW reused it after the outbreak of war in Europe.[58] In this context the figure of the saboteur took on a new dimension, associated with an internal enemy in the service of a foreign power.

Starting in 1917, the federal authorities initiated a campaign of repression against the IWW which conflated sabotage and treason. Conversely, during the war, the French government paid scant attention to the possibility of sabotage serving (intentionally or unintentionally) the interests of Germany. The immediate rallying of the French working class to the "Sacred Union" as of August 4, 1914 suddenly made the threat of "mobilization sabotage" disappear, though previously it had considerably worried the authorities.[59] Before the war, beginning in 1909-10, the CGT had begun to distance itself from insurrectionary doctrines, and Gustave Hervé himself renounced his anti-patriotism upon his release from prison in 1912[60] – paradoxically, the same year the IWW published a translation of one of his texts, dating from 1905, denouncing patriotism.[61] Only certain anarchist groups continued to advocate a form of destructive sabotage intended to prevent France from entering the war, but their projects remained a "dead letter." During the conflict, thus, there exists almost no record of any sabotage in France, whether in the form of slowdowns or acts of destruction, even after 1917.

Therefore, while the term "sabotage" spread and continued to designate rather disparate acts, the method was not publicly associated with a clan-destine practice likely to weaken the country in its war against Germany.[62] In the United States, however, the Wobblies' attitude seemed more ambig-uous. As a precautionary measure, the IWW ceased calling for anti-militarist actions after the declaration of war on April 6, 1917, but it did not endorse the government's war efforts. Nevertheless, in the eyes of state and fed-eral government officials the union remained highly suspect for having established itself among the immigrant agricultural workers of the West, and supposedly for receiving German money as early as 1915.[63] As IWW strikes multiplied during the war years, the union posed a real threat to federal war production,[64] as well as to industries in Western states that sub-jected it to "criminal syndicalism" laws they adopted or tried to adopt in 1917–18.[65]

In this context, the question of sabotage became central, and the debates that had ceased to trouble France continued in the United States. (In 1917 the Cornell Dramatic Club, for instance, adapted the French play *Sabotage*, staged in Paris in 1910.[66]) The defense of this mode of action by the IWW proved a decisive role in the ferocious repression targeting the IWW. From then onward, Wobblies were no longer merely accused of advocating vi-olence but were also denounced as traitors. When the United States was still officially neutral but providing material aid to the Allies, the country was the scene of a sabotage campaign orchestrated by Germany. German agents acting on US soil were suspected of having committed nearly 200 acts of sabotage before the United States' entry into the war, including the destruction of an ammunition dump on Black Tom Island and of a Kingsland, New Jersey munitions factory in 1916.[67] Many Americans be-lieved the IWW also acted on behalf of Germany, or, at the very least, that the context of war justified launching a new campaign of repression against the organization.

After the adoption of the Espionage Act on June 15, 1917 (supplemented in April 1918 by the Sabotage Act, and by the Sedition Act in the following month), the California Commission of Immigration and Housing and eight Western governors again demanded federal intervention to end IWW intrigues, to which Wilson agreed in the summer of 1917.[68] Whatever the motivations, the repression that fell upon the union focused on sabotage. Documents published by the IWW since the beginning of the 1910s in support of this tactic were used to affirm that the Wobblies had advocated violence and clandestine action for years. Moreover, the anti-militarist stances of the organization, albeit prior to April 6, 1917, allowed the enemies of the IWW to accuse it of obstructing the war effort. As a result, hundreds were arrested and 93 militants were sentenced to federal prison, some of them (including Haywood) for 20 years, in the mass trial in Chicago in 1918.[69]

If this history is well known, the extent of the transformations in the concept of sabotage at the time is not. In vainly attempting to prove that the IWW received German money,[70] those campaigning against the union contributed substantially to giving this concept a new dimension. Whereas to IWW militants the term "sabotage" indicated, first and foremost, a form of direct action confined to the workplace, during the war it became synonymous with subversive and clandestine acts in the service of a foreign power. It is necessary to examine in detail who precisely took part, and at which times, in this concept's redefinition. For, indeed, the process involved a multitude of actors. Among the many enemies of the IWW, for example, the National Civic Federation, a conservative think tank created in 1900, played a decisive role. During the year 1918, this organization strove to explain that, in spite of the impossibility of proving any connection between the IWW and Germany, the defense of sabotage by Wobblies and its practice by German agents sufficiently proved their collusion.[71]

No doubt the German government itself used the term sabotage, at least as of January 1915, to designate the clandestine acts of its agents in the United States,[72] although later sources should be read with skepticism as they tended to use the term in an anachronistic way, especially during the deliberations of the Mixed Claims Commission between 1922 and 1939, which intended to determine responsibility for the acts committed on US soil prior to April 6, 1917.[73] Contrary to what the National Civic Federation asserted, this did not prove that IWW methods directly inspired the German government. However, the extension of the definition of the term "sabotage," and the appropriation of this term by a multitude of actors on an international scale, reveal this concept no longer remained the preserve of a fraction of the workers' movement.

Conclusion

Studying the IWW from the standpoint of the practices and concepts it used highlights the influence of French revolutionary syndicalism on the organization but also qualifies it. Certainly, sabotage as a concept originated with the CGT, itself inspired by the Scottish practice of "ca'canny." However, the IWW redefined it according to the American context. Despite the very limited conception of sabotage promoted by the IWW, its enemies associated this tactic with a form of treason in wartime. Paradoxically, a rather reductive version of sabotage, while being denounced in the United

States as an antipatriotic practice, subsequently contributed to the emergence of a new and much broader concept that included subversive and clandestine acts in the service of a foreign power. However, it was in the United States—rather than in France—that sabotage was conceptualized as such and this transformation occurred. Further research is necessary to determine whether we might observe a similar process in other countries, particularly in Soviet Russia, which created the "All-Russian Extraordinary Commission for the Struggle Against Counterrevolution and Sabotage" (the Cheka) in December 1917. Regardless, the defense of sabotage by the IWW, far from being the pale imitation of a French syndicalist tactic quickly reduced to nothing by the federal government, gave rise to a concept adapted to the US context that indirectly contributed to the international dissemination of yet another iteration of the concept after 1918.

Notes

1 Sébastien Albertelli, *Histoire du sabotage: De la CGT à la Résistance* (Paris: Perrin, 2016).

2 Ralph Chaplin, *Wobbly: The Rough-and-Tumble Story of an American Radical* (Chicago, Ill.: University of Chicago Press, 1948), p. 207.

3 Emile Pouget, *Le Sabotage* (Paris: Marcel Rivière, 1910), p. 3; Emile Pouget, *Sabotage*, with introduction by Arturo Giovannitti (Chicago, Ill.: Charles H. Kerr, 1913), p. 37.

4 Dominique Pinsolle, "Du ralentissement au déraillement: le développement du sabotage en France (1897–1914)," *Histoire, Economie et Société* 4 (2015): 56–72.

5 Eldridge F. Dowell, *A History of Criminal Syndicalism Legislation in the United States* (Baltimore, Md.: Johns Hopkins University Press, 1939), p. 36.

6 For the latest research on this topic, see Eric Thomas Chester, *The Wobblies in their Heyday. The Rise and Destruction of the Industrial Workers of the World during the Word War I Era* (Santa Barbara, Calif.: Praeger, 2014).

7 The IWW subsequently published this speech, made in support of Vincent Buccafori, a shoe-maker charged with murder, in *The General Strike* (Chicago, Ill.: IWW Publishing Bureau, 1917).

8 Paul F. Brissenden, *The IWW: A Study of American Syndicalism* (New York: Columbia University, 1920), pp. 53–4.

9 The first occurrence in the Library of Congress's Chronicling America: Historic American Newspapers database is in *The Sun*, April 28, 1907: "Workmen urged to crime. Sabotage as it is advocated in France."

10 *Washington Standard* (Olympia, Wash.), October 21, 1910.

11 Austin Lewis, "Sabotage," *International Socialist Review* (October 1910): 202–5.

12 Philip S. Foner, *History of the Labor Movement in the United States*, vol. 4 (New York: International Publishers, 1997), p. 160.

13 Peter Carlson, *Roughneck: The Life and Times of Big Bill Haywood* (New York: W.W. Norton, 1983), pp. 151–2.

14 Carlson, *Roughneck*, p. 152 ; William D. Haywood, "In prison with Hervé," *International Socialist Review* (March 1911): 513–16.

15 Haywood, *The General Strike*, p. 4.

16 André Narritsens and Pierre Vincent, "La grève des cheminots d'octobre 1910," *Les Cahiers de l'Institut CGT d'histoire sociale* 115 (September 2010): 6–11.

17 Christian Chevandier, *Cheminots en grève, ou la construction d'une identité, 1848– 2001* (Paris: Maisonneuve et Larose, 2002), p. 89.

18 François Caron, "La grève des cheminots de 1910. Une tentative d'approche," in *Conjoncture économique, structures sociales: hommage à Ernest Labrousse* (Paris: École Pratique des Hautes Études-Mouton, 1974), pp. 201–19.

19 Brissenden, *The IWW*, p. 270.

20 Howard Zinn, *A People's History of the United States* (London/New York: Longman, 1994), p. 320.

21 Pinsolle, "Du ralentissement au déraillement," p. 59.

22 Haywood, *The General Strike*, p. 4.

23 Haywood, *The General Strike*, p. 5.

24 Pinsolle, "Du ralentissement au déraillement," pp. 66–9.

25 Guillaume Davranche, *Trop jeunes pour mourir: Ouvriers et révolutionnaires face à la guerre, 1909–1914* (Paris: Libertalia/L'insomniaque, 2014), pp. 114–25.

26 J. Anthony Lukas, *Big Trouble: A Murder in a Small Western Town Sets Off a Struggle for the Soul of America* (New York: Simon & Schuster, 1998), pp. 201–40.

27 *La Guerre Sociale*, March 24, 1909.

28 Haywood, "In prison with Hervé," p. 514.

29 Davranche, *Trop jeunes pour mourir*, pp. 171–3.

30 Brissenden, *The IWW*, pp. 284–6.

31 Brissenden, *The IWW*, p. 286.

32 Zinn, *A People's History*, pp. 329–30.

33 Zinn, *A People's History*, p. 333.

34 Ira Kipnis, *The American Socialist Movement, 1897–1912*, reprint edn. (Chicago, Ill.: Haymarket, 2004), pp. 391–5.

35 "New clash in socialists' ranks," *Indianapolis News*, May 20, 1912, in Morris Hillquit Papers, Reel 8, International Institute of Social History, Amsterdam.

36 John Spargo, *National Convention of the Socialist Party: Held at Indianapolis, Ind., May 12 to 18, 1912* (Chicago, Ill.: Socialist Party, 1912), pp. 122–37.

37 Brissenden, *The IWW*, p. 280.

38 William Trautmann, *Direct Action and Sabotage* (Pittsburgh, Pa.: Socialist News Co., 1912).

39 Salvatore Salerno (ed.), *Direct Action and Sabotage: Three Classic IWW Pamphlets from the 1910s* (Chicago, Ill.: Charles Kerr, 1997), pp. 7–8.

40 Trautmann, *Direct Action and Sabotage*, pp. 23–4; Albertelli, *Histoire du sabotage*, pp. 27–8.

41 Geoff Brown, *Sabotage: A Study in Industrial Conflict* (Nottingham, UK: Spokesman, 1977), pp. 5–8.

42 Trautmann, *Direct Action and Sabotage*, p. 26.

43 Pouget, *Le Sabotage*.

44 Salerno, *Direct Action and Sabotage*, p. 10.

45 Salerno, *Direct Action and Sabotage*, pp. 71–88.

46 Pouget, *Sabotage*, p. 14.

47 Industrial Workers of the World, *"Jersey Justice" at Work: First Decision on the Advocacy of Sabotage in the United States Courts* (New York: n.p., 1913), pp. 1–3.

48 Elizabeth Gurley Flynn, "Sabotage," December 21, 1913, Austin Lewis Papers, Bancroft Library, University of California, Berkeley.

49 Salerno, *Direct Action and Sabotage*, pp. 12–13.

50 Elizabeth Gurley Flynn, *Sabotage: The Conscious Withdrawal of the Workers' Industrial Efficiency* (Cleveland, Ohio: IWW Publishing Bureau, April 1915). The original edition is preserved in the Kheel Center archives (IWW Records, Box 1) at Cornell University. This research was supported by the John Nolen Research Fund of Cornell University.

51 Flynn, *Sabotage*, p. 5.

52 Chaplin, *Wobbly*, p. 207.

53 Albertelli, *Histoire du sabotage*, pp. 72–83.

54 Austin Lewis, "Some matters of law in prosecutions under Criminal Syndicalism Law of California" and "The sabotage question" [1919?], Austin Lewis Papers, Bancroft Library.

55 Brissenden, *The IWW*, pp. 328–30.

56 Melvyn Dubofsky, *We Shall Be All: A History of the Industrial Workers of the World* (Chicago, Ill.: Quadrangle, 1969), p. 290.

57 Chester, *The Wobblies in their Heyday*, p. 17.

58 Chester, *The Wobblies in their Heyday*, pp. 12–26.

59 Paul B. Miller, *From Revolutionaries to Citizens: Antimilitarism in France, 1870–1914* (Durham, N.C.: Duke University Press, 2002), pp. 150–61.

60 Jean-Jacques Becker, "Antimilitarisme et antipatriotisme en France avant 1914: le cas de Gustave Hervé," in *Enjeux et Puissances. Hommages à Jean-Baptiste Duroselle* (Paris: Publications de la Sorbonne, 1986), pp. 101–13.

61 "Excerpts from the Publications of the Industrial Workers of the World showing that this organization advocates revolution, destruction of property, sedition and lawlessness," 1915–17, Folder 1, Simon J. Lubin Papers, Bancroft Library; Gustave Hervé, *Patriotism and the Worker* (New Castle, Pa.: IWW Publishing Bureau, 1912).

62 Albertelli, *Histoire du sabotage*, pp. 80–3.

63 Chester, *The Wobblies in their Heyday*, pp. 16–17.

64 Chester, *The Wobblies in their Heyday*, pp. 133–4.

65 Dowell, *A History of Criminal Syndicalism*, p. 49.

66 *New York Daily Tribune*, December 11, 1910; Cornell Dramatic Club, playbill for Ch. Hellem, W. Valcros and Pol d'Estoc, *Sabotage*, 1917, Folder 8, Box 43, Cornell University Department of Theatre Arts Records, Rare and Manuscripts Collections, Cornell University.

67 Jules Witcover, *Sabotage at Black Tom: Imperial Germany's Secret War in America, 1914–1917* (Chapel Hill, N.C.: Algonquin, 1989), p. ix.

68 Chester, *The Wobblies in Their Heyday*, pp. 143–51.

69 Chester, *The Wobblies in Their Heyday*, p. 180.

70 Chester, *The Wobblies in Their Heyday*, p. 149.

71 National Civic Federation, *The Sinister Forces of Sabotage*, 1918, National Civic Federation Records, Reel 404, Box 453, New York Public Library; *New York*

Tribune, July 21 and August 14, 1918; Ralph M. Easley and Thomas Everett Harré, *The i.w.w., an Auxiliary of the German Espionage System: History of the i.w.w. Anti-War Activities, Showing How the i.w.w. Program of Sabotage Inspired the Kaiser's Agents in America* (n.p., 1918).

72 Richard R. Doerries, "Deutsche Sabotage in den Vereinigten Staaten von Amerika im Ersten Weltkrieg: Die Jahre der amerikanischen Neutralität, 1914–1916," in Manfred Berg, Michaela Hönicke, Raimund Lammersdorf, and Anneke de Rudder (eds.), *Macht und Moral: Beiträge zur Ideologie un Praxis amerikanischer Aussenpolitik im 20 Jahrhundert* (Münster, Germany: Lit Verlag, 1999), pp. 71–86.

73 In 1931, for example, the journal *Liberty* reproduced a circular of November 2, 1914 sent by German General Headquarters to military representatives, in which the word sabotage is not used, but which was nevertheless presented as the "sabotage circular." S. Sutherland, "German spies in America, Part I," *Liberty* 8:8 (February 21, 1931): 7–12, in Politisches Archiv des Auswärtigen Amts, Berlin, Deutsches Generalkonsulat.

3

Living Social Dynamite:
Early Twentieth-Century
IWW–South Asia Connections

Tariq Khan

Neither the East, ancient or modern, nor the West, nor again a union of the two, but something higher than both, will save us. Some noble souls dream of the interchange of ideas and ideals between the East and the West, but that will not give us much. Barbarism added to barbarism remains barbarism still. Above the East and the West, far from the present misery of both, shines the light of truth, freedom and social cooperation, that beckon us.

Har Dayal, 1912[1]

Founded in Chicago in 1905, the Industrial Workers of the World (IWW) played a crucial part in the social circuitry of a radical, transnational complex of networks connecting revolutionary movements on every inhabited continent. This chapter discusses the influence of the IWW in the anti-colonialist movement that defied British authority in Hindustan—mainly the part of British India consisting of present-day India and Pakistan. Wobblies admired Indian rebels as serious insurgents who took direct action against elite power. Historian Kornel Chang wrote, "Within IWW circles, no figure was held in higher esteem than the South Asian revolutionary."[2] The Ghadr movement acted as the major connection between the IWW and the people's struggle for a free Hindustan. The chapter introduces the Ghadr movement, why it formed in the US West, its connection to the IWW, and the significance of that connection.

"Ghadr" (sometimes transliterated as "Ghadar" or "Gadar") is an Urdu word that translates to "mutiny" or "revolt." Ghadr's immediate purpose was exactly that, to embolden and empower both Indian soldiers to mutiny against their British officers and Indian workers to take up arms against colonial authority. The Ghadr Party operated in India but formed in the Indian diaspora, founded in 1913 by migrant Indian intellectuals and laborers. It was headquartered in the San Francisco Bay area at its Yugantar Ashram, named in honor of the Bengali revolutionists. British authorities were aghast to discover that Ghadr supporters, bases, plots, and propaganda operated throughout the diaspora—in cities and towns along the North American West Coast, Mexico, Panama, the Caribbean, British Guiana, the Netherlands, Germany, Morocco, Southern Africa, Madagascar, Réunion, Aden, Sudan, Egypt, Turkey, Mesopotamia, Persia, Afghanistan, Burma, Siam, Singapore, the Dutch East Indies, Australia, the Philippines, Japan, Hong Kong, Tien-Tsin, and almost anywhere else that Indian migrant laborers and revolutionists traveled.[3]

The Ghadr movement was simultaneously destructive and constructive. From 1914 to 1917, it was responsible for anti-British attacks, *dacoities* (bandit raids), assassinations and attempted assassinations, weapons-smuggling operations, acts of infrastructural sabotage, and attempted mutinies. These activities led to two of the most sensationalized trials of the era: the "Lahore conspiracy case" of 1915, in which a British colonial court sentenced over 40 Indian conspirators to be executed and more than 200 to be imprisoned, most with life sentences; and the dramatic "Hindu-German conspiracy" trial held in San Francisco from November 1917 to April 1918. During the latter trial, defendant Ram Singh shot dead co-defendant Ram Chandra in the courtroom, with a pistol hidden in his turban, just as Ram Chandra was about to testify concerning the activities of Ghadr. A US marshal then immediately shot Ram Singh dead. The remaining 34 defendants were found guilty under the 1917 Espionage and Sedition Acts and sentenced to varying prison terms in the infamous Leavenworth Federal Penitentiary.[4]

Ghadr activity, however, was not all sedition, conspiracy, and armed insurgency. While members engaged in acts of violence and destruction to demoralize British agents and weaken the Empire's ability to control India, they also worked to build counter-infrastructure and autonomous communities: spaces in which Indians could organize, develop skills, and meet needs without the corrupting influence of colonial dependency. For example, in Salwant (a Punjabi village in Hoshiarpur) Ghadarites Balwant Singh and Arur Singh organized a society to build a veterinary hospital, school, library, and court that operated outside the authority of the state. These projects were not separate from insurgent activities but a complement to them. Ghadarites did not envision a dichotomy between prefigurative politics and insurrectionary politics as many on the radical Left do today. For them it was a given that the two must go together. Colonial police traced the cutting of telegraph lines, destruction of railway lines, and the looting of arms and ammunition from government armories to that very same village.[5]

South Asian Revolutionaries in America

Landowning former enslavers in the Caribbean islands, Guiana, and Suriname brought South Asians to the Americas in significant numbers beginning in the 1830s. These landowners used indentured Indian "coolie" labor to replace enslaved African labor. The United States and Canada, however, did not see significant numbers of South Asian immigrants until the start of the twentieth century; even then, the numbers were small compared with Eastern and Southern European immigrant groups. Between 1899 and 1913, fewer than 7,000 South Asians entered the United States, and by 1914 there were about 10,000 South Asians in the United States and Canada combined. Of those, most were men and a majority Punjabis (from a region of Hindustan now split between Indian and Pakistan), who worked as migratory agricultural laborers along North America's West Coast. A more socially and economically privileged minority of 200–300 among them were intellectuals who came to study or teach at universities such as Stanford and the University of California, Berkeley.[6]

Ghadr sprang from politicized communities formed by these intellectuals and laborers. Social and economic divisions and hierarchies that existed in India began to break down in the Indian diaspora, and new solidarities were carried back. In North America, South Asians who had been divided by caste, class, and religious lines in India experienced common racism and xenophobia. Regardless of their social status in India, they were just "Hindoos" in the eyes of many white North Americans. The term Hindu (often spelled "Hindoo") was a racial, not religious, designation that white North Americans used to describe all South Asians regardless of religion or caste. Since whites targeted them not for being a particular religion or caste, but for being Indians, they united as Indians to defend themselves from white supremacy.

Economic downturns led to white scapegoating of Indians. From 1907 to 1910 Indians were victims of organized white supremacist vigilante attacks in Washington state, Oregon, and California. They also faced racist discrimination in immigration policy, with lawmakers in both the United States and Canada seeking ways to ban South Asians. A 1910 Immigration Commission report referred to Indians as "universally regarded as the least desirable race of immigrants thus far admitted to the United States."[7] South Asians immigrants quickly recognized that it was in their interests to put class, caste, and religious barriers aside to organize for their common advancement. Hindus, Sikhs, and Muslims together founded the Ghadr Party, which included privileged intellectuals as well as exploited laborers. Its tricolor flag represented its religious pluralism, described by British colonial police who found the flag among insurgents in Lahore, Peshawar, and Ferozepur as including "yellow for the Sikhs, red for Hindus and blue for Muhammadans as advocated by the Ghadr."[8]

Historian Maia Ramnath writes that Indian revolutionaries in North America organized for two purposes, to fight British imperialism and protect the South Asian immigrant community from racism. Further, they sought to arouse a consciousness among Indian immigrants that their personal experiences of racism and xenophobia were deeply connected to larger systems of imperialism: that to fight the former required fighting the latter. This message resonated powerfully throughout the Indian diaspora in the United States and Canada. Within a few months of its founding, Ghadr had 5,000 members and 72 branches in North America alone.[9]

During this period of Ghadr formation, the IWW also organized in the same parts of the United States and Canada. The decade of 1910–20 was one of lively and intense radical activity for both the IWW and the Ghadr movement. The organizations were entwined in several significant ways. There was an overlap in membership in the IWW and Ghadr, with the IWW serving as a gateway into the international revolutionary anarchist movement for some Ghadarites. They shared much of the same space—geographic as well as political and ideological—and similar mobilization strategies. Outsiders perceived the two as connected since British authorities partly attributed Ghadr's radicalism to IWW influence, and US popular culture represented the two groups as part of the same social and political space. And North American law enforcement targeted members of both groups with the same anti-anarchist and anti-immigrant laws, resulting in incarcerated Wobblies and Ghadarites becoming fellow prisoners. Many Wobblies and Ghadarites were united by the shared experience of economic exploitation, racism, xenophobia, state repression, and anti-authoritarian resistance.

Pandurang Khankhoje and Har Dayal

It is difficult to know the extent of membership overlap between the Iww and Ghadr but it definitely existed, as Kornel Chang confirms in his book *Pacific Connections*.[10] At the very least, two of Ghadr's most influential organizers and founders, Pandurang Khankhoje and Har Dayal, were Wobblies. Khankhoje organized the military wing of the Ghadr movement, while Har Dayal organized the educational and propaganda wing. It was Har Dayal, against the wishes of Khankhoje, who insisted on the name "Ghadr" for the organization.[11]

Khankhoje had an impressive biography. Born around 1885 into a relatively privileged Brahmin family in the Central Provinces (present-day Maharashtra), as a youth he became a nationalist agitator involved in several anti-British projects, including a circus that was actually a ruse to hide nationalist activities from the police. His family disapproved of his actions and alienated him. At the age of 19, hounded by police, his comrades captured and imprisoned, and with no family support, he decided to leave India. A French Messageries Maritimes captain smuggled him out of the country, beginning a lifelong journey that led Khankhoje into collaborations and friendships with Sun Yat-sen's Chinese revolutionaries, the US labor movement, the anarchist Partido Liberal Mexicano (PLM), Emiliano Zapata's Zapatistas, and anti-imperialists in Berlin, Constantinople, Aleppo, Baghdad, and Russia, until he finally obtained asylum in Mexico in 1924, where he worked as a respected agricultural scientist. He is still remembered in Mexico for his contributions to both the Mexican Revolution and Mexican agriculture. In particular, he developed a high-yield corn strain, "Maize Granada," that Diego Rivera commemorated in a mural that hangs in the Palacio de Bellas Artes in Mexico City. In 1949, the Mexican government even sent Khankhoje to India as a diplomat to forge relations with the newly independent nation.[12]

For all of Khankhoje's travels and connections, he credited the IWW with introducing him to socialism and the US labor movement. In 1910 Corvallis State Agricultural College (present-day Oregon State University) accepted him as a student. As he needed a job to pay his expenses, he sought employment at a lumber mill near Astoria since he had heard that other Indian immigrants worked there. He hitched a ride with some lumberjacks and approached the boss, who took one look at Khankhoje, saw that he was a "black Hindu," and told him there was no work for him there. During this period the IWW had been organizing energetically in lumber mills and camps throughout the Pacific Northwest, including the one that rejected Khankhoje. Upon hearing what happened, a Wobbly organizer employed there approached the boss and used his leverage as a labor leader to pressure the boss into hiring Khankhoje as a lumberjack. Khankhoje wrote of those days: "We stayed in log cabins and every night after work we sat around a campfire and listened to the lectures of the old labour leader who had got me my job. This was the first time I had heard of the labour movement in America and it was my first introduction to socialist thought."[13] Khankhoje became a Wobbly not out of any prior ideological commitment to the labor movement, of which he knew little at that point, but from direct economic necessity—he needed a job and the IWW helped him get one. The socialism the IWW introduced to Khankhoje later made its way into the Ghadr party's vision for a new India.

Har Dayal, likewise, was a larger-than-life character. He was born in 1884 in Old Delhi, like Khankhoje in circumstances of relative privilege. His family was Kayastha, an intellectual/literary caste with occupations in the universities, the legal profession, and government record keeping. His father had a high-status job working for the British in the District Court at Delhi. As such, Har Dayal had access to education at a level that most Indians of his time did not. He excelled scholastically: he was the first Punjabi to receive a state scholarship, which he used to undertake postgraduate studies at St John's College, Oxford, beginning in 1905. The British granted such scholarships to outstanding Indian students with the expectation that they would enter government service. Secretly, however, Har Dayal was attracted to anticolonialism and anarchism. Once at Oxford, he made a "pilgrimage" to meet the famed Russian anarchist-communist Peter Kropotkin, who was exiled from his native Russia, living in London, and serving as editor for the revolutionary journal *Freedom*. Har Dayal held Kropotkin in high regard, referring to him in a later IWW speech as "the Saint Francis and Saint Bernard of Labor."[14]

Har Dayal became very involved in India House, a space at Oxford alight with Indian students discussing and debating Indian nationalism and independence from British rule. After two years at Oxford he resigned from his state scholarship as an act of protest against British authority. He had entered an arranged marriage at the age of 17, and it appears to have been a happy union. His wife Sundar went with him to Oxford, against the wishes of both families, because the couple did not want to be apart. When Har Dayal denounced his scholarship and increased his involvement in the nationalist movement, Sundar's parents were furious, accused him of destroying her life, and made her move back in with them, forbidding him to see her. Sundar was pregnant with a daughter, Shanti, whom the family also banned Har Dayal from seeing.[15]

Alienated from his family and having destroyed his chances of a civil service career, Har Dayal set off as a traveling philosopher. He returned to India, went again to England, then Paris, Algiers, and Martinique, making contacts in radical and intellectual circles wherever he went. In 1911 he sailed to Massachusetts to study Buddhism at Harvard but did not enroll in any courses. He heard there were thousands of Punjabi Sikhs living on the West Coast ready to be organized into a political force, so he moved to Berkeley. After a short while he left for Hawai'i, perhaps to meet Sun Yat-sen, then in Honolulu. There he lived a short while in a cave on Waikiki Beach, where Japanese Buddhist fishermen treated him as a sage, fed him, and discussed Buddhism with him. At this time he also studied Marx, Hegel, and Kant.[16]

Har Dayal returned to Berkeley and immersed himself in radical and intellectual circles. He received a faculty appointment at Stanford University as a lecturer on Indian philosophy in the Spring 1912 semester, which was renewed for the 1912–13 academic year. In the Bay area in 1912, Har Dayal became involved with the IWW. It is not clear how this happened but, in the Bay area radical circles Har Dayal associated with, it must have been almost impossible for him not to cross paths with Wobblies. He became secretary of the Oakland branch of the IWW.[17]

He also started a monastic order for anarchists called the Fraternity of the Red Flag, which combined Hindu and Buddhist asceticism and self-discipline with anarchist politics and goals. Joining the order required no less than a year-long term as an initiate; the taking of vows of poverty, homelessness, humility, purity, and service; and faith in the "eight principles of radicalism." These principles included the abolition of government, religion, patriotism, and racism, as well as "The establishment of the complete economic, moral, intellectual and sexual freedom of woman." The order also intended to establish Modern Schools based on the ideas of martyred Spanish anarchist educator Francisco Ferrer i Guardia, the "promotion of industrial organization and strikes (in cooperation with the I.W.W. and the Syndicalist movements)," and "In Asia and Africa, it will further the movements of progress and revolt in various countries."[18] Here we can see Har Dayal fusing anarchist education, Wobbly syndicalism, and anticolonial insurgency, which sums up his politics at that point in his life rather well.

A "female comrade," identified as E. Norwood in the Mexican anarchist paper *Regeneración*, donated to Har Dayal 6 acres of land and a house on a hill near Oakland. It had a view of the sea and served as the monastery of the Order of the Red Flag. Named the Bakunin Institute, after the great Russian anarchist theorist and organizer Mikhail Bakunin, it was also intended to be the location for the Modern School, in which Norwood offered to teach for free. The Bakunin Institute operated for at least two years, and saw visits from revolutionaries such as the Flores Magón brothers and other Mexican anarchists, whose PLM movement Har Dayal and his comrade Pandurang Khankhoje openly supported. Khankhoje even led a squad of Ghadarites on a foolhardy military reconnaissance expedition into Mexico to support the PLM and Zapatistas and to gain experience in insurgency tactics. After crossing the border, he found the situation to be far more violent than he had expected and decided the plan was unfeasible.[19]

Har Dayal endeavored to contribute to an internationalist consciousness among the Wobblies and other leftists with whom he organized. In January 1913, prior to the founding of Ghadr, he spoke at the Oakland IWW hall to educate Wobblies about Indian resistance and British repression in Hindustan. He told his fellow Wobblies that he planned "to establish an association based on I.W.W. principles for the benefit and uplifting of the people of India." Five days later he delivered a speech in Jefferson Square Hall about the revolutionary labor movement in France. He said that the unions there were the most advanced he had seen in his travels, and spoke highly of the "Anarchist Society of France," which he claimed he had joined when living there. The IWW, said Har Dayal, was the US organization that most closely resembled the French movement. He also urged the workers to "love one another among the labouring-class, but hate, hate the rich." He pointed to the US flag that hung near the podium and said state flags were a "sign of slavery." William C. Hopkinson, an undercover British intelligence agent sent to the Bay area to spy on Indian nationalists, attended both meetings and reported that "Of all the Indian agitators" in North America, "Har Dayal is the most dangerous."[20] A Ghadarite later discovered Hopkinson in Vancouver and assassinated him in 1914 in retaliation for the killing of two Ghadarites.[21]

Transnational Comrades

Har Dayal's attraction to the IWW makes sense in light of the significant commonalities between Wobblies and Ghadarites. Philosophically the IWW and Ghadr shared more in common with Diogenes than Plato. Both groups shared a common affinity for parrhesia—bold, plain, and unvarnished truth—over sophistry and metaphysics. Just as the Wobblies derided preachers who taught workers to await "pie in the sky" in the afterlife, rather than class struggle in the here and now, Har Dayal derided the Indian gurus who mystified people's minds with metaphysics while ignoring actually existing suffering on earth: "While so much transcendental nonsense is being perpetrated, famines are desolating the land, pestilence and malaria hang like a pall on town and country, and there is not a single decent representative institution, technical institute, laboratory or library in the whole country."[22]

Further, as a faculty member in academia, he felt constricted by what anticolonialist and antiracist organizers today contemptuously refer to as "respectability politics." Part of what attracted Har Dayal to the IWW was that it was a society in which he could speak unencumbered by respectability politics. Shortly after finishing his first semester as a Stanford faculty member, he gave a speech to the Wobblies in which he commented what a breath of fresh air it was to be among them. He said that it "was a great pleasure to stand out boldly for my ideas. I hate hole-and-corner hypocrisy and silence."[23] It appears that this aversion to sophistry was an attitude he developed as a youth before he ever left India; British intelligence confiscated a letter Har Dayal wrote to a friend in 1905 in which he registered his disgust with bourgeois assimilationist Indian reformers, declaring, "No, when I write I shall dip my pen in my heart's blood and write about what I feel and think .... Depend upon it, plain speaking carries conviction to the heart, while sophistry only perplexes honest men."[24] This orientation to parrhesia partly explains why Har Dayal recognized the bold, radical, plain-speaking, scrappy fighters of the IWW as comrades.

Har Dayal's speeches to Wobblies and anarchists in the United States show some of the similarities in the politics of the IWW and Ghadr. He taught that working-class resistance must be organized transnationally and revolution must be global, because "Should one nation acquire freedom, the rich of another nation will crush it." The rich, he believed, devised patriotism to instill in the poor a false consciousness and keep the workers of the various countries from uniting across borders. Just as the Wobblies saw electoral politics, parliamentary democracy, and even the tactic of running socialist candidates for office as a dead end, Har Dayal told audiences that these supposed progressive and even socialist politicians were opportunistic cowards who served the capitalist function of taking the steam out of truly revolutionary people's movements. Both the IWW and Ghadr preferred direct action of organized people's movements instead of rallying behind politicians. However, direct action, said Har Dayal, did not necessarily mean terrorism. As an example he pointed to the martyrdom of Francisco Ferrer, who threatened the system and was executed "not for killing, but for his greater love. A man who lives and acts in the interests of freedom is himself living social dynamite."[25]

The IWW resisted militarism, as did Ghadr. Most soldiers were recruited from the ranks of the working class, only to go to kill impoverished workers in another country, or sacrifice their own bodies, minds, and lives for the sake of the rich who exploited everyone below them while giving nothing in return. The IWW worked to instill in workers a sense of global working-class consciousness against jingoism. Likewise, Ghadr worked to instill a sense of solidarity among Indians living under the British Raj and a sense of solidarity with other colonized peoples. Har Dayal's *Ghadr* newspaper, distributed in India and throughout the diaspora, often pointed out the British strategy of sowing enmity between Hindus and Muslims to keep people divided, stupid, and obedient. Further, said *Ghadr*, "With Indian money and with Indian troops China, Burma, Afghanistan, Egypt, and Persia have been subdued."[26] This shows that Ghadr cultivated a sense of transnational anti-colonial consciousness; that unlike the Indian bourgeois nationalists, Ghadr thought in terms of global socialist revolution, not mere national independence.

This consciousness can be attributed in part to IWW influence. However there were also other influences at work. Khankhoje's introduction to transnational anticolonialism came from Sun Yat-sen's students he met in Japan. When they asked him and a comrade how it was that Indian soldiers could help the British plunder China, "We had no answer."[27] Just as the IWW encouraged workers to fight their own bosses rather than fighting in the rich men's wars, Ghadr encouraged Indian soldiers to mutiny against their commanders. Among Indian soldiers, British authorities found several Ghadr leaflets with messages such as "Imperialism is gangsterism on a large scale."[28] Organizing within military barracks was a primary reason the Raj found Ghadr so dangerous.[29]

The IWW and Ghadr shared much ideologically: both were syndicalist, anti-imperialist, anticapitalist, antiracist, direct action-oriented, and insistent that revolutionary initiative must come out of the ranks of the subaltern. As Har Dayal told his fellow Wobblies, "The rich and respectable cannot lead us." He also absorbed some level of feminist consciousness from the IWW and anarchist movements. In a speech he called his "frank confession of faith," he asserted that the labor movement and the woman's movement must join ranks: "The workers and the women are two enslaved classes and must fight their battles together."[30] Ghadr, however, remained a largely male-dominated affair, partly because the Indian population in North America, where Ghadr was based, overwhelmingly consisted of men, but also because the society those men came out of was highly patriarchal and organized along strict gender lines.

Nevertheless, women played a significant role in the Ghadr movement. A few examples are Gulab Kaur, "Madam" Bhikaji Cama, and Agnes Smedley. Gulab Kaur was a Punjabi woman who joined a Ghadr branch in the Philippines. Among her many contributions to the movement, she posed as a journalist to smuggle weapons and propaganda to Ghadr insurgents. British agents eventually captured, tortured, and imprisoned her at Lahore. Madam Cama is still remembered in India for her work in the Mumbai slums during a plague outbreak and as the person who boldly raised the Indian independence flag—a tricolor flag with a Hindu sun and Muslim crescent on it—at the International Socialist Conference in Stuttgart, Germany in 1907. She became involved with Ghadr after meeting Ghadarites in the United States. Smedley, a socialist-feminist and journalist from the United States, aided the Ghadr Party with communications and propaganda.[31]

Communications and propaganda was one of the main ways non-Indian socialists, anarchists, and Wobblies supported the Ghadr movement. For example, Irish anarchist and Wobbly Ed Gammons produced English-language literature for Ghadr. However, Gammons later betrayed the anarchist movement and Ghadr by becoming a paid informant for the British government.[32]

In terms of organizing strategies, both the IWW and Ghadr placed the highest importance on cultural production, using leaflets, newspapers, folk music, and homespun poetry as tools to mobilize subaltern peoples. Maia Ramnath writes that both the IWW and Ghadr "sourced a prolific wellspring of militant propaganda, newspapers, pamphlets, and volumes of singable poems in the 1910s and 1920s: where the IWW had the *Little Red Songbook*, Ghadar had *Ghadar-di-Gunj*."[33] Much of this material possessed influence far beyond the organizations themselves.

Outsiders also recognized the IWW and Ghadr as connected. The British Foreign Office reported that Har Dayal "became a member of the Industrial Workers of the World, the most lawless labour movement which has ever existed, and was on intimate terms with Anton Johan[n]sen [an anarchist and Wobbly], one of the accused in the California dynamite conspiracy case." British Ambassador Spring-Rice wrote to the US Secretary of State to convince the United States to crack down on Ghadr, saying "efforts are being made [by Ghadr] to affiliate some of the Industrial Workers of the World, one of whom is now in Berlin," and claimed that the organization was storing weapons and ammunition at New York and San Francisco.[34] US officials likewise saw this connection. US immigration inspector Charles Riley reported, "As evidence of their proficiency in the art of 'blowing people up,' I was assured that most of the members of the Hindu nationalist party were also 'IWWs'."[35]

The IWW and Ghadr were connected not only in law enforcement and state department circles but also in popular culture. IWW association became part of the Indian rebel "type." In his 1916 novel *The Little Lady of the Big House*, Jack London created a character clearly based on Har Dayal named Dar Hyal, described as:

> a revolutionist, of sorts. He's dabbled in our universities, studied in France, Italy, Switzerland, is a political refugee from India, and he's hitched his wagon to two stars: one, a new synthetic system of philosophy; the other, rebellion against the tyranny of British rule in India. He advocates individual terrorism and direct mass action. That's why his paper, *Kadar*, or *Badar*, or something like that, was suppressed here in California.[36]

The character Dar Hyal narrowly escapes deportation officers and hides out at a camp in the woods with a small group of social outsiders who spend their days reading and debating philosophy. One of his accomplices is a character named Terrence McFane, an "epicurean anarchist" who got "mixed up in some i.w.w. riot for free speech or something."[37] Giving Dar Hyal's comrade the Irish name McFane perhaps also played on Ghadr's actual ties to the Irish independence movement.

War and Repression

Har Dayal really did narrowly escape a brush with immigration inspectors in March 1914, after being arrested under the 1903 Immigration Act, which the US Government created specifically to exclude and deport anarchists. However, he did not hide in the woods of California; rather, he traveled to Switzerland and carried on Ghadr organizing in Europe. He still considered US Wobblies to be his comrades in the struggle. In October 1915 he sent two letters from Amsterdam to anarchist Alexander Berkman in New York, asking Berkman if he could send any radicals to meet him in Amsterdam to aid in the struggle against Britain. Har Dayal specified, "They should be real fighters, i.w.w.'s or anarchists."[38]

While no evidence exists that Berkman complied with this request or even responded, the state used these letters as evidence against Berkman and his life-long accomplice Emma Goldman. The two were arrested in June 1917 for conspiring against the draft and sentenced to prison. The Department of Justice took special interest in the case, wanting Berkman and Goldman deported. Based on Har Dayal's letters to Berkman, Attorney-General Gregory charged that Goldman and Berkman were "working in conjunction with German spies in foreign countries." Goldman admitted that she knew Har Dayal from his days in Berkeley, and she called him a "great idealist," but claimed that she would never have complied with a request to send anarchists to fight for Ghadr's cause because she did not think "outsiders can free a country."[39] The United States had allied with the United Kingdom in the war against Germany, and in the wartime political atmosphere, to work against the British Empire was to be pro-German; and so to be a friend of Ghadr meant to be an enemy of the United States.

The war also brought heightened hysteria, jingoism, xenophobia, racism, and state repression that criminalized dissent. Chang writes, "The converging radicalism of the IWW and South Asian revolutionaries caused widespread alarm and would justify an enormous expansion in state surveillance around the time of the First World War."[40] In addition to being targeted by the 1903 Immigration Act, radical leftists had to contend with the 1917 Espionage Act. Wobblies, Ghadarites, socialists, black radicals, PLM organizers, Irish republicans, and other "undesirables" soon became prison mates in Leavenworth Federal Penitentiary. In this space Wobblies, Ghadarites, and Mexican anarchists continued working as co-conspirators. Historian Christina Heatherton writes: "Incarcerated for their resistance to militarism, capitalism, and racism, prisoners transformed Leavenworth into an organizing space, a laboratory for new ideas and tactics, or, as one federal surveillance file called it, 'A University of Radicalism'."[41]

Ghadr organizer Taraknath Das and famous Wobblies like "Big Bill" Haywood, black longshore workers organizer Ben Fletcher, and artist Ralph Chaplin gathered the Wobblies and other radicals in a corner of the prison yard, which they called "the campus," to hold classes and discussions on cutting-edge politics, philosophy, art, and the revolution in Russia. Mexican anarchist Enrique Flores Magón and Wobbly Aurelio V. Azuara taught Spanish classes. Taraknath Das taught classes on Vedanta philosophy and organized the prison library, which quickly became filled with anarchist and socialist periodicals and books. Within their prison walls they continued forging revolutionary transnational solidarity.[42]

Nevertheless, both the IWW and Ghadr suffered greatly under the extraordinary repression of the First World War and the subsequent era of fascism and Red Scares. Neither organization fully recovered. The rise and decline of both were intertwined. That the lives and fates of these two organizations were so connected confirms that the IWW significantly influenced the South Asian movement, and vice versa. Further, the IWW–Ghadr connection shows that the IWW contributed not only to anti-capitalist labor struggles but also to transnational anti-colonialist and anti-imperialist ones.

Notes

1 Quoted in Emily C. Brown, *Har Dayal: Hindu Revolutionary and Rationalist* (Tucson, Ariz.: University of Arizona Press, 1975), pp. 95–6.

2 Kornel Chang, *Pacific Connections: The Making of the U.S.-Canadian Borderlands* (Berkeley, Calif.: University of California Press, 2012), p. 116.

3 The most informative works on the Ghadr movement are: Maia Ramnath, *Haj to Utopia: How the Ghadar Movement Charted Global Radicalism and Attempted to Overthrow the British Empire* (Berkeley: University of California Press, 2011) and Brown, *Har Dayal*. See also Savitri Sawhney, *I Shall Never Ask for Pardon: A Memoir of Pandurang Khankhoje* (New Delhi: Penguin, 2008); T. R. Sareen, *Selected Documents on the Ghadr Party* (New Delhi: Mounto, 1994); Bhai Nahar Singh and Kirpal Singh (eds.), *Struggle for Free Hindustan: Ghadr Movement* (New Delhi: Atlantic, 1986); Harish K. Puri, *Ghadar Movement: Ideology, Organisation, and Strategy* (Amritsar, India: Guru Nanak Dev University Press, 1983); F. C. Isemonger and J. Slattery, *An Account of the Ghadr Conspiracy, 1913–1915* (Berkeley, Calif.: Folklore Institute, 1998); *Ghadr Party's Lahore Conspiracy Case: 1915 Judgment* (Meerut, India: Archana, 2006); *The Ghadr Directory* (Patiala, India: Punjabi University Publication Bureau, n.d.); Maia Ramnath, *Decolonizing Anarchism: An Antiauthoritarian History of India's Liberation Struggle* (Oakland, Calif.: AK Press/ Institute for Anarchist Studies, 2011).

4 *New York Times*, April 24, 1918; Ramnath, *Haj to Utopia*, pp. 89–94; Puri, *Ghadar Movement*, pp. 99–103.

5 Isemonger and Slattery, *An Account of the Ghadr Conspiracy*, pp. 95–6; Ramnath, *Haj to Utopia*, pp. 52–3.

6 For more specific numbers, see notes 2-4 in Ramnath, *Haj to Utopia*, pp. 242–3.

7 Ramnath, *Haj to Utopia*, p. 24.

8 Isemonger and Slattery, *An Account of the Ghadr Conspiracy*, p. 121.

9 Ramnath, *Haj to Utopia*, pp. 24–37.

10 Chang, *Pacific Connections*.

11 Sawhney, *I Shall Never Ask for Pardon*, pp. 103–4.

12 Sawhney, *I Shall Never Ask for Pardon*.

13 Sawhney, *I Shall Never Ask for Pardon*, pp. 82–3.

14 Quoted in Brown, *Har Dayal*, p. 110.

15 Brown, *Har Dayal*; Ramnath, *Decolonizing Anarchism*, pp. 80–109.

16 Brown, *Har Dayal*; Ramnath, *Decolonizing Anarchism*, pp. 80–109.

17 Ramnath, *Decolonizing Anarchism*, pp. 80–109; Brown, *Har Dayal*.

18 Quoted in Brown, *Har Dayal*, pp. 114–15.

19 Kenyon Zimmer, *Immigrants Against the State: Yiddish and Italian Anarchism in America* (Urbana, Ill.: University of Illinois Press, 2015), 106; Brown, *Har Dayal*; Ramnath, *Decolonizing Anarchism*, pp. 80–109; Sawhney, *I Shall Never Ask for Pardon*.

20 Brown, *Har Dayal*, pp. 132–3.

21 Richard Popplewell, *Intelligence and Imperial Defence: British Intelligence and the Defence of the Indian Empire 1904–1924* (London: Frank Cass, 1995).

22 Har Dayal, "The wealth of the nation," *Modern Review* (July 1912), pp. 43–50; Brown, *Har Dayal*, p. 102.

23 Quoted in Brown, *Har Dayal*, p. 110.

24 Isemonger and Slattery, *An Account of the Ghadr Conspiracy*, pp. 1–2.

25 Brown, *Har Dayal*, pp. 111.

26 Sareen, *Selected Documents on the Ghadr Party*, p. 83.

27 Sawhney, *I Shall Never Ask for Pardon*, p. 43.

28 Sareen, *Selected Documents on the Ghadr Party*, p. 178.

29 Isemonger and Slattery, *An Account of the Ghadr Conspiracy*; Puri, *Ghadar Movement*; *Ghadr Party's Lahore Conspiracy Case*; Sareen, *Selected Documents on the Ghadr Party*; Singh and Singh, *Struggle for Free Hindustan*.

30 Brown, *Har Dayal*, p. 110.

31 Kesar Singh, *Gadar Di Dhee Gulaab Kaur* (Chandigarh, India: Unistar, 2014); Geraldine Forbes, *Women in Modern India* (New York: Cambridge University Press, 1996); Agnes Smedley, *Agnes Smedley: The Life and Times of an American Radical* (Berkeley, Calif.: University of California Press, 1988); Agnes Smedley, *Daughter of Earth* (New York: Feminist Press, 1987).

32 Zimmer, *Immigrants Against the State*, pp. 108–9, 142.

33 Ramnath, *Haj to Utopia*, p. 67.

34 Sareen, *Selected Documents on the Ghadr Party*, pp. 58, 69.

35 Chang, *Pacific Connections*, p. 99.

36 Jack London, *The Little Lady of the Big House* (New York: Macmillan, 1916), p. 117.

37 London, *The Little Lady of the Big House*, p. 115.

38 Brown, *Har Dayal*, pp. 208–9.

39 Richard Drinnon, *Rebel in Paradise: A Biography of Emma Goldman* (Boston, Mass.: Beacon Press, 1970), pp. 206–7.

40 Chang, *Pacific Connections*, p. 121.

41 Christina Heatherton, "University of radicalism: Ricardo Flores Magón and Leavenworth Penitentiary," *American Quarterly* 66:3 (2014): 559.

42 Tapan Mukherjee, *Taraknath Das: Life and Letters of a Revolutionary in Exile* (Calcutta, India: National Council of Education, 1997); Heatherton, "University of radicalism"; Ramnath, *Haj to Utopia*, p. 66.

4

IWW Internationalism and Interracial Organizing in the Southwestern United States

David M. Struthers

In the contested space of the Southwestern United States that previously had been Native American land, New Spain, and northern Mexico, the Industrial Workers of the World (IWW) was a syndicalist labor union that promoted a beautiful ideal for a better world. The IWW's organizational foundation in the region grew from locals in Los Angeles, Phoenix, and San Francisco. Yet historians need to balance attention to the formal consolidation of these locals with the grassroots organizing undertaken by loosely affiliated, or even unaffiliated individuals, in the name of the IWW. In a dispersed productive landscape requiring mobile labor to satisfy the demands of capitalist agriculture, mining, and infrastructure development, most IWW locals experienced ebbs and flows in membership. Formal organizations and members with their red cards held the center of gravity, with other organizers and workers passing through their orbits and crossing national boundary lines.

This chapter sketches out the institutional history and instances of radical organizing inspired by the IWW in Los Angeles and across the Southwest. It also identifies key points of transmission when the IWW's on-the-ground internationalism spread outward to nearby Mexico and even more distant Japan.[1]

Internationalism is commonly understood as solidarity across a national border.[2] The IWW in the region engaged in this practice, but the racial and national diversity of immigrants in the region gave workers the opportunity to extend international solidarity to multiracial fellow workers in their own communities: a local internationalism. A common practice in most locations where the IWW organized, it took a broad form in the Southwestern

United States, where the diversity of types of employment and races of laborers combined with continued mobility. Multiracial migratory laborers and miners hundreds of miles from the nearest city, speakers carted away from soapboxes by police during free speech fights, bindlestiffs in hobo "jungles" or wintering in cities, organizers traversing state lines and national borders, foreigners fighting in the Mexican Revolution, and dockworkers who served as human connections between local, national, and global happenings all shaped the union's regional character.

The Regional Organizing Landscape

In California's two largest cities, many leftists rolled their existing institutions into iww-affiliated organizations after the iww's foundation. In San Francisco, George Speed, an eclectic radical who once had belonged to the Knights of Labor, joined others in forming an industrial union club in response to the "Industrial Union Manifesto" issued in Chicago in January 1905, the document that announced the iww's forthcoming founding convention in July 1905. In Los Angeles the socialist-oriented Emancipation Club reformed itself as an iww local directly after the Chicago convention. Mortimer Downing, a member of an anarchist club in Los Angeles, joined this iww local shortly after its formation. Both Speed and Downing became prominent national figures in the iww and eventually served prison time during the First World War.[3]

In its first year the iww had a limited presence outside of San Francisco and Los Angeles and its membership remained largely white and English-speaking. These early iww locals functioned as clubs and vehicles for propaganda, lacking the power to insert themselves into syndicalist labor organizing at the point of production. The groups in both cities maintained institutional and personal links to one another, but focused upon their local spheres. Nevertheless, this period saw one of the earliest transmissions of iww ideals abroad. In 1905 and 1906 the Japanese anarchist Denjiro Kotoku traveled through California and met with workers while speaking and organizing. He shared the stage with iww organizers on a few occasions, organized Japanese laborers, and incorporated iww ideals into his own vision after returning to Japan (see Zimmer, Chapter 1).[4]

In the early twentieth century, Los Angeles and San Francisco functioned as hubs that connected two major migratory circuits. The first saw workers traveling along the West Coast to labor in Alaska's fishing industry, the Pacific Northwest's timber and related trades, California's vast agriculture industry, and in San Francisco itself. At the southern end of this circuit,

Los Angeles also connected to inland southern California agricultural centers such as Redlands and Holtville, developing San Diego, and then eastward to Phoenix and the copper belt in Arizona and Northern Mexico. The racially and ethnically diverse workers transiting through these labor circuits—migrants from Mexico, Europe, Asia, the Eastern United States, and elsewhere—brought with them organizing traditions and cultural perspectives that shaped their engagement with the labor movement.

The organizing landscapes of California, Arizona, and Mexico also influenced the regional path of the IWW. The American Federation of Labor (AFL) dominated the trade union movement in California. Similar to most American locales, AFL locals and trade councils concentrated the power of white, so-called skilled workers, while actively excluding most non-whites and women. Strongest in cities, the few times the AFL ventured to organize agricultural workers, it quickly reached the limits of its methods, structure, and racism. Such was the case with the California State Federation of Labor's failed United Laborers organizing campaign between 1909 and 1913.[5]

In the mining camps of Arizona, California, Colorado, and Utah the Western Federation of Miners (WFM) led union organizing. The WFM, an active force in the creation of the IWW, split from the organization in 1907, and eventually reaffiliated with the AFL in 1911. Apart from joint WFM-IWW organizing in Goldfield, Nevada between 1906 and 1908, the IWW attempted to organize this essential sector of the regional economy in competition with the WFM. In the American West the WFM forged its own path toward organizing non-Anglo workers. In Arizona copper camps local conditions shaped what Philip Mellinger described as the WFM's "ethnically tolerant inclusion"—a reminder that trade unions often spoke with multiple voices and local members could work for more inclusive organizations.[6]

The Socialist Party of America (SPA) and to a lesser degree the Socialist Labor Party (SLP) also remained active forces in the region. SPA locals existed in Los Angeles, San Diego, Globe, and Bisbee. The Anglo-led Socialist Party in Los Angeles included European immigrants of many ethnicities and nationalities, and African American socialist George Washington Woodbey often spoke in Los Angeles and San Diego during this period. However, no African American socialist group emerged, and Anglos in the West also directed their racism toward Asians, the "indispensable enemy" of California's white working class, in Alexander Saxton's crucial formulation, which further constrained the prospects for interracial organizing by both the AFL and SPA. Mexicans and Spaniards in Los Angeles jointly formed a socialist group affiliated with the SPA to advance their interests in 1907, and this organization remained active until around 1911. Rafael Carmona, Anselmo Figueroa, and Lázaro Gutiérrez de Lara all took public roles in the Mexican Branch of the SPA in Los Angeles, and each also belonged to the Partido Liberal Mexicano (Mexican Liberal Party, or PLM).[7]

The IWW belonged to this broad confluence of forces that collectively formed the regional left and labor movement. The syndicalist union organized multiracial workers in locations and industries often disregarded or excluded from other unions, and distinguished itself from the SPA by limiting its engagement in politics and consistently defending nonwhite workers. Collaboration and conflict occurred across ideological difference.

The Ground-Up Growth of the Regional IWW

Two interrelated strands of organizing led to the IWW's regional growth. First, Mexican organizers deeply involved with the revolutionary PLM expanded the perspective and ranks of the Wobblies, while also working on both sides of the border to push Mexico along the path to revolution. Part of a multinodal network, Phoenix-based Mexican organizers for the IWW and PLM saw important early success before being supplanted by Los Angeles-based IWW and PLM militants. Second, mostly white IWW organizers agitated among multiracial regional laborers and agricultural workers. All regional organizing occurred with extremely limited financial support and independently from the national IWW.

Fernando Velarde personally connected many of the region's overlapping organizational currents. As Devra Weber noted, Velarde "organized Mexicans with the WFM, belonged to Daniel De Leon's Socialist Labor Party, organized and voted for the Socialist Party, joined the PLM, and organized for the IWW."[8] In 1906 Velarde, along with Rosendo Dorame, added a Spanish-speaking branch to Phoenix IWW Local 272. One of the first locals in the region outside of California, Local 272 soon had a majority of Mexican members. In August 1908, Velarde informed the *Industrial Union Bulletin* that he had started collecting funds to finance a Spanish-language IWW newspaper. The next year the Phoenix local commenced publishing *La Union Industrial*, the second Spanish-language IWW newspaper, which continued until 1911. Newspapers like this served the vital function of facilitating communication and building community across space— especially important in bridging the Southwest's vast distances.[9]

La Union Industrial came on the heels of an earlier publishing effort. In 1908 the indefatigable Fernando Palomares, a Mayo Indian, and Joseph Ettor, the son of Italian immigrants, published *Libertad y Trabajo*, backed by Los Angeles Local 12, to which Palomares belonged. The pair only released a few issues, as Palomares' organizing drew him elsewhere. The newspaper included IWW content as well as the writings of PLM leader Ricardo Flores Magón. Ettor lived in Los Angeles at the time, organizing sailors and dockworkers for the IWW in San Pedro, the port of LA. He signed up 22 members, including 17 Italians, in the summer of 1908. Ettor went on to notoriety when police arrested him along with Arturo Giovannitti on murder charges during the 1912 strike in Lawrence, Massachusetts, but Ettor cut his teeth organizing out West. *La Union Industrial* and *Libertad y Trabajo* supplemented a handful of other radical Spanish-language newspapers published in the region, such as the PLM's *Revolución* and *Regeneración*, and the affiliated *La Voz de la Mujer* and *El Mosquito*.[10]

Mexican organizing in Los Angeles and the borderlands drew on the *mutualista* tradition to form Club Liberales, associated with the PLM, and other local community organizations. Mexican IWW organizing also fit within this tradition. Devra Weber characterized Mexican involvement with the IWW in the following way: "Mexicans' complex histories and cultural contexts framed and shaped their involvement with the organization, and linked the diverse concerns of Mexican members. Their perspective decenters the IWW by framing it as part of a spectrum of organizations attempting to counteract dispossession. Yet in doing so, Mexicans also expanded the IWW."[11] Neither the PLM nor the IWW demanded the singular allegiance of their supporters, and IWW growth among Mexican workers corresponded to the growth of the PLM up to 1911. The organizers that most directly led to the growth of the IWW among Mexican workers—including Fernando Palomares, Fernando Verlarde, and Pedro Coria—were Mexican or Native American and also organized with the PLM.

As the national IWW endured organizational changes by splitting with the SLP and its supporters, new locals sprouted up in the Southwest. By 1908, IWW locals operated in San Diego (Local 245), in the inland citrus town of Redlands (Local 419), the Imperial Valley town of Holtville (Local 437), and the Arizona copper town of Globe (Public Service Local 100). These locations illustrate the IWW's appeal across different industries, from agriculture, to infrastructure projects, to mining.

The organizing of the legendary Wobbly Frank Little brings to life the second strand of IWW organizing in the Southwest. Little and many others like him spread the IWW's message in a direct, personal way, like Mexican IWW-PLM organizers. Little is often mistakenly identified as Native American or various percentages thereof: "Half Indian, half whiteman, All I.w.w."[12] Wobbly Ralph Chaplin remembered, "Frank Little boasted of being a half-breed."[13] While this appears to be a willful distortion by Little, he undeniably found his place among itinerant and multiracial miners and laborers in the western United States, and Franklin Rosemont characterized him as being "widely regarded by fellow Wobs as the union's single greatest organizer."[14]

Little's travels are the stuff of IWW legend. During one trip in 1908, Little wrote to the *Industrial Union Bulletin* to share his experiences as a "hobo miner." He first left Prescott, Arizona for Octave with a friend. A manager recognized Little from his earlier organizing in Clifton so they traveled on to Congress and Wickenburg. They then left Arizona for California, "the state of little matches and big scabs," where he attended a meeting of the WFM-affiliated Mojave Miners' Union. He praised the local's former radicalism but lamented that the mine owners now controlled the union. Little managed to speak in the town before he and his traveling companion dropped from the high desert down into the inland fruit-producing valleys. After a short stay in southern California, they proceeded north into the Sierra mining town of Graniteville. Little got a job though quickly found himself blacklisted for his labor agitation.[15]

Little spent that summer in Fresno, spreading the IWW gospel among the city's multiracial workforce. He noted the presence of Russians, Armenians, Japanese, Mexicans, Italians, and "other Latins," and chartered a "Latin-American" SPA local with nine members. He called for further organizing for the "real Revolution."[16] His efforts helped charter Fresno IWW Local 66 in October 1909, which soon raised the funds to rent a union hall. Fernando Velarde and Fernando Palomares also contributed to organizing this IWW local. The IWW's 1910 free speech fight in Fresno began when police prevented a "Mexican socialist" speaking at a street meeting. Frank Little had a permit to hold a public gathering, but the police claimed that permission did not extend to the Mexicans present.[17]

The Wobblies' growing strength in the Southwest, and in turn the region's importance to the organization as a whole, became visible as early as 1909. The national leadership increased their personal support for regional organizing. Bill Haywood toured southern California in 1909, lecturing in Rialto, San Bernardino, Hemet, El Centro, Brawley, Upland, Redlands, Santa Ana, San Diego, and Escondido.[18] Also in 1909, the IWW's *Industrial Union Bulletin* relocated to Spokane, Washington. The name changed to the *Industrial Worker*, and it served as the IWW's official West Coast voice in English. Along with *La Union Industrial* in Phoenix, the IWW now had two newspapers with local content for workers within the American West's migratory circuits. However, very little financial support flowed from the national organization; instead, Southwest organizers with the language skills and cultural entrée helped expand the IWW from the grassroots. They built a regional support base, gave voice to the ideal of industrial unionism across a broad swath of industries, and expanded the organization's institutional footprint, increasingly allowing it to put radical ideals into action.

A New Militancy

Southern California led the way in this militancy as the two strands of organizing, Mexicans with ties to the PLM and multiethnic whites, drew closer together. A series of free speech fights across the West best illustrate the IWW's insurgent direct action. Its first major free speech fight kicked off in Spokane, Washington in 1909. Despite brutal treatment by local police and jailors, the IWW prevailed in March 1910.[19] In Fresno, the repression of IWW street speaking and organizing through the spring, summer, and fall of 1910 gave rise to a similar struggle, but within a more racially diverse workforce. The *Industrial Worker* publicized the struggle and asked fellow workers to travel to the city to take part. Many heeded the call, including a group of about 50 Wobblies and sympathizers from Los Angeles.[20]

In the summer of 1910, while Frank Little and others geared up for the free speech fight in Fresno, San Diego saw a remarkable spurt of interracial IWW organizing. A new IWW branch, Mixed Local 13, formed there in December 1909 and grew through the spring of 1910. Its members soon raised the funds to establish an office and reading room. In June, Local 13 elected Fernando Palomares, who went by the name Francisco Martinez in his IWW organizing, as its corresponding secretary. In July the local reported a membership of 90, though some left town to work elsewhere. This recurrent pattern was a double-edged sword that made organizing more difficult in a single location, but also helped expand IWW ideals through regional circuits. IWW organizing picked up speed throughout the summer. By August, Local 13 held two street meetings a week in English and another "two or three" in Spanish. It also reported 50 Mexicans interested in forming a Mexican local, who soon became members of IWW Public Service Local 378.[21]

A few weeks after Local 378 applied for a charter, Mexican laborers for the gas company walked off the job in the "first strike to be pulled off in this city for a number of months." Anglos and some Italians on the jobsite earned $2.25 for a nine-hour day, while Mexicans and the rest earned $2.00 for the same work.[22] The strikers demanded $2.50 and an eight-hour day for all workers, regardless of race. The strike soon extended from the gas plant to the "pick and shovel" and "concrete men" employed by the Barber Asphalt Company. When the Mexican workers walked off these jobs, the owners tried to replace them with Anglo and Italian strikebreakers. The scabs worked on "Tuesday, but Wednesday morning the Mexicans and American i.w.w. men got them to quit." Local 378 held the "biggest street meeting that was ever held in San Diego" in support of this strike, where around 200 people listened to Fernando Palomares, the poet, author, and organizer Laura Payne Emerson, and others for three hours. Another meeting followed, with 250 attending, and still more workers joining the strike. The *Industrial Worker* reported, "Five Greeks and a couple of Italians and Americans who at first refused to strike quit work today." In the same issue, San Diego Wobblies called for IWW members fluent in Italian, Spanish, Japanese, and Greek to come to the city.[23]

In September, San Diego Local 13 appealed to California and Arizona locals via the pages of the *Industrial Worker*. It claimed that "during the last month we have pulled off several strikes and have won two of them," with some workers still off the job. Palomares, José Ruiz, and "some of the other Mexican boys" had trained a number of other Mexican IWW speakers. In total, 75 workers for the gas company walked off the job before winning a wage increase to $2.25 for all workers. It also claimed that "only i.w.w. men" would henceforth be employed as excavators for the gas company. It is unclear whether they won an eight-hour day. The AFL, meanwhile, organized the rest of the company's employees.[24] The success of the gas strike still left the asphalt workers off the job, and Local 13 proclaimed "the beginning of the great uprising of the oppressed and poorly paid Mexican laborer in America and Mexico." The prominent PLM speaker Lazaro Gutiérrez De Lara joined the organizing, traveling from Los Angeles to San Diego. While it is not clear how the concrete strike ended, it likely failed. The local did not report on it again, although it did continue organizing to establish a citywide standard of $2.50 for an eight-hour day.[25]

In October, the IWW held a public meeting at San Diego's Germania Hall to commemorate the murder of Spanish anarchist and educator Francisco Ferrer i Guardia. The "Spanish speaking fellow workers" of Local 373 and the members of Local 13 marched behind a red IWW flag from their headquarters on Fourth Avenue to the hall.[26] Still in San Diego, Palomares reported that the IWW had 200 members in the city, including 100 Spanish speakers. When Local 378 finally received its formal charter from the IWW headquarters in Chicago that October, it elected José Ruiz president, E. Vasquez recording secretary, and Francisco Martinez (Palomares) secretary-treasurer.[27] Laura Payne Emerson reported that in response to continued IWW street meetings that fall—"nearly every night in both Spanish and English"—local merchants "formed a 'club' to stop street speaking."[28] This led to police arresting two IWW members in November. Local 378 wrote to the *Industrial Worker*: "Workers, Fresno first, then San Diego," sowing the seeds of the San Diego free speech fight in 1912.[29]

The San Diego IWW locals did not neglect broader issues during their local actions. They lambasted the California SPA's support for Asiatic exclusion while still having the "nerve to wear the little emblem of the theirs—that button where the workers of America are clasping hands with the foreign worker and with the inscription, 'Workers of the World, Unite'."[30] The IWW call for Japanese organizers to come to San Diego showed that it backed this criticism with action. Another example of the reach of the IWW's outlook came from farther out in its network. The union celebrated when "fifty members of the Pima tribe of Indians who were employed by the government in building bridges at Phoenix, Arizona recently struck for an eight hour work day and won their strike."[31] The *Industrial Worker* did not claim this as an IWW action, but made clear its support.

The San Diego locals articulated a broad vision that extended out through the borderlands and into Mexico: "The Mexican workers of the United States want to organize in the i.w.w. and co-operate with their fellow slaves in Mexico and organize them. An organization of the syndicalists in Mexico is being formed secretly." To support this drive, they asked the IWW General Executive Board to appoint Spanish-speaking organizers for California, Arizona, New Mexico, and Texas. In 1910, the Phoenix local reached a membership of 500, still with a Mexican majority. Local 437, encompassing both Holtville and El Centro, also expanded.[32]

As Palomares publicly organized workers in San Diego, he and many others quietly laid the groundwork for an armed incursion into Baja California, part of a broader attempt to ignite armed revolution in Mexico. In August 1910, three PLM leaders—Ricardo Flores Magón, Librado Rivera, and Antonio Villareal—returned to Los Angeles after a stint in prison in Florence, Arizona for earlier transborder agitation. In September, the *Industrial Worker* informed its readership that this group would soon resume publication of the PLM newspaper *Regeneración*.[33] Throughout this period the PLM and the IWW cooperated extensively. In 1910, as Devra Weber has noted, "Arizona and California locals" in the PLM's "network formally merged with Mexican IWW branches."[34] In late 1910 and early 1911, as IWW supporters took to the streets in Fresno to demand freedom of speech and their right to organize, the PLM began fighting in Baja California, 450 miles to the south. Events in Baja illustrate the confluence of the two strands of IWW organizing in the region.

The Baja Raids helped launch the Mexican Revolution. The PLM-led force largely crossed over from California in January 1911, and seized Mexicali and then Tijuana. The insurgents were defeated after Francisco Madero displaced Porfirio Díaz as president and turned federal troops on the rebels in June 1911. The rebels demonstrated a remarkable amount of interracial solidarity, and included Mexicans as well as Anglos, Italians, African Americans, and others. Hundreds of Wobblies, mostly channeled through the Holtville local—which also helped smuggle arms across the border—as well as anarchists, particularly Italians, joined the rebel army in Baja California. Many more in the IWW sphere of influence supported those fighting in Mexico. The outbreak of the Mexican Revolution also dramatically impacted IWW organizing in Phoenix. The pull of the revolution drew away almost the entire Phoenix IWW's Mexican membership. However, these men did not join the insurgency in Baja California, instead joining groups fighting elsewhere in Mexico.[35]

The Baja Raids and Fresno free speech fight overlapped temporally and organizationally: an extraordinary display of the ability of radicals in the region to rally hundreds of supporters in locations roughly 500 miles apart. In Fresno, the IWW achieved a limited victory, ensuring its ability to hold public meetings. To the south, the cooperation between the PLM and IWW continued after defeat in Baja California, through the organizations' mutual support during the court cases that followed. Many of the participants in the Baja Raids, particularly non-Mexicans, stayed in San Diego after returning across the border, and fed the initial wave of support for the free speech fight there. This struggle grew out of repression during IWW organizing in the fall of 1910, and eventually boiled over in 1911 when these idle radicals lingered in town. The fight kicked off in earnest in 1912 and garnered national support and attention as word traveled about the brutality of the city's vigilantes and authorities alike.[36]

1913 brought the Wheatland hop riot, where a dizzyingly diverse workforce of 27 different nationalities joined forces to better their lot, held together by a shared sense of solidarity rather than official union membership (see Pinsolle, Chapter 2). A few common themes drew together these interconnected events during these intense years. IWW organizing, its ideals, and even its songs effectively rallied racially diverse workers toward cooperation in labor struggles as well as armed revolution south of the border. The mobility of IWW members and sympathizers across vast distances facilitated these actions. But as IWW ideals and members moved, sustainable victories remained elusive because of the same mobility that empowered these struggles.[37]

The organizational strength of the PLM diminished through continued arrests of its leaders after the Baja Raids, and the shifting revolutionary landscape within Mexico. Yet the PLM labored on, working to influence events in both Mexico and the United States. The IWW continued to grow in Los Angeles, especially its Mexican membership, and it replaced the PLM as the leading radical Mexican organization in the years immediately before the First World War. Mexican Wobblies concentrated on organizing Mexican workers on both sides of the border into the IWW rather than on choosing sides in the ongoing Mexican Revolution.[38]

In 1913, Wobblies in Los Angeles started to publish another newspaper, *Huelga General*, to replace the now defunct *La Union Industrial*. It only lasted about a year because of a lack of local funds or national IWW support. That same year, the Spanish and English-speaking members of the IWW shared a Los Angeles office a few blocks from the plaza, the center of the city's multiracial working class. In 1915, the IWW regained a Spanish-language voice with *El Rebelde*, published in Los Angeles. This newspaper consolidated a new wave of Mexican IWW organizing by Aurelio V. Azuara, a Spanish immigrant, who joined Tomás Martínez, Armando M. Ojeda, and longtime PLM supporters Pedro Coria and Fernando Velarde. These men became—or remained, in the case of Velarde—the leading public voices and on-the-ground local facilitators of Mexican IWW organizing in southern California and Arizona. As *El Rebelde* rolled off the press, these organizers cycled through managing their duties with the paper in Los Angeles and organizing in Clifton, Morenci, Metcalf, Jerome, Bisbee, and Trona in Arizona, as well as in places like Shasta County in Northern California. IWW organizing significantly contributed to the dramatic, and brutally suppressed, copper strikes in Arizona during the First World War.[39]

War, Repression, and Decline

The United States' entry into the First World War brought with it the combined repression of the IWW by federal, state, and local governments, with vigilantes added to the mix. Authorities arrested hundreds of IWW members and sympathizers throughout California and Arizona. Repression led Pedro Coria to flee to Tampico, Mexico where he had recently traveled on an organizing trip. The IWW spread internationally through this kind of grassroots transnationalism. Coria's direct connection to the foundation of the IWW in Tampico during the peak of wartime repression in the United States illustrates this crucial interpersonal component of IWW internationalism (see Aguilar, Chapter 7). In this regard the IWW functioned similarly to the transnational anarchist movement which, Davide Turcato observed, "shaped up more often as networks of militants than as formal organizations."[40] Furthermore, Anton Rosenthal has documented how the Wobbly press and migration both extended the reach of individuals:

> In the period between the fall of the Baja commune and the establishment of a central I.W.W. administration within Mexico, the Wobblies carried out a concerted propaganda campaign through their press, which was established in ports and border cities such as Los Angeles, Phoenix and Tampa. Mexican workers who had migrated to work on mines in Arizona had already encountered the I.W.W., and many of them returned to work in Northern Mexico, bringing syndicalist ideology and strategy home with them.[41]

The transmission of IWW ideals, union forms, and practices came through the complementary practices of on-the-ground organizing, the press, and the movement of people.

Clearly the IWW declined in the 1920s, but this occurred slowly over the decade and not as a sudden rupture during the First World War. In 1918 and 1919, the Los Angeles IWW organized closer to home, among San Gabriel Valley citrus workers. In 1923 and 1924, the union organized San Pedro dockworkers. In retaliation, the Ku Klux Klan, which included many prominent local citizens, attacked its headquarters. The vigilantes severely burned 12-year-old May Sundstedt with scalding coffee and murdered her mother Lisa, who succumbed to her injuries a few days after the attack. After the IWW's 1924 split, the Emergency Program faction, led by Mortimer Downing, relocated its headquarters to Los Angeles from Chicago, but failed to establish a viable organization. One of the last large-scale industrial actions organized by the IWW in the region came in 1931, among workers constructing the Boulder Dam.[42]

Recognizing continued IWW organizing in the 1920s allows for a more complex understanding of its regional decline, rather than solely blaming wartime repression. Postwar criminal syndicalism legislation in many Western states contributed, as did shifting regional migration patterns, increased urban development, and shifting terrain on the left with the rise of the Communist Party. Immigration restriction passed in 1921 and 1924 and a decline in immigration during the Depression also reduced the immigrant labor pools that had organized under the IWW banner. Mexican labor organizing in the region found outlets in new organizations that built on the IWW-PLM legacy, including communist-led unions. But both older organizations served as points of reference and inspiration for Mexican radicals for decades to come.[43]

The IWW in the US Southwest consciously nurtured a remarkable form of local cooperation to create a multiracial union. Organizers and workers carried this on-the-ground internationalism through regional migration paths as they traveled to organize or to scratch out a living. When Wobblies called for interracial organizing, it was not an internationalism to emerge after some future revolution. Diverse migrant streams and regional labor practices pulled racially diverse workers together into close proximity, giving them an opportunity to put their ideals to action.

Notes

1 Salvatore Salerno, *Red November, Black November: Culture and Community in the Industrial Workers of the World* (New York: State University of New York Press, 1989), p. 204; Devra Anne Weber, "Wobblies of the Partido Liberal Mexicano: reenvisioning internationalist and transnational movements through Mexican lenses," *Pacific Historical Review* 85:2 (2016): 188–226.

2 Perry Anderson, "Internationalism: a breviary," *New Left Review* 14 (2002): 5–25.

3 *Common Sense*, July 15, 1905; Salerno, *Red November, Black November*, p. 87; Hyman Weintraub, "The I.W.W. in California: 1905–1931," MA thesis, University of California, Los Angeles, 1947, pp. 17, 281.

4 *People's People*, February 17, 1911; George Elison, "Kotoku Shsui: the change in thought," *Monumenta Nipponica* 22:3–4 (1967): 449.

5 Richard Steven Street, *Beasts of the Field: A Narrative History of California Farm Workers, 1769–1913* (Stanford, Calif.: Stanford University Press, 2004); David Marshall Struthers, "The world in a city: transnational and inter-racial organizing in Los Angeles, 1900–1930," PhD dissertation, Carnegie Mellon University, Pittsburgh, Pa., 2010.

6 Philip J. Mellinger, *Race and Labor in Western Copper: The Fight of Equality, 1896–1918* (Tucson, Ariz.: University of Arizona Press, 1995), p. 167; Katherine Benton-Cohen, *Borderline Americans: Racial Division and Labor War in the Arizona Borderlands* (Cambridge, Mass.: Harvard University Press, 2009); Phylis Cancilla Martinelli, *Undermining Race: Ethnic Identities in Arizona Copper Camps, 1880–1920* (Tucson, Ariz.: University of Arizona Press, 2015).

7 *Common Sense*, May 4, 1907; Philip S. Foner (ed.), *Black Socialist Preacher: The Teachings of Reverend George Washington Woodbey and His Disciple, Reverend G. W. Slater, Jr.* (San Francisco, Calif.: Synthesis, 1983); Mellinger, *Race and Labor in Western Copper*, p. 151; Alexander Saxton, *The Indispensable Enemy: Labor and the Anti-Chinese Movement in California* (Berkeley, Calif.: University of Cali-

fornia Press, 1971); Ethel Duffy Turner, *Ricardo Flores Magón y el Partido Liberal Mexicano* (Morelia, Michoacán: Editorial "Erandi", 1960), p. 138.

8 Weber, "Wobblies of the Partido Liberal Mexicano," p. 204.

9 *Industrial Union Bulletin*, August 22, 1908.

10 *Industrial Union Bulletin*, July 25, 1908; *Revolt*, March 16, 1912; Melvyn Dubofsky, *We Shall Be All: A History of the i.w.w.* (Chicago, Ill.: Quadrangle, 1969), p. 248; Mary Gallagher, *An Interview with Mary Gallagher on the i.w.w.*, *Tom Mooney* (Berkeley: University of California, Bancroft Library, Regional Oral History Office, 1955), p. 17; Weber, "Wobblies of the Partido Liberal Mexicano," p. 209.

11 "Wobblies of the Partido Liberal Mexicano," p. 226.

12 *International Socialist Review*, September, 1917.

13 Ralph Chaplin, *Wobbly: The Rough-and-Tumble Story of an American Radical* (Chicago, Ill.: University of Chicago Press, 1948), p. 195.

14 Box 14, Folder 9, Frederick W. Thompson Collection, Archives of Labor and Urban Affairs, Wayne State University; Franklin Rosemont, *Joe Hill: The iww and the Making of a Revolutionary Workingclass Counterculture* (Oakland, Calif.: pm Press, 2015), p. 237.

15 *Industrial Union Bulletin*, December 12, 1908.

16 *Industrial Worker*, June 10, 1909.

17 Street, *Beasts of the Field*, p. 604; Weber, "Wobblies of the Partido Liberal Mexicano," p. 205; *Industrial Worker*, April 30, 1910.

18 *Common Sense*, February 20, 1909.

19 Dubofsky, *We Shall Be All*, p. 183.

20 Box 9, Folder 15, Frederick W. Thompson Collection; Ione Elizabeth Wilson, "The *i.w.w.* in California, with special reference to migratory labor (1910–1913)," ma thesis, University of California, 1941, p. 12; Street, *Beasts of the Field*, p. 612.

21 *Industrial Worker*, August 6, April 30, May 21, July 9, July 16, 1910; Weber, "Wobblies of the Partido Liberal Mexicano," p. 218.

22 *Industrial Worker*, August 20, 1910.

23 *Industrial Worker*, August 27, 1910.

24 *Industrial Worker*, September 3, 1910.

25 *Industrial Worker*, September 10, October 15, September 3, 1910.

26 *Industrial Worker*, October 15, 1910.

27 *Industrial Worker*, October 15, 1910.

28 *Industrial Worker*, September 10, 1910.

29 *Industrial Worker*, November 17, 1910.

30 *Industrial Worker*, September 17, 1910.

31 *Industrial Worker*, October 15, 1910.

32 *Industrial Worker*, November 2, 1910; *The Road to Freedom*, June 1932; Mellinger, *Race and Labor in Western Copper*, p. 89.

33 *Industrial Worker*, September 17, 1910.

34 Weber, "Wobblies of the Partido Liberal Mexicano," p. 208.

35 David Struthers, "'The boss has no color line': race, solidarity, and a culture of affinity in Los Angeles and the borderlands, 1907–1915," *Journal for the Study of Radicalism* 7:2 (2013): 79; *The Road to Freedom*, June 1932.

36 Rosalie Shanks, "The i.w.w. free speech movement," *Journal of San Diego History* 19:1 (1973): 25–33.

37 Carleton H. Parker, *The Casual Laborer and Other Essays* (Seattle, Wash.: University of Washington Press, 1920), p. 173; Struthers, "'The boss has no color line'," p. 81.

38 *El Rebelde*, March 18, 1916.

39 *Los Angeles Times*, December 28, 1913; Eric Thomas Chester, *The Wobblies in Their Heyday: The Rise and Destruction of the Industrial Workers of the World During the World War I Era* (Santa Barbara, Calif.: Praeger, 2014), ch. 2; Mellinger, *Race and Labor in Western Copper*.

40 Davide Turcato, "Italian anarchism as a transnational movement, 1885–1915," *International Review of Social History* 52 (2007): 411.

41 Anton Rosenthal, "Radical border crossers: the Industrial Workers of the World and their press in Latin America," *Estudios Interdisciplinarios de América Latina y el Caribe* 22:2 (2011): 49.

42 Nelson van Valen, "The Bolsheviki and the orange growers," *Pacific Historical Review* 22:1 (1953): 39–50; "Cleaning up the harbor: the suppression of the i.w.w. at San Pedro, 1922–25," *Southern California Quarterly* 66:2 (1984): 147–72; Errol Wayne Stevens, *Radical L.A.: From Coxey's Army to the Watts Riots, 1894–1965* (Norman, Okla.: University of Oklahoma Press, 2009), pp. 142–64; *Industrial Worker*, July 18, 1931.

43 *El Luchador*, February 1, 1936; Douglas Monroy, "Anarquismo y Comunismo: Mexican radicalism and the Communist Party in Los Angeles during the 1930s," *Labor History* 24 (1983): 34–59; Devra Weber, *Dark Sweat, White Gold: California Farm Workers, Cotton, and the New Deal* (Berkeley, Calif.: University of California Press, 1994), pp. 85–6.

5

Spanish Anarchists and Maritime Workers in the IWW

Bieito Alonso
(translated by Kevan Antonio Aguilar)

Spanish emigrants to the United States in the early twentieth century typically had proletarian backgrounds. Largely unskilled, these workers migrated to different parts of the Americas in search of jobs or occupations that other European migrants rejected owing to their difficulty or limited duration. Until the global financial crisis of 1929, this transnational group of workers helped erect some of the most iconic infrastructure projects of the period, from the tobacco factories of Tampa to the Panama Canal. This same group also labored aboard American ships that crossed the Atlantic and other oceans. Spanish maritime workers recognized themselves as the workforce that moved commerce from one continent to the next, invisible laborers that helped transform the United States into a world power.

Although many Spanish maritime laborers did not settle permanently in the United States, they nevertheless participated in many labor struggles. Spaniards joined the unions of their professions and became actively involved in proletarian immigrant struggles they helped foster. Among the most important of Spanish maritime workers' efforts, during the first third of the twentieth century, was their formation of the ethnic-based Unión de Fogoneros, Cabos y Engrasadores del Atlántico (Stokers, Sailors, and Oil Workers Union of the Atlantic, or UFCEA). The organization emerged at the end of the nineteenth century as a union for maritime workers without links to other union structures in North America. In 1909–10 it affiliated with the International Seamen's Union (ISU) and then, in 1913, joined the ranks of the Industrial Workers of the World (IWW). The history of the IWW is thus also one of anarchist Spanish maritime workers struggling for the recognition of their labor, achieving social dignity, and mobilizing compatriots in the struggle against capital.

Similar processes of international migration and transnational organizing increased syndicalism's sway among maritime workers in Australia, New Zealand, and Chile in the same era. Spanish Maritime workers drew inspiration from their comrades in the Confederación Nacional del Trabajo (National Confederation of Labor or CNT), formed in Spain in 1910, and community labor organizing in Paterson, New Jersey, where anarcho-communists, individualist anarchists, and syndicalists all discussed labor matters. Their own migratory experience also guided them, much like Spanish workers in Cuba who organized unions with anarchist sympathies.[1]

Enter Pedro Esteve

In 1892, the Catalan anarchist Pedro Esteve arrived in New York, fleeing the repression unleashed by Spanish authorities against the libertarian movement. Esteve's arrival proved a crucial moment in the organizing of Spanish sailors in the Atlantic. That same year in the Port of New York the UFCEA was formed, the first association of Spanish-speaking workers in the United States. With few labor affiliations and little organizational structure, the union persisted until 1902, the year that marked the first strike by Spanish sailors. Although the reasons for the union's collapse are unknown, possibly members of the group grew disillusioned by the racist attitudes towards Spanish-speaking sailors displayed by some of its delegates.

In 1895 Esteve moved to Paterson, New Jersey, a location that hosted a multiethnic and polyglot anarchist community with a predominantly Italian immigrant population. In Paterson he renewed his friendship with Errico Malatesta, with whom he shared a commitment to organizational anarchism and revolutionary syndicalist action. Esteve favored collective organizing because he understood the mobilization and organized resistance of the working class as essential in the fight against the state and capital. Anarchists, Esteve proposed, should be near workers, in factories and workshops, guiding them toward anarchism. Anarchists should also join unions and turn them into instruments of struggle for social revolution.[2]

Esteve left Paterson in 1902 to participate in a nation-wide propaganda tour to organize miners. Under his leadership, the Paterson group decided to assist Colorado miners by providing monetary support and publishing news of their struggle in the pages of their newspaper, *La Questione Sociale*.[3]

Pedro Esteve, Spanish
anarchist ideologue and
activist. Drawing from the
US *New York Herald*,
July 7, 1900.

For a few months Esteve also collaborated with the Western Federation of
Miners and United Mine Workers, the former of which played a key role
in the formation of the IWW. He assisted Italian miners in a wave of strikes
they organized throughout Colorado and Utah. Esteve ultimately sought
to contribute to the mobilization of unskilled immigrants who had been
abandoned by the American Federation of Labor (AFL), and encouraged
them to organize and disseminate revolutionary anarchist ideas.[4]

In June 1905 Esteve traveled to Chicago to participate, as an unofficial
observer, in the founding convention of the IWW. In the IWW, Esteve and
Italian anarchists found an organization that could accommodate their
militant demands while allowing them to organize alongside workers
of different nationalities (see also Zimmer, Chapter 1). Esteve became a
leading organizer within the Italian and Spanish-language radical movements in the United States. Many anarchists acknowledged that he greatly
influenced workers, but also remembered him as a gentle, idealistic, and
generous person whose character displayed a strong sense of honor and
moral integrity.[5]

From the ISU-AFL to the IWW

By 1907 the newly founded Marine Firemen, Oilers, and Water-Tenders
Union (MFOW), an affiliate of the ISU-AFL, had incorporated the remnants
of the Stokers Union into an ethnic section of their union.[6] Over time,
relations between the stokers and ISU administration improved to the point

that the latter's leader, Andrew Furuseth, did not hesitate to publicly acknowledge the level-headedness of the "Latin" leaders (Juan Martínez,
Secundino Brage, José Berenguer, and Jaime Vidal) and their understanding
of union affairs. In February 1910 the Spanish stokers, representing 85 percent of the Atlantic Coast Marine Firemen's membership, accepted their
integration into the ISU and began to reform their organization. With
institutional and financial support from the ISU, the union launched a
campaign to agitate and recruit workers in all ports on the Atlantic coast
while promoting the regeneration of the union's inner workings with the
appointment of a new general delegate, the Galician Frank Ernesto.

While the reconfiguration of the Marine Firemen received praise from
Furuseth, another event occurred with profound consequences for the
organization. In May, shortly after the union joined the ISU, the anarchist collective Cultura Proletaria (Proletarian Culture, also known as Solidaridad
Obrera or Worker Solidarity) was formally established in Brooklyn. The
group merged libertarian political exiles and a small group of migrant
workers—cigar makers and stokers (also known as "firemen")—of mainly
Spanish origin. They aimed to publish a Spanish-language anarchist
weekly, *Cultura Proletaria*, to propagate the virtues of social struggle and
serve as a meeting point for the scattered and fragmented community of
Spanish workers. They began publication in the spring of 1911, printing
issues at the local hall of the Stokers Union on the docks near West Street.
Editor Jaime Vidal was among those who had pushed for the union's
incorporation into the ISU.

Vidal, a libertarian from Barcelona, had worked closely with Francisco
Ferrer i Guardia in his Modern School project before going into exile in
London. During his time in exile, between 1897 and 1903, he made close
contacts with other anarchists throughout Europe and the United States,
eventually relocating to Paterson, New Jersey in 1904. Paterson's polyglot anarchist community warmly welcomed him upon his arrival. There,
Vidal encountered an enclave of anarchism, which, as the *New York Herald*
warned, permeated the Italian, German, French, and Spanish communities
and various other foreign residents.[7] Multilingual intellectuals helped translate for their comrades at meetings and sustained relations between these
radical immigrant communities. The inter-ethnic solidarity established by
the immigrants' shared interest in anarchism facilitated the incorporation
of various immigrant communities in the predominantly Italian-speaking
Paterson movement. Within this community, the Italian anarchists' cosmopolitan outlook proved essential in mobilizing the multiethnic labor force

during times of struggle. Soon after arriving, Vidal also met Pedro Esteve, an influential man in Vidal's future militant ideological drift.

While ideologically far from the unionist model of the ISU-AFL, the Spanish anarchists found no great difficulty in organizing within its structure. The AFL allowed for the autonomy of union locals, and structurally it did not have the statutory ability to interfere in their internal affairs. The anarcho-syndicalist group that led the Atlantic Coast Marine Firemen valued this organizational autonomy. This "consolation" appealed to the Galician anarchist sailor Antonio Ucha, who justified the Spaniards' relationship to the ISU by arguing, "we have neither God nor country, and lately, we organize and affiliate with the International without losing our autonomy, despite having neither leaders nor pastors in our midst."[8] Nonetheless, the ISU's structural limitations, as a craft rather than industrial union, forced Spanish libertarians as well as other anarchist immigrants to pursue a "modern" and revolutionary syndicalist tendency, as defined by Jaime Vidal.[9]

The union tactics applied by these new Spanish labor leaders, despite the ISU's organizational restraints, seemed nearly identical to revolutionary syndicalist models. Direct action, understood as the direct negotiation between workers and employees without the mediation of the state or another body, emphasized the general strike as the primary instrument of collective mobilization. On multiple occasions, Juan Martínez and Pedro Esteve publicly defended anarcho-syndicalism's promise of solidarity that transcended vocation, and the incorporation of all workers without exclusion. Such a model seemed useful to respond to the multiple actors and interests that navigated the maritime world, which relished in its isolated nature. Maritime labor remained a sector that negotiated largely through informal boycotts, strikes, and other acts of solidarity within a single port rather than as a united social movement. Accordingly, port unions often succumbed to a cyclical process of formation, rupture, and reformation.[10]

Organizing under the ISU, though, provided immediate results. The Marine Firemen formed locals in the main Atlantic ports and established relations with Spanish-speaking workers. The dues and financial support accrued by the union's membership led to publication of a new periodical, *Cultura Obrera*, which included a four-page booklet in English edited by Pedro Esteve. The ISU, however, remained under the control of George Bodine and Ed Anderson, who feared the Spanish syndicalists could take control of the organization and transform it into a "radical" union. This produced what Stephen Schwartz characterized as the hybridization of radical American unionism with Spanish syndicalism.[11]

The pages of *Cultura Obrera* persistently promoted the virtues of industrial unionism in contrast to trade unionism. The fundamental challenge facing trade unionism, according to the industrial unionists, was the ability to merge as many territorial federations as possible in an effort to forge the basis of a true industrialist structure. The differences between the syndicalist model of industrial unionism and rigid separation of craft unionism also stemmed, in part, from the anarcho-syndicalists' unwillingness to negotiate legislative initiatives for the grievances of seafarers.

In the summer of 1911, anarcho-syndicalist leaders of the Atlantic Coast Marine Firemen considered transferring their industrialist principles to the rest of the districts and imposing their organizational model on the whole ISU. Recognized for their mobilizing success, the radical sectors won additional strength in the face of the immediate celebration of the ISU's sixth convention in Baltimore in December 1911. Despite opposition, "radical" delegates such as Spaniards Jaime Vidal and José Filguerira took control of the Marine Firemen's three districts (Atlantic, Pacific, and Great Lakes).

Although the ranks of the Marine Firemen may have viewed the results of the convention positively, they gravely misunderstood the inner workings of the ISU. This misreading was fueled by poorly contained euphoria and a flagrant underestimation of the power of "conservative" leaders including Andrew Furuseth. Faced with the prospect of "radical" groups taking control of a large part of the organization, the response of the ISU leadership was relentless. It not only mobilized the majority of membership in elections, it also aimed to strangle economically entities that were hostile to its practices. This included the suppression of economic aid ($30 a month) given by the Marine Firemen to *Cultura Obrera*. The voluntarism of the anarcho-syndicalists and their allies was not enough to prevent a clear internal defeat which was a culmination of grave strategic errors. The leadership of the Atlantic Coast Marine Firemen had only two alternatives: accept defeat and fold into the dominant craft union orientation or abandon the ISU.

Radical workers chose the latter, and stated their position in *Cultura Obrera*: "After the Baltimore Convention, we have nothing in common with the International."[12] Indeed, in the first months of 1912 the pages of *Cultura Obrera* hosted a torrent of articles and editorials highlighting the virtues of industrial unionism and consolidation of the craft federations. The thin alliance between the Spanish stokers and the ISU definitively broke that summer.

In June 1912, the shipping companies tossed out the agreement reached with the union the previous year as it came up for renegotiation. The refusal of the companies to implement the contract provoked a strike by dissident ISU-affiliated Spanish sailors and stokers in the Port of New York, who organized a new labor entity, the Federación de los Obreros del Transporte de América (National Transport Workers Federation of America, FOTA). Violent clashes and boycotts by non-Latin stokers backed by the ISU plagued this strike. It ended with the defeat of the Spanish sailors. By December, the FOTA took its final step away from the ISU and requested affiliation with the IWW.[13]

Within six months, the FOTA integrated itself within the IWW with little resistance, except for a small collective of individualist anarchists led by Dionisio Freijomil who opposed the merger. The Spanish maritime workers' affiliation with the IWW officially began in April 1913. *Cultura Obrera* started to publish an English edition, *Labor Culture*, and became an official IWW periodical. The newspaper was published in Brooklyn, sharing office space with the anarchist Center for Social Studies.[14] Pedro Esteve became editor of *Cultura Obrera* as well as secretary of the Spaniards' Marine Transport Workers (MTW) local.[15]

Other Ports, Other Leaders

Spanish sailors organized and agitated in many ports beyond New York during the early part of the twentieth century, including Philadelphia, one of the largest manufacturing centers and ports in the country. The lack of job security for unskilled laborers and constantly changing employer demands on workers there had produced a surplus labor population. On May 14, 1913, Philadelphia longshore workers struck, demanding a wage increase of 10 cents per hour and a ten and a half hour workday on night shifts and Sundays. Strikers quickly invited IWW organizers, who helped win the strike and formed a union which organized relentlessly over the next ten years. By August 1913 the IWW's MTW Local 8 had created what historian Bruce Nelson called "the most striking example of class solidarity between blacks and whites in this country."[16]

With the docks under workers' control, the IWW launched a recruitment campaign aimed at maritime workers. Among others, Local 8 hired Manuel Rey, a Galician anarchist who led a Spanish-speaking libertarian group, La Sociedad Pro-Prensa (the Pro-Press Society), composed largely of Latin sailors and longshore workers.[17] Rey, who arrived in Philadelphia in 1910 as a boatswain on a cargo ship from Cuba, never considered himself an "authentic" syndicalist despite being an IWW organizer. He argued that "[Syndicalism] is not true anarchism because it is built on hierarchy and authoritarianism."[18] However, unlike other Spanish anarchists who opposed the IWW, Rey accepted union activism as a means to promote anarchism and moral regeneration among workers. He explained, "Anarchism is as old as man …. Anarchism is the natural philosophy of life; and through the process of education we may be able to make of every human being a man, a man who can think freely and do the best he can for himself and his fellow human beings."[19]

Anarchism galvanized Rey and the other 500 Spanish sailors attracted to IWW organizing in the port of Philadelphia. Rey and the workers held regular meetings and established a Spanish library filled with IWW literature, musical scores, and novels. Sailors voraciously read articles in *Cultura Obrera* and *El Rebelde*, published in Los Angeles (see Struthers in Chapter 4), while organizing at the port. What is more, the racial dynamics between the ISU and Spanish organizers became a major point of contention. Manuel Rey staunchly opposed the racist and discriminatory language used by ISU organizers in Philadelphia, who largely organized in the interest of Anglo-American workers. ISU organizers despised black workers and immigrants from South and Southwest Europe, whom they viewed as incapable of assimilation and hostile to unionization. The contention found its way onto the ships, where heated debates between the racially divided stokers regarding the ISU's exclusion of blacks and "undesirable foreigners" broke out. ISU loyalists retorted by accusing the IWW of being an organization run by a handful of "foreigners." The ISU's discrimination and xenophobic policies ultimately led many sailors and longshoremen to join the IWW throughout 1913.[20]

Manuel Rey proved an invaluable asset to the IWW, as the only national organizer of Spanish descent who worked for the Union. While other Spanish organizers such as Jaime Vidal, Juan Martínez, and the former stokers' leaders decreased in prominence on the New York docks, Rey became the recognized leader of Latin sailors in the Atlantic. Both Vidal and José Vilariño, secretary of the Marine Firemen during the strike of 1911, moved to Los Angeles in 1913 and published the short-lived anarchist newspaper *Fuerʒa Consciente*. Rey's affiliation with the union came to an abrupt end on September 5, 1917, when the Justice Department raided 64 IWW offices across the country. Six Wobblies were arrested in Philadelphia, including Rey, accused of interfering with the Selective Service Act, violating the Espionage Act, conspiring to strike, violating the rights of employers, and using the postal service to commit fraud against businessmen.[21]

The arrest of Manuel Rey not only left Local 8 without one of its key organizers but also took away the Spanish maritime workers' main leader. The IWW rushed to hire another organizer with experience among maritime workers to maintain ties with the port's Spanish sailors. Genaro Pazos, another Galician anarchist, soon took the position. A former collaborator on *Cultura Obrera* who defended the incorporation of the Atlantic Coast Marine Firemen into the IWW, Pazos participated in MTW propaganda campaigns throughout Atlantic ports, and raised funds for the IWW General Defense Committee.[22] Nonetheless, the repression continued. In the spring of 1918 Philadelphia police prevented mass public events and meetings on ships. In this repressive context, Pazos understood the need to increase the frequency of internal assemblies to maintain workers' mobilization and sustain solidarity for imprisoned leaders. Members sold "freedom bonds" to liberate Philadelphia Wobblies Ben Fletcher, Rey, John Walsh, and others, and to assist their family members.

Because of the state's heightened attacks on the IWW, the MTW held a national convention in May 1919. Genaro Pazos represented the sailors of Philadelphia. By then, he maintained correspondence with sailors scattered across the Atlantic, including close ties with Gerardo Malvido, a Galician who served as secretary for the MTW organizing committee in the port of Buenos Aires. In their correspondence, Malvido noted the great interest of workers in Spain and Cuba in the IWW's organizing model, and viewed the union as being on the same level of the powerful maritime union La Naval, based in Barcelona.[23]

Soon after, Wobblies began to discuss the formation of a Revolutionary International Marine Transport Workers Federation, a new organization grouping all Atlantic sailors, though this project never came to fruition. In addition to a complex organizational model, the proposed federation suffered the negative effects of the global economic crisis that permeated throughout commercial shipping following the First World War. Employers curbed expansion throughout the early 1920s, leading to massive layoffs. With fewer workers to mobilize, many of the MTW's primary organizers returned to their countries of origin.[24]

The proud and aggressive Wobbly organizing in Philadelphia paved important roads for multiethnic labor mobilizations in the nation's greatest Southern port, New Orleans. Between 1880 and the 1920s labor organizers established a remarkable and long-lasting multiethnic labor campaign, although New Orleans was a racist stronghold of the US South. Eric Arnesen described it as "the most powerful biracial labor movement in the nation."[25] In the summer of 1913 one of the biggest citrus monopolies, the United Fruit Company, locked out stokers from their vessels in the ports of New York,

Boston, Philadelphia, and New Orleans. Maritime workers in New Orleans produced the greatest response, largely due to the influence of the MTW among sailors. On June 2, 1913, the MTW launched a total work stoppage on ships owned by the United Fruit Company and demanded collective control of the ships. The strike quickly erupted in violence, with clashes between workers and private security guards paid for by the company. Four sailors were killed, including two members of the strike committee. Dozens of Wobblies were wounded and arrested, including the remaining members of the strike committee. One of the most prominent members of the organization was the Spanish stoker Frank Prego, brother of the Galician CNT leader José Prego, the first director of the confederation's Galician publication *Solidaridad*. Charged with the illegal possession of weapons and sentenced to 12 years in prison, Prego eventually was deported to Spain in 1918.[26]

As was seen in earlier organizing campaigns, the connection between unions on both sides of the Atlantic displayed the transnational dynamics of the labor movement among Spanish sailors. Their objective, as always, was to form a single global union of all Atlantic maritime workers. The decline in union organization and agitation was perhaps the most profound consequence of the defeat on the New Orleans docks. It embodied a point of no return in maritime trade unionism. Despite the solidarity among workers, the disadvantages of calling a general strike in the maritime sector outweighed its prospects. Subsequently the mobilization failed. The United Fruit Company defeated the IWW and regained control of its shipments, and the ISU absorbed radicalized workers into its ranks.

Repression

While the first Red Scare targeted immigrant workers, it also destroyed a dense network of cultural centers, publications, left-libertarian societies, and other institutions of revolutionary movements. These elements had galvanized the most combative and conscious sectors of workers, for whom radical organizations not only offered opportunities to foster a space of dignity, but also facilitated integration into American society. Spaniards—whether businesspeople, anarchists, or common laborers— suffered the consequences of the US anti-Bolshevik hysteria. Some were deported, others imprisoned in the United States. Most sought isolation or fled to places less hostile.[27]

All the while, the anarchist press on both sides of the Atlantic called for solidarity and support despite the increasing pressures on the Iberian immigrant community:

There are currently thousands of prisoners in North America whose families have not been notified [of their imprisonment]. They were disappeared when going to work and nobody knows where they are. One periodical, *Cultura Obrera*, was initially saved ... but it has been suppressed. Some of those that edited it have been imprisoned while others who were Spaniards just arrived in Vigo, uprooted.[28]

Manuel Rey's case is particularly interesting, not only because of the severity of his sentence but also the national dimension of the process. After a five-month trial, Rey and 93 other IWW leaders were found guilty of espionage. Rey and 14 others, those deemed the most dangerous or charismatic, received the harshest sentence of 20 years in prison and a $20,000 fine. Along with the rest, Rey went to prison in Leavenworth Federal Penitentiary.[29]

During his time in Leavenworth, Rey established a close friendship with the Mexican anarchist Ricardo Flores Magón, and came into contact with Lilly Sarnoff, a Russian anarchist known by the pseudonym Ellen White. Rey's relationships with Flores Magón and White stimulated his libertarian yearnings. He served as a liaison between the prisoners and their defense committees, a labor that frequently earned him punishments.[30] Nonetheless, Rey kept writing articles and collaborative works which were published in the anarchist press. The August 1919 edition of the IWW periodical *One Big Union Monthly* published one of Rey's poems, "Thoughts of a deal-living soul." He also published an untitled poem in the New York-based publication *The American Political Prisoner* in 1922.

In addition to the aid received by the General Defense Committee, the Workers Defense Union (WDU) offered Rey financial support. However, Rey and a small group of Wobblies openly disagreed with the IWW and WDU's policy of rejecting individual prisoner support, and instead demanding collective liberation. In the opinion of the IWW leadership, only a unified response could provide the leverage to achieve amnesty of all political prisoners. Harry Weinberger, Rey's defense lawyer, argued that clemency to one individual did not negatively affect the labor movement, and submitted a clemency petition on Rey's behalf. Some imprisoned Wobblies, however, openly criticized the Spanish anarchist as undermining the group's collective struggle against imprisonment.[31]

By 1922, the most radical wing of the prisoners created the Workers Prison Relief Committee, which aimed to prevent disunity among jailed militants. Its first public statement called for solidarity among the dissenting prisoners: "This committee is a class conscious proletarian group primarily interested in the strengthening of the labor movement. We are not romantics who seek to alleviate the personal situations of each person."[32] It specifically condemned Rey's plea for clemency, but Rey and other immigrants continued to propose individual petitions for clemency based on their legal status as foreigners. Their mental and physical deterioration was ultimately a more pressing concern than a hypothetical act of solidarity.[33]

The determination of Rey to receive individual support demonstrated the limitations of IWW principles, which were unable to prevent individual initiatives concerning the pursuit of freedom. In fact individual requests for clemency were eventually accepted by the organization, but this did not stop Rey and other dissidents from being expelled from the very union they had helped build. The union's expulsion of prisoners was done by means not so different from the undemocratic practices of the United States, with the decision being made in a secret clandestine meeting which was not advertised and so did not receive public comment. Ultimately, federal authorities released Rey on December 22, 1922 on the condition that he accept deportation to Spain and never return to the United States.[34] Rey arrived in the Port of Vigo in early 1923, but after a brief visit with his family he returned clandestinely to the United States. Following an anonymous complaint, Rey was deported again in 1925. That same year, however, he returned to the United States by crossing the Mexican border under the alias Louis G. Raymond, a name he maintained until his death at the Stelton anarchist colony in New Jersey on December 14, 1989, at the age of 101.

The release of Rey marked the beginning of the end of the Spanish Wobbly activism. Initially inspired by libertarian ideas disseminated by Spanish sailors and longshore workers throughout the Atlantic, the ideological basis of this movement ended in 1925, devoid of newspapers and workers to sustain it. Along with the transfer of Vidal to California, *Cultura Obrera* ceased publication in 1922. Pedro Esteve, the ideological heart of the movement, resigned from the IWW after becoming disillusioned with its "authoritarianism," and died in 1925.[35] Nevertheless, what remained of the Spanish libertarian movement reaffirmed its commitment to anarchist principles with the revival of *Cultura Proletaria*, which ran from 1927 to 1953. Through it all, Spanish anarchists held on to the prophetic words of Manuel Rey: "Another century may pass before people truly understand the significance of anarchism. We cannot lose heart."[36]

Notes

1   Marcel van der Linden, *Workers of the World: Essays toward a Global Labor History* (Leiden, Netherlands: Brill, 2008), 374–5.

2 Susana Sueiro, "Un anarquista en la penumbra: Pedro Esteve y la velada real del anarquismo transnacional," *Alcores: Revista de Historia Contemporánea* 15 (2013): 43–66.

3 Salvatore Salerno, "I Delitti della Razza Bianca (crimes of the white race): Italian anarchists' racial discourse as crime," in Jennifer Guglielmo and Salvatore Salerno (eds.), *Are Italians White? How Race is Made in America* (New York/London: Routledge, 2003), p. 119.

4 *Cultura Obrera*, September 11, 1926.

5 Sueiro, "Un anarquista en la penumbra," p. 57.

6 Hyman Weintraub, *Andrew Furuseth: Emancipator of the Seamen* (Berkeley, Calif.: University of California Press, 1959), p. 102.

7 Kenyon Zimmer, *Immigrants against the State: Yiddish and Italian Anarchism in America* (Urbana, Ill.: University of Illinois Press, 2015), p. 102.

8 *Cultura Obrera*, July 24, 1912.

9 *Cultura Obrera*, November 22, 1911.

10 David Montgomery, *Workers' Control in America: Studies in the History of Work, Technology, and Labor Struggles* (Cambridge: Cambridge University Press, 1979), p. 194.

11 Stephen Schwartz, *Brotherhood of the Sea: A History of the Sailors' Union of the Pacific, 1885–1985* (Somerset, N.J.: Transaction, 1986), pp. 38–40.

12 *Cultura Obrera*, January, 1912.

13 Schwartz, *Brotherhood of the Sea*, p. 42.

14 *Cultura Obrera*, August, 1913.

15 Paul Avrich, *Anarchist Voices: An Oral History of Anarchism in America* (Oakland, Calif.: AK Press, 2005), p. 393.

16 Bruce Nelson, *Divided We Stand: American Workers and the Struggle for Equality* (Princeton, N.J.: Princeton University Press, 2000), p. 134.

17 Peter Cole, *Wobblies on the Waterfront: Interracial Unionism in Progressive-Era Philadelphia* (Urbana, Ill.: University of Illinois Press, 2007), p. 66.

18 Avrich, *Anarchist Voices*, p. 395.

19 Avrich, *Anarchist Voices*, p. 396.

20 Although we have no specific data on the workers' political identities, we know that up until May of 1916 the foreign section of Local 8 contained 200 members, with an overwhelming majority from Spain.

21 Rey was arrested for organizing a strike in Buffalo, New York on June 5, 1917 and again for agitating in Niagara Falls on July 21.

22 Cole, *Wobblies on the Waterfront*, p. 91.

23 Cole, *Wobblies on the Waterfront*, p. 104.

24 Cole, *Wobblies on the Waterfront*, p. 105 *et passim*.

25 Eric Arnesen, "Biracial waterfront unionism in the age of segregation," in Calvin Winslow (ed.), *Waterfront Workers: New Perspectives on Race and Class* (Urbana, Ill.: University of Illinois Press), p. 24.

26 *Industrial Worker*, July 24, 1913.

27 *Tierra y Libertad* (Barcelona), January 15, 1919.

28 *Tierra y Libertad*, January 15, 1919.

29 Stephen Martin Kohn, *American Political Prisoners: Prosecutions under the Espionage and Sedition Acts* (Westport, Conn.: Praeger, 1994), p. 127.

30 Inmate Number 13111, Records of the Bureau of Prisons, Leavenworth Penitentiary, Record Group 129, National Archives and Records Administration, Kansas
City, Mo.

31 Letter from Harry Weinberger to Lilly Sarnoff, May 14, 1922, Box 23, Folder 1,
Harry Weinberger Papers, Sterling Memorial Library Collection, Yale University.

32 Douglas C. Rossinow, *Visions of Progress: The Left-Liberal Tradition in America*
(Philadelphia, Pa.: University of Pennsylvania Press, 2008), p. 96.

33 Eric Chester, *The Wobblies in Their Heyday: The Rise and Destruction of the Industrial Workers of the World during the World War I Era* (Santa Barbara, Calif.:
Praeger, 2014), p. 211.

34 Kohn, *American Political Prisoners*, p. 127.

35 Avrich, *Anarchist Voices*, p. 393.

36 Avrich, *Anarchist Voices*, p. 396.

Part II

The IWW in the Wider World

6

The IWW and the Dilemmas of Internationalism

Wayne Thorpe

By its very name the Industrial Workers of the World (IWW), now well into its second century, suggests an international organization.[1] Its history is certainly international: though founded in 1905 in Chicago, its influence quickly extended into Canada and Mexico. In countries further afield, groups identified with it, adopted its name, and established official or semi-official branches. But that is not to say that the IWW regarded itself in 1905 as a self-standing world organization or a labor International. Founded as an industrial rival of the craft-based American Federation of Labor (AFL), the IWW also encouraged radical industrialism beyond the borders of the United States. Some delegates in Chicago in 1905 favored the name "Industrial Union of America" to indicate the national character of the organization, while others favored "Industrial Workers of the World" to symbolize the fact that the working class, rather than the organization founded in Chicago, was itself world-wide. Lucy Parsons preferred the "American Branch of the Industrial Workers of the World."[2] This chapter focuses not on the repercussions or outposts of the IWW in countries beyond the United States, but first, on the evolution of the organization's international policy over its first three decades. The main contours of that policy did not change markedly thereafter. Second, it examines the positions taken by the General Executive Board or the conventions of the IWW.[3] One way to delineate that evolution is to ask: did the IWW consider, seek, or decline membership in the formal labor Internationals that existed in these years, or offer itself in lieu of them? What international options did the IWW have?

The Socialist Option

In 1905 labor's international options consisted of the Second Socialist International, founded in 1889, and the International Secretariat of National Trade Union Centers, founded in 1901, the former largely the political, and the latter the trade union, arm of the international social democratic movement. The IWW made a single appearance at the assemblies of each. Still debating its own views on political action, the IWW delegated Fred Heslewood to attend the 1907 congress of the Second International held in Stuttgart, Germany. On a major congress issue, Heslewood unsuccessfully opposed linking unions to political parties. He regretted that few wage earners were present. Most delegates were socialist intellectuals, well-fed and "eligible to [enter] any fat man's race."[4] The following year, the IWW's affirmation of its exclusive reliance on direct action and its independence from all political parties precluded further association with the Second International, which insisted that affiliates endorse political action. That left the Berlin-based International Secretariat, administered by Carl Legien, the head of the massive German trade union federation. Although dominated by social democratic unions, the International Secretariat did not require a pledge of political action. This permitted the Confédération Générale du Travail (General Confederation of Labor, CGT) of France, its only revolutionary syndicalist affiliate, to promote democratizing and radicalizing the Secretariat.

That its founders in 1905 directed it to enter into relations with the International Secretariat is an indicator that they did not consider the IWW itself to be a labor International. In August 1909, the IWW applied for membership in the Secretariat, which admitted only one union organization from each country. In 1909, the Secretariat had 20 national affiliates with nearly 6 million members, but as yet no affiliate from the United States. Legien long had courted the AFL. For his part, AFL leader Samuel Gompers was deeply suspicious of the socialism of most national affiliates of the Secretariat, but also eager to secure international recognition for his organization. He could take consolation, moreover, in the fact that the Secretariat sidestepped contentious issues, deferring them to the Second International. The Secretariat, therefore, had refused CGT proposals to put the general strike and antimilitarism on its agenda, prompting the French to boycott the Secretariat's 1905 and 1907 conferences. The French nevertheless agreed to host the 1909 conference in Paris, which Gompers attended as a guest.

Having lingered in Europe to study the labor movement, Gompers found the CGT to be greatly different "in both organization and methods" from the AFL, and the large, highly organized German trade unions the most similar to it.[5] The AFL joined the International Secretariat in 1910. Its longevity and size (1 million members in 1909) favored the AFL's bid to represent US labor in the International Secretariat. But for Legien, the AFL had additional appeal: it was moderate, whereas the IWW was revolutionary; and it was an opponent, and the IWW a potential ally, of the French CGT. That the IWW's application to the Secretariat had preceded that of the AFL was inconvenient to Legien, but he simply temporized, not presenting it to the 1909 conference.

The domestic rivalry between the IWW and the AFL took the international stage in Budapest, dominating the Secretariat's 1911 conference. Speaking for the IWW, William Z. Foster challenged the presence of the AFL. As Foster described it, Legien tried "to steam-roller me," but as "a 'wobbly' from the West and not so easily squelched, I took the floor and caused … a hubbub."[6] In the words of James Duncan, the AFL delegate, the "misguided and vulgar i.w.w. man" invoked "force and language too vile to repeat."[7] Only the French CGT supported Foster's condemnation of AFL complicity with employers, and the IWW's repudiation of class collaboration. The CGT's plea that the interests of unity dictated that both US unions be enrolled fell on deaf ears. All remaining national affiliates rejected admission of the IWW. Not only did the IWW suffer a rebuff in Budapest; to add insult to injury its delegate Foster, who had spent a year in Europe and was impressed by the French CGT, returned to the United States to encourage the IWW to abandon "dual unionism" in favor of boring from within existing unions, as the CGT advocated. In February 1912, Foster paid his last dues to the IWW. He joined the AFL craft union of railway car workers and soon launched the Syndicalist League of North America.[8]

For the IWW, the International Secretariat proved no option at all. The Budapest decision closed that door, whereupon *Solidarity* declared on September 16, 1911: "Up with the New International, typified by the C.G.T. and the I.W.W.!" But by 1913 another door appeared ajar, though it was not thrown open for nearly a decade. Syndicalist organizations beyond France, barred, like the IWW, from the Secretariat, also began to consider their own international options. These syndicalist groups included the 100,000-strong Unione Sindacale Italiana (Italian Syndicalist Union), the Confederación Nacional del Trabajo (National Confederation of Labor) in Spain, smaller organizations in Sweden, the Netherlands, and Germany, along with revolutionary unions in Latin America. Nearly all of them looked to the French CGT, perhaps 500,000 strong in 1910–11, for inspiration. As one Belgian put it, the French were "the older brothers" of the syndicalist movement, while Armando Borghi observed, "we in Italy were the daughters of France."⁹ Embattled minorities in their own countries, they sought to overcome their domestic isolation and enhance their own sense of legitimacy and purpose by deepening their ties with like-minded organizations beyond their borders. Some favored an International of their own, a major issue pondered at the First International Syndicalist Congress held in London in September 1913. European syndicalists saw the IWW as a part of their family.

Despite its earlier bid to enter the socialist-dominated Secretariat, the IWW was much closer in spirit and outlook to the syndicalists who met in London. Along with them, the IWW supported the *Bulletin international du mouvement syndicaliste*, published from Paris by the Dutch syndicalist Christiaan Cornelissen to keep the revolutionary unions informed about one another. The IWW also shared with European syndicalists an insistence on the autonomy of workers, the primacy and independence of revolutionary unions, the importance of economic organization, and direct action at the point of production. In organizational emphasis they differed, with prewar syndicalists favoring federations of craft unions to preserve local autonomy over the industrialism endorsed by the IWW. The *Industrial Worker* observed in 1913 that the IWW "represents a higher type of revolutionary labor organization." But "in international affiliations," it added, the IWW "is more closely allied with the revolutionary syndicalist than any other body." Three months later, speaking of the proposed syndicalist congress, it wrote: "Let its most important work be the formation of a connecting link between the revolutionary syndicalists and industrialists of all countries."¹⁰ The IWW, noting the costs involved and its own almost simultaneous convention, did not send a formal delegate to London. General Secretary Vincent St John's letter to the organizers, however, emphasized that abstention should not "be construed as opposition to the Congress" or to formation of a revolutionary International, which the IWW hoped soon to see and which it was willing to help finance.¹¹ Nine European and three Latin American countries were more formally represented. The CGT, committed to working within the International Secretariat, boycotted the meeting. The London assembly, still hoping to win French support, postponed the question of establishing a specifically Syndicalist International to a later congress. Between 1909 and 1911, the IWW had sought to join the French effort to revolutionize the Secretariat. In 1913, finally, it lent its blessing to a separate revolutionary labor International.

The hopes of the syndicalists for more formal international bonds were derailed by the outbreak of war in 1914. The 1913 London congress had reiterated syndicalist opposition to war, and the European organizations represented there—from Germany, Italy, the Netherlands, Sweden, and Spain—refused to support the defensive or war policies of their respective governments. So did the IWW. In contrast, most of the national affiliates of the Second International and the International Secretariat (or, as it was known after 1913, the International Federation of Trade Unions) supported their governments during the war, including initially the French CGT. It is an irony worth noting that those labor organizations that most fully honored labor internationalism during the First World War tended to be those systematically excluded from the labor movement's international institutions. The high cost of the IWW's resistance to war is well known.

The Communist Option

War brought with it the Russian Revolution, followed in 1919 by the founding of the Third or Communist International (Comintern), and its bid to unite the global revolutionary movement under its own banner. The purported workers' revolution in Russia captured the attention of radicals everywhere, who made of it, as the Italian syndicalist Armando Borghi recalled, "our polar star. We exulted in its victories. We trembled at its risks .... We made a symbol and an altar of its name, its dead, its living and its heroes."[12] The appearance of soviets, seemingly a new form of occupational representation, held inescapable appeal for those who had no sympathy for prewar socialist parliamentarism. Some Wobblies could celebrate the early Comintern as the realization of the program and ideals of the IWW. As "Big Bill" Haywood said, "here is what we have been dreaming about; here is the IWW all feathered out."[13] Enthusiasm penetrated the IWW's General Executive Board as well. It unanimously voted in August 1919 to establish a Committee on International Relations to enter into fraternal relations with the communists and syndicalists of Russia and Europe, the industrial unionists of Canada and Australia, and "to provide for the representation of the i.w.w. as a constituent member of the Third International."[14] This decision, however, never was confirmed by an IWW convention. Before 1919 ended, the Spanish and Italian syndicalists similarly declared for the Comintern, before their fervor ebbed. The early enthusiasm for the Russian Revolution remained alive for some radical unionists; for others it yielded to more cautious assessment. This ambivalence could be felt by individual Wobblies. George Hardy, who favored the IWW's entry into the Comintern, was elected IWW general secretary at the May 1920 convention. During the vote, as Hardy recorded, a delegate called out: "'God damn it,

I'll vote for you although I know you're a politician'—already recognition of my changed outlook."[15]

The Second Comintern Congress in the summer of 1920 endorsed the primacy of political action, the necessity and preeminence of communist parties, and repudiated "dual unionism." The hopes of most syndicalist delegates that an autonomous revolutionary labor International would emerge from Moscow evaporated. "All my beautiful illusions came to fall one by one," wrote the Spaniard Angel Pestaña, "withered and dead, like the petals of the rose fall when they lack the sap of the plant."[16] The IWW did not have a delegate in Moscow, but the congress's results hopelessly divided its Board. Three motions were put before it: first, that the IWW affiliate with the Comintern (failed); second, that it not affiliate (passed); third, that it affiliate with reservations about engaging in parliamentary action (passed). The Board decided to put this confusing compendium of motions in a referendum to the membership, but such protest and uncertainty followed (all motions reportedly failed) that the Board declared the ballot void at the end of 1920.[17] The Board removed Hugh R. Richards as editor of *Solidarity* in October 1920, because of his undue sympathy to the communist cause, and John Sandgren as editor of *One Big Union Monthly* in December 1920, for undue hostility to it (see Zimmer, Chapter 1).[18]

To circumvent resistance to Comintern policies by revolutionary unions like the IWW that repudiated parliamentary action and political parties, Moscow proposed to establish a separate Red International of Labor Unions (Profintern). European syndicalists, in turn, summoned an international conference in Berlin in December 1920 to seek common ground regarding the proposed Profintern, whose founding congress would meet in 1921. Delegates from the British Shop Stewards movement, the United States, the Netherlands, Germany, France, Sweden, and Argentina were present. The Spanish and Italian delegates had been jailed en route in Italy. Representing the Russian unions and the Provisional Council of the Proftintern, S. Belinsky was also seated, though he remained hostile to a syndicalist assembly preceding that of the Profintern. The IWW delegate in Berlin, its general secretary George Hardy, had urged IWW entry into the Comintern, with "reservations," but also wrote that what the IWW and the syndicalists wanted was "a purely industrial international."[19] He endorsed the "Berlin declaration" requiring that the new revolutionary labor International be free of all political influence. "Russia will have to come into line," Hardy wrote back to Chicago. But he also unsuccessfully proposed that the "Berlin declaration" endorse "the dictatorship of the proletariat" and that all organizations represented at the Profintern's congress should accept its decisions.[20] Hardy accepted Belinsky's invitation to travel onward to Moscow, where the spell of the revolution and its leaders led him to alter his views. He now assured Lenin that he accepted the necessity of a disciplined political party and would work for the communists upon his return to the United States. Hardy's term expired in 1921. On March 18, 1922, *Industrial Solidarity* reported his expulsion from his local union. He later worked in England for the Anglo-Saxon section of the Profintern. "To help to overcome the anarchist and syndicalist prejudices in the international trade union movement," his memoir records, "was made my special task."[21]

The 1921 founding congress of the Profintern significantly changed the picture for the IWW. The "Berlin declaration" formed the IWW's mandate, and George Williams, the union's delegate, favored affiliation before he left for Moscow.[22] The Profintern Congress, however, rejected "dual unionism" generally, explicitly condemned the policies of the IWW, and called for the national coordination of communist parties and labor unions and the international coordination of the Comintern and the Profintern. In a long report, Williams lamented the congress: the credentials committee determined the course of the proceedings; delegates from revolutionary unions "might better have stayed home;" congress decisions "were made before it started." For organizations like the IWW to maintain a "separate existence" "was an unpardonable crime." The assembly reminded Williams of a massive trial, "in which the high priests of the Communist International were sitting in judgment over the 'criminal' Syndicalists." At year's end the IWW Board, having studied the congress resolutions and Williams's preliminary report, concluded that affiliation with the Profintern, which it dismissed as "the Communist Party, thinly disguised," was "not only undesirable but absolutely impossible."[23]

Although this judgment of December 1921 would never be reversed, the issue of relations with the communists continued to reverberate within the IWW. As a leading labor historian put it, "Communism became topic number one in the IWW; when Wobblies weren't fighting over it in their halls or in the streets, they debated the issue in their newspapers and conventions."[24] Profintern head Alexander Lozovsky issued "An appeal to the rank and file of the IWW," lamenting, "We have searched in vain for one correct statement in the report of Joe [George] Williams." The IWW press, he claimed, "abounds with anarchist phraseology" and was more critical than the capitalist press in its coverage of the first proletarian state. The syndicalists of Europe remained divided over a Syndicalist International and, in any event, the Profintern wanted a united political and economic

"The ass in the lion's skin or 'all dressed up and no place to go'," *One Big Union Monthly*, October 1920

front. If the rank and file broke with IWW officials, those diluters of "revolutionary spirit," the IWW would be welcome at the second Profintern Congress. This appeal drew a 24-page hostile reply from the IWW Board.[25]

While some members who embraced communism simply left the IWW, others campaigned openly to convert it.[26] The Red International Affiliation Committee, headed by Harrison George, adopted this tactic and worked to reverse the IWW's decision regarding the Profintern. It argued that the IWW must affiliate internationally, that the Profintern was nearest "in harmony with its own best interests," above all since it endorsed "revolutionary industrial unionism." There was also "an insignificant anarcho-syndicalist" International at Berlin, "which profanes the name of the First International of Marx, whose science they despise and ignore." The Profintern, moreover, renounced "syndicalist prejudices toward a revolutionary party."[27] But while some committed communists worked openly to convert the IWW to the Profintern, others, like Vern Smith, found it more effective to work behind the scenes. Smith served as the editor of the IWW's weekly, *Industrial Solidarity*, for nearly three years in the mid-1920s.

The Syndicalist Option

On the heels of the communist option another quickly appeared, with which it became inextricably intertwined for a time. The IWW did not stand alone during 1921–22 in seeing both the reformist International Federation of Trade Unions (formerly the International Secretariat), now sitting in Amsterdam, and the politicized Profintern in Moscow, as unpalatable. Syndicalist organizations met for preliminary discussions in Germany in June 1922. The IWW, lamenting that notice arrived too late to send a delegate, elaborated its views. The lessons of the Russian Revolution included that an International had to be free of political influence, unlike the Profintern, which was controlled by the "Russian Communist Party." The Board stressed that affiliates of the Syndicalist International should be autonomous in dealing with distinctive national circumstances. It also emphasized the IWW's "Industrial Unionism," declaring craft unions and federations merely divisions "clustered around their own particular interests." The syndicalist assembly, it concluded, "is without doubt the most important event in the history of the International labor movement."[28] The syndicalists reassembled to found the Berlin-based International Working Men's Association (IWA) in December 1922. With the founding of the IWA, the choice for revolutionary unions was no longer "Amsterdam or Moscow," but "Berlin or Moscow." Organizations in 15 European and 14 Latin American countries eventually affiliated with Berlin. The IWA hoped to win the IWW's affiliation as well. The IWW had identified with the syndicalists before 1914 and its immediate postwar conventions also specified them as potential partners in a revolutionary labor International. Two years earlier the IWW had participated in the syndicalist conference in Germany and embraced the "Berlin declaration." Now that the IWW and most syndicalist organizations had rejected the Profintern, the way seemed open to unite in the new IWA.

Yet that affiliation, urged by the IWA and pondered within the IWW for over a decade, never happened. In the early 1920s, the IWW faced an array of profound challenges: continuing judicial persecution, attempts to assist imprisoned Wobblies, increasing divisions between centralizers and decentralizers, changing economic conditions, and pressure from communists within and outside the organization. Competition between supporters of the Profintern and the prospective Syndicalist International only exacerbated tensions. The IWW's 1922 convention sought to defuse the issue. Anticipating two greatly differing revolutionary Internationals in Moscow and Berlin, neither of which the IWW could enter "without forfeiting fundamental principles," the convention adopted temporary neutrality, while maintaining "friendly intercourse with both."[29] The issue of international affiliation drew lightning, threatening the fragile internal unity of the IWW. Neutrality appeared to be a useful lightning rod.

The IWA also tried to deal with more substantive issues that might work against the IWW's affiliation, especially that of its industrialism. The IWW, in its 1922 reply to the Profintern, had described itself as a non-syndicalist organization, as supporting direct action, as "an economically militant organization, which acts upon the theory that the workers learn to fight by fighting." It placed "no reliance upon political action." The IWW constituted "an economic working-class organization," whose "unit is the industrial union."[30] The IWA Secretariat responded in 1923 that this self-characterization of the IWW fit syndicalist views and aims "almost to a tee." While syndicalism had originally developed on a craft basis, this was not a matter of principle, as syndicalists increasingly advocated industrial organization and the IWA included explicitly industrialist national affiliates, including the Chilean administration of the IWW.[31]

Beset by external challenges and profound internal differences, IWW had a membership hovering around 25,000 in the early 1920s.[32] Supporters often saw the IWW's most pressing need as that of organizational rebuilding, with the international issue being important but highly divisive and best deferred. A friendly but candid letter of May 1923 from the IWW Board to Rudolf Rocker of the IWA Secretariat is revealing in several respects. First, it reiterated that neutrality towards Berlin and Moscow was temporary. "International affiliation has occupied our attention very much …. We know that sooner or later we will have to take some step towards this end." Second, it noted that the issue was explosive, both because of wider public suspicions about the loyalty of the IWW and because within the labor movement in the United States "every international has its partisans who are continually and severally condemning the other." Prudence required minimizing such disputes. Third, it frankly acknowledged that the IWW needed to concentrate on rebuilding at home and, therefore, "that there be no unnecessary wrangles on Internationals …. We hope you can understand this important point." The Board suggested that the IWA should similarly concentrate on strengthening its European components. Building an effective and genuine International required the absorption of the working class through "contact and experience."[33] The IWA was itself beleaguered by 1923, both by competition within the left from the communists and by hostile states. Its largest affiliates had fallen victim to repressive right-wing governments in Spain and Italy, and its affiliates elsewhere, except in Sweden, failed to sustain their membership levels of 1919.

Tensions between centralists and decentralists, reinforced by regional factors, had shaken the iww in 1913, but drove it on the shoals in 1924. After a virtual split, which witnessed a precipitous membership decline and ongoing infighting in the iww, it clung to its policy of international non-alignment. Its conventions to the mid-1920s had sometimes agreed to hear speakers appeal for the Profintern (James P. Cannon in 1923, Harrison George in 1925), and sometimes refused (1924). The iwa simultaneously but inconclusively corresponded with the iww's Board and saluted its conventions. In 1926, Rudolf Rocker of the iwa Secretariat visited iww headquarters in Chicago. Still, the international issue remained unresolved. The work of undeclared communists within the iww further muddied the waters.

Vern Smith, the editor of *Industrial Solidarity*, could not openly support the Profintern but he did work to discredit the iwa. In October 1923, for example, Smith asked C. E. Payne, the editor of the *Industrial Worker* in Seattle, to publish a denunciation of the iwa, including charges that it endorsed scabbing. This, Smith explained, would "avoid serious injury" to the iww, "which at present seems to be lined up too much with the ... outfit in Berlin .... I think this is a pretty bad outfit, but will admit that they had me fooled too, for a long time." Payne's terse reply: "You go to hell!" Refusing to publish the material Smith sent, Payne demanded: "Who put you up to sending it out here, anyhow?"[34] In August 1924, Smith attacked the Berlin International more directly in *Industrial Solidarity*. He accused it of "treacherous ... attacks" on the iww in Mexico, and although his editorial offered no evidence, of fiscal malfeasance. "What kind of a bunch is this anyway, that slanders us among our Mexican fellow workers, steals our money, and then scolds us for not sending them more?"[35] The iwa was astonished at these charges in an official iww journal. iwa Secretary Augustin Souchy, suspecting communist "machinations," asked the iww Board either to sanction the editorial or repudiate it.[36] The Board did neither; nor did *Industrial Solidarity*'s attacks on the iwa end there. Smith was removed from editorial functions only in August 1926, when the French journal *La Vie Ouvrière* printed part of a report to the Profintern by US Communist Party leader Earl Browder, a former Wobbly himself, which inadvertently revealed Smith to be a communist mole in a position of influence within the iww.[37]

The Industrialist Option

Socialist, communist, and syndicalist strands had all been woven into the fabric of the iww's international policy by the mid-1920s, without having produced a clear or dominant pattern. But a fourth strand—an industrialist strand—must be considered as well. That strand did not simply highlight the industrialist form of organization, but also emphasized the role of the IWW itself in the capacity of a world organization or a labor International stressing industrialism. This returns us to our starting point: that the name Industrial Workers of the World itself implies a labor International. After all, there were organizations outside the United States deemed to be IWW "administrations."

The claim that the IWW was itself an international organization, moreover, provided one means of defense against partisans of labor Internationals in Moscow and Berlin who sought to win its allegiance. It only came to the fore after the First World War, when the enthusiasm for the Comintern ebbed. From 1921 or so this assertion was sometimes advanced. In 1930, reviewing 25 years of international policy, Board chair Joseph Wagner wrote, "from its very inception, the i.w.w. was international in sentiment and scope."[38]

Some qualifications and complications should be noted here. Despite Wagner's claims, the conception of the IWW as a labor International did not predominate in the early association. The IWW repeatedly pondered bringing itself under the umbrella of socialist, communist, or syndicalist international organizations. The labor unions outside the United States that bore the IWW name, moreover, did not necessarily regard themselves as members of an international organization. The largest of them, the Chilean IWW, identified with and immediately joined the new IWA. Supporters in other nations sometimes compelled the IWW to clarify its own policies or complicated relations with otherwise sympathetic foreign labor organizations. In Sweden, for example, when maritime workers founded an IWW branch, the country's national syndicalist organization objected. The IWW's Board responded by ruling in 1920 "not to issue industrial charters in countries where there are already organizations in existence with a program similar to ours."[39] Later Boards did not observe the same policy. In Mexico a new Confederación General de Trabajadores (General Confederation of Labor) emerged in 1921, with perhaps 36,000 members. Based on decentralized principles, it soon joined the IWA. Some former Wobblies were influential within it. Other members of the Mexican IWW, having failed to convince the new organization to accept centralism and industrialism, continued to maintain their own smaller organization. The two could announce an alliance, oppose the government, and resist AFL influence in Mexico, but frictions remained. Finally, the IWW union most active internationally (notably in Latin America and Europe), the Marine Transport Workers Industrial Union (MTW), urged the IWW to enter the

IWA. The MTW even approached the IWA, in October 1933, about entering in its own name.[40]

Despite ambiguities complicating the concept of the IWW as a labor International, the industrialist strand periodically recurred in the weave of the Wobblies' international policy. Prior to the First World War the IWW, without precluding joint participation in a new International, had pointed to industrialism as distinguishing it from its nearest allies, the syndicalists. When the Board reported to the 1920 IWW Convention that "the international field has never looked better for a realization of a World International" of the IWW,[41] it expressed optimism that a global organization incorporating syndicalists and industrialists might emerge, but also recognized that the IWW based in Chicago itself was not, or not yet, that International. The unifying principles to which the Board alluded, moreover, were those of non-political direct action. But the emergence of the communist-oriented Proftintern and the syndicalist IWA in 1921–22 had a double effect on the IWW. Internally, it left supporters of these Internationals dueling within it. Externally, it drew off many revolutionary unions in other countries, potential partners of the IWW, circumscribing its international focus considerably. Both effects encouraged an increased inwardness, or at least self-sufficiency. Against this backdrop, the IWW's 1925 convention struck the industrialist note more clearly than previously. The IWW intended to provide the working class with a "world-wide organization revolutionary in philosophy and industrial in structure." Noting its far-flung "administrations and branches" the convention instructed the Board to investigate the calling of "a world congress of the I.W.W."[42]

However optimistic or desperate this proposal may have been, it bore no fruit in an IWW beset by problems and weakened by a nearly incapacitating internal split. The IWW held seven conventions from 1919 to 1925, but managed only four between 1926 and 1935. A world IWW congress seemed unlikely. The 1925 proposal nevertheless signaled a new emphasis in international relations. For the next decade or so the syndicalist and the industrialist proved to be the major strands in proposed international strategy. While each had advocates, the international issue was less fiercely contested than in the first half of the 1920s; the IWW felt rather than fought its way toward a resolution over the next decade. For one camp, industrialism and self-sufficiency were the guiding features in that they favored, at least for the time being, strengthening ties with IWW "branches" elsewhere, particularly in Europe. In the early 1930s this position, promoted above all by Joseph Wagner, prevailed. Speaking to the 1932 convention, Board chair Albert Hanson saw the international choice as "affiliation with existing labor unions which recognize the class war" (the IWA) or, Hanson's preference, "establishing the I.W.W. on a world-wide basis." As if to remove long-standing ambiguity on the point, the convention endorsed Wagner's declaration that the IWW "is a Working Class Union of the World," and its branches were not "affiliates but integral parts of the General Organization." It also directed the IWW to improve contact with groups outside the United States and to assist in summoning a European conference of the IWW. Secretary Treasurer Herbert Mahler voiced concerns that some branches might affiliate with the IWA. At the same time, however, the convention directed the Board to cooperate with the IWA.[43]

A second camp, promoted above all by the MTW, argued for the necessity of more formal international links beyond IWW outposts, particularly during a global depression. By the nature of the field in which it organized, the MTW was the most active IWW union internationally and many foreign "administrations" were primarily the work of seamen, the "missionaries" of the movement.[44] The MTW, however, concluded that establishing IWW branches elsewhere was not an adequate international strategy. In 1931, the MTW petitioned the IWW to ally with "existing syndicalist organizations of various countries who are of the same principles," whereupon the MTW would send its foreign members into national syndicalist unions.[45] As for the IWA, circumstances had no more favored it than they had the IWW. In Europe alone, the rise of fascist and quasi-fascist governments had led to the suppression of the IWA's Italian and Portuguese affiliates, and the ascent of Hitler in 1933 spelled the end of its German affiliate and the flight of the IWA's headquarters from Berlin. Nevertheless, the syndicalists persisted in their overtures to the IWW. In 1933 they published a brochure in English, *The International Working Men's Association: Its Purpose – Its Aim – Its Principles*, which directly addressed IWA relations with the IWW.

The MTW resolved in 1933 that if the IWW did not affiliate with the IWA, it would seek admission on its own as an industrial union organization. The IWW Board soon insisted to MTW members that the provisions of both the IWW and the IWA prohibited components of a larger body to affiliate. The IWA took another view, though with much hesitation: either the MTW could affiliate, with IWA congress approval, until its parent organization did so, or it could enter the proposed IWA international industrial federation of marine workers then being formed (but which failed to materialize).[46]

With no significant progress with its overseas branches and the IWA's brochure in hand, the IWW decided to act. Its 1934 convention resolved to put the question of affiliation with the IWA to a ballot. It decided to disseminate the brochure, but when it ordered additional copies, US custom officials seized the shipment as seditious material. The anticipation of the affiliation issue triggered an internal debate ("For Members Only") in the *General Organization Bulletin* well before the 1934 convention. Those opposed to affiliation, Secretary Treasurer (former Chair) Joseph Wagner and Fred Thompson being the most visible, advanced four main arguments. Wagner raised first the centralist–decentralist issue and, second, that the IWA urged incorporating small farmers, eking out an existence, into agricultural unions against larger landowners. Thompson vociferously argued, third, that the referendum was unconstitutional, since the IWW constitution declined alliances with political parties or anti-political sects. Thompson asserted that the IWA was anti-political, comprised of "anarchistic freaks." He added that it was anti-clerical and atheistic, a "bughouse clique of professional Jesus-killers." Frank Cedervall, also no friend of rhetorical restraint, mused that MTW membership could not be increased "by making the IWW an Anarchistic, Farmer Loving, Jesus Killing, Anti-Political sect." Fourth, Thompson argued that the IWW was itself "an international body with more than one national administration." How could one international body join another on the basis of a referendum in the United States only?[47]

The supporters of affiliation countered these arguments, and offered far more contributions to the debate. They urged the IWW not to be dogmatic. The centralist-decentralist issue was "most bitterly contested" and willfully "misrepresented." The IWA admitted revolutionary unions whatever their structure. Autonomy meant "the IWW will deal with the farmer as it sees fit." Britt Smith, recently paroled as a Centralia prisoner, pointed out that neither the 1934 convention, nor the IWW Board, nor the membership itself saw the issue as constitutional. The rank and file determined these issues, or was there some hidden power unknown to them? "We might just as well have a dictatorship." Fred Hansen, himself a delegate at the 1934 IWW convention, scoffed at the union itself being international. He further observed that the IWA does not "ask the IWW to kill Christ or anybody else," and Wobblies could have whatever political and religious views they chose. Was it constitutional for the Chilean IWW to have affiliated with Berlin? Others pointed out that the IWA organized revolutionary economic movements just like the IWW. The IWW could affiliate without imposing views on Wobblies, and that the question was a constitutional one therefore defied the imagination. Would affiliation undermine propaganda with US workers? "This is silly." Harry Owens, a sailor whose internationalist commitment would cost his life in the Spanish Civil War (see White, Chapter 13), contrasted the IWW as an international body ("How? When? Where?") with the larger membership and the many countries affiliated with the IWA. (The Spanish IWA affiliate alone was then far larger than all IWW bodies combined.) Had the Chilean IWW, by affiliating, lost its identity? The Canadian IWW, for its part, could make up its own mind. Owens resisted "a policy of isolation." H. Streisant observed that "theoretically the IWW is international; practically, it is not. It has few foreign (geographical) connections." Ethics and effectiveness should prevent the IWW from forming dual unions in countries with syndicalist organizations. How would the IWW respond if the IWA pursued the same policy in the United States?[48]

There were procedural issues as well. The first ballot, issued in July 1935, supported affiliation by a slight majority of 17 votes. Some industrial unions, including those in forestry and metal and machinery, protested about the speed and results of the first referendum. A second was held and those opposed to affiliation prevailed. The 1936 IWW convention, in reporting the ballot results from 1935, hoped that "continuous cooperation and harmony will exist" between the IWW and the IWA. This convention also rejected the MTW motion to affiliate with the IWA.[49]

In any event, few international options were left to the IWW by 1940. Fear of the Nazis' rise to power in Germany prompted the 1935 Comintern Congress to endorse the Popular Front and unity on the left. The Profintern, in consequence, was dismantled in 1936–37. In 1939, Franco's nationalists won the Spanish Civil War. This victory, in Rudolf Rocker's opinion, "sealed the fate" of the IWA as a viable labor International,[50] although Sweden harbored it during the Second World War and it survives still today.

Conclusion

The decision in the mid-1930s completed the evolution of the IWW's international policy, at least in its major outlines. Warp and weft, for 30 years, had interlaced in the fabric of international policy before a clear pattern emerged. The socialist, communist, syndicalist, and industrialist strands constituted the warp in the weave, each coming to the fore at one time or another. The evolving needs of the IWW constituted the weft: the need for an international policy that would respect its organizational integrity; harmonize with its own revolutionary goals, industrialist aspirations, and commitment to direct action and workers' autonomy; and win something like a consensus from its membership, or at least not disrupt internal unity. The IWW's ambiguity about its own international role inevitably colored the process, notably after 1921.

The IWW tested the alternatives that were, or appeared to be, open to it for three decades. It unsuccessfully had sought a voice, a permanent and revolutionary one, in the councils of the largely social democratic International Secretariat before 1914. The Comintern and the Profintern had fired and then dashed powerful hopes. The contest over communism had severely shaken the IWW. Even before 1914, the IWW had viewed the syndicalists as next of kin. However, reservations about entering into an international organization which was anarcho-syndicalist and not pro-grammatically industrialist proved decisive. Despite being poorly phrased and conducted, referenda seemed to demonstrate that in neither the relatively robust IWW of 1920 nor the diminished one of the mid-1930s could communist or syndicalist internationalism command a clear allegiance. It is tempting to see the development of the international policy of the IWW between 1905 and the mid-1930s as the natural unfolding of what was implicit within it from the start. But to argue that the trajectory of the IWW's international policy was predetermined is to read history backward, to project some future stage onto its beginning. The strand of industrialism and self-sufficiency came to dominate in the weave of the IWW's international policy, but it took over 30 years to do so. That pattern was far from predictable in 1905.

Notes

1   An earlier version of this paper, much revised and expanded here, appeared in the *Anarcho-Syndicalist Review* 42–43 (Winter 2006), pp. 13–18.

2   *Proceedings of the Founding Convention of the Industrial Workers of the World* (New York: Labor News Company, 1905), pp. 295, 299.

3   While this chapter discusses debates on the issue, an examination of the views of IWW locals is beyond its scope.

4   *Industrial Union Bulletin*, August 7, 1907. See also *Industrial Union Bulletin*, August 10, 1907; and *Report of the IWW to the International Socialist and Labor Congress at Stuttgart (1907)* (Chicago, Ill.: IWW, 1907).

5   *American Federationist*, February 1910, pp. 149–51.

6   William Z. Foster, *Pages from a Worker's Life* (New York: International Publishers, 1939), p. 291. See also *Solidarity*, September 16, 1911.

7   *American Federationist*, November 1911, p. 901.

8   See William Z. Foster, *From Bryan to Stalin* (New York: International Publishers, 1937), chap. 6.

9   *La Vie Ouvrière*, April 5, 1913, p. 405; Armando Borghi, *Mezzo secolo de anarchia (1898–1945)* (Naples, Italy: Edizione scientifiche italiane, 1954), p. 120.

10 *Industrial Worker*, January 9 and April 3, 1913.

11 St John to Guy Bowman, August 9, 1913, reproduced in *Stenographic Report of the 8th Annual Convention of the IWW* (Chicago, Ill.: IWW, 1913), p. 13. The convention

nevertheless instructed George Swasey, campaigning in Britain for the IWW, to participate informally in the assembly. See Swasey's report in *Solidarity*, October 25, 1913.

12 Armando Borghi, *L'Italia tra due Crispi* (Paris: Libreria Internazionale, n.d.), p. 91.

13 Ralph Chaplin, *Wobbly: The Rough-and-Tumble Story of an American Radical* (Chicago, Ill.: University of Chicago Press, 1949), p. 87.

14 Reproduced in *One Big Union Monthly* (hereafter *OBU Monthly*), November 1920.

15 George Hardy, *Those Stormy Years: Memoirs of the Fight for Freedom on Five Continents* (London: Lawrence & Wishart, 1956), p. 130.

16 Angel Pestaña, *Consideraciones y judicios acerca de la Tercera Internacional* (Madrid: ZYX, 1968 [1922]), p. 15.

17 "Memorandum on IWW general referendum ballot on the question of joining the Third International," 5210, Box 1, File 6, IWW Archives, Kheel Center for Labor-Management Documentation and Archives, Cornell University (hereafter Kheel Center). See also *Solidarity*, December 18, 1920; *OBU Monthly*, January 1921.

18 See *Solidarity*, October 23, 1920; *OBU Monthly*, January 1921.

19 *OBU Monthly*, October and December 1920.

20 *Solidarity*, January 22, 1921; see also *Industrial Worker*, February 5, 1921; *Minutes of the 13th Convention of the IWW* (Chicago, Ill.: IWW, 1921), pp. 62–9.

21 Hardy, *Stormy Years*, pp. 133–7, 164.

22 *Minutes of the 13th Convention*, pp. 46–7.

23 George Williams, *The First Congress of the Red Trade Union International at Moscow, 1921* (Chicago, Ill.: IWW, 1921), pp. 9, 18, 13, 55–6. See also *Industrial Solidarity*, December 17, 1921.

24 Melvyn Dubofsky, *We Shall be All: A History of the IWW*, 2nd edn. (Urbana, Ill.: University of Illinois Press, 1988), p. 463.

25 Alexander Lozovsky, "An appeal to the rank and file of the IWW," 1922, pp. 1, 3–4, Box 25, Folder 26, (see also the IWW "Reply," Box 25, Folder 28), IWW Records, Walter P. Reuther Library of Labor and Urban Affairs, Wayne State University (hereafter IWW Records). This was printed in *The I.W.W. Reply to the Red Trade Union International (Moscow)* (Chicago, Ill.: IWW, 1922).

26 John S. Gambs, *The Decline of the I.W.W.* (New York: Russell & Russell, 1966 [1932]), p. 89, estimates that by the early 1930s perhaps 2,000 Wobblies had joined the Communist Party.

27 Committee statement, n.d. [late 1923 or early 1924], Box 25, Folder 32, IWW Records.

28 "International Position of the I.W.W.," Box 164–I, IWW Records.

29 *Minutes of the 14th Convention of the IWW* (Chicago, Ill.: IWW, 1922), p. 34.

30 *I.W.W. Reply*, pp. 17–18.

31 IWA to the IWW, February 2, 1923, Box 22, Folder 22, IWW Records.

32 Estimates vary but here I follow Eric Thomas Chester, *The Wobblies in Their Heyday: The Rise and Destruction of the Industrial Workers of the World during the World War I Era* (Santa Barbara, Calif.: Praeger, 2014), pp. 209–10.

33 IWW Board to Rudolf Rocker, May 11, 1923, Box 22, Folder 22, IWW Records.

34 Smith to Payne, October 10, 1923, and Payne to Smith, October 14, 1923, Smith Papers, Kheel Center.

35 *Industrial Solidarity*, August 13, 1924.

36 Souchy to the IWW, September 19, 1924, IWW Records, Box 22, Folder 23. Joe Fisher asked Vern Smith to draft a reply (dated October 7, 1924) from the Board to the IWA. Smith explained that Diego Abad de Santillán, an IWA official, had accused the IWW of imperialism in Mexico in *Nuestra Palabra*, the newspaper of the Mexican affiliate of the IWA. Fisher refused to send Smith's reply. Smith Papers, Kheel Center.

37 Smith presents his own view in "Report on change of editors in official organs of IWW," Smith Papers, Kheel Center.

38 Wagner, "International relations of the IWW," *Twenty-Five Years of Industrial Unionism* (Chicago, Ill.: IWW, 1930), p. 69. But see also Williams, *The First Congress*, p. 59; *IWW Reply*, p. 23.

39 *OBU Monthly*, October 1920, p. 54, and August 1920, p. 51.

40 MTW to the IWA, 9 October 1933, in *Taetigkeit der Internationalen Arbeiter-Assoziation 1933–1935* (n.p.: IAA, n.d.), pp. 99–100.

41 *OBU Monthly*, June 1920, p. 16.

42 *Minutes of the 17th Constitutional General Convention of the IWW* (Chicago, Ill.: IWW, 1925), p. 18.

43 *Minutes of the 20th Constitutional General Convention of the IWW* (Chicago, Ill.: IWW, 1932), pp. 10, 12, 16.

44 *Industrial Solidarity*, November 25, 1922.

45 *Proceedings of the 19th General Convention of the IWW* (Chicago, Ill.: IWW, 1931), pp. 8–9. See also *Minutes of the 20th Convention*, p. 33.

46 *Taetigkeit der Internationalen Arbeiter-Assoziation*, pp. 99–100. For the Board's statement, see *Industrial Worker*, December 3, 1933 (I owe this reference to Kenyon Zimmer).

47 See the *General Organization Bulletin* (*GOB*) from 1934 to 1936, especially January 1934 (Wagner), August and November 1935 (Thompson), and September 1935 (Cedervall). Ralph Chaplin also opposed affiliation, but on grounds that it would change the IWW (August 1935).

48 *GOB*, February 1934 (N. Boorus), December 1935 (Smith), September 1935 (Hansen), December 1935 (J. M. DeWitt), September 1935 (Owens), January 1934 (Streisant).

49 *Minutes of the 22nd Constitutional General Convention of the IWW* (Chicago, Ill.: IWW, 1936), pp. 2, 23.

50 Peter Weinand, *Der "geborene" Rebell: Rudolf Rocker Leben und Werk* (Berlin: Kramer, 1981), p. 328.

7

The IWW in Tampico:
Anarchism, Internationalism, and
Solidarity Unionism in a Mexican Port

Kevan Antonio Aguilar

On the morning of July 2, 1917, 15,000 workers affiliated with the Industrial Workers of the World (IWW) and the anarchist labor confederation La Casa del Obrero Mundial (House of the World Worker or COM) brought the Port of Tampico in Mexico to a standstill. The unions called for a general strike targeting Mexican, US, and British oil companies located throughout the Eastern Gulf region of Mexico. Workers marched from their dilapidated tenements to obtain better living conditions for themselves and their families. They called for salaries and conditions comparable to the white American drillers, who received better treatment, higher salaries, and segregated housing away from the Mexican oil workers. Such stipulations were commonplace in IWW strikes throughout the world, yet the ideological parameters of their demands emerged out of the workers' specific political landscape.

The strike commenced just two months after the United States entered the First World War to support its British allies. Both nations grew increasingly concerned over the security of one of the war's most precious commodities—oil. Tampico, located in the state of Tamaulipas and Mexico's primary oil-exporting port, was also of strategic importance for the country's various military factions vying for governmental control. Francisco "Pancho" Villa's recent attacks in New Mexico and encroaching proximity to US and British-owned oil refineries located in Tampico prompted an increased surveillance of revolutionary activities in Mexican border towns and ports. For Tampico's port workers, the eight-month presence of six US destroyers idling in the Pánuco River, which separates the city from the neighboring state of Veracruz, offered a constant reminder of

Cover of
Germinal,
September 6,
1917

the prospects of foreign military intervention. One IWW-affiliated newspaper, *Germinal*, called on oil workers to defy the threat of US invasion and
prepare for a "war of all the wretched of the earth in open revolt against
the murderers of humanity."[1] *Germinal*'s proclamation looked outward—
past the refineries, oil fields, and seas—to the class struggles enveloping
the world. The IWW's influence in the port came from the organization's
adaptability to local social and political conditions, thereby allowing the
port to become a significant nodal point within a world engulfed in social
revolutions of many ideological flags.

The city's relationship to myriad international trade networks—
connecting the United States, the Caribbean, Spain, and South
America—created a heterogeneous population deeply intertwined in both
global capital and transnational radical movements. Tampico's significance
to both the Mexican Revolution and global revolutionary struggles of the
early twentieth century emerged from the port's geographical relationship

to other sites of radical contestation and the ways in which urban, rural, and foreign workers defined their politics within the context of a global revolution. From 1915 to 1930, Wobblies organized with local anarchists and communists in Tampico and the neighboring working-class *barrio* of Doña Cecilia (now Ciudad Madero) against the centralization of the labor movement under the Mexican revolutionary governments, foreign exploitation, and the suppression of anti-capitalist struggles throughout the world.

With over a quarter of Tampico's population connected to the petroleum industry, the port provided a unique environment for the prospects of revolutionary syndicalism, global solidarity networks, and industrial unionism. While many studies of the Tampico labor movement emphasize its significance to the Mexican Revolution, few detail the social and cultural impacts of the IWW's various transnational campaigns among the port's working-class communities.[2] In contrast to the increasingly nationalist scope of Mexico's military factions, the IWW's ideological framework provided an organizing space that complemented the port's cosmopolitan political landscape. Wobblies from Tampico and around the world coordinated with local radicals to promote anarchism, internationalism, and anti-imperialism while persistently resisting state cooptation. The city's relationship to various social movements and capitalist interests throughout the Atlantic and Pacific worlds demonstrated the radical worldview of Wobbly organizers and rank-and-file members.

Origins of the IWW in Tampico, 1915–20

From its first mobilizations in Tampico, the IWW integrated its vision of revolutionary syndicalism with the existing political views of the city's working-class communities. The port's laborers were, as Myrna Santiago describes, "born political," enraged by decades of foreign management in the growing industrial hub along with a lack of social prosperity. Anarchism and other anti-capitalist ideologies permeated the Huasteca region as far back as the 1850s; by 1907, cells affiliated with the anarchist Partido Liberal Mexicano (Mexican Liberal Party, or PLM), led by Ricardo and Enrique Flores Magón, emerged. Starting in the 1910s, the PLM's newspaper *Regeneración* helped fortify "a new vocabulary and set of ideas" for the port's working class.[3] In conjunction with the arrival of foreign revolutionaries from Europe, the United States, and other parts of Latin America, workers were emboldened by a lexicon of internationalism and anti-imperialism. This mixture of local and immigrant laborers quickly forged a transnational network of radical activity within which Tampico's IWW branch germinated.

Between 1915 and 1917, Mexican Wobblies affiliated with the PLM moved from the US Southwest and Northern Mexican mining hubs to the port to escape escalating repression. Pedro Coria, one of the IWW's most prominent organizers during its Bisbee, Arizona mining strikes, fled to Tampico to evade federal indictment in late 1916, and helped establish the IWW's Marine Transport Workers Industrial Union (MTW) Local 100 in January 1916. In 1917, members of IWW Local 602 from Los Angeles joined Coria in Tampico to help with Local 100 (see Struthers, Chapter 4).[4]

Wobblies also forged ties with the local branch of the COM, which founded its Tampico branch in 1915. Ricardo Treviño, an IWW and PLM organizer, arrived in Tampico from San Antonio, Texas and quickly rose to be a prominent Wobbly in the port.[5] By 1917, the COM had formed 14 craft unions and the IWW established two industrial unions. The IWW's influence came through its collaboration with the COM as well as with the US headquarters of the IWW. At some points, the union's influence expanded beyond its own capacity. In February 1919, an IWW member-at-large from Tampico contacted the publishers of the IWW's Spanish-language paper, *La Nueva Solidaridad* (*New Solidarity*), requesting that administrators send more copies of the newspaper and additional Spanish-language literature.[6] Similar to many IWW hubs outside of the United States, however, the Tampico branch largely depended on local networks to sustain itself. Though Spanish-language literature sent from the United States provided a valuable resource to workers, the local anarchist press functioned as the primary means of disseminating news of the IWW's local activities.

From 1916 to 1918, Treviño assisted the COM's local newspaper, *Tribuna Roja* (*Red Tribune*), which produced the city's first articles on radical labor. While most Wobblies in the port were Mexican, they interacted frequently with "fellow workers" (IWW members) and anarchists from the United States and elsewhere. Spanish anarchists such as Jorge D. Borrán and Vicenta Cabrera also allied with the IWW and assisted in forming the Tampico branch of a New York-based anarchist group, Germinal. The new organization quickly forged bonds with the IWW, COM, and Centro Femenil de Estudios Sociales (Women's Center of Social Studies), led by Cabrera and Maria Márquez. Women were of particular importance to the city's radical sectors; Cabrera and Marquez both worked as administrators for the Grupo Germinal and accrued much of group's donations through worker outreach. Women such as Cabrera and Marquez served as intermediaries for transnational revolutionary campaigns and reaffirmed the internationalist worldview of Tampico's rank-and-file by incorporating local struggles into a global context.

While most IWW members in Tampico were of Mexican origin, the port served as a harbor for migrating radicals from the United States, Latin America, and Europe. Wobblies from Los Angeles established a small farm outside of González, Tamaulipas as a way station for organizers heading to the port. One Wobbly, Ret Marut—an enigmatic German anarchist who became a world-famous novelist under his pen name, B. Traven—wrote extensively on Tampico's revolutionary struggles.[7] Many South American and European political exiles arrived by boat and joined local campaigns upon arriving in Tampico.[8] Regardless of nationality, the city's Wobblies and other radicals embraced the struggles of their newly adopted home as their own. Although frequently labeled "foreign agitators" by the Mexican and US governments, Tampico's working class viewed them as comrades in arms. Mexican workers saw in the ideals and actions of radical immigrants the same aspirations to forge a new world from the shell of the old.

The IWW and its COM allies created a cultural sphere of influence among the local working class. Both groups worked out of the same building, actively produced anarchist publications, and held joint union and organizational meetings.[9] On any given night of the week, the IWW-COM headquarters buzzed with activity; various unions affiliated with the two groups met three nights a week, with Tuesdays and Sundays reserved for general assemblies and internal propaganda meetings. Bartenders, taxi drivers, service laborers, construction workers, and seamen all frequented the building and became acquainted with one another through the various services provided by the organizations.[10] Educational lectures frequently commenced between union meetings, utilizing the pedagogical influences of Catalan anarchist Francisco Ferrer i Guardia. In their attempts to fortify a radical working-class culture, COM and IWW members aimed to steer workers away from what they perceived as capitalist vice and threats to "social morality." Lectures and articles frequently condemned activities such as drinking, cockfighting, the running of the bulls, and gambling.[11] In order to expand radical thoughts beyond the workplace, Wobblies and anarchists aimed to empower workers both in their professions and their homes. They perceived the creation of alternative forms of community congregation, distinct from the lure of capitalism, as an integral part of fortifying a stronger network of radicals in the city.

As radical consciousness spread throughout the working-class neighborhoods surrounding the ports, Mexican Wobblies began to look beyond their immediate surroundings and towards their role in other North American IWW campaigns. The dissemination of IWW literature in Tampico gives an indication of the scope of such transnational perspectives. Wobbly-affiliated periodicals, which disseminated between 2–3,000 copies for little to no cost on a weekly basis, provided the context for the union's struggles. Along with the persistent interaction with foreign radicals coming in and out of the port, the dissemination of literature and verbal recitation of radical ideas informed local workers of the various IWW campaigns occurring throughout the United States. Despite rapid inflation counteracting the higher salaries of petroleum laborers between 1918 and 1928, over 200 of Tampico's IWW militants contributed funds to international solidarity defense campaigns in Arizona, Colorado, and other parts of the United States.[12] During this time, the local activities of the Tampico IWW branch connected the local struggles of petroleum workers with the fights of workers beyond the borders of Mexico.

Internationalism and Anti-Imperialism

The Tampico IWW's pedagogical and cultural activities helped fortify a belief in the imminence of a global revolution. Unlike other parts of Mexico, Tampico's revolutionary movements were uniquely bound by shared ideological and mobilizing practices. The port's communists and anarchists collaborated more often than they succumbed to ideological disagreement. Whereas foreign Wobblies in Mexico City frequently immersed themselves in various skirmishes between party-based communist groups and anarcho-syndicalist organizations, the Wobblies in Tampico focused their attention on collaborating with communists and anarchists to unionize the petroleum industry. As seen in various other radical movements during this time, the ideological positions of the Wobblies, early communists, and anarchists were virtually synonymous. Their collective dedication to worker control of the means of production encouraged cross-ideological collaboration among radical groups such as the IWW, the COM, and, by 1921, the Confederación General de Trabajadores (General Confederation of Workers, or CGT). José C. Valadés, a CGT communist with strong anarchist leanings, reflected on the labor movement's multifaceted political ideologies:

> There existed a general idea: social welfare. A pragmatic doctrine: extinguish the bourgeois state. A longing: to sow fraternity. Hence, the questions concerning domestic ideologies were distinct from our dreams.

We wanted to follow the example of the Russians [before] Lenin became the terrible dictator.[13]

While the influence of the Russian Revolution served as a unifying point for Mexican leftists, the working class maintained a strong anti-authoritarian tradition. US-born Wobblies and foreign radicals affiliated with the Comintern, however, downplayed the ideological sentiments of Mexico's various radical movements as the consequence of a politically and economically underdeveloped country.

Some US-born Wobblies overlooked the anti-statist nature of the Mexican left and labor movement to focus attention on reconciling the IWW with Soviet communism. Linn A. Gale, an American Wobbly and self-proclaimed "Lenin of the Americas," came to Mexico to avoid conscription into the First World War draft and quickly attempted to form both a Communist Party of Mexico and an IWW branch in Mexico City. Through the English-language periodical, *Gale's Magazine*, Gale aimed to attract US Wobblies and radicals to Mexico by emphasizing Mexicans' sympathies for the IWW.[14] Rather than viewing all Americans as imperialists, Gale argued that the Mexican working class understood the differences between foreigners with radical politics and those who exploited them, such as Samuel Gompers of the American Federation of Labor:

> When a "Wobbly" comes to Mexico, the peon knows the difference instantly. He feels a kinship for the "Wobbly," believing the latter is actually an under-dog like himself and is on the level in his promises. He has an idea that i.w.w.'ism [sic] is something not distinctly American and this appeals to him, for he has come to associate "Americanism" with robbery and slavery. The word "world" in the name "Industrial Workers of the World" sounds pleasanter to him than the word "American" in the name "American Federation of Labor."[15]

While exalting Mexican workers' solidarity to US-born labor radicals, Gale fell short of acknowledging the laborers' agency in determining their own political ideologies, distinct from their US counterparts:

> Internationalism, although he [the Mexican] usually only incompletely understands the word, seems to him a desirable thing, but he detests "Americanism." The only "Americanism" he knows is misery, wretchedness and abuse, and if he had no other reason this would be sufficient to perpetually prejudice him against the Gompers organization.[16]

As affirmed in his numerous articles published both in his own magazine and IWW periodicals, Gale promoted a paternalistic stewardship of Mexican workers by foreign organizers, with little interest in grassroots organizing in Mexican communities.

Such aims contrasted starkly with the ideals and tactics of IWW organizers of Mexican descent, who persistently called for an end of top-down political structures and, instead, proposed mutual aid and the reciprocal allocation of support for campaigns and communities beyond national boundaries. Vanguardism under the auspices of the Communist International (Comintern), as promoted by Gale as well as the leader of a rival Communist Party faction, Indian anti-imperialist Manabendra Nath Roy, demonstrated the cultural illiteracy of many foreign radicals regarding the conditions and aspirations of Mexico's anti capitalist movements.[17] What is more, the publication of Gale's writings in US-based IWW literature demonstrated the organizational limitations of American Wobblies to provide solidarity for their Spanish-speaking Mexican counterparts. By April 1921, these disparities in tactics reached an apex when Gale joined the state-backed labor federation, the Confederación Regional Obrera Mexicana (Region Confederation of Mexican Workers, or CROM), while continuing to write on behalf of the Mexican IWW branches for the English-language IWW press. Mexican Wobblies demanded that the Chicago-based newspapers cease the publication of Gale's articles, as they did not reflect their organizing efforts occurring on the ground. Following his deportation from Mexico in 1921, Gale collaborated with the US government in order to avoid prison time for draft evasion, naming radicals located in both the United States and Mexico.[18]

By the end of the First World War, Mexico's social revolution became increasingly complicated owing to various power struggles and sectarian conflicts. Linn Gale's and M. N. Roy's attempts to incorporate Mexico's radical movements into the Comintern emphasized a nationalist convergence of revolutionary movements—an aspiration that directly contradicted many existing organizations' anti-statist praxes. Tampico's anarchist and Wobbly contingents adamantly opposed any support or relation to the Mexican state during the 1918 National Labor Congress in Coahuila. While the Congress led to the formation of the CROM, anarchists and Wobblies from Tampico disapproved of collaborating with the state in every capacity.

The Tampico delegation's disapproval of a centralized national labor organization exposed deep-rooted ideological differences between anarchists, communists, and labor reformists. By 1918, prominent IWW and COM organizer Ricardo Treviño resigned from the radical labor movement to join the state-backed Partido Laborista Mexicano (Mexican Labor Party). In his memoirs, Treviño chastised the anarchists' utopian proposals: "[T]he anarchist radicalism and intransigency created the environment and feasible conditions for new struggles and sterile sacrifices, unnecessary and detrimental to the development of the country's Worker Organization [CROM]."[19] Vicenta Cabrera, speaking on behalf of the Grupo Germinal's anarchist women's center and as an ally of the IWW, opposed the nationalist sentiments of the conference's labor reformists and called for regional labor organizing and transnational labor solidarity. After chastising the congress's lack of women, she explicitly reiterated the anarchist call for expropriation as opposed to modest reforms, stating, "Not only do we need bread, comrades, we need the land!"[20] Cabrera's sentiments reflected the demands proposed by IWW and COM unions in their strikes against foreign oil industrialists and state profiteers; the oil below the workers' feet represented a source of their own wealth, not that of the Mexican state. Rather than supporting the national unification of the labor movement, Cabrera called for the expansion of the country's social revolution. Whereas the Mexican government aimed to consolidate control through the CROM, organizers with the IWW reaffirmed their anti-statist ideals and called for a transnational labor movement.

The refusal of Tampico organizers to concede to the Mexican state was rooted in their experiences in the port. Foreign extraction of local resources, unequal pay, squalid living conditions, and racial segregation produced a social environment ripe for radical organizing.[21] While Wobblies utilized wildcat strikes, direct action, and demonstrations to bring about change in Tampico, acts of international solidarity forged bonds between Wobblies of various countries in the face of state suppression. Wobblies in Mexico frequently distinguished between foreign opponents and "fellow workers," and ensured that their actions reflected such distinctions. Solidarity unionism, in turn, aimed to coordinate a global reconstruction of labor based on equity and need. Such a vision required a programmatic effort to not only implement but also sustain it. As conditions worsened for IWW members around the world, Tampico's radical sectors mobilized to counter what they perceived as an affront to their own revolutionary struggle.

Solidarity Unionism In Action: Transnational Prisoner Support

Beyond strikes, solidarity with political prisoners provided a method of expanding political consciousness amongst the port's working-class communities. As the IWW in the United States faced debilitating repression under the federal Espionage and Sedition Acts of 1917–18 and many states' criminal syndicalism laws, Tampico's radical working class attempted to alleviate the associated financial burdens through donations to the union's general defense campaigns. Throughout 1918, Wobblies Santiago Martínez and Pedro Coria called upon petroleum and construction workers to support radical campaigns throughout the world. In particular, they encouraged workers to preserve the visions of social revolution characterized in the Wobbly and anarchist periodicals, plays, and education circles that had radicalized them and their communities. As state suppression of the IWW in the United States increased, Martínez and Coria utilized workers' consciousness as a means to galvanize support for imprisoned organizers being "buried alive in penitentiaries." Creating a transnational network of financial support, demonstrations, and publicity for struggles in the United States linked Wobbly prisoners to Tampico's working class. The two organizers summarized their call for the global unification of Wobblies and fellow travelers by exclaiming, "Rebellious workers from north to south and from east to west, all to form One Big Union!"[22]

On March 30, 1918, Pedro Coria called upon Tampico maritime workers to support imprisoned Wobblies in the United States by putting the internationalist ideals of anarchist revolution into practice. Before escaping federal indictment and deportation, Coria had organized with the PLM and the IWW throughout California, Texas, and Arizona. When not organizing workers, Coria frequently contributed articles to the IWW-COM newspaper *Germinal* to stress the importance of the transnational solidarity networks that he himself had utilized to flee the United States. Coria's pleas to Tampico's working class to support the IWW's General Defense Committee, which conducted prisoner support for Wobblies, strengthened the union in both Mexico and the United States.

In an article entitled "To the organized and unorganized workers of Mexico and Latin America," Coria invoked May Day, the international holiday commemorating the execution of the Haymarket martyrs, as the historical basis of worldwide solidarity against capitalism. Noting the September 5, 1917 raid of US IWW locals and subsequent indictment of 166 organizers, Coria called on the port's maritime workers to join other industrial unionists in sending financial support for those imprisoned. Coria invoked the historical precedents of IWW support for Mexican radicals in the overthrow of Mexican dictator Porfirio Díaz, particularly from co-founder "Big Bill" Haywood and Latino Wobblies in the Southwest. He concluded by noting the importance of solidarity unionism to the struggle against global capitalism:

Let us understand, fellow workers of Latin America, that if we allow our comrades to be sent as victims to the gallows, we will be complicit in this criminal act. We also suffer from this brutal industrial imperialism as they extend their economic tyranny over Mexico and South America. Therefore, it is our duty to respond to the persecution of our comrades in the North with our class solidarity through the One Big Union, to lead by the slogan "an injury to one is an injury to all."[23]

For Coria, the Red Scare not only drove him from the United States, it also hurt the struggle for global revolution. Further, the article encapsulated the worldview of Tampico's working class as members of a global struggle forged by groups such as the IWW. Wobblies from around the world sent contributions to post bail for their fellow workers in the United States, though these attempts at solidarity could not fully counteract the ferocious repression of the IWW.

In August and September 1919, the IWW headquarters in Chicago received over $6,000 in donations from fundraisers organized in Tampico for the prisoners, and an additional $5,000 collected for the General Defense Committee. These donations helped 30 of the 118 Wobblies imprisoned at Leavenworth Penitentiary in Lawrence, Kansas go free on bond. Attacks against the union persisted despite these efforts; another 30 Wobblies were imprisoned by November.[24] Nonetheless, Coria and the Tampico Wobblies remained dedicated to international solidarity campaigns into the 1920s and 1930s.

Coria published numerous articles throughout March and April 1918 in support of various anarchists and Wobblies, including Emma Goldman and three of the PLM's leaders—Librado Rivera, Enrique Flores Magón, and Ricardo Flores Magón—also imprisoned at Fort Leavenworth, the latter three owing to their anti-militarist articles in *Regeneración*.[25] Tampico's support of the Wobblies, PLM leaders, and US anarchists represented a continuity of transnational anti-imperialist organizing in opposition to military conscription and the suppression of the radical left. Yet just as the IWW in the United States faced the repercussions of the Red Scare, so too did Tampico's Wobblies.

The IWW in Tampico encountered opposition on both sides of the US–Mexico border. The mainstream Spanish-language press in both countries warned readers of "the terrible threat of bolshevism" in Tamaulipas. According to the San Antonio-based newspaper *La Prensa*, "impartial" informants notified the periodical that three Wobblies from Russia, Poland, and Catalonia had recently spent exorbitant amounts of money publishing thousands of copies of a newspaper, *El Bolsheviki*, in Tampico, and distributed it throughout the eastern part of the country. Fearing the consequences of "Bolshevik" organizing so close to the border, *La Prensa*'s publishers declared, "We Mexicans here [in Texas] are beginning to feel the prejudices that have created global calamity."[26] Newspapers in Mexico City also commented on the suspected influence of Bolshevism amongst the port workers, and American businesspeople collaborating with US senators alleged that members of the Tampico anarchist organization Grupo Hermanos Rojos (Red Brothers Group) and IWW organizers worked as agents for Moscow and published *El Bolsheviki* to promote communism in the port.[27] Despite these sources' claims of widespread dissemination of the periodical, the Mexican military had confiscated all copies before its release. The military also raided a local shop producing the Hermanos Rojos's other publication, *El Pequeño Grande*, and confiscated it along with its printing press; a Russian organizer in the shop was deported as well.[28] Furthermore, one of the leading members of the Hermanos Rojos, José Allen, worked as an informant for the US consulate in Mexico City, and encouraged political infighting among the various radical organizations.[29] Although it is unknown whether Allen was the informant that notified the press of the new publications, US-backed infiltrators clearly functioned at the highest levels of the Mexican radical movements.

Even after the sweeping suppression of the IWW in the United States during the late 1910s and early 1920s, Tampico Wobblies continued to support prisoners of the global class war. By the mid-1920s, the rise of fascism represented a new front for international solidarity campaigns. Along with comrades in Tampico's CGT unions, Wobblies called for the boycott of Italian ships following the suppression of anarchists under the dictatorship of Benito Mussolini. Radicals in the city also offered refuge for the children of Italian anarchist prisoners through the various maritime networks between Europe and Tampico.[30] By fomenting ties to European popular struggles against fascism, Wobblies and fellow travelers in Mexico stimulated a cyclical network of financial and practical solidarity. Such campaigns expanded the worldview of radical working-class communities, as localized struggles became internationalized and affirmed by workers in different geographic, political, and economic conditions.

Another important example of long-term IWW organizing in Tampico could be seen during the trial of the Italian-American anarchists Nicola Sacco and Bartolomeo Vanzetti. When the pair were convicted of robbery and murder in 1921, radical movements throughout the world responded to what they perceived as yet another attempt to suppress radical organizing.

Wobblies and anarchists in Mexico and many other nations responded with demonstrations that attracted workers, including conservatives, who opposed the United States' racial prejudices.[31] Subsequently, the United States became the central target of the port's Wobblies and others opposed to the trial. On November 16, 1921, a group of 300 radicals, including a number of uniformed soldiers, demonstrated outside of the US consulate in Tampico to protest the sentencing of Sacco and Vanzetti.[32] Upon the 1926 announcement of the two men's sentence of execution, the IWW organized a march through the streets of Tampico before descending upon the US consulate.[33] On August 23, 1928—the first anniversary of Sacco and Vanzetti's executions—workers affiliated with the Federation of Labor of Tampico, a long-standing IWW ally, and the Mexican Communist Party marched to the US consulate to celebrate the memories of the fallen anarchists. The march lasted for three hours, bringing traffic and commerce to a standstill. Three workers were arrested, charged with insulting the Mexican military.[34]

Workers and radicals in the city continued to uphold the memory of the fallen Italian anarchists. On November 7, 1930—the 13th anniversary of the Bolshevik revolution—30 men and three women labeled "communists" were arrested after a parade outside the US consulate. Protesters lambasted the US and Mexican governments as well as the press while shouting the names of Sacco and Vanzetti throughout the demonstration. The police also raided the offices of the Labor Federation.[35] Despite growing suppression of the radical labor movement under President Plutarco Elías Calles, Wobblies, anarchists, and communists continued organizing throughout the 1930s to sustain the country's revolutionary elements of organized labor.[36] While left-leaning labor unions certainly faced the brunt of various government policies to oppose worker-controlled industries, the earlier organizing campaigns forged a legacy of deep distrust of foreign monopolies and collaboration with the state.

Conclusion

As the 1930s commenced, the persistent suppression of the remaining vestiges of anti-authoritarian labor movements continued, resulting in the decline of IWW activities in Tampico. State arbitration of labor grievances and the violent suppression of collective organizing outside of the influence of the Mexican state decimated the IWW's capacities to organize effectively. With the severance of diplomatic relations under Calles's presidency, approximately 1,400 Mexican Communist Party members were forced underground until the ascension of President Lázaro Cárdenas in 1934.[37] IWW dues from Tampico continued to trickle into the IWW general headquarters in Chicago as late as 1930, though active organizing dissipated after years of state suppression. Nonetheless, the memory of the Wobblies and other revolutionary syndicalists fostered new forms of dissent within the state-supported labor federations. Even during the nationalization of the oil industry in 1938, workers maintained anti-authoritarian ideals regarding how and why they organized.[38] A new generation of workers reaffirmed earlier struggles against foreign exploitation, but under the veil of national autonomy rather than anarchist or communist revolution. Still, the notion of internationalism remained a key component of the city's collective consciousness. Universal declarations of hope and camaraderie exemplified the legacy of years of bloody struggle forged on the docks, in the factories and union halls, and on the streets of Tampico.

Acknowledgments

My deepest thanks to Amie Campos, Wendy Matsumura, and Josh Savala for providing valuable suggestions for this essay. All translations from Spanish are my own.

Notes

1   *Germinal* (Tampico), July 2, 1917.
2   Anton Rosenthal, "Radical border crossers: the Industrial Workers of the World and their press in Latin America," *Estudios Interdisciplinarios de América Latina y el Caribe* 22:2 (2011), pp. 39–70; Peter DeShazo and Robert J. Halstead, "Los Wobblies del Sur: the Industrial Workers of the World in Chile and Mexico," unpublished manuscript, University of Wisconsin, 1974, pp. 1–57; S. Lief Adleson, "The cultural roots of the oil workers' unions in Tampico, 1910–1925," in Jonathan C. Brown and Alan Knight (eds.), *The Mexican Petroleum Industry in the Twentieth Century* (Austin, Tex.: University of Texas Press, 1992), pp. 36–62; Norman Caulfield, "Wobblies and Mexican workers," *International Review of Social History* 40:1 (1995), pp. 51–75; Aurora Mónica Alcayaga Sasso, "Librado Rivera y los Hermanos Rojos en el movimiento social y cultura anarquista en Villa Cecilia y Tampico, Tamaulipas, 1915–1931," PhD dissertation, Universidad Iberoamericana, 2006; Myrna I. Santiago, *The Ecology of Oil: Environment, Labor, and the Mexican Revolution* (Cambridge: Cambridge University Press, 2009).
3   Santiago, *Ecology of Oil*, p. 208.
4   Caulfield, "Wobblies and Mexican workers," p. 57; Devra Anne Weber, "Wobblies of the Partido Liberal Mexicano: reenvisioning internationalist and transnational movements through Mexican lenses," *Pacific Historical Review* 85:2 (2016), p. 223; Alcayaga Sasso, "Librado Rivera," pp. 57–8.

5 Ricardo Flores Magón, *Dreams of Freedom: A Ricardo Flores Magón Reader*, ed. Chaz Bufe and Mitchell Cowen Verter (Oakland, Calif.: AK Press, 2005), p. 13.

6 In the same periodical, a response to the request noted that José Zapata, a local Wobbly organizer, could be contacted to receive more materials from the general headquarters. *La Nueva Solidaridad* (Chicago, Ill.), February 15, 1919.

7 Heidi Zogbaum, *B. Traven: A Vision of Mexico* (Wilmington, N.C.: SR Books, 1992), p. 2.

8 Santiago, *Ecology of Oil*, pp. 218–19.

9 Kirk Shaffer, "Tropical libertarians: anarchist movements and networks in the Caribbean, Southern United States, and Mexico," in Steven Hirsch and Lucien van Der Walt (eds.), *Anarchism and Syndicalism in the Colonial and Postcolonial World, 1870–1940* (Leiden, Netherlands: Brill, 2010), p. 311.

10 *Tribuna Roja: Órgano de la Casa del Obrero Mundial* (Tampico), May 3, 1916; Alcayaga Sasso, "Librado Rivera," p. 100.

11 Alcayaga Sasso, "Librado Rivera," p. 53.

12 Numbers calculated from the names of Tampico Wobblies that appeared in *La Nueva Solidaridad* and *Solidaridad* between 1918 and 1928.

13 José C. Valadés, *Memorias de un joven rebelde: Mis confesiones, 2a. parte* (México, D.F.: Universidad Autónoma de Sinaloa, 1986), p. 103.

14 Daniela Spenser, *Stumbling Its Way through Mexico: The Early Years of the Communist International* (Tuscaloosa, Ala.: University of Alabama Press, 2011); *New Solidarity*, April 23, 1921; *New York Times*, September 18, 1921.

15 *One Big Union Monthly*, November 1919.

16 *One Big Union Monthly*, November 1919.

17 Daniela Spenser and Richard Stoller, "Radical Mexico: limits to the impact of Soviet communism," *Latin American Perspectives* 35:2 (2008), pp. 57–70.

18 *New Solidarity*, April 23, 1921; *New York Times*, September 18, 1921.

19 Ricardo Treviño, *El movimiento obrero en México: Su evolución ideological* (Mexico City: The Author, 1948), p. 53.

20 *Vida Libre* (Tampico), May 25, 1918.

21 Santiago, *Ecology of Oil*, pp. 148–202.

22 *La Nueva Solidaridad*, November 31, 1918.

23 *Fuerʒa y Cerebro* (Tampico), March 30, 1918.

24 *One Big Union Monthly*, November, 1919.

25 Javier Torres Parés, *La revolución sin frontera: El Partido Liberal Mexicano y las relaciones entre el movimiento obrero de los Estados Unidos, 1910–1923* (Mexico City: UNAM, 1990), pp. 197–200; Christina Heatherton, "University of radicalism: Ricardo Flores Magón and Leavenworth Penitentiary," *American Quarterly* 66:3 (2014), pp. 557–81.

26 *La Prensa: Diario Popular Independiente* (San Antonio, Tex.), January 23, 1919.

27 Jonathan C. Brown, *Oil and Revolution in Mexico* (Berkeley, Calif.: University of California Press, 1992), p. 317.

28 Santiago, *Ecology of Oil*, p. 244.

29 Spenser, *Stumbling Its Way Through Mexico*, pp. 137–8.

30 *Nuestra Palabra* (Mexico City), August 14, 1924.

31 *Industrial Solidarity*, October 8, 1921.

32 *La Prensa*, November 21, 1921.

33 *La Prensa*, November 28, 1926.

34 *La Prensa*, August 25, 1928); *El Tucsonense* (Tucson, Ariz.), August 25, 1928; Valentín Campa, *Mi testimonio: Experiencias de un comunista mexicano* (Mexico City: Ediciones de Cultura Popular, 1978), p. 27.

35 *San Diego Union*, November 9, 1930.

36 Jürgen Buchenau notes that the number of strikes under the Calles administration went from 136 to seven between 1924 and 1928 due to the use of state arbitration as a means of resolving labor conflicts. *Plutarco Elías Calles and the Mexican Revolution* (Lanham, Md.: Rowman & Littlefield, 2007), p. 126.

37 Barry Carr, *Marxism and Communism in Twentieth-Century Mexico* (Lincoln, Neb.: University of Nebraska Press, 1992), p. 46.

38 Alberto J. Olvera, "The rise and fall of union democracy at Poza Rica, 1932–1940," in Brown and Knight, *The Mexican Petroleum Industry*, p. 67.

8

The Wobblies of the North Woods: Finnish Labor Radicalism and the IWW in Northern Ontario

Saku Pinta

Northern Ontario occupies a unique place in the socioeconomic structure of Ontario, Canada. The economy of "New Ontario," as it was known in the colonial phraseology of the late nineteenth and early twentieth centuries, has traditionally been dominated by primary resource extraction, above all mining and forestry. The expansive, sparsely populated northern hinterland sits in sharp contrast to the much more populous political, manufacturing, and financial centers of the south. As historian Jean Morrison remarked, "the splendors of Toronto's financial district ... could be explained, in part, by northern Ontario's scarred landscape."[1] Large-scale settlement began in the 1880s, with the construction of the Canadian Pacific Railway (CPR), and later, other regional railroads built to open the region up to resource development. The discovery of massive mineral deposits in Sudbury in the 1880s and Cobalt in the early 1900s drove further settlement, as did the harvesting of the region's enormous timber wealth. At the turn of the last century, the logging industry grew rapidly thanks in part to regulations that required pulpwood cut on Crown land to be processed in Ontario and the elimination of tariffs on exports of newsprint to the United States. From the 1920s to the mid-1940s, logging operations typically employed 20,000 to 30,000 workers in Ontario, providing the wood supply that fed the demands of the burgeoning saw mill and pulp and paper industries.[2]

It is in this setting that the Industrial Workers of the World (IWW) emerged as a significant force in the labor movement during the first decades of the twentieth century, especially amongst the Finnish lumber workers who constituted a plurality and perhaps even a majority of the Canadian IWW membership after the mid-1920s. Although the IWW experience in northern Ontario has not escaped the attention of Canadian labor historians, previous research has concentrated chiefly on the interwar period in the region surrounding modern-day Thunder Bay—an era best known for the intense rivalry between the IWW Lumber Workers Industrial Union No. 120 and the similarly named Communist-led Lumber Workers Industrial Union of Canada (LWIUC)—and has relied heavily on English-language sources.[3] The origins of the movement, especially within the Finnish community, are not well known. This chapter examines the history of the IWW in northern Ontario before 1918, the year that the Canadian federal government outlawed the organization. It demonstrates that the Wobblies built up a well-organized base of support in the logging industry earlier than has previously been assumed. The period under consideration is also notable in that it reveals the beginnings of the divisions that later bisected the Finnish-Canadian socialist movement into opposing political and anti-parliamentary factions.

The Finnish North American Socialist Movement, 1906–14

The Finnish-Canadian socialist movement did not develop in isolation, but rather was shaped by its close relations with the much larger Finnish-American immigrant left through a shared language, personal and organizational contacts, and news and information exchanged through a vibrant press.[4] People and ideas flowed easily across the porous US–Canada border—particularly in the region around the western Great Lakes—until the early 1920s, when the United States passed more restrictive immigration laws.

Between the years of 1893 and 1914, over 300,000 Finns immigrated to North America. Of this number, approximately 22,000 Finns arrived in Canada, the majority of whom settled in Ontario.[5] Oiva W. Saarinen notes, "From the 1880s to World War II, Finns in the labour force consisted largely of farmers and unskilled workers in the resource industries … as most came from rural areas with limited skills in the trades."[6] Like other immigrant groups, they imported their culture, language, and a variety of institutions that helped newcomers adapt to their surroundings. The Finnish socialist hall, a fixture in many rural and urban communities, stands out in this regard. As historian Varpu Lindström writes, the halls served as multi-purpose community centers, doubling "as schools, employment exchanges, cultural centres, gymnasiums, libraries and counselling centres, and the socialist leaders gave not only political but social, moral, and economic guidance."[7] The socialist hall, and the many practical services that it provided, helped left-wing ideas secure a receptive audience in the Finnish diaspora.

Finnish socialist groups and clubs proliferated across North America in the early twentieth century, and discussions soon centered on the creation of nationwide socialist organizations. The Finnish Socialist Federation (FSF), founded in August 1906 in Hibbing, Minnesota, became the first and largest foreign-language federation of the Socialist Party of America. By 1907, the FSF produced three newspapers in its Eastern, Central, and Western Districts, as well as a variety of monthlies and other literature. This print media enjoyed a large readership in Canada, and in 1907 Finnish Leftists established the newspaper *Työkansa* (*The Working People*) in Port Arthur, Ontario. The Finnish Socialist Organization of Canada (FSOC), founded in 1911 and largely modeled on the FSF, affiliated to the Social Democratic Party of Canada (SDPC) that same year. Thirteen of the 24 founding socialist groups that formed the FSOC were located in northern Ontario. By 1914, the FSOC had grown to 64 local branches with over 3,000 members, constituting a majority of the SDPC's membership.[8]

The Finnish IWW movement developed out of the radical left wing of the FSF and FSOC, and while the Wobblies found adherents among Finnish socialists early on, not all socialists embraced the doctrine of revolutionary industrial unionism. A longstanding rift in the FSF between pro and anti-IWW groups became an all-encompassing factional conflict by 1914. In what became known as the "first schism," radical left-wing branches of the FSF, located primarily in the Central and Western Districts, were expelled from the federation or voluntarily withdrew.[9] Radicals were pejoratively labeled "syndicalists" or "anarcho-syndicalists" by the social democratic faction, terms that all but a tiny segment of the Finnish IWW movement rejected.[10] The radicals, in turn, referred to the social democrats as "yellow socialists" or "opportunists." The expelled branches launched the newspaper *Sosialisti* (the *Socialist*, later renamed *Industrialisti* or the *Industrialist*) in Duluth, Minnesota in June 1914 and retained stock ownership of the Work People's College, a residential labor college in Smithville, Minnesota which was an important educational institution attended by Finnish immigrants on both sides of the border. FSOC branches in Canada helped sustain the labor college through fundraisers and the purchase of shares until 1915. It is evident, for example in *Työkansa* editorials appealing for increased Canadian enrolment, that the Work People's College was regarded not as a Finnish-American institution, but as an institution intended for the benefit of the entire Finnish North American working class.[11] As will be seen later, the factional struggle in the FSF created an analogous schism in the FSOC which centered on the IWW, support for the Work People's College, and the Finnish Wobbly press.

The Wobblies and the Western Federation of Miners, 1906–13

In the early twentieth century, over the same period that Finnish immigrants began forming nationwide socialist federations, the Western Federation of Miners (WFM) embarked on an eastward expansion from its well-established strongholds in the Western United States and Canada into the hard-rock mining districts around the Great Lakes basin. The WFM arrived in the western Great Lakes region with a well-earned reputation for labor militancy, a status later reinforced by its affiliation to the IWW, as the WFM served as the IWW Mining Department between 1905 and 1907.

The WFM came to northern Ontario with the mining boom that followed the discovery of silver during the construction of the Temiskaming and Northern Ontario Railway in 1903. Many of the miners who flocked to the area were veterans of the fierce class warfare waged between the WFM and mine owners in the West. On March 24, 1906, miners founded the Cobalt Miners' Union Local 146 of the WFM. IWW union organizers like Vincent St John and Robert Roadhouse toured the mining camps of the north during these years, spreading the message of direct action and industrial unionism.[12] As late as 1909, two years after the WFM exited the IWW, William "Big Bill" Haywood lectured at the Orpheum Theatre in Cobalt as part of a cross-country speaking tour. Cobalt's *Daily Nugget* newspaper reported that Haywood delivered two lectures "under the auspices of the Cobalt Miners' Union" on the topic of "The class struggle in the West," describing the lecture as "very fiery" with "lots of applause."[13]

The miners' embrace of the Wobblies in the early days outlived the brief WFM-IWW alliance and was also felt further afield. Richard Brazier first encountered the IWW in Cobalt in 1906 and fondly recalled the miners' songs and the "gusto" with which they sang them. When he came across the IWW again in Spokane, Washington in 1907, Brazier joined the union immediately. The Cobalt miners' musical culture consequently factored into the creation of the IWW's *Little Red Songbook*, as Brazier was a member of the committee that produced the first edition, contributing 15 of its 24 songs.[14]

From its beachhead in Cobalt, by 1910 the WFM had established new locals in mining camps in Elk Lake, Gowganda, South Porcupine, Silver Centre, Swastika, and Boston Creek.[15] Cobalt, South Porcupine, and Silver

Centre all had large Finnish contingents and FSOC locals.[16] The sizeable Finnish mining workforce required the WFM to hire union organizer John Välimäki from Michigan, who frequently toured the mining communities in Ontario, a role later taken on by Frank Snellman.[17] The mines in the Sudbury basin – especially the Canadian Copper Company mines in Copper Cliff, Creighton, and Crean Hill – also had large Finnish communities and FSOC locals, but aggressive company resistance to unionization kept the WFM out of this district for all but a brief period between 1913 and 1915.[18]

When the WFM reaffiliated to the AFL in 1911, miners sympathetic to IWW ideas and methods were outraged at what they regarded as a regression to conservative trade unionism. The 1912–13 South Porcupine miners' strike is indicative of these attitudes. The strike began on November 16, 1912, to protest about a wage reduction and demand an eight-hour workday. Some 1,200 miners of Local 145, which had become the largest WFM branch in Ontario, participated in the strike. It was a long, bitter, and violent affair, intensified by the introduction of armed private detectives by the Hollinger Mining Company.[19] Finnish miners referred to the area as "Canada's Siberia" because of the ominous atmosphere reminiscent of a penal colony.[20] Four months into the strike, Local 145 President Jack Barry published an article in the *International Socialist Review* affirming the Local's adherence to industrial unionism and the tactic of the general strike. "We, as an organization," wrote Barry, "would not stand for the workers in one camp digging out the war chest to defeat the members of the organization in a sister local only a few miles away."[21]

A letter published in the *Industrial Worker* claimed that agitation for a general strike was met with enthusiasm in the unorganized mines in Copper Cliff, Sudbury, and the steel mills in Sault Ste. Marie. The WFM Executive Board, however, sought compliance with the Industrial Disputes Investigation Act—legislation that required 30 days of notice for industrial action as a cooling off period—and threatened "non-support" in the event of illegal strike actions.[22] When WFM president Charles Moyer then visited South Porcupine, his nearly three-hour speech provoked a heated response from the striking miners. Jaakob Taipele, a member of the Finnish strikers' aid committee and correspondent for *Työkansa*, wrote that Moyer's talk included commentary on "William Haywood's bad deeds" in the WFM. Jack Barry was the first miner to take the floor. Barry declared that "it is not harmful to the organization of the working class when workers struggle against capitalism, this incites workers to organize. But when union leaders fight one another it impedes workers' unity." Taipele noted, "After this speech dozens of workers took to the floor and each one gave Moyer a tongue-lashing."[23]

The Sault Ste. Marie IWW Mixed Workers' Union, 1912–14

In the mid-1920s the IWW signed up as many as 3,000 miners and railroad workers in the Sudbury and Timmins-South Porcupine areas in what were apparently fairly short-lived locals; beyond this, the union was never able to establish a stable presence in Ontario's mining industry.[24] The situation was different in the logging camps, where the IWW found its most ardent supporters and established its most powerful unions. The arrival of the IWW in the logging industry was precipitated by the labor radicalism in the mines. Finnish miners were a part of a highly mobile workforce which also found work in forestry, where many carried their union creed forged in the conflicts with mine companies. The labor organizers who established the first IWW local in the logging industry in 1911—Verner Venhola and several others—hailed from Copper Cliff, a mining "company town" dominated by the Canadian Copper Company. Venhola was a member of the Copper Cliffin Nuorisoseura (Young People's Society of Copper Cliff)—an FSOC-affiliated group—and attended the Work People's College in 1913. In the 1920s, the IWW gained control of the Copper Cliff Young People's Society and went on to operate several labor halls in Sudbury, the last of which, Workers' Hall on 28 Alder Street, closed in 1938.[25]

The lumber workers' group to affiliate first with the IWW, likely formed in the winter of 1911, was organized not in the Sudbury district, but on the Algoma Central Railway line north of Sault Ste. Marie. In January 1912, a notice appeared in *Työkansa*, written on behalf of a group of 40 lumber workers in Wabos, Ontario, proposing a three-day camp workers' festival to be held in Sault Ste. Marie in the spring, timed to coincide with the end of the logging season. The purpose of the festival was to organize the *kämppäjätkät*, or "camp lads," as workers in the logging and railway camps came to be known, into a union. Verner Venhola served as the recording secretary for the group.[26]

The camp workers' festival attracted over 200 attendees. A meeting of lumber workers convened on the second day of the festival and formed a *Sekatyöläisten Unio* (Mixed Workers' Union), promptly electing a seven-member executive. The assembled workers deferred the question of affiliation to either the AFL or the IWW, and the executive was entrusted with the task of acquiring, as quickly as possible, information about both organizations. Later that month, the Mixed Workers' Union—now boasting

96 members and the tidy sum of $10,046—unanimously endorsed affiliation to the ɪᴡᴡ after vigorous discussion and debate.[27]

The formation of the Mixed Workers' Union represented a significant breakthrough for the ɪᴡᴡ in northern Ontario. It came at a time when massive ɪᴡᴡ-led strikes in 1912—like the famous Fraser River railway strike in British Columbia and the Lawrence "Bread and Roses" textile strike—captured the headlines and sympathies of working-class people across the continent. The ꜰꜱᴏᴄ branch in Sault Ste. Marie organized a fundraiser in support of the Lawrence strikers, raising more funds than any other Ontario branch.[28] The large Finnish ɪᴡᴡ membership in the lumber mills of Grays Harbor, Washington also struck in March 1912.[29] *Työkansa* as well as Finnish-American socialist newspapers such as *Toveri* (*Comrade*) and *Työmies* (*The Worker*), which circulated widely in the camps along the Algoma Central line, carried the news of these labor conflicts. Also significant was the formation of the ɪᴡᴡ's National Industrial Union of Forest and Lumber Workers in 1912, which demonstrated the union's commitment to organizing loggers.

The Sault Ste. Marie ɪᴡᴡ Mixed Workers' Union represented a major snub to the *Työkansa* and ꜰꜱᴏᴄ leadership. These evolutionary socialists, influenced by the ꜱᴅᴘᴄ and the moderate Fitchburg, Massachusetts-based newspaper *Raivaaja* (the *Pioneer*), favored the ᴀꜰʟ.[30] The ꜰꜱᴏᴄ locals in Port Arthur and Fort William attempted to form a lumber workers' union in February 1911, but it proved to be a failure. In May of 1911, the union executive made the unilateral decision to apply for affiliation to the ᴀꜰʟ, as they felt it was impossible effectively to build the union without belonging to a larger organization. The application was accepted that summer on the condition that the union be named the Laborers' Protective Union of Ontario (ʟᴘᴜ), thus conforming to the ᴀꜰʟ federal labor union model designed to consolidate unskilled workers in occupations outside of existing craft union jurisdictions. However, by January 1912 the ʟᴘᴜ was moribund, having dwindled to 22 members.[31]

The Schism Between the IWW and Social Democrats in the FSOC

The Mixed Workers' Union, like the ʟᴘᴜ, proved to be a short-lived affair, dissolving some time in 1914. One source hostile to the ɪᴡᴡ later claimed that the union failed because low initiation fees did not allow the organization to build up a sufficient treasury, and when the main agitators left the area, the union collapsed.[32] The impressive income that the union claimed appears to refute the first claim, but organizer Verner Venhola had indeed returned to Copper Cliff shortly after the formation of the union, and left to study at the Work People's College soon after. However, the principal cause for the local's disappearance was the sectarian split in the FSOC that paralleled the ideological divide within the Finnish-American left.

The FSOC leadership rallied to support the social democratic faction in the FSF, and moved to purge IWW supporters by securing a mandate to do so from its membership. In an FSOC referendum held in June 1915, 990 members voted in favor of officially severing all ties to *Sosialisti*, with 220 opposed. A second referendum question on the Work People's College saw 979 members vote to discontinue support of the school, with 175 opposed. From this point onwards, the FSOC officially forbade its members from serving as agents, correspondents, or supporters of *Sosialisti*, and local branches barred from supporting the Work People's College in any form, on threat of expulsion.[33] FSOC membership fell substantially, from 3,062 in 1914 to 1,867 a year later.[34] Between August 1915 and October 1916, a steady stream of FSOC members were expelled from multiple branches for distributing *Sosialisti*.[35] Finnish Wobblies were incensed at the "excommunications," as they called them, regarding the expulsions as an attack on freedom of speech, and thus in violation of basic socialist principles.

In June 1915 *Työkansa* went bankrupt, in part because of an overly ambitious effort to publish as a daily, but the expulsion or resignation of radicals from the FSOC may have also contributed. Its successor, *Vapaus* (*Liberty*), did not begin publishing until June 1917. Finnish socialists in Canada relied on Finnish-American newspapers in the interim, including *Sosialisti*, which appealed for Canadian subscribers. By July 1915, *Sosialisti* had eight local correspondents in seven Canadian towns or cities, five of them in Ontario.[36] The ideological division within the Finnish immigrant left in Canada now took on a much more hostile tone. As one Sault Ste. Marie correspondent for *Sosialisti* later declared, "it would be just as good for us to join the Catholic Church in Canada and vote to expel the bishops and priests from its leadership, until it becomes an industrial organization, as it would be for us to join the AF of L."[37]

The Re-Emergence of the IWW in Sault Ste. Marie, 1916–18

The Sault Ste. Marie Work People's College Support Ring, founded on December 25, 1916, became the first Finnish pro-IWW group in Canada to definitively break ties with the FSOC. The 34-member group pledged to advance the cause of industrial unionism and revolutionary socialism, and soon established its headquarters at Hussey Hall.[38] The revived IWW presence grew quickly thanks to the foothold the Wobblies had secured in the region in 1912. Several members, like Dave Mansonen, Work People's College alumnus John Huppunen, and August Torttila had been involved with the region's first IWW local. By far the most prominent members were John J. Wilson (an Anglicized version of his given name, Johan Filsson) and his wife Fanny Wilson.

The founding of the Work People's College Support Ring followed months of agitation and fundraising for the IWW-led Minnesota Iron Range miners' strike.[39] An account of one such "magnificent and rousing entertainment and agitational" fundraiser held at Hussey Hall, where "Italians and Finns jointly acted for the benefit of the Minnesota strikers," appeared in *Sosialisti*. Speakers in three languages addressed the assembled audience: John J. Wilson in Finnish, Giuseppe Mancini and Umberto Martignago ("Albert Martigvage") in Italian, and C. N. Smith in English. Finns Fanny Wilson and John Palokangas read poetry, including a poem by Giordano Bruno. Songs followed in Italian, Finnish, and English, and the Finnish and Italian orchestras played the dance that followed. The account concluded with a moving statement of internationalist principles: "let this be a demonstration that the global working class, once we have come to understand one another, will not be blinded by national and ethnic hatred and plunged into the bloody games of war against each other."[40]

In late 1916, the FSOC branch in Sault Ste. Marie founded the AFL-affiliated Lumbermen and Laborers' Union. Arthur Salo, a Finnish-American union organizer, was dispatched to the Algoma Central, and FSOC speaker Sanna Kannasto traveled to the area in support of the initiative.[41] Wobblies accused the union of accepting "jobbers" (subcontractors) into the union who, as bosses with the power to hire and fire, had opposing class interests to those of the workers they employed.[42] By October 1917, some branches had quit the union, sending their charter back to the AFL. The FSOC responded by sending Victor Rossi, a former Wobbly, to tour the camps in an effort to revive the union.[43]

Meanwhile, on November 11, 1917, a branch of the IWW General Recruiting Union (GRU) formed in Sault Ste. Marie.[44] One of the first GRU socials at Hussey Hall was a Joe Hill memorial event which featured songs from the IWW songbook and the launch of a new local publication, *Nouseva Voima* (*Rising Power*).[45] Membership in the IWW grew rapidly. By December 1917, some 415 Finnish workers were involved in IWW affairs in Sault Ste. Marie. Of this total, 163 worked in the camps along the Algoma Central. The only other known IWW presence in northern Ontario at this time was in the James Hongon Company camp near Port Arthur, which had a total of 55 members.[46]

The 1918 Algoma Central Log Drivers' Strike

In late April 1918, the IWW struck at several logging camps on the Algoma Central. The strike, which primarily involved log drivers, was almost certainly the first successful coordinated labor action to be waged by a lumber workers' union in Ontario. Details of the strike are scarce, even in the pages of *Industrialisti*, likely owing to the watchful eye of the Canadian press censor and fears that too much publicity could attract unwanted attention from the authorities. Indeed, the Ontario Provincial Police (OPP) carried out surveillance on the Algoma Central, and even obtained the minutes of one of the strike committees, revealing that plans for the strike were well under way by late March.[47]

The key to the strike's success was its strategic timing, coinciding with the annual log drive when the spring snow melt and rains combined to raise the volume of water carried by the rivers. Logging subcontractors settled the strike quickly in order to avoid disruptions during this critical period which could have risked the security of the pulpwood supply to the paper mills. The IWW proclaimed victory in a short announcement released on May 1 and published on the front page of *Industrialisti*. Log drivers secured a $4.00 wage for an eight-hour day, after having first rejected an offer of $3.75 for a ten-hour day.[48] While the eight-hour day was established in nearly every camp along the Batchewanna River, where the well-organized Wobbly presence was largely concentrated, camps on Mile 140 and 138 "stood like a wall" but negotiated a ten-hour workday on the condition that travel time from the bunkhouses to work areas would be paid.[49] Nick Viita, who joined the IWW at a camp on the Algoma Central in 1917 at age 15—later becoming one of the union's most outstanding Canadian leaders—recalled that the workers had also won clean mattresses and blankets in 1918.[50]

An Enemy Language and an Unlawful Organization

Between February and May of 1918, radicals withdrew from FSOC branches at an increasing rate, establishing their own independent workers' organizations committed to the IWW and class struggle. Pro-IWW Finns in Copper Cliff and Port Arthur formed Marxian clubs, and by April 1918, as many as ten new Finnish radical groups had formed across Canada.[51]

That summer, a five-member committee formed in Sault Ste. Marie, committed to forming a central organization to coordinate activity between these groups.[52] This growing radical sentiment was bolstered by the worker uprisings that engulfed Russia and Germany in the postwar era—events which appeared to support the view that revolutionary change on a global scale was a concrete possibility.

However, the anti-immigrant and anti-radical hysteria that gripped the Canadian federal government ultimately thwarted these efforts. On July 31, 1918 the Canadian press censor placed a ban on *Industrialisti* because of the radical views expressed in the paper, preventing it from being mailed from the United States to its approximately 1,500 Canadian subscribers.[53] Less than two months later, in September 1918, passage of Order-in-Council PC 2381 and PC 2384 listed Finnish as an enemy language and outlawed the IWW, along with 13 other organizations, including the FSOC.[54] The repression was swift. In mid-October, police conducted raids on 50 homes in Sault Ste. Marie, arresting 15 Russian and Finnish individuals on charges related to membership in an unlawful organization or possession of banned literature. John J. Wilson, one of the five Finnish Wobblies arrested in the raids, received a sentence of three years imprisonment or a $1,000 fine for his membership in the IWW, and opted to pay the fine rather than go to jail. Having contracted influenza, Wilson died of pneumonia at the age of 32 on December 16, 1918, shortly after his release from Kingston Penitentiary. Finnish and Italian workers attended his funeral and gave speeches. His body was lowered to the tune of the Finnish revolutionary song *Barrikaadimarssi* (*The Barricade March*). Afterwards, the Canadian government provided a refund of $800 of the original $1,000 fine to Wilson's widow Fanny and his two children.[55]

The FSOC successfully appealed the ban on their organization on the condition that they cease political activity. In a letter to the Director of Public Safety, dated December 12, 1918, secretary J. W. Ahlqvist wrote that from its founding the FSOC had opposed to the IWW and "a large part of the activity of our organization has been a constant struggle against syndicalist and anarcho-syndicalist concepts."[56] Decades later, IWW organizer Nick Viita still bitterly recalled this betrayal.[57]

Conclusion

After the Canadian government banned the IWW, the union went underground. IWW delegates continued to collect dues and kept the organization going, at great risk to themselves, but did so "without any brass banding" and "avoided any fanfare about it."[58] Wobblies and members of the Finnish Organization of Canada (FOC), the successor to the FSOC, again found a common organizational home in the Lumber Workers Industrial Union of Canada's IWW-influenced One Big Union (OBU), founded in 1919. Predictably, old rivalries resurfaced as the FOC grew closer to the nascent Communist Party of Canada and sought to affiliate the OBU to the Red International of Labor Unions, or Profintern. The pro-IWW faction—the dominant force inside the OBU—fiercely resisted this proposal. In 1924, lumber workers in the OBU voted to affiliate to the IWW, and in that same year, the Communist-led FOC established the Lumber Workers Industrial Union of Canada (LWIUC) as a competing labor organization. For a five-year period, from 1930 to 1935, the FOC accepted the first major departure from its longstanding "boring from within" labor strategy with the adoption of the Communist International's Third Period policy. This directed affiliated parties to form revolutionary unions independent of either the AFL or TLC. By this time, the Communist LWIUC had become the most powerful union in the north woods. With the shift to the Popular Front strategy in 1936, the LWIUC in Ontario affiliated en masse to the Lumber and Saw Mill Workers Union, a branch of the AFL-affiliated United Brotherhood of Carpenters and Joiners. The IWW, meanwhile, gradually faded into obscurity in the north woods, but Finnish Wobblies continued to operate halls, cultural organizations, and cooperatives, and to distribute *Industrialisti*, well into the 1970s.

Labor historian Mark Leier, in his study of the IWW in British Columbia, argues that the Wobblies are deserving of serious attention, and moreover that they posed a "realistic historical alternative."[59] Such an approach offers a useful counterweight to studies shaped by hindsight. Applying this perspective to the Finnish IWW experience in northern Ontario suggests the use of direct action to wrest concessions from employers and the rejection of timed contracts were not "utopian" or "infantile," as the union's detractors have claimed. Rather, this was the de facto method of labor organization in the logging industry—indeed, in most industries, outside of a small segment of skilled occupations—until the passage of Order-in-Council PC 1003 in 1944, the legislation that first codified labor law and established the legal framework for collective bargaining in Canada. Labor union contracts were the exception, not the rule, during the first three decades of the twentieth century, and the AFL and TLC were simply not concerned with organizing "unskilled" workers. While labor union density increased after PC 1003, helping to secure important gains for the working class, it also ushered in a more bureaucratized labor unionism. We would do well to reflect on the example of the Finnish Wobblies in relation to the Faustian bargain between labor and capital—union legality in exchange for labor peace—in our own post-Keynesian era, as well as how historical models of non-contractual labor organization could help revive the working-class movement, and what kind of community infrastructure is required to sustain such movements.

Acknowledgments

The author wishes to thank the following for their support: Trudy Russo and Kathleen Traynor from the Northern Studies Resource Centre at Lakehead University, Kaija Pinta, the Wobbly Research group, and the editors of this volume. All translations from original Finnish-language sources are by the author. This work is dedicated to the memory of Jean Morrison.

Notes

1   Jean Morrison, "The working class in Northern Ontario," *Labour/Le Travail* 7 (1981): 151.
2   Ian Radforth, *Bushworkers and Bosses: Logging in Northern Ontario, 1900–1980* (Toronto, Ont.: University of Toronto Press, 1987), pp. 18–19, 27.
3   See Radforth, *Bushworkers and Bosses*, pp. 107–33; J. Peter Campbell, "The cult of spontaneity: Finnish-Canadian bushworkers and the Industrial Workers of the World in Northern Ontario, 1919–1934," *Labour/Le Travail* 41(1998): 117–46; Michel Beaulieu, *Labour at the Lakehead: Ethnicity, Socialism, and Politics, 1900–35* (Vancouver, BC: University of British Columbia Press, 2011), pp. 179–209; and Michel Beaulieu, "Spittoon philosophers or radical revolutionaries? The Canadian administration of the Industrial Workers of the World, 1932–35," *Ontario History* 105:2 (2013): 183–211.
4   Auvo Kostiainen, "Contacts between the Finnish labour movements in the United States and Canada," in Michael Karni (ed.), *Finnish Diaspora I: Canada, South America, Africa, Australia and Sweden* (Toronto, Ont.: Multicultural History Society of Ontario, 1981), pp. 33–48; A.T. Hill, "Historic basis and development of the lumber workers organization and struggles in Ontario," unpublished manuscript, 1952, p. 1.
5   See Reino Kero, *Migration from Finland to North America in the Years between the United States Civil War and the First World War* (Vammala, Finland: Vammalan Kirjapaino, 1974), p. 45; Marc Metsaranta (ed.), *Project Bay Street: Activities of Finnish-Canadians in Thunder Bay Before 1915* (Thunder Bay, Ont.: Thunder Bay Finnish-Canadian Historical Society, 1989), pp. 15–19.
6   Oiva W. Saarinen, *Between a Rock and a Hard Place: A Historical Geography of the Finns in the Sudbury Area* (Waterloo, Ont.: Wilfred Laurier University Press, 2013), p. 178.

7 Varpu Lindström, *Defiant Sisters: A Social History of Finnish Immigrant Women in Canada* (Beaverton, Ont.: Aspasia, 2003), p. 139.

8 See Michael Karni, "The founding of the Finnish Socialist Federation and the Minnesota strike of 1907," in Michael Karni (ed.), *For the Common Good: Finnish Immigrants and the Radical Response to Industrial America* (Superior, Ont.: Työmies Society, 1977), pp. 65–86; Yrjö Raivio, *Kanadan Suomalaisten Historia I* (Copper Cliff, Ont.: Canadan Suomalainen Historiaseura, 2005), p. 403; Arja Pilli, *The Finnish-language Press in Canada, 1901–1939: A Study in the History of Ethnic Journalism* (Turku, Finland: Institute of Migration, 1982), pp. 36, 58–73; Metsaranta, *Project Bay Street*, pp. 75–88.

9 Douglas Ollila, Jr., "From socialism to industrial unionism (iww): social factors in the emergence of left-labor radicalism among Finnish workers on the Mesabi, 1911–19," in Michael Karni, Matti Kaups, and Douglas Ollila, Jr. (eds.), *The Finnish Experience in the Western Great Lakes Region: New Perspectives* (Turku, Finland: Institute for Migration, 1975), pp. 156–71.

10 William Risto, who was expelled from *Sosialisti* in 1916, was the most prominent spokesperson for the doctrine of revolutionary syndicalism in the Finnish iww movement. Risto appears to have maintained a small following after his expulsion and published a book outlining his views. See William Risto, *Vallankumouksellinen Syndikalismi* (New York: Carl Päiviö ja Gusti Alonen, 1916).

11 Auvo Kostiainen, "Work People's College: an American immigrant institution," *Scandinavian Journal of History* 5:4 (1980): 295–309; Saku Pinta, "Educate, organize, emancipate: the Work People's College and the Industrial Workers of the World," in Robert H. Haworth (ed.), *Anarchist Pedagogies: Collective Actions, Theories, and Critical Reflections on Education* (Oakland, Calif.: PM Press, 2012), pp. 45–68; *Työkansa*, July 4, 1911.

12 *Official Proceedings of the Fifteenth Annual Convention of the Western Federation of Miners, 1907*, pp. 155–9; Mike Solski and John Smaller (eds.), *Mine Mill: The History of the International Union of Mine, Mill and Smelter Workers in Canada since 1895* (Ottawa: Steel Rail Publishing, 1984), pp. 57–63.

13 *Daily Nugget*, October 9, 1909. My thanks to Charlie Angus for providing me with a copy of the original newspaper clipping.

14 Richard Brazier, "The story of the i.w.w.'s 'Little Red Songbook'," *Labor History* 9:1 (1968): 91–105; Archie Green, David Roediger, Franklin Rosemont, and Salvatore Salerno (eds.), *The Big Red Songbook* (Chicago, Ill.: Charles H. Kerr, 2007), p. 42.

15 Solski and Smaller, *Mine Mill*, pp. 58–62.

16 Raivio, *Kanadan Suomalaisten Historia*, p. 403.

17 See *Työkansa*, November 7, 1911; William Eklund, *Builders of Canada: History of the Finnish Organization of Canada, 1911–1971* (Toronto, Ont.: Finnish Organization of Canada, 1987), p. 133.

18 Solski and Smaller, *Mine Mill*, pp. 97–100.

19 Peter Vasiliadis, "Dangerous truth: interethnic competition in a Northeastern Ontario goldmining community," PhD diss., Simon Fraser University, 1984, pp. 83–102; Charlie Angus and Louie Palu, *Mirrors of Stone: Fragments from the Porcupine Frontier* (Toronto, Ont.: Between the Lines, 2001), pp. 15–18.

20 *Työkansa*, March 18, 1913.

21 *International Socialist Review*, March 1913.

22 *Industrial Worker*, March 20, 1913.

23 *Työkansa*, May 19, 1913.

24 "Notes from reminiscences of Nick Viita," recorded by Fred Thompson, Lake Worth Florida, February 1968, included in a letter to Jean Morrison, October 20, 1970. My thanks to Jean Morrison for providing me with a copy of this letter.

25 Oiva W. Saarinen, *Between a Rock and a Hard Place: A Historical Geography of the Finns in the Sudbury Area* (Waterloo, Ont.: Wilfred Laurier University Press, 2013), pp. 127–9; *Vapaus*, March 7, 1922; Einar Jouppi, "Ruumillisen Kultuurin Vainioilta Keski-Ontariossa," *Uuden Ajan Joulu*, 1942, p. 22.

26 *Työkansa*, January 19, 1912.

27 *Työkansa*, April 12, June 5, 1912.

28 *Työkansa*, March 1, 1912.

29 Aaron Goings, "Red harbor: class, violence, and community in Grays Harbor, Washington," PhD diss., Simon Fraser University, 2011, pp. 94–8.

30 *Työkansa*, September 29, October 6, March 7, 1911.

31 *Työkansa*, February 14, April 11, July 28, May 23, October 17, October 6, 1911; January 26, 1912.

32 *Sosialisti*, March 11, 1916.

33 *Sosialisti*, June 8, 1915.

34 Raivio, *Kanadan Suomalaisten Historia*, p. 404.

35 See *Sosialisti*, August 20, December 17, 1915, May 10, October 9, 1916.

36 The first *Sosialisti* correspondents were from Fort William, Steelton, Toronto, Copper Cliff, and Sault Ste. Marie, Ontario; Chase River, British Columbia; and Nummola, Saskatchewan. *Sosialisti*, July 14, 1915.

37 *Sosialisti*, November 7, 1916.

38 *Sosialisti*, December 29, 1916.

39 For the most recent analysis of the strike see Gary Kaunonen, "The fanned flames of discontent: a Solidarity-inspired history of the identity/ideology, cultural history, and rhetorical strategies of the Wobblies during the 1916 Minnesota iron ore strike," PhD diss., Michigan Technological University, 2015.

40 *Sosialisti*, September 19, 1916.

41 *Sosialisti*, December 4, 1916.

42 *Industrialisti*, May 8, 1917.

43 *Industrialisti*, October 12, November 9, 1917.

44 *Industrialisti*, November 20, 1917.

45 *Industrialisti*, November 22, 1917.

46 *Industrialisti*, December 19, 1917.

47 Ian Radforth, *Bushworkers and Bosses: Logging in Northern Ontario, 1900–1980* (Toronto, Ont.: University of Toronto Press, 1987), p. 113.

48 *Industrialisti*, May 3, 1918.

49 *Industrialisti*, May 28, 1918.

50 "Notes from reminiscences of Nick Viita."

51 *Industrialisti*, February 18, May 4, 1918.

52 *Industrialisti*, June 14, 1918.

53 *Industrialisti*, August 1, 1918.

54 Barbara Roberts, *From Whence They Came: Deportation from Canada, 1900–1935* (Ottawa: University of Ottawa Press, 1988), p. 81.

55 *Industrialisti*, January 28, February 5, March 25, 1919; Gregory S. Kealy and Reg Whitaker (eds.), *R.C.M.P. Security Bulletins: The Early Years, 1919–1929* (St. John's, NL: Canadian Committee on Labour History, 1994), pp. 362–82.

56 Raivio, *Kanadan Suomalaisten Historia*, p. 414.

57 *Industrialisti*, October 13, 1970.

58 "Notes from reminiscences of Nick Viita."

59 Mark Leier, *Where the Fraser River Flows: The Industrial Workers of the World in British Columbia* (Vancouver, BC: New Star Books, 1990), p. 1.

9

"We Must Do Away with Racial Prejudice and Imaginary Boundary Lines": British Columbia Wobblies before the First World War

Mark Leier

Transnationalism may seem an odd concept to apply to people moving back and forth across the US–Canadian border. As settler-colonial states largely populated by immigrants from around the world, neither country is a "nation-state" in the sense of a community sharing a common language, heritage, economy, and culture, especially during the years of the Wobblies' greatest influence. "American" and "Canadian" were formal, legal labels signifying citizenship rather than a national identity, and citizenship did not erase privileges and stigmas of race and ethnicity. Furthermore, capital and workers flowed easily across the border, and the two countries developed in broadly similar economic and political ways, making national differences less obvious. As Samuel Gompers, longtime head of American Federation of Labor (AFL), put it, "when the Yankee capitalist" crossed the border to "oppress Canadian workingmen ... it was but natural that the Yankee 'agitator' should follow."[1]

That did not mean, however, that the border did not matter. Labor organizers could expect very different reactions in the two countries. When the IWW launched free speech fights in Victoria and Vancouver, British Columbia (BC) between 1909 and 1912, the battles were won with relative ease. In contrast, IWW members in free speech fights in San Diego, California and Everett, Washington in the same period were met with firehoses, beatings, long prison terms, and murder at the hands of vigilantes and police. The two-year strike of coal miners on Vancouver Island between 1912 and 1914 saw workers thrown out of company housing, the militia deployed, and mass arrests, but nothing like the violence of Ludlow, Colorado, where nearly 200 people, including 13 women and children, were killed in armed skirmishes and the blaze caused when the state militia set the strikers' tent city on fire. Despite the similarities between the two countries, then, the "national" boundary between Canada and the United States could mean a great deal, and so the question of transnational experience still has some meaning.

Gompers also proved mistaken in his assessment of the cross-border movement of union organizers. It was not one-way and not limited to "Yankee" AFL craft unionists. Wobblies in and from British Columbia demonstrated a practical transnationalism as they crossed between the two states to work and organize, and in doing so they proclaimed a radical internationalism while articulating their interests as workers.

Transnationalism and internationalism began at the IWW's founding convention. Canadian-born John Riordan, representing the American Labor Union (ALU), and James Baker, representing the Western Federation of Miners (WFM), traveled 2,000 miles from the Kootenay region of British Columbia to participate in the deliberations. The two had learned from their experience as miners and union organizers that nationalism was nothing more than an ideology cynically deployed by both governments and capitalists to divide workers. When the ALU and WFM struck in British Columbia, they were red-baited and branded as "foreign" unions. Yet the same governments and corporations that denounced the influence of American unions colluded to bring American scabs across the border to break strikes. Conservative craft unions were no better. Canadian and American unions might use the rhetoric of nationalism to compete with each other for members and influence, but they were quick to unite and encourage their members to break the strikes of industrial unions. By 1905, Riordan and Baker were convinced that a new union movement—militant, organized by industry rather than craft, and based on international solidarity—was the only solution for workers, so they headed to Chicago.[2]

At the IWW convention, Baker suggested that "that the word 'international' be used ... wherever 'national' occurs; as 'national president' and 'national secretary-treasurer' have no place here." When some delegates proposed calling the new union the Industrial Workers of America to avoid appearing too ambitious, Riordan had two objections. The first was the desire to avoid national chauvinism which would potentially alienate workers not as enlightened as they should be. There were, he said, some Canadian organizations and some "patriotic Canadians who do not agree with the name of an organization defining itself too closely .... It creates more or less of a prejudice when you define things so closely as to name or designate international boundary lines." This reflected the acute competition between independent Canadian unions and the so-called international unions from the United States that Gompers encouraged to organize in Canada. Riordan's second objection came from his experience with conservatives in both Canadian and American unions who worked with the Canadian government against the radical industrial unionism of the WFM and ALU. Solidarity had to be based on class and commitment, not national boundaries, and many workers in Canada "realize the fact that they must be cosmopolitan in a matter of this kind. They do not want to recognize international boundary lines. I for one do not." He insisted the new union be called the Industrial Workers of the World.

Riordan was a popular figure at the convention, where he allied himself with the anarchists and revolutionary syndicalists present (see Zimmer, Chapter 1). He had been a Canadian delegate to ALU conventions and a member of its executive board, and when he was nominated for a position on the IWW's executive board, he was referred to as "a brother who is well-known in the northwest and Chicago and especially Canada." In the subsequent balloting, Riordan topped the polls, though this was in part of the reflection of the voting scheme that gave the delegates votes according to the membership of their unions.[3] The executive, however, was largely made up of unionists who were not dedicated syndicalists; as the radical IWW member William Trautmann put it, "only John Riordan ... was in full agreement with the principles and methods of the industrial union movement. All the others were plain 'Reactionaries' to say the least."[4]

Over the next year, Riordan literally put his stamp on the organization. Forced to pay the bloated expenses submitted by the conservatives such as IWW president Charles O. Sherman, Riordan stamped "For Graft" on the receipts to signal his disgust. At the same time, according to Trautmann, Riordan "organized the educational department of the IWW, to his everlasting credit."[5] Despite this, or because of it, the conservative faction purged Riordan from the executive board shortly before the 1906 convention. Their victory, however, proved short-lived, for at the second annual convention Riordan, Trautmann, Vincent St. John, Fred Heslewood, and other radicals, including Daniel De Leon, unseated Sherman and abolished the office of president (see Zimmer, Chapter 1).[6]

We know very little about Riordan, but his life is an example of Canadian-US transnationalism. He moved back and forth across the border throughout his life. Born in Ontario, he moved to Michigan and then to BC by 1900. There he was elected financial secretary of the Phoenix Miners' Union Local 7 of the WFM and was the local's delegate to the 1901 WFM convention in Salt Lake City. In 1903, Riordan ran for the provincial legislature as a candidate for the Socialist Party of British Columbia, a radical party with links to De Leon and his Socialist Labor Party. Riordan finished second in a three-way race and received about 30 percent of the votes cast. In 1905, the *Boundary Creek Times* reported that Riordan "leaves shortly for Chicago where he will establish his permanent home," and he took up the position of general-secretary of the ALU a few months before the IWW convention.[7] He returned to Canada, and in 1907 spoke to a "monster parade" of Phoenix, BC miners to celebrate the acquittal of "Big Bill" Haywood on the charge of murdering former Idaho governor Frank Steunenberg. He was also elected to the position of vice president of the Phoenix Public Service Union No. 155, IWW. Some time after 1910, he moved to Brimley, Michigan, but the bonds of family and the harsh reality of class brought him back to Canada in 1914. His brother Frank had continued working in the copper mine in Phoenix until he was killed along with two other mineworkers in a rock fall. After settling his brother's affairs, John Riordan returned to the United States. He appears to have played no further role in the IWW or radical politics, though he was remembered with respect and some fondness in Trautmann's memoirs, written more than 20 years after the two fellow workers had battled the conservatives and pie cards in the union.[8]

The British-Canadian Wobbly Robert Gosden was also instrumental in helping to shape the IWW. Gosden emigrated to Nova Scotia around 1910, and made his way to Prince Rupert, BC shortly afterwards. He took part in a strike of road construction laborers there, and by late 1911 had headed south to San Diego. He may even have joined with other Wobblies to take part briefly in the Mexican Revolution. By early 1912, he returned to San Diego, getting arrested during its free speech fight. From his prison cell, Gosden contributed to the IWW press, notably weighing in on the debate over industrial sabotage the union had recently taken up (see Pinsolle, Chapter 2). Gosden was an advocate of sabotage, including the destruction of machinery. Strikes and free speech fights, he argued, had produced very little. The IWW strategy of the general strike to take over the means of production was no closer in 1912 than it had been in 1905, and the union's membership was still small, perhaps 100,000 across the entire United States. But that was enough, he continued, "to tie up every industry at any time if we use sabotage, and by such action alone will we have the liberty to organize in the industries so that we can feed and clothe the world's workers when the class war has ceased." In another piece, he commented directly on transnationalism. "Democracy is the order in jail," he wrote. "The aristocrat of labor bums his cigarette from his Oriental brother, and the white man argues with black. All race prejudices are swept aside." Furthermore, fellow prisoners from Japan and China were "well informed" on industrial unionism and staunch allies in the class war. Released from jail after nine months, Gosden was deported to Canada, but as the *Industrial Worker* noted, "as the IWW is not particularly patriotic and there is a class struggle in Canada, we fail to see how a system based on theft has gained by making the change."[9]

The cross-border activities of Gosden and Riordan are important reminders that the objective links of class and the subjective links of class experience easily crossed the lines drawn by governments. Due to those links, American Wobblies such as John H. Walsh found ready audiences for their message of militancy and solidarity in BC. Walsh is better known for helping to create the IWW's famous *Little Red Songbook*, and for his role at the 1908 IWW convention. Along with his wife, whose first name has been lost to history, Walsh organized a delegation of West Coast Wobblies known as the "Overalls Brigade" to ride the rails to Chicago for the convention. Nicknamed "the bummery" by Daniel De Leon, the western delegation joined with Trautmann, St. John, and others to defeat the DeLeonites and assert the IWW's syndicalist character by disavowing political action. The year before, Walsh had led a month-long strike of Vancouver longshore workers in IWW Lumber Handlers Local 526.

Other US Wobblies came across the border to organize, agitate, and educate. Joseph Ettor, who played a crucial role in the Lawrence "Bread and Roses" textile strike in 1912, organized teamsters into an IWW local in Vancouver five years earlier. IWW speakers such as Lucy Parsons, "Big Bill" Haywood, and Elizabeth Gurley Flynn stopped in BC during their speaking tours, as did "Mother" Jones, who was born in Ireland, trained as a teacher in Toronto, and was a delegate at the IWW founding convention. Edith Frenette, a friend of Gurley Flynn, traveled with her husband and brother-in-law to organize loggers in the northern region of Vancouver Island, where she gave birth to her daughter Stella in 1911 and saw her issued with IWW card number 11014 (see Mayer, Chapter 14).[10]

The most famous Wobbly to cross from the United States into Canada was Joe Hill. An immigrant from Sweden, Hill travelled to BC in 1912 during a strike of "navvies" building the Canadian Northern Railway line. There he penned songs for the strikers, including the classic "Where the Fraser River flows," still sung by workers in the province. Other American

During the IWW strike against the Canadian Northern Railway, Joe Hill wrote "Where the Fraser River flows." Courtesy of BC Archives collections.

Wobblies joined the strike, and if they did not leave songs, they left a practical message of transnational solidarity. Henry McGuckin left his home in Paterson, New Jersey and made it to Washington State in late 1911. There, he heard Wobblies give impassioned soapbox speeches about industrial unionism, the need for a workers' revolution, and the ongoing Aberdeen free speech fight. McGuckin volunteered to join in the free speech fight as Tommy Whitehead signed him up in the IWW. Whitehead had been elected to the IWW executive board in 1908, along with Joe Ettor, St. John, and Trautmann, as part of the syndicalist, anti-De Leon group, and edited the IWW newspaper the *Industrial Worker* in 1916. In 1919, with the arrests of hundreds of Wobblies during the United States's first Red Scare, he served as the acting general secretary-treasurer of the union.

After Aberdeen, Whitehead asked McGuckin to go to Vancouver, BC, where another free speech fight had broken out. McGuckin hiked, camped out in hobo jungles, and rode the rails to Vancouver to participate in the open-air street meetings where IWW and Socialist Party of Canada organizers proselytized and organized. In another example of transnationalism, one IWW speaker, Jack Graves, "very English," McGuckin observed, "got up on the soapbox, and I have never heard a better or clearer presentation of industrial unionism and socialism." From Vancouver, McGuckin went to Kamloops, BC, a railway junction town, where he walked up and down the line in a circuit that took six days, staying in the makeshift construction camps as he signed up workers in the IWW and distributed its newspapers and *Little Red Songbook*. He had spent nearly four months organizing when the strike broke out. Tommy Whitehead left the United States to meet him in Kamloops and become one of the strike coordinators. The intervention of the police and mass arrests soon broke the strike. McGuckin spent over four months in jail, and Whitehead was released early only because the terrible prison conditions nearly cost him his sight.[11]

This strike gives us another way to examine the transnationalism of the IWW across the US-Canadian border. Much of what we know about IWW members and transnationalism is restricted to the lives of famous immigrants such as Joe Hill and activists of some prominence such as J. H. Walsh. Riordan and McGuckin were more typical IWW members, but their stories also are accessible because they were white and male, and more able, in the case of Riordan, to take part in public matters such as union elections. In the case of McGuckin, his experiences were recorded with the aid of his university-educated son. That we know more about them reflects the reality of class, race, and gender in their period and in the universities of ours. Although labor, gender, and immigration history have been established academic disciplines for at least 40 years, this work has largely been done by scholars limited to sources created in English. Only recently have historians tackled primary sources in other languages, which are rarely as plentiful and well-curated as the newspapers, government documents, company records, and union materials created in the dominant language.

Episodes such as the 1912 strike, however, give us some limited access to less visible aspects of the IWW's transnationalism. The IWW insisted on organizing all workers, regardless of their nationality, race, or ethnicity. This contrasted sharply with the view of the craft unions that belonged to the AFL and the Canadian Trade and Labour Congress (TLC). R. S. Maloney, the AFL "fraternal delegate" to the 1907 TLC convention in Winnipeg, undoubtedly thought he was making a broad, inclusive statement when he told Canadian unionists that "We speak a common language, are descendants from the same races, inhabit the same land and our labor problem with all its ideals, aspirations and ambitions is alike for both of us."[12] However, Maloney's conception of the working class excluded indigenous peoples, African-Americans, the one-third of Canadians who were Francophone, non-Anglophone immigrants, women, and the so-called unskilled; in short, the great majority of people. The workers Maloney and the AFL ignored made up the IWW's target constituency, and represented many of the workers it organized in the 1912 railway strike. We get a glimpse of this reality from a Vancouver newspaper editorial that racialized and denounced the strikers:

> The word "wap" [sic] in the United States language denotes a mammal whose place in the animal kingdom is that of a closely allied species to man, who works on the railway grade when he is not on strike or in town pursuing pleasures equally noisome in bottles and in skirts. He wears foot-rags instead of socks, and he has other names beside the poetical word "wap" in our abundantly endowed language. "Bohunk" is one of them and "hunk" is another .... The "waps" are the lower animals among the makers of the grade .... swept up from all parts of Europe. They are turbulent, moody, superstitious, and often wicked. They are very amenable to the intrigues of agitators. They come of mother-forgotten races feudal even yet, and misery, hopelessness, and even hunger have not been long disestablished from their lives. Italians, Bulgar, Russ, Wallachian, Croat, Hun, they have little regard for sanitary regulations, do not wash, and seldom change their shirts ....

The only advantage to the "wap," the editorial concluded, was that the railroad could not be constructed without their cheap labor, "unless coolie labor were employed," an even more hated group which the paper knew its white, respectable readers would not accept. The use of Chinese labor, after all, had been explicitly forbidden under the terms of the government charter issued for the new railway.[13]

The steady organizing work of Wobblies like Henry McGuckin and J. S. Biscay paid off when, in March 1912, over 4,000 "waps" overcame differences of nationality, language, and culture to strike against the terrible conditions in the construction camps. They did more than walk off the job: they created a model of a workers' society in the bush country of British Columbia. They built new, clean camps to live in, brought in supplies, and organized the camps to keep order. They ran classes in socialist theory and created a rough system of rules and administration. As one newspaper reported on one of the camps, it was "a miniature republic run on Socialistic lines, and it must be admitted that so far it has been run successfully." The strike eventually was defeated when police arrested hundreds of Wobblies, but conditions for the railway workers improved considerably. As McGuckin concluded, "a strike is part of the total struggle, and where it has forced better conditions that are enjoyed by other members of the working class, it cannot be called a defeat." It did more than that: it proved that transnationalism and internationalism could forge a workers' organization along lines of class and across nationality and ethnicity.[14]

The 1912 strike offers yet another insight into the transnationalism of the iww. Fred Thompson, born in St John, New Brunswick in 1900, joined the iww in San Francisco in 1922 and wrote a history of the union in 1955.

In it, Thompson maintained that the nickname "Wobbly" came from a Chinese restaurant owner who extended credit to the striking railway workers. Unable to pronounce the letter "W," he would ask workers if they were in the "eye wobble wobble." Mortimer Downing, a longtime member of the IWW and an editor of the *Industrial Worker* in the 1920s, gave a different place and date for the story, suggesting the word was coined "up in Vancouver, in 1911" where "we had a number of Chinese members." While later Wobblies such as the singer Utah Phillips have held that "it's a story that we're not particularly proud of, because it's a racist perception" and folklorist Archie Green concluded there is "no evidence for the Chinese lingual tale," earlier generations, typified by Los Angeles Wobbly Mortimer Downing, thought "it hints of a fine, practical internationalism, a human brotherhood based on a community of interests and of understanding."[15]

The organization of the transnational, multi-ethnic workforce of the province was not restricted to the 1912 strike. The lumber handlers local Walsh aided in its 1907 strike was nicknamed "the Bows and Arrows" after the large number of indigenous workers who worked on the Vancouver waterfront and joined the union. It also included, as Walsh noted with some pride, "Scotch, French, Swede, Indian, German, Norwegian, half-breed, Dane, Japanese, Arabian, Italian, Chillian [sic], Filipino, Negro, Russian, Mexican, American, Portuguese ... I might say here that not one of the membership, although composed of eighteen different nationalities, has proven untrue to his obligation." The polyglot membership also gave the union a great advantage, Walsh explained: "when you go down to the mill with a body of pickets that can talk every language under the sun ... when a fellow comes along to say 'No savvy,' he soon learns that won't work." In the northern seaport of Prince Rupert, an IWW organizer declared, "when the factory whistle blows it does not call us to work as Irishmen, Germans, Americans, Russians, Greeks, Poles, Negroes or Mexicans. It calls us to work as wage-workers, regardless of the country in which were born or color of our skins. Why not get together, then ... as wage-workers, just as we are compelled to do in the shop."[16]

The IWW defended this internationalism in the face of the racism of other BC unions. When the Sandon local of the WFM announced that it "vigorously condemns the employment of Asiatic help in any capacity" and called upon "its friends and members to use every lawful and honorable effort to secure the banishment of the present Orientals" and halt further immigration, the *Industrial Worker* condemned the miners in strong language. It first noted that the WFM had left the IWW for the AFL, and so it was clear "they don't know very much about industrialism" or "the profit system we are living under." As long as labor was a commodity, "bought and sold upon the market, its price being regulated to a large extent by supply and demand .... what difference it makes to workers whether BC is black, white or yellow is hard to understand." The answer was instead for "workers to own the means of production themselves." To do that, the paper continued:

> we must educate and organize on class lines; we must do away with racial prejudice and imaginary boundary lines; we must recognize that all workers belong to the international nation of wealth producers, and we must clearly see that our only enemy is the capitalist class and the only boundary line is between exploiter and exploited .... We must organize all workers regardless of sex, creed, color or nationality into One Big Industrial Organization.

This was more than a rhetorical flourish. As historian Kornel Chang observes, the IWW "made significant efforts to organize and ally with Chinese, Japanese, and South Asian workers in the Pacific Northwest." This included building links with radical Chinese and Indian nationalists, whose nationalism took the form of an anti-imperialism based on socialist ideas of class and colony (see Khan, Chapter 3).[17]

The historian E. P. Thompson famously noted that class consciousness is the way in which class experiences "are handled in cultural terms: embodied in traditions, value-systems, ideas, and institutional forms."[18] As immigrant and migratory workers, transnationalism was a lived experience for Wobblies and the workers they sought to organize. The class consciousness the IWW sought to build was based on an internationalism that explicitly refused the racialized, racist logic of capital, the nation-state, and conservative trade unions. It could, and often did, transcend the border between the United States and Canada and the broader borders of race and ethnicity.

Notes

1   Robert H. Babcock, *Gompers in Canada: A Study in American Continentalism before the First World War* (Toronto, Ont.: University of Toronto Press, 1974), p. 36.
2   Paul Craven, *"An Impartial Umpire": Industrial Relations and the Canadian State, 1900–1911* (Toronto, Ont.: University of Toronto Press, 1980), especially ch. 8; Judy Fudge and Eric Tucker, *Labour before the Law: The Regulation of Workers' Collective Action in Canada, 1900–1948* (Toronto, Ont.: Oxford University Press,

2001), especially ch. 2; Babcock, *Gompers in Canada*; Mark Leier, *Red Flags and Red Tape: The Making of a Labour Bureaucracy* (Toronto, Ont.: University of Toronto Press, 1995).

3 *The Founding Convention of the IWW: Proceedings* (New York: Merit, 1969), pp. 28, 297, 322, 437, 492, 510, 543, 547.

4 William E. Trautmann, "Fifty Years War, Book #2, The Rise and Fall of the Industrial Workers of the World," cited in Jay Miller, "Soldier of the class war: the life and writing of William E. Trautmann," PhD diss., Wayne State University, 2000, p. 135.

5 Trautmann, "Fifty Years," cited in Miller, "Soldier of the class war," p. 144.

6 For the 1906 convention, see Paul F. Brissenden, *The IWW: A Study of American Syndicalism*, 2nd edn. (New York: Russell & Russell, 1957), ch. 5; Melvyn Dubofsky, *We Shall Be All: A History of the Industrial Workers of the World* (New York: Quadrangle, 1974), ch. 5; Trautmann cited in Miller, "Soldier of the class war," p. 163.

7 *Greenwood Weekly Times*, March 31, 1900; *Electoral History of British Columbia, 1871–1986* (Victoria, BC: Elections British Columbia, n.d.); *Boundary Creek Times*, February 21 or 3 March, 1905—the microfilmed copy of the newspaper has "21 February" printed as the date, but that has been scratched out and "3 March" written in; *Phoenix Pioneer*, April 29, 1905.

8 *Phoenix Pioneer*, August 3, 1907; January 11, 1908; August 22, 1914. I am grateful for the help of Kevin Caslor for helping unearth details of Riordan's life. See Miller, "Soldier of the class war," *passim*, for Trautmann on Riordan and his work in the IWW. A pie card is a highly paid union official concerned primarily with maintaining friendly relationships with management.

9 Mark Leier, *Rebel Life: The Life and Times of Robert Gosden, Revolutionary, Mystic, Labour Spy*, 2nd edn. (Vancouver, BC: New Star, 2013).

10 Richard Brazier, "The Story of the IWW's Little Red Song Book," in Archie Green, David Roediger, Franklin Rosemont, and Salvatore Salerno (eds.), *The Big Red Songbook* (Chicago, Ill.: Charles H. Kerr, 2007), pp. 375–90; Heather Mayer, "Beyond the rebel girl: women, Wobblies, respectability, and the law in the Pacific Northwest, 1905–1924," PhD diss., Simon Fraser University, 2015; Brissenden, *The IWW*, ch. 9; Dubofsky, *We Shall Be All*, ch. 6; Mark Leier, *Where the Fraser River Flows: The Industrial Workers of the World in British Columbia* (Vancouver, BC: New Star, 1990).

11 Franklin Rosemont, *Joe Hill: The IWW and the Making of a Revolutionary Working-class Culture* (reprint edn., Oakland, Calif.: PM Press, 2015); Henry E. McGuckin, *Memoirs of a Wobbly* (Chicago, Ill.: Charles H. Kerr, 1987), pp. 34–48; Leier, *Where the Fraser River Flows*, pp. 47–53.

12 Maloney quoted in Babcock, *Gompers in Canada*, p. 36.

13 *Vancouver Sun*, April 6, 1912.

14 Leier, *Where the Fraser River Flows*; McGuckin, *Memoirs*, pp. 42–8.

15 Whatever we might conclude about racism and the "I Wobble Wobble" etymology, both stories are almost certainly false. See Archie Green, "The name Wobbly holds steady," in *Wobblies, Pile Butts, and Other Heroes: Laborlore Explorations* (Urbana, Ill.: University of Illinois Press, 1993). Green notes that it "remains too vivid a story, has circulated widely, and carries 'the truth' of folktales long believed," p. 194.

16 *Industrial Union Bulletin*, November 2, 1907. The Prince Rupert Wobbly is cited in A. Ross McCormack, *Reformers, Rebels, and Revolutionaries: The Western Canadian Radical Movement, 1899–1919* (reprint edn., Toronto, Ont.: University of Toronto Press, 1991), p. 102.

17 *Industrial Worker*, November 31, 1912; Kornel Chang, "Mobilizing revolutionary manhood: race, gender, and resistance in the Pacific Northwest borderlands," in Moon-Ho Jung (ed.), *The Rising of Color: Race, State Violence, and Radical Movements across the Pacific* (Seattle, Wash.: University of Washington Press, 2014), p. 92. Chang also argues that the IWW's gendered and racialized concept of "revolutionary manhood" may have "disrupted but ultimately reinforced the hegemonic discourse of race and gender," p. 96.

18 E. P. Thompson, *The Making of the English Working Class* (reprint edn., London: Penguin, 1980), p. 9.

10

Wobblies Down Under:

The IWW in Australia

Verity Burgmann

On the other side of the Pacific Ocean, the Industrial Workers of the World (IWW) became a significant force within a labor movement that was already industrially strong and represented by a politically successful Labor Party. This chapter explains why the IWW appealed to workers in a national context very different from that of the United States, investigates the type of workers who became Wobblies "down under," discusses the distinctive strategies of this far-flung IWW, and tells the tale of how it met its particular and peculiar fate.

The IWW's Appeal to Australian Workers

The militant workers who joined IWW clubs established by the De Leonite Socialist Labor Party beginning in 1907 tended to reject its enthusiasm for "political action." Australian working-class political action already had brought about the world's first Labor governments at the state level in 1899 and the federal level in 1904. Labor was, again, in power federally in 1908–09, 1910–13, and 1914–17 as well as at the state level for much of this period in most of the country's six states. The failure of Labor governments to meet radical workers' expectations, however, convinced them that a political party could not act as the shield of the revolution, and instead encouraged many to view the parliamentary process as having nothing to offer a revolutionary working-class movement.[1]

For instance, in August 1907, Hunter Valley coalminers deleted the reference to political—as in electoral—action before adopting the IWW

Preamble. They argued that if workers came together on the industrial field they could control events on the political field. At least as early as 1906, Colliery Employees Federation president Peter Bowling had established contact with the Western Federation of Miners in the United States.[2] On October 30, 1909, a conference of trade unions in Melbourne, in a paraphrase of the non-political 1908 IWW Preamble, urged:

> all trade unions and wage workers to organize industrially with the object of obtaining possession of the fruits of their industry, recognizing that the employing class and working class have nothing in common, and that poverty and want will continue until the wage workers unite on the industrial field as a class to abolish the wage system.[3]

As these discontented workers developed their own non-political versions of the Preamble, it is unsurprising that they turned to the Chicago IWW after 1908. At a meeting to launch an Adelaide IWW Club, "overalls brigader" Harry Clarke presented Chicago literature and a further meeting was called to discuss the two alternatives (see Leier, Chapter 9). At the adjourned meeting on May 6, 1911, the gathering resolved to form a Chicago-line local, which subsequently became the Australian Administration of the IWW with the right to charter further locals on the Australian continent. Militant workers in Sydney agreed in September 1911 that, "any industrial movement that is bossed by any political movement cannot live."[4]

The Adelaide Local issued a charter to a Sydney Local on October 13, 1911. John Dwyer of the Sydney Local, commenting on the state Labor government's recent strikebreaking action against miners, declared, "a party that can send up trainloads of armed Police to Lithgow is a queer crowd to carry the flag of emancipation." This Sydney Local published its own version of the Preamble, with a significant addition: "knowing that all attempts to bring Emancipation of the Proletariat about, by means of any kind of political party has and must end in failure, therefore we reject parliamentary action."[5] Its 1911 recruiting leaflet warned workers:

> The Capitalist Class and their political agents—many who are called friends of the workers—plan to keep you under the yoke of tyranny by offering you what they are pleased to call working class legislation, such as Arbitration Courts, Wages Boards, Labor Exchanges, National Insurance and Workers' Compensation, etc., on condition that you smother your discontent, and have nothing in common with those who desire you to act for yourselves.[6]

Labor governments further aided the growth of the Chicago IWW by confirming its dire warnings against political action. "I was absolutely convinced," explained leading Wobbly Tom Barker, "after seeing [Labor] politicians ... that a strong and even ruthless working-class body was necessary to see that people were properly protected and properly paid."[7]

The strength of the IWW in North America stemmed from discontent with weak, conservative, ineffective craft unionism rather than disillusionment with working-class parliamentary politics, which had not been tried seriously. In Australia, by contrast, it was the precocious nature of the political labor movement that explains the appeal of the Chicago IWW. It expressed and reinforced the strong feelings of resentment felt by many workers towards their elected representatives. Operating in a country with almost universal suffrage and compulsory electoral registration, the Australian IWW was truly non-political, informed by the unique experience of the inability of Labor governments to unmake capitalist social conditions.

The Australian administration was shifted from Adelaide (Local 1) to Sydney (Local 2). In January 1914, the Sydney Local began publication of *Direct Action*, a dynamic newspaper enlivened by Syd Nicholls's superb cartoons. From this point, the Sydney Local grew rapidly and new general workers' locals, based on locality rather than industries, sprang up across the country: Broken Hill, Port Pirie, Fremantle, Boulder City, Brisbane, Melbourne, Tottenham, Perth, Mount Morgan, and Cairns (an all-Russian local). In addition, there were individual Wobblies, especially in remote areas. IWW active membership probably never exceeded 2,000 in a population of 4.5 million, slightly smaller in proportion than IWW membership in the United States. However, *Direct Action* influenced the wider labor movement with a circulation around 10–15,000, on top of the fact that copies were passed from hand to hand.

In a peculiarly strong position to indulge in polemic based on evidence, *Direct Action* emphasized the futility of political action, the betrayals by Labor politicians, and their huge salaries and perks. The Australian IWW's best-known song was "Bump me into Parliament," which ridiculed the pretense of Labor MPs to advance working-class interests while enjoying the pomp and circumstance of parliamentary life. The lyrics include:

Come listen, all kind friends of mine,
I want to move a motion,
To build an El Dorado here,
I've got a bonzer[8] notion.

Chorus:
Bump me into Parliament,
Bounce me any way,
Bang me into Parliament,
On next election day.

Oh yes I am a Labor man,
And believe in revolution;
The quickest way to bring it on
Is talking constitution.[9]

Also to the tune of "Yankee Doodle" was "Hey! Polly," which began:

The politician prowls around,
For workers' votes entreating;
He claims to know the slickest way
To give the boss a beating.

Chorus:
Polly, we can't use you, dear,
To lead us into clover;
This fight is ours, and as for you,
Clear out or get run over.[10]

The conditions for the comparative success of the Wobblies in Australia were provided by those within the labor movement whom they opposed.

Who Were the Australian Wobblies?

Principal speakers for the IWW disproportionately included activists experienced in labor movements of other parts of the planet, whose principal reference point in theory and practice was, literally, the workers of the world. Global mobility is a distinctive feature of the Wobbly phenomenon. Patterns of movement were freer then than they would become after the First World War, when trade barriers and immigration restrictions became more systematic. Mining, construction, and heavy industry provided employment opportunities for footloose single men; cheap sea travel linked Britain, its dominions, and America; and an efficient mail service and print capitalism allowed ready communication from one worksite to another.

Foremost amongst Wobbly orators was Donald Grant, born in 1888 in Inverness, Scotland, who migrated to Australia in 1910. He found work in a paper mill, and later as a dental mechanic. He forsook the Sydney-based

International Socialists for the iww. Tall, with thick red hair brushed back and a strong Scottish accent, he attracted huge crowds to Sunday meetings in the Sydney Domain.[11] Fellow Wobbly Betsy Matthias recalls him as "Curly-headed, Scotch, poetic Donald!" whose speeches eclipsed all others.[12] Contemporary activist Fred Farrall claims he was:

> an orator that could hold his own with anybody in the country, anybody. The average politician wouldn't be in the race. His command of the language and the way he could use it could be devastating. He could humiliate anyone. And he could recite yards of Robert Burns and Shelley and those poets who upheld the rights of the common people.[13]

Labor movement leader Henry Boote, writing in 1917 when Grant had been jailed "for fifteen years for fifteen words," noted:

> For years he was the most popular orator of the Sydney Domain. Sunday after Sunday thousands surrounded the stump from which he spoke. His pungent satires upon capitalistic society evoked the laughter and applause of vast audiences. His eloquent appeals for working-class solidarity stirred them to the depths of their being.[14]

John Benjamin King, a hefty Canadian born in 1870, had worked as a miner, teamster, stoker, and engine-driver, and had been an iww organizer in Vancouver and Auckland before arriving in Sydney in 1911 (see Derby, Chapter 11). The police believed he had been sent in an official capacity by Chicago headquarters, but, like the American sailors they noticed speaking from the iww platform, King had come of his own accord. Though not in Grant's league, he was a fine orator with a boisterous and aggressive style. During his 1914 speaking tour as general organizer, *Direct Action* billed him as "a convincing and earnest expositor of scientific organization, and Marxian Economics."[15]

Charlie Reeve, a thickset Cockney with straight, well-oiled, long dark hair was, according to his security file, only 5 feet 1 inch tall and "very much tattooed on the arms, hands and fingers." Born in 1887, he arrived in Sydney in 1907 after experience in the American iww, and worked as a bricklayer. The police regarded him as "one of the most aggressive speakers of the i.w.w." His fellow members, according to Grant, thought him "a bloody madman" who "would fight the whole world—so long as it was looking on." Tony McGillick remembers a more poignant side to Reeve, that he was a master at painting word-pictures of the sad lot of the worker: "He would describe a cold morning when it was still dark, when the worker would awaken to the shrill peal of the alarm-clock, with the prospect of a day of weary toil for little reward."[16] In jail in 1921, Reeve mused how his thoughts always strayed to the Domain on Sundays: "I am there with you, at my be-loved meetings, rubbing shoulders with Men from all parts of the World, and can feel the unspoken wish and determination to strive for a better world. With all their faults, I love my class."[17] After his term in jail Reeve lived in a homosexual relationship with another Wobbly, a Danish sailor called Carl Jensen, who worked as a laborer at Sydney's White Bay power station.[18]

Tom Barker was born at Crosthwaite in Westmoreland, England in 1887 of Lakeland farming stock. He started working on farms at age 11, then went to Liverpool at about 14 to work in a milk-house. In 1905, he joined the army, where he trained young horses, took an army certificate of education, and became a lance-corporal. Invalided with slight heart trouble in 1908, he worked on the Liverpool railways. In June 1909 he migrated to New Zealand, joining the Auckland tramway company as a conductor. In 1911 Barker became secretary of the New Zealand Socialist Party's Auckland branch, but he left around the end of 1912. Sacked from the tramways, he went organizing for the iww and became involved in the general strike of 1913, three charges of sedition being laid against him. A key figure of the New Zealand iww, he was imprisoned in January 1914 then placed under a £1,500 bond. He came to Sydney in February 1914.[19] Barker soon became the leading figure in the iww down under, until his deportation to Chile towards the end of the war (see de Angelis, Chapter 16).

Though not a great orator, Tom Glynn was a gifted writer and edited *Direct Action*. Born in Galway, Ireland in 1881, he arrived in Australia in 1900, then served as a trooper in the Boer War. He remained in South Africa as a sergeant in the Transvaal Police and was suspended for refusing to shoot a Zulu boy during an uprising. By 1907 he was active in New Zealand radical politics, leaving the Wellington De Leonites to join a larger socialist party, hoping to split off its "revolutionary element." By 1910 he was back in Johannesburg in the tramway service, becoming general secretary of the South African Industrial Workers Union. He played a leading part in the 1911 tramway strike, for which he was jailed (see van der Walt, Chapter 18). After becoming prominent in radical journalism in South Africa, in late 1911 he left for Ireland and the United States, where he joined the iww, and finally worked his way back to Australia in 1912 as a stoker, after which he worked mainly as a tramway conductor in Sydney.[20]

Of the 89 Sydney Local members in late 1911, 15 had continental European names. Three presented American dues cards; another three had transferred from the Auckland Local. On the membership list police obtained in 1916, most of the 1,091 surnames and given names were "Anglo-Celtic," including 56 "Mac/Mc" names, 16 "O" names, and many other Irish ones such as Maloney or Murphy. There were 84 names signifying continental European origin, mainly Scandinavian or German, of whom ten gave their occupation as seaman.[21] Of the 75 Wobblies prosecuted under the Unlawful Associations Act during September 1917, 27 were born overseas, mostly in the British Isles. Of the Sydney Twelve, whose arrest and trial are outlined below, only John Hamilton from Victoria and Bill Teen from Tasmania were Australian-born. Three were from England (Reeve, Besant, Beatty); two from Ireland (Glynn, Larkin); two from Scotland (McPherson, Grant); one from New Zealand (Moore); one from Canada (King); and one from Russia (Fagin). A glazier who arrived in Sydney in 1910 via Wales and the United States, Fagin had been a member of the Socialist Party of America. He was one among many Russians, Bulgarians, and Italians who formed ethnic networks within the IWW. There were German and Austrian-born members, too, some of who were interned enemy aliens of considerable concern to the authorities.[22]

The Wobbly as foreigner became a stereotype deliberately exaggerated by opponents. While a significant proportion of the most public propagandists of the movement did hail from the geographically dispossessed tribe of internationally itinerant radical activists, a large proportion of the membership belonged to the nomads of the domestic labor movement: migratory rural workers in railway construction, lumber, wood, agriculture, and sheep and cattle grazing. The occupation of "laborer," common in Wobbly records, denoted the kind of unskilled worker who pursued employment wherever and whatever it might be.

However, unlike the American hoboes largely ignored by institutionalized labor, nomads were respected within the Australian labor movement—revered rather than reviled. Among the labor movement's strongest participants, they were especially active in the new unions formed late in the nineteenth century. Itinerant workers' high standing reflected the fact that Australia was primarily an extractive and large-scale grazing economy absolutely dependent on the labor of migratory workers; the United States was a more industrialized economy in which transient workers played a vital but smaller role.

Wobbly Bill Beattie claimed, "The bulk of our membership was composed of bush and construction workers who travelled by necessity."[23] Barker recalled:

We had the Home Guard, from Sydney, but most of the members worked in the country, came into Sydney from time to time, took out their card, and would take a bundle of papers and sell them wherever they went. Often they worked as miners until the shearing season came, then went up to North Queensland, started to shear and followed the sun until they got down to Victoria, which was quite a long time .... That was a time of great unemployment, backward industry and vast movements of working people, especially single men. Migratory people looked for support when they came to a new place and if they found an i.w.w. branch they knew they were amongst friends, and that created a solidarity of spirit that was something more than words ... wherever there was an i.w.w. branch you could go there for friendship and help and also to get on to a job.[24]

Military intelligence observed that IWW influence in the Queensland meat works was strongest in the freezing departments which hired itinerant workers; more skilled, domiciled workers were less tainted.[25] Tom Audley recalls that Bill Casey, who wrote "Bump me into Parliament," was "a real hobo type."[26] *Direct Action* ran frequent reports from Wobblies "on the track," which typically contained tales of a cowed boss quickly conceding the demands of Wobblies they had unwittingly hired.

Wobblies did not last long on jobs, with the result that they and their propaganda dispersed all over the continent. When Jimmy Seamer, a mining industry union activist during the First World War, was asked whether the Wobblies moved about a lot, he commented, "Yeah, and they was pushed about, too."[27] *Direct Action* editorialized:

To be "fired" simply means a change of jobs, and a change is good for all. It is not good to be in one job too many years. It has a tendency to make one too contented. The more one roams around, the more experience he gets, and he is more fitted to fight the industrial battle.[28]

Military intelligence stressed the nuisance value of the nomadic agitator fomenting discontent: "Quinton ... travels over a considerable area of the Darling Downs country; therefore has special opportunities for spreading the teachings of the i.w.w."[29] Reporting on trouble in the northern cane fields in 1918, the censor noted: "Shepard and others of the i.w.w. gang appear to carry a good stock of literature with them—they are always on the move and they disseminate their criminal doctrines at every halting place." The censor referred to Norman Jeffery as one of many Wobblies "touring the country disseminating, by their soap box orations, the doctrine which our Government ... has thought fit to denounce."[30] There are numerous examples of the wandering Wobbly fanning the flames of discontent the length and breadth of the continent, roaming because their limited skills could not secure them stable employment.

This stereotype—caricatured in secondary literature and revered by Wobblies themselves—deserves qualification. Examination of the Broken Hill Local minute books, for example, reveals that this local of miners flourished as a stable institution. One duty of the management committee was to go to the local hospital on Sundays to visit sick fellow-workers and deliver their copies of *Direct Action*.[31] Francis Shor argues that the Broken Hill Local affords a corrective to notions of the IWW as a loose affiliation of migratory militants; he draws a picture of a community-based membership in an established setting of working-class solidarity and militancy. By the end of 1916 the Broken Hill Local exceeded 100 members, and even after the jailing of many members, it retained an organizational life and identity that guaranteed its social significance.[32]

When police raided Sydney Local headquarters in September 1916, they obtained "documentary evidence" with which they compiled a list of 1,091 IWW members, with addresses and occupations, and duly forwarded it to military intelligence. Two categories of Wobbly reveal themselves from the residential addresses: the itinerant worker, and the stationary worker living in the inner city.[33] Such domiciliary characteristics typified the less skilled sector of the working class from which Wobblies disproportionately came. The IWW, *Direct Action* announced:

> carries on its agitation principally amongst the unskilled workers. By organising the lowest paid workers and gaining better conditions for them, it has the tendency to force the higher paid grades and "aristocrats of labor" to get busy and fight for more concessions if they would keep ahead of the "common labourer."[34]

Contemporary activist Fred Coombe claimed it was from "right amongst the working class" that the IWW gained its support, from "the hard workers," such as laborers and miners.[35]

Early membership in the Sydney Local, a general workers local, consisted of nine laborers, four wharfies (longshoremen), three miners, two wireworkers, one gardener, one shearer, one glazier and one signalman.[36] By late 1911, this Local had 89 members: 35 laborers, 8 miners, 7 seamen, 5 wharfies, 3 gardeners, 3 timber-getters, 2 carpenters, 2 engineers, 2 stonemasons, 2 bakers, and 1 painter, canvasser, tinsmith, signalman, shearer, glazier, wireworker, dental mechanic, boilermaker, shearer, painter and docker, engine-driver, conductor, automobile-driver, carter, fitter, elevator operator, and hairdresser.[37] Though the 1916 list compiled by police used broader categories, the occupational breakdown was similar, with the vast majority in unskilled or semi-skilled employment. Well over a third of the men (375) classified themselves as laborers: 42 wharfies, 66 miners, 56 seamen, 44 firemen (including ship and railway firemen), 35 factory workers, 69 building workers, 55 metal workers, 71 transport workers, 55 hotel and retail trade workers, 13 rural workers, and 8 postal workers. There also were 92 skilled workers, such as fitters, electricians, plumbers, mechanics, printers, and cabinet-makers. There was a sculptor, a musician and 2 vaudeville artists, and a few non-manual workers—a schoolteacher, 6 public servants, 7 clerks, and one draughtsman. The 20 females included 7 in the clothing trade, 2 public servants, 1 laundress, 1 typist, 1 governess, 1 housekeeper, 1 laborer, 1 clerk, 2 married women, and 3 who declined to provide an occupation.[38]

What Were They Like?

Wobblies have been cited as representative of Australia's "national character" because they recruited many members from the nomadic rural proletariat, and manifested attitudes and values of the national type based on this mythologized worker: loyalty to one's mates, antagonism towards authority, and contempt for middle-class virtues such as sobriety, industry, formal education, and religious observance.[39] The inventive genius of imported Wobbly argot easily absorbed local cultural mores. Wobblies successfully played on widely accepted themes. Mr. Simple, the Mr. Block of down under, believed in the promises of respectable, middle-class Labor "pollies." Like the Australia of national mythmaking, the predominantly masculine IWW adopted a pose of extreme toughness. Though rebel girls were welcomed, Shor's designation of the Australian IWW as an example of "virile syndicalism" fits.[40] Rowan Day has studied this masculinist Wobbly culture taken to violent extremes in the outback in his study of the killing by enraged Wobblies of a country policeman, an act roundly condemned by the union's leadership.[41]

The recruiting card issued to new Wobblies listed "Pamphlets you should read": *Advancing Proletariat*, *The Social Evil*, *The Immediate Demands of the I.W.W.*, *Industrial Union Methods*, *Arbitration and the Strike*, *Job Control*, and *Direct Action*. The Preamble on this card served as a concise expression of IWW ideology and was known well by most members, often by heart. Embodying much Marxian theory and proletarian wisdom in blunt terminology, this Preamble was considered much better than the sacred texts of socialist sects. The IWW scorned the "scientific socialist" who, according to *Direct Action*, quoted *Capital* by the page but was useless in struggle:

> Glib-tongued theory is of little help in the class struggle unless it is backed by class loyalty and class action …. A man is not what he thinks, but what he does. It is easy to think war, or think strike, or to theorise on tactics, but it takes real manhood and real womanhood to back up these theories and these thoughts in the actual everyday battle of the working class.

Talk and education were necessary, *Direct Action* argued, but class activity and loyalty were more important. "The capitalist system cannot be theorised out of existence, nor can it be effaced by a plentiful supply of platitudinous piffle." The fact remains that "analysis of the capitalist system of exploitation is only more or less of academic interest; the matter of vital importance is the remedy for putting a stop to that exploitation." Experience had proven that the members worth having were those whose understanding was of a practical bent, suited for revolutionary action.[42]

Peter Rushton identified the good, the bad, and the ugly Wobbly: "The organization attracted the disgruntled, the larrikin, the army dodger, the criminal, and those who joined merely for companionship. It also appealed to the idealist."[43] Norman Rancie insisted, "We had amongst our members men and women of high ideals, intellectuals, men holding responsible positions, men of integrity, clean living family men and home lovers." Contemporary activist Tom Payne recalled that Wobbly Mark Anthony was "a man with a big heart," who returned regularly to Clunes to look after his mother and family, filling up their larder before returning to Broken Hill. There were heroes, too: Alexander Horrocks lost one eye from a fall of earth while saving a mate in a mine accident. However, Fred Farrall described his Wobbly cousin Roly Farrall as a contradiction of his political views, having no respect for other people, least of all his wife Jean, frequently a victim of Roly's drunkenness, "But he was a character."[44]

That the Wobblies were "characters" is indisputable. Socialist May Brodney disliked the "exhibitionalism" of the IWW, and dismissed it for making "a cheap appeal to emotionalism rather than logic," yet wrote: "give them their due they were most entertaining …. The language was colourful & speakers were fluent & had their following." The *Sydney Morning Herald* conceded that the Wobbly "has an enthusiasm in his ideas which gives him an almost fearful impetus in the promulgation of his views, and the infection of others with his doctrines." The *Bulletin* commented:

"Misguided they are, of course, and all that; but how the enthusiasm of these i.w.w. people shames Liberals and Laborites." To Wobblies, workers had a choice: One Big Union or Barbarism. Wobbly energy levels indicated the vehemence with which they adhered to their class-struggle philosophy, and the extent to which they were formed from that section of the working class that had nothing to lose in seeking to change the world.[45]

What Did They Do?

Australian IWW Locals had little choice but to "bore from within" rather than practice "dual unionism." This departure from North American IWW practice was an adaptation to Australian circumstances. In 1916 union density was 47.5 percent in Australia, compared with 12.2 percent in the United States. The Australian IWW was not aiming to organize workers neglected by trade unionism, but hoping to change the basis on which all workers were organized. Thus, most Wobblies also belonged to established unions. Within them, Wobblies criticized craft unionism, sectionalism, and the emergence of a union bureaucracy, especially when numerous and better remunerated than the workers it served. A security file on the IWW noted, "there has been a growing movement on the part of the i.w.w. men to join Unions so that the principles of their organization might be more widely promulgated."[46] They understood that boring from within could only succeed if relations with other unionists were reasonable. In private IWW correspondence seized by police, Wobblies advised each other not to alienate craft unionists.[47] Tom Barker expressly warned the miners establishing the Tottenham Local in 1915 not to "antagonise the crafties," for "they are the material we have to work upon, and therefore every care should be taken to keep their good will."[48]

By boring from within, Wobblies spread their ideas. Military intelligence noted that IWW theories had "struck deep into the militant unions."[49] New South Wales Labor Premier Holman regretted "the secret but steadily growing influence of the Industrial Workers of the World over union organisations."[50] Jimmy Seamer recalled: "You met Wobblies wherever you went …. All militants followed the Wobblies …. They had a foot in everywhere."[51] The effects of the Australian IWW locals' decisions to make a political virtue out of industrial necessity were significant. In relegating dual unionism to long-term aspiration and boring from within in the meantime, Wobblies down under secured considerable protection. Australian employers could not easily isolate and physically intimidate Wobblies, because they worked within a strong union movement with the added respectability of sponsoring a party regularly in government. Where American Wobblies were confronted violently by employers and their thugs, Australian Wobblies were simply hemmed in, while sheltered, by the labor movement itself.[52]

In the United States, the iww was internally riven by concern that anti-war activity would distract from organization at the point of production and invite government repression, which explains its reticence on the war and withdrawal of anti-war pamphlets it had produced. By contrast, in Australia, no organization opposed the outbreak of war as promptly and vociferously as the iww. The front page of *Direct Action* for August 10, 1914 declared:

WAR! WHAT FOR? FOR THE WORKERS AND THEIR DEPENDENTS: DEATH, STARVATION, POVERTY AND UNTOLD MISERY. FOR THE CAPITALIST CLASS: GOLD, STAINED WITH THE BLOOD OF MILLIONS, RIOTOUS LUXURY, BANQUETS OF JUBILATION OVER THE GRAVES OF THEIR DUPES AND SLAVES. WAR IS HELL! SEND THE CAPITALISTS TO HELL AND WARS ARE IMPOSSIBLE.

On August 22, Tom Barker urged: "LET THOSE WHO OWN AUSTRALIA DO THE FIGHTING. Put the wealthiest in the front ranks; the middle class next; follow these with politicians, lawyers, sky pilots and judges. Answer the declaration of war with the call for a GENERAL STRIKE."

The iww threw itself wholeheartedly into campaigning against the war and Australian involvement. In so doing, it increased rather than diminished its opportunities to organize at the point of production because its anti-war activity won it many supporters amongst workers critical of the senseless slaughter. The threat of conscription gave the iww its greatest opportunity to have its voice heard, and it expanded rapidly in this period.[53] "Great crowds used to come to our anti-conscription meetings," Tom Barker recalls, "up to a sixth of the population of Sydney gathering around and trying to hear the speakers."[54] The iww became established in the patriotic mind as the source of disloyal infection, and confirmed in the radical working-class mind as the center of anti-militarist resistance. As the labor movement divided over the war, Australia's involvement in it, and conscription, the role of the iww in encouraging this regrouping into left/anti-conscription and right/pro-conscription forces was crucial. By acting as a "radical flank" entirely opposed to the war, iww campaigning helped at least to defeat conscription in referenda in 1916 and 1917.[55]

By November 1916, Labor Prime Minister Hughes complained that the

IWW was "largely responsible for the present attitude of organised labor, industrially and politically, towards the war."[56] Three-quarters of federal Labor politicians indicated they would refuse to pass a Conscription Act. Prime Minister Hughes blamed the IWWs, "foul parasites" who had "attached themselves to the vitals of labour."[57] Hughes appealed to "organised labour" to cast out from its midst those who dominated the anti-conscription wing of the movement: "Extremists—I.W.W. men, Revolutionary socialists, Syndicalists, 'red-raggers' ... who seek to use labour for their own purposes."[58] Hughes's desire to beat back IWW influence within the labor movement sealed the fate of those he blamed for fomenting opposition to him and his kind from within that movement.

What Happened to Them?

In Australia, the repression of the IWW was engineered by the right wing of the Labor Party—in government—to prevent the union from seizing control of the labor movement, if not of the means of production. Labor governments at the federal and state level cast the IWW as an enemy agent. While the Australian Wobblies did not endure the privatized retribution inflicted upon their American fellow-workers—beatings, lynchings, intimidation, and torture by individual patriots—the state-sponsored suppression of the Australian IWW, which occurred before American criminal syndicalism legislation, proved sufficiently draconian to achieve the eradication of the IWW as a viable organization, notwithstanding successor organizations and its formal re-emergence after 1928.[59]

Repression was facilitated by the framing of 12 Wobblies tried late in 1916 for treason-felony: plotting arson on Sydney business premises.[60] With public hysteria aroused by this case, the Hughes National Labor government enacted the Unlawful Associations Act, passed on December 19, 1916, under which any member of the IWW could be imprisoned. In the next few months, 103 Wobblies were jailed, usually for six months with hard labor, and many more were sacked from their jobs. Twelve foreign-born Wobblies were deported; at the same time, US authorities were shipping American Wobblies to Australia, the ships passing each other in the Pacific.[61]

The final irony was that the labor movement, whose right-wing political representatives had suppressed the IWW, was also responsible for releasing the Twelve—proof that the strategy of boring from within had earned Wobblies acceptance within the wider labor movement. The agitation was so strong that the movement to release them included all manner of labor organizations: trade unions, labor and trades hall councils and regional industrial councils, left-wing parties, and even sections of the Labor Party.[62] Union after union committed itself in support of the release campaign and to industrial action if necessary. The Twelve were released in stages by New South Wales Labor Premier Storey during 1920 and 1921, bowing to the strength of the labor movement campaign to defend those whom fellow workers saw as their most militant, but still their own. *Labor News* boasted that the liberated men owed their freedom to the fact that Labor was in power.[63] In departing jail, it is unlikely any of the Twelve sang "Polly, we can't use you dear."

Conclusion

Though the Australian IWW was a direct transplant from the United States and remained recognizable as such, it adapted to local circumstances. The extent to which the IWW down under flourished in a different setting was attributable to distinctive characteristics developed in intelligent response to the environment in which it operated. Had it been obliged to toe a "Chicago line," its local impacts would have been less remarkable. In contrast with the Communist movement that succeeded it, the IWW's commitment to freedom of militant working-class maneuver is worth celebration.

Notes

1 Verity Burgmann, *Revolutionary Industrial Unionism: The Industrial Workers of the World in Australia* (Melbourne, Vic.: Cambridge University Press, 1995), pp. 11–26.
2 Robin Gollan, *The Coalminers of New South Wales* (Melbourne, Vic.: Melbourne University Press, 1963), pp. 122–5; R. Wright to J. F. Neill, Nov. 17, 1909, IWW Sydney Branch Correspondence, 262/1, Mitchell Library, Sydney.
3 *Industrial Worker*, January 8, 1910.
4 Handwritten notes, J. N. Rawling Collection, N57/131, Noel Butlin Archives, Canberra; Correspondence between H. J. Hawkins and P. Christensen (April–June 1911), E. Moyle, G. G. Reeve, D. Mallon (June–July 1911), IWW Papers, A1333/4, Mitchell Library; Adelaide Local, Organised May 1911, Fred Hancock Papers, Mitchell Library; E. A. Giffney to Fellow-Workers, Sept. 20, 1911, John Dwyer Papers, Mitchell Library.
5 Correspondence between J. Dwyer and E. Moyle, Nov. 1911, John Dwyer Papers, Mitchell Library.
6 Sydney Local, IWW, "Manifesto of the Industrial Workers of the World," n.d. [(1911]), IWW Papers, Mitchell Library.
7 Tom Barker, "Self-portrait of a revolutionary," *Society for the Study of Labour History Bulletin* 15 (Autumn 1967): 20.
8 Contemporary vernacular meaning "brilliant" or "wonderful."
9 IWW, *Rebel Songs* (Melbourne, Vic.: IWW, 1966), p. 15.
10 IWW, *Songs of the Industrial Workers of the World*, 3rd Australian edn. (Sydney, NSW, c. 1916), p. 64.
11 Frank Farrell, "Donald Grant," *Australian Dictionary of Biography* (Melbourne, Vic.: Melbourne University Press, 1966), 9: p. 75; W. J. McNamara, "Donald Grant—a tribute," *Labour History* 19 (November 1970): 63.
12 *Solidarity*, May 4, 1918.
13 Author interview with Fred Farrell, June 1, 1984.
14 Henry Boote, *The Case of Grant: Fifteen Years for Fifteen Words* (Sydney, NSW: Worker Print, 1918), p. 7.
15 Australian Archives (AA) 1979/199 Item WA1024A Vol.1, p.4; Peter Rushton, "The IWW in Sydney, 1913–1917," MA thesis, University of Sydney, 1969, pp. 87–8; *Direct Action* (hereafter DA), May 1, 1914.
16 AA: ACT/CRS/A3932 Item SC292 Pt.3, 1979/199 Item WA1024A Vol.1, p.4; Rushton, "The IWW in Sydney," p. 89; Tony McGillick, *Comrade No More* (West Perth, WA: T. J. McGillick, 1980), p. 36.
17 Charlie Reeve, State Penitentiary, June 4, 1921, to Dear Little Mother, 2, Charles Reeve Collection, Mitchell Library.

18 Author interview with Leo Kelly, January 20, 1986; Burgmann, *Revolutionary Industrial Unionism*, pp. 95–6.

19 Tom Barker, St Pancras Town Hall, October 23, 1959, to John Playford, Rawling Collection; AA1979/199 Item WA1024A Vol.1, 2; Barker, "Self-portrait," p. 19.

20 AA1979/199 Item WA1024A Vol.1, 3; Correspondence between Glynn and others, various dates, SLP of Australia Records, National Library, Canberra; Rushton, "The IWW in Sydney," pp. 62–3, 86–7.

21 List of names of members I.W.W. Sydney Local (Chicago) 1908 Preamble Organised December 27, 1911, Hancock Papers; List No.1, AA: ACT CRS CP404/1, Bundle 1.

22 AA1979/199 Item WA1024A Vol.1; Minutes, Broken Hill Local, 1916–17, State Archives of NSW (SANSW); Frank Cain, *The Wobblies at War, A History of the IWW and the Great War in Australia* (Melbourne, Vic.: Spectrum, 1993), p. 259; Rushton, "The IWW in Sydney," pp. 211–12; Francis Shor, "Masculine power and virile syndicalism: a gendered analysis of the IWW in Australia," *Labour History* 63 (November 1992): 98.

23 Bill Beattie, "Memoirs," *Labour History* 13 (November 1967): 35.

24 Eric Fry (ed.), *Tom Barker and the IWW* (Canberra: Australian Society for the Study of Labour History, 1965), pp. 20, 34.

25 Item 17/4/18; Item 15/5/18 (A6286, 1st Military Dt, 26/12/17–29/6/18).

26 Pat Gowland and Norm Saffin interview with Tom Audley, February 17, 1978.

27 Author interview with Jimmy Seamer, August 29, 1985.

28 *DA*, December 2, 1916.

29 Item 22/1/18, A6286, 1st Military Dt, 26/12/17–29/6/18.

30 F. Ellis, Innisfail, 7/8/18, to A. Shepard, Ayr, Item 24/8/18, A6286, 1st Military Dt, 3/7/18–30/10/18; Mary Jeffrey, 6/3/19, to Norman, Item 26/3/19, A6286, 1st Military Dt, 1/3/19–7/6/19.

31 Minutes, Broken Hill Local, 29/4/17, SANSW.

32 Shor, "Masculine power," pp. 97–8.

33 List No.1, AA: ACT CRS CP404/1.

34 *DA*, July 14, 1917.

35 Author interview with Fred Coombe, May 15, 1984.

36 List of names of members attending first meeting IWW Sydney Local who signed list going to Ed. Moyle Gen. Sec. Treas., Hancock Papers.

37 List of names of members I.W.W. Sydney Local, (Chicago) 1908 Preamble Organised December 27, 1911, Hancock Papers.

38 List No.1, AA: ACT CRS CP404/1.

39 Peter Rushton, "The revolutionary ideology of the Industrial Workers of the World in Australia," *Historical Studies* 15:59 (October 1972): 446.

40 Shor, "Masculine power," pp. 83–99.

41 Rowan Day, *Murder in Tottenham: Australia's First Political Assassination* (Sydney, NSW: Anchor Books Australia, 2015).

42 *DA*, December 18, 1915, July 7, 1917, February 28, 1914.

43 Rushton, "Revolutionary ideology," p. 431.

44 Author interview with Tom Payne, October 25, 1985; *Bulletin*, reprinted in *Solidarity*, November 24, 1917; *Argus*, December 16, 1916; Author interview with Fred Farrall, June 1, 1984.

45 Draft of May Brodney's autobiography, LT10882/8/23; May Brodney, "Histor-tions," State Library of Victoria; *Sydney Morning Herald*, September 30, 1916; Bulletin, December 14, 1916.

46 IWW, Statement giving a brief outline of the activities of the above organization in Australia, AA AA: ACT Branch, CRS A456 Item W26/148 P.H.B.

47 Detective Moore's Report re History and Proceedings of the IWW, SANSW.

48 Quoted in Cain, *The Wobblies at War*, pp. 73–4.

49 Items 5/6/18, 18/2/18, 1st Military Dt, 26/12/17–29/6/18 and Item 12/3/19, 1st Military Dt, 1/3/19–7/6/19, A6286, AA Canberra; Item WA1024A, Vol. I, Investigation Branch Reports, Summaries 1–25, AA1979/199, AA Canberra.

50 *Argus*, 12 Oct. 1916.

51 Seamer interview.

52 Burgmann, *Revolutionary Industrial Unionism*, pp. 159–80.

53 Notebook 1, Ted Moyle Collection in possession of Jim Moss, Adelaide; Rushton, "The IWW in Sydney," p. 190, Appendix III.

54 Fry, *Tom Barker*, p. 27.

55 Verity Burgmann, "Syndicalist and socialist anti-militarism 1911–1918: how the radical flank helped defeat conscription," in Phillip Deery and Julie Kimber (eds.), *Fighting Against War: Peace Activism in the Twentieth Century* (Melbourne, Vic.: Leftbank Press, 2015), pp. 55–78.

56 L. C. Jauncey, *The Story of Conscription in Australia* (Melbourne, Vic.: Macmillan, 1968), p. 223.

57 Quoted in *DA*, January 22, 1916.

58 *DA*, January 30, 1916; *Sydney Morning Herald*, October 25, 1916.

59 Burgmann, *Revolutionary Industrial Unionism*, pp. 246–76.

60 Ian Turner, *Sydney's Burning* (Melbourne Vic.: Heinemann, 1967).

61 Frank Cain, "The Industrial Workers of the World: aspects of its suppression in Australia, 1916–1919," *Labour History* 42 (May 1982): 57–8; Notebook 2, Ted Moyle Collection; Shor, "Masculine power," p. 98.

62 Burgmann, *Revolutionary Industrial Unionism*, pp. 229–45.

63 *Labor News*, August 7, 1920.

Ki Nga Kaimahi Maori Katoa ("To All Maori Workers"): The New Zealand IWW and the Maori[1]

Mark Derby

Of all the international labor movements of the early twentieth century, the Industrial Workers of the World (IWW) has been described as "certainly the most consistent in organizing workers of color."[2] The Wobblies' commitment to working-class solidarity across racial and ethnic, as well as national, lines is attested to by its polyglot publications, the status of leaders such as the African American longshoreman Ben Fletcher, and its influence on other multiracial organizations such as South Africa's Industrial and Commercial Union.[3] The IWW's anti-racism, like other aspects of its revolutionary syndicalist platform, took varying forms in the many different countries and communities in which it emerged. The Australian IWW's address to non-white minorities, according to Verity Burgmann:

> centred on the issue of immigrant workers.... Apart from expressing sincere regret at the plight of the Aborigines and indicting British imperialism for its hand in this, *Direct Action* otherwise ignored the Aboriginal issue; the IWW wrongly judged it as lacking industrial significance.[4]

The New Zealand and Australian branches of the IWW shared much in common, including many mutual members, due in part to their countries' geographic proximity, shared heritage of colonization, and interchanging workforces. However, distinct features of the relations between New Zealand's indigenous Maori population and its Pakeha (non-Maori) majority were reflected in that country's IWW. In particular, the New Zealand IWW newspaper, the *Industrial Unionist*, published a series of articles in the Maori language, written by a Pakeha Wobbly, Percy Short.[5] A house-painter and decorator by trade, Short also worked as a licensed translator and teacher of the Maori language. He helped to found the vigorous Auckland local of the IWW and was a member of its newspaper's editorial collective. This inclusion of material in the language of the indigenous minority may make New Zealand's *Industrial Unionist* unique among Wobbly newspapers of any colonized country.

The New Zealand Wobblies' appeal to Maori signified far more than simple political inclusiveness or even anti-racism. In the early twentieth century, the Maori population could count on few political allies among the non-Maori majority and faced many powerful opponents, overt and otherwise. They represented less than 10 percent of the country's population, were mostly of the poorest class, and their loyalty to the state remained questionable in the wake of bitter land wars against the government and British Crown 50 years earlier. The Wobblies could empathize with those alienating characteristics and were further inclined to admire Maori for their pre-colonial traditions of communal society and collective property ownership.

Percy Short: Maori-Speaking Radical

Percy Short was born in Wellington in 1881, and later moved north to the much smaller, rural town of Feilding, a service center for the surrounding large sheep farms.[6] Its population was then made up of predominantly Pakeha settlers of British origin. The Maori of the Feilding area belonged to the small Ngati Kauwhata tribe and were based around their *marae*, or communal meeting place, called Aorangi, about 2 miles outside the town. Aorangi Marae had its own bakery, blacksmith, and Maori-owned store.[7] Its people lived and worked collectively, supporting themselves from a combination of subsistence agriculture and seasonal labor on the surrounding sheep stations.

In this district, as in the country generally, Maori were a marginalized minority within the general population, a rural semi-proletariat routinely ignored and frequently despised by the settler majority. Within both races, however, there were exceptions to this pattern, and Short, a dapper young man with a waxed moustache, proved one of them. By means unknown to his present-day descendants, he had learned to speak the Maori language fluently, gaining qualifications as a translator and interpreter. From around 1908 he taught night classes in "the language of the Maori Race, including conversational Maori."[8] In later life, especially when outside New Zealand,

Percy Short, circa 1912. Courtesy of Lynley Short, his granddaughter.

he occasionally claimed to be of Maori ancestry himself, but there is no evidence to support this and his family disputes it.[9]

It was unusual at that time (and remains so today) for Pakeha such as Short to become competent in the language of New Zealand's indigenous people. In this respect, however, the Maori language offered advantages over the indigenous languages of other colonies, or former colonies, of Britain such as Australia. Although the major tribal groups spoke differing dialects, their native tongue was essentially the same from one end of the country to the other. Students of the language drew upon a substantial body of written Maori, since the first Christian missionaries had made efforts to learn the language and render it in written form, primarily to teach converts the scriptures. Maori took avidly to reading and writing and became literate in their own language even when they spoke little or no English. They published a number of Maori-language newspapers, but few publications other than some religious materials and official notices and journals were routinely printed in both languages. Even when Maori lived in close proximity with Pakeha, as in Feilding in the early twentieth century, the two races occupied separate social realms, with little communication between them.

Organizing the Maori Workforce

One vigorous national organization that attempted to bridge the divide between the races was the New Zealand Shearers Union. Maori played a vital part in the national shearing industry, usually working in teams based around extended families, a system that accorded with the traditionally communal nature of Maori life.[10] From the 1880s, when it began printing its rules in their language, the Shearers Union made special efforts to recruit and retain Maori members.[11] These efforts were likely prompted less by a spirit of inclusiveness than by the fear that Maori might undermine union rates, or act as strikebreakers during disputes.[12]

The union succeeded in recruiting a large percentage of the Maori shearing workforce, and some Maori held leading positions within it. The first president of the Gisborne and East Coast branch was a champion shearer named Raihania Rimitiriu, and a fellow Maori, James Morgan, was branch secretary. In 1909, the union's Maori members called for specific representation and the union appointed a Maori organizer, Henry Hawkins.[13] At the union's 1910 annual conference, Morgan was elected vice-president "representing the Maori race."[14] That year also saw the launch of the union's monthly newspaper, the *Maoriland Worker*.[15]

Industrial Unionism in New Zealand

Among the rural communities in the Feilding district, the Shearers Union likely had a significant Maori membership and served as a rare progressive force in a community dominated by the "wool kings," the owners of the large sheep stations. However, it was not the only one. By 1911, Feilding also had an active branch of the New Zealand Socialist Party (NZSP), with Percy Short as its secretary. He described the party in this period as:

a flourishing organization ... its membership comprised many varieties of socialists—anarchists, single-taxers, step-at-a-timers, revolutionaries, two-wingers (political and industrial), Christian socialists, rationalists, materialists and Fabian idealists, not to mention the anti-

Parliamentarians—the syndicalists. The Socialist Party never had a class war policy, though most of its members managed to be followers of Marx. It sold thousands of pounds worth of socialist literature.[16]

A group of socialist immigrants from the United Kingdom had formed the NZSP in 1901, having been attracted to New Zealand by its reputation for advanced social experimentation, and in particular its universal franchise and state-sponsored system for compulsory arbitration of industrial disputes. Since the 1890s, that system had suppressed industrial unrest and sustained a placid parliamentary coalition representing craft unions and liberals.

By 1905 the militant wing of the labor movement, comprising larger, semi-skilled unions representing miners, dockworkers, laborers, and shearers, chafed under the restrictions of compulsory arbitration. Less than a year after the IWW was formed in the United States, the first strike in 15 years took place in New Zealand mines, and two years later the miners' unions broke away from the compulsory arbitration system to negotiate directly with employers using the strike weapon. These unions formed the nucleus of the avowedly socialist and syndicalist-dominated New Zealand Federation of Labor (FOL), known as the "Red Fed," formed in 1909.[17]

From 1906 the small, combative NZSP championed opposition to the arbitration system and espoused De Leonite revolutionary industrial unionism.[18] Its journal, *Commonweal*, began reporting on IWW activities in the United States and distributing radical literature such as the US weekly *Appeal to Reason*. In March 1908 *Commonweal* reported a visit by NZSP party organizer Edward Fitzgerald to the small mining town of Denniston: "Comrade Fitzgerald has aroused the Workers on this hill to see that this system will fall …. he showed the fallacy of arbitration, and also the need for a branch of the IWW in Denniston." Later that year the IWW preamble was adopted at the NZSP's annual conference.[19] In 1910 militants from the anti-conscription movement formed an IWW Club in Christchurch. They applied to join the FOL as a New Zealand branch of the IWW and were admitted in June 1911.[20]

The fast-growing Federation assumed control of the *Maoriland Worker* from the Shearers Union in 1911, and expanded it into an impressive national weekly whose masthead proclaimed it, "A Journal of Industrial Unionism, Socialism and Politics." Percy Short contributed occasionally.[21]

With the IWW as a syndicalist grouping on its left, the FOL's constituent unions achieved considerable success in winning improved conditions and rates of pay.[22] With the exception of an element of the Shearers Union, almost none of its individual members were Maori, who were unofficially excluded by geographic and social divides. Most waged workers lived in the towns, but the Maori population remained overwhelmingly rural.

The IWW was especially active in Auckland, the country's biggest city and its first port of call for overseas ships. It was thronged with young single men raring for excitement and confrontation. The loose-knit and untested Auckland Wobblies received powerful reinforcement in November 1911 when three Chicago-style, anti-De Leonist Wobblies from Canada, including J. B. (Jack) King, arrived on a visiting ship. Two young English radicals on board, Alec Holdsworth and Charlie Blackburn, had been strongly influenced by the three Canadians during their long voyage.[23] By the time all five disembarked in Auckland, they were primed to make an explosive impact on the locals.

"In a very short time," Holdsworth later recalled, "Jack [King] was on the street expounding Industrialism (One Big Union) and Marxism in the vernacular."[24] He was backed up by at least 25 local Wobblies, including the heavily tattooed fishmonger Charlie Reeve (see Burgmann, Chapter 10).[25] Every Sunday they drew thousands to their platform down by the wharves. "We had little or no objections around the soapbox," according to Holdsworth. "Attention was good, collections were good—and we had no other source of income."[26]

The 1912 Waihi Strike

In early 1912, King left Auckland to spread the Wobbly message around the North Island, eventually settling in Waihi, a company town economically dependent on Australasia's largest gold mine. There he led a Marxist economics class, enrolled about 30 miners in an IWW local, and soon played a leading part in a mass strike that shut down the mine.[27]

The FOL held its annual conference shortly after the Waihi strike began, with King attending as a Labourers Union delegate. He convinced the Federation to adopt the first part of the IWW Preamble into its own constitution. His motion for a general strike in support of the Waihi miners was lost, but he found support from other delegates, including future Labour Prime Minister Peter Fraser, who said, "With such propagandists I have no quarrel, whose work must undoubtedly advance the revolutionary working class movement."[28]

By August 1912, with the strike still not settled, King's name was raised in Parliament as a dangerous agitator and potential saboteur. He left for

Australia just ahead of the police, and became a stalwart of the Wobblies' Sydney local.[29]

The strike had, by then, spread to a coalmine in the town of Huntly.[30] The managers of both mines called for strikebreakers to reopen their stalled operations, specifically targeting Maori. The *Maoriland Worker* claimed in October 1912 that "emissaries of the employers are travelling among the Maoris and by every possible device practically kidnapping some of them into scabbery."[31] Waihi strike leader Herb Kennedy later claimed that two-thirds of the scabs at Waihi were "half-breed Maoris, the pahs [Maori villages] in the Thames country having been circularized for this purpose."[32] Maori were some of the most notoriously violent strikebreakers, including a tall thug named Peter Leaf, known from his sinister appearance as the "Snake charmer."[33] However, other Maori were successfully discouraged from strikebreaking in the mines. When five Maori were recruited as scabs at Huntly, "the Maori members of the Union brought inside pressure to bear on their fellows to cease work."[34]

After six months on strike, the political tide turned sharply against the Waihi miners. Squads of mounted police attacked their picket lines, and when police encouraged violence between strikers and scabs, brawls broke out between the warring parties in the streets. Vigilante squads of strikebreakers then ran riot through the town, forcing strike leaders and their families to leave their homes overnight. Alec Holdsworth saw a boatload of terrified Waihi women and children arrive in Auckland, and he and other local Wobblies scoured the countryside to feed them. The Auckland Wobblies marched as a body at the funeral parade for a murdered striker, Fred Evans.[35]

The NZ Wobblies' Newspaper

The brutal crushing of the Waihi strike had the effect of dispersing hardened and angry strikers around the country. Several of them joined IWW groups, including 16-year-old George Phillips, who served as the Auckland local's secretary for the next three years.[36] The IWW also gained defectors from among the most active and effective members of the NZSP. English-born Tom Barker had migrated to New Zealand in 1909 and worked as a tram conductor in Auckland, serving as secretary of its NZSP branch from 1911. Two years later he began organizing for the IWW (see also Burgmann, Chapter 10, and de Angelis, Chapter 16).[37] Percy Short, who had by then left Feilding for Auckland, also joined the IWW and remained a close friend of Barker's throughout his life.[38] Alec Holdsworth later recalled that:

> All boats from America were met by one or more of us wearing our IWW badge, in case there should be a Wobbly on board with the appropriate swag [of rebel literature]. But it was a precarious source of supply, so we set to and got out our own newspaper, the *Industrial Unionist*.[39]

This, the first IWW periodical in the Southern Hemisphere, was launched as a monthly in February 1913. A lively, attractive broadsheet, filled mainly with material reprinted from overseas Wobbly and other publications, it also featured irreverent local content. Five Wobblies, including Holdsworth and Short, collectively edited the paper.[40]

The *Industrial Unionist* (*IU*) traced local versions of international political currents, such as the policy of "boring from within" politically broader institutions. In New Zealand this debate focused on whether the Federation of Labor (later the United Federation of Labour, or UFL) should be remodeled on IWW lines, with all unions in each industry combining into a single, national industrial union, "ultimately allowing for the formation of One Big Union throughout the entire country."[41] The defeat of the Waihi strike weakened IWW influence within the FOL, which, by 1913, was routinely referred to in the *IU* as the "FOOL."[42] At the same time, the *Maoriland Worker* deplored "the malicious attempt of the employers to identify the UFL with the IWW."[43]

Although membership details are lacking, no Maori are known to have been paid-up IWW members or regular readers of the *IU*. Nor does the New Zealand IWW appear to have addressed Maori or other racial questions in its political program or the main, English-language, sections of its paper. However, many Maori must have encountered IWW agitators and workmates through their workplaces. To reach out to this barely organized section of the workforce, Short drew on his Maori-language expertise.

Maori-Language Articles

Beginning with its sixth issue, the *IU* included articles in Maori, written by Short but attributed to and evidently endorsed by the entire editorial collective. These skillfully combined traditional Maori expressions with translations of IWW propaganda. Several were followed by an appeal, also in Maori, for subscriptions to the newspaper, indicating that their purpose was active recruitment and not simply pre-emption of possible strikebreaking. Collectively, the articles amount to an embryonic Marxist economic analysis in the Maori language, using authentically Maori metaphors and cultural values:

In the past, the work of one person went towards the wellbeing of everyone, of the whole tribe. The thoughts of one were the thoughts of everyone. The people of old worked and ate together. They lived and died together. However, the custom has changed completely …. Now all the wealth belongs to the bosses: the land, the mines, the ships, the great machines, the trains and much more. All we can do is go to the people who control our belongings and beg for work. Our wealth is being stolen by the wealthy – the capitalists …. Stick together! Let us unite our thoughts! Be resolute! Be brave! Workers of the whole world, unite; you have nothing to lose, you have the world to win.[44]

Short's article in the following issue acknowledged the devastating loss of land and resources by Maori. Just as Maori had violently resisted the loss of their lands in the past, he wrote, all workers should now form a single tribe to recover and retain their possessions:

When your land has passed into the hands of the Pakeha, it has gone forever. All that remains to you are your physical bodies as an article of sale which you may sell to your master, just as though you were a horse or a dog. Therefore, rise up! Come to the rescue of your own people, and this union, the iww, will come to your assistance.[45]

In this and later articles Short appealed to Maori on their own terms, using familiar expressions, concepts and arguments such as their historical experience of land loss through questionable private sales: "Following the introduction of the musket, the land sharks arrived. Soon the bulk of your lands had been taken from you, and the sharks occupied it instead."[46] Another article summarized the Marxist theory of surplus value, indicating that Short resisted patronizing or underestimating his Maori readers.[47]

Less often, he addressed the general anxiety within the labor movement that the low-paid and casually employed Maori workforce might become strikebreakers. In September 1913, he recalled the Waihi miners' strike and deplored the actions of those Maori who had acted as strikebreakers and paid thugs.[48] Elsewhere, he likened them to those Maori who sided with the government during the Land Wars of the previous century, a comparison bound to rankle with their descendants.[49]

The 1913 Waterfront Strike

By late 1913, the vigorous Auckland iww local decided to expand its activities elsewhere in the country. Tom Barker acted as a roving emissary, riding with the tramps on railway freight cars.[50] Holdsworth says, "He went without money and was without price. But he had a bundle of potential rebels in his bag—a pile of Industrial Unionists—each one more for the Revolution."[51] Barker's journey was interrupted at Wellington by the outbreak of a waterfront strike. He promptly organized a program of speakers and music opposite the wharves, and led guerrilla attacks on parties of mounted "special constables" (untrained volunteer police reinforcements) recruited from rural districts.

The strike soon spread to other industries and other cities, and striking dock workers eventually shut down every port, paralyzing the country's export-based economy. For several days, a general strike in Auckland brought commercial activity in the city almost to a standstill. The government enlisted thousands of strikebreakers and special constables, and reinforced the regular police with armed military detachments. Historian Eric Olssen described "unprecedented scenes of violence and civil disorder in New Zealand during the 1913 strike, the most significant strike in the country's history."[52]

During the strike, production of the *IU* increased from monthly to twice weekly, with each issue urging a general strike to bring down the government. Barker said, with engaging frankness, "When we got an edition out we went down on the streets and sold it, the next day we went on the booze and the following day got the next edition out."[53]

Short managed to supply only one further Maori-language article once the strike began, urging Maori workers to join the strikers and resist appeals to act as strikebreakers and special constables:

> The leading figures of the shipping companies and the Government mean to destroy the unions of New Zealand workers, so that they can succeed in lowering their wages. The newspapers are concealing the most important point. These bosses are looking for people to act as policemen to fight us. None of you should participate in these treacherous dealings. It is disgusting work .... It was these bosses who confiscated your land, they who shot your ancestors in days gone by. This gang of thieves is your enemy – people without heart .... We are all workers together, we are ever one tribe—the tribe of workers.[54]

The same issue exulted, in English, that "The Maoris have protested against the Government enroling [sic] Maori for 'special' duty during the present industrial trouble, and pointed out that they greatly resented the acceptance of two Maoris [for this role]."[55] This likely refers to a speech given to a

Wellington strike meeting, through an interpreter, by Te Heuheu Tukino, the powerful chief of a large central North Island tribe. He said that when he heard that "members of my race" were being enrolled as special constables, he sent messages to Maori in all parts of the country, asking them:

> to refrain from participating in the present struggle, by remaining neutral and not signing on as special police. It is quite clear to us that the struggle you are fighting is for a fair and just cause, and ... that the present Government is using the same tyranny against us as they are using against you at the present time.[56]

The extent to which Short's articles contributed to this stance cannot be known. It is notable, however, that very few Maori appear to have acted as either special constables or strikebreakers in 1913.

No new Maori-language material appeared in the *IU*, whose pages instead were devoted to urgent updates on strike developments around the country. One of those, from Auckland, reported that Chinese greengrocers, whose ethnic group faced ridicule and discrimination from the white-majority population, "have been approached and it is understood that they are favourable to a proposal not to supply scab restaurants etc with greengrocery and fruit."[57]

As the strike grew more violent and widespread, the *IU* claimed a relatively enormous circulation of 5,000. Barker sold copies in the street until he was arrested and charged with sedition. The arrests of other strike leaders, and the government's recruitment of more than 10,000 strikebreakers and special constables, finally broke the strike. The *IU* ceased production at the end of November, and as in the aftermath of the Waihi strike, many Wobblies not already in jail scattered far and wide to avoid retribution.

Barker was released on a £1,500 bond, and promptly jumped bail and left for Sydney. There he, Reeves, and other New Zealand Wobblies rejoined Jack King and greatly strengthened the Australian IWW.[58] Those remaining in New Zealand disappeared into remote parts of the country to organize rural workers.[59] The outbreak of the First World War soon afterwards empowered the New Zealand government to finish the job of destroying labor militancy. All strikes in essential industries became illegal, rights of free speech and assembly were severely curtailed, and a wide range of publications were banned, including all by the IWW.[60] The government also imposed exceptionally harsh conscription laws. Some Wobblies served jail sentences for opposing conscription; others set up an escape route for conscientious objectors, smuggling them in the coalbunkers of ships to Australia, where conscription was not imposed.[61] These measures shattered the mettlesome movement that Barker, Short, and others had built up, but also saw it disperse internationally. The New Zealand IWW proved a short-lived yet resilient and adaptable organization, capable of surviving severe state repression by reforming elsewhere.

Percy Short in Europe

Short was among those who left the country, and in February 1914 he traveled to Europe.[62] He saw this trip as an opportunity to communicate with like-minded European syndicalists, an instance of IWW transnationalism extending from the world's periphery to its political centers, rather than the reverse, as is often assumed. In May 1914, he visited the Paris headquarters of the Général Confédération des Travailleurs (General Confederation of Labor, or CGT), meeting executive members Léon Jouhaux, Charles Marck (who, said Short, "had worked 18 months at the docks in London, and was an intimate friend of Ben Tillett's"), and Christiaan Cornelissen, editor of the *Bulletin international du mouvement syndicaliste*:

> They asked me a number of questions concerning the labour organisations in New Zealand and Australia, and Cornelissen made notes of my replies for publication .... They were extremely interested in my account of the class war in the Antipodes, and were jubilant with the success of the direct action propaganda. This organization has no time whatever for politics, and is very hostile to the French Socialist Party, which they said is very active just before the elections.[63]

Short was also interviewed by the anarchist archivist and historian Max Nettlau, to whom he gave a highly colored version of Maori support for revolutionary syndicalism, and of his own ethnic origins. Nettlau gained the impression that:

> our comrade is Maori by birth, the son of a native of New Zealand, the people who are more and more pushed aside but keep standing tall with extraordinary energy and endurance .... [Revolutionary syndicalist] propaganda is particularly successful amongst Maori because of the past of this people with their indigenous communism. Amongst Maori, a worker who acts as a scab and steals the bread out of their comrades' mouths is basically unheard of because their old sense of solidarity stemming from their tribal customs prohibits such actions.[64]

In the United Kingdom, Short offered public lectures, illustrated by "a splendid set of slides," on "The Maori race in New Zealand—from cannibalism to civilization." His promotional literature features, somewhat oddly, a photograph of himself as a Maori woman, with facial tattoo, pipe, and typical costume.

Post-IWW Addresses to Maori

After two years abroad Short returned to Feilding and started a family.[65] He married Annie, an Englishwoman, and they had a son, John, three years later. Although called to enlist in 1917, he managed to avoid military service.[66] Short continued working as a house painter and periodically a licensed translator, traveling to district courts to represent Maori land claimants and defendants.[67]

The pre-war revolutionary socialist movement, he observed sadly, had been eliminated:

> Craft unions had captured nearly all the militant labour unions .... The socialist movement finally became moribund. It was kept somewhat alive in theory by the formation [in 1916] of the NZ Labour Party, which finally detached itself from the everyday struggles of the mass of wage workers.[68]

The IWW itself was not resurrected, and its commitment to addressing the Maori people and their political concerns was not sustained by successor organizations on the left, despite repeated efforts by Maori themselves. An atypical exception was a Maori-language article in a 1916 issue of the newspaper of the New Zealand Waterside Workers Union, which had a significant Maori membership. Under the heavily ironic headline "Te Matau a te Pakeha" ("Pakeha wisdom"), the writer warned Maori readers not to trust such wisdom, which fattened the lazy man (the employer) while leaving the workers hungry.[69]

In 1928, a Maori delegate to a conference of the New Zealand Workers Union, the successor of the Shearers Union, urged the organization to run a regular column in the Maori language.[70] The following year, Maori executive members of the Watersiders Union suggested publishing the union rules in Maori. Nothing came of either proposal.[71] Only when Maori were thought to be at imminent risk of scabbing, it appeared, did white unionists make efforts to address Maori on equal terms.

The New Zealand Communist Party (NZCP), formed in 1921, made only cursory efforts to address Maori political concerns, despite repeated urgings from the Comintern to do so.[72] In 1935, the party finally produced a number of articles and at least one pamphlet in the Maori language.[73]

Unlike other former Wobblies who joined the NZCP and struggled to work within it, Short remained a fellow traveler, though he admired the achievements of the Soviet Union. By 1931 he had returned to his hometown of Wellington, and spent the rest of his life working as a painter and paperhanger. He became secretary of his local branch of the Friends of the Soviet Union (FSU), and tried to learn Russian.[74] In 1935, he wrote to the USSR's Acting President of the Society for Cultural Relations with Foreign Countries, requesting an official invitation for a FSU-organized delegation of Maori performers to the Soviet Union. "They are born entertainers, exceptionally fine singers in both their own and the English language."[75] Short also appealed to Maori to take part in this delegation, through a Maori-language article in the FSU newsletter *Soviet News*.[76] The prospect of Muscovites entertained by floor-shaking *haka* during the height of Stalinist purges is intriguing. However, no invitation materialized and the proposal did not proceed.[77]

Short continued to correspond with his contact within the USSR, however, hoping for support to publish his lifelong researches into traditional Maori society. His application of Marxist theory to Maori custom, he evidently hoped, would challenge the findings of authoritative ethnologists such as Lewis Henry Morgan and even Friedrich Engels:

> I believe that I am the only person who is making use of this rich ethnographical harvest and explaining its nature by the aid of dialectical materials.... The Maoris, being a communistic people, are extremely interested in your social system, and it is impossible to find a single individual who is hostile to it, especially when they are informed of the freedom enjoyed by the small nationalities within your country. They know what it means to be suppressed by an imperialist nation.[78]

Upon his death in 1944, Short left many pages of unpublished notes on *punaluan* (polygamous) marriage, cannibalism, leadership, and other features of pre-colonial Maori life. However, it is his handful of Maori-language articles for the *IU* that proved his most significant contribution.

Short's published addresses to Maori exemplify the observation that "The IWW can be seen as a precursor to today's social justice movements."[79] In sharp contrast with the pre-First World War period, many of the political concerns his articles raised, such as the historical loss of tribal lands, now stand at the center of New Zealand political life. In the country's labor movement, the nearest present-day equivalent to the Wobblies is the vig-orous and effective Unite Union, representing workers in the fast food and other minimum-wage industries. Maori and their fellow Polynesian New Zealanders are prominent within the leadership, as well as the membership, of Unite, a development which Percy Short and his fellow New Zealand Wobblies could hardly have envisaged, but one in which they would surely have rejoiced.

Notes

1 Modern written Maori generally includes the macron, a line above some vowels to indicate whether they should be pronounced in their long form. It has been de-cided not to include macrons in this chapter. To read a version of the chapter with macrons added, go to: http://libcom.org/tags/mark-derby

2 Peter Cole and Lucien van der Walt, "Crossing the color lines, crossing the con-tinents: comparing the racial politics of the iww in South Africa and the United States, 1905–1925," *Safundi* 12:1 (2011): 77.

3 Cole and van der Walt, "Crossing the color lines," pp. 69–96. See also A. Rosen-thal, "Radical border-crossers: the Industrial Workers of the World and their press in Latin America," *Estudios Interdisciplinarios de América Latina y el Caribe* 22:2 (2011): 39–70.

4 Verity Burgmann, *Revolutionary Industrial Unionism: The Industrial Workers of the World in Australia* (Cambridge: Cambridge University Press, 1995), p. 85.

5 Apart from its short-lived newspaper, no records of the New Zealand iww are known to have survived, hindering a substantial study of its activities. See however Francis Shor, "Bringing the storm: syndicalist counterpublics and the Industrial Workers of the World in New Zealand, 1908–1914," in Pat Moloney and Kerry Taylor (eds.), *On the Left: Essays on Socialism in New Zealand* (Dunedin, New Zealand: Otago University Press, 2002), pp. 59–72; Stuart Moriarty-Patten, "A world to win, a hell to lose: the Industrial Workers of the World in early twentieth century New Zealand," ma thesis, Massey University, New Zealand, 2012.

6 For access to Percy Short's unpublished papers, I am grateful to his granddaughter, Lynley Short.

7 *Te Ao Hou*, November 1973, p. 49.

8 *Feilding Star*, June 10, 1908; March 7, 1911.

9 Lynley Short, personal communication.

10 Tom Murray et al., "Towards a history of Maori and trade unions," in John E. Martin and Kerry Taylor (eds.), *Culture and the Labour Movement* (Palmerston North, New Zealand: Dunmore Press, 1991), p. 51.

11 John E. Martin, *Tatau Tatau—One Big Union Altogether: The Shearers and the Early Years of the New Zealand Workers Union* (Wellington: NZ Workers' Union, 1987), p. 8.

12 Murray et al., "Maori and trade unions," p. 51. The US iww also carried out inter-racial organizing on these grounds, termed "stomach equality" by David Roediger (quoted in Cole and van der Walt, "Crossing the color lines," p. 79).

13 Martin, *Tatau Tatau*, p. 42.

14 Martin, *Tatau Tatau*, p. 44.

15 "Maoriland" was a common alternative name for New Zealand in the late nineteenth and early twentieth centuries.

16 Handwritten account of NZSP, Percy Short unpublished papers, Short family collection.

17 Erik Olssen, *The Red Feds: Revolutionary Industrial Unionism and the New Zealand Federation of Labour 1908–1913* (Auckland, New Zealand: Oxford University Press, 1988), p. 27.

18 Olssen, *The Red Feds*, p. 17.

19 Olssen, *The Red Feds*, p. 34.

20 Olssen, *The Red Feds*, p. 66.

21 *Maoriland Worker* (hereafter *MW*), April 25, 1913.

22 Cybele Locke, "Solidarity across the 'colour' line? Maori representation in the *Maoriland Worker*, 1910–1914," *New Zealand Journal of History* 48:2 (2014): 56.

23 A. Holdsworth to H. Roth, "Biographical notes—Tom Barker,"MS-Papers- 6164–007, Turnbull Library, Wellington

24 Holdsworth and Roth, "Tom Barker."

25 Burgmann, *Revolutionary Industrial Unionism*, pp. 39, 95.

26 Holdsworth and Roth, "Tom Barker."

27 Olssen, *The Red Feds*, p. 128.

28 H. Roth, "New Zealand 'Wobblies': the story of the Industrial Workers of the World," *Here and Now* (March 1952): 6–7.

29 Burgmann, *Revolutionary Industrial Unionism*, p. 38.

30 Locke, "Solidarity," pp. 56–7.

31 *MW*, November 22, 1912; Locke, "Solidarity," pp. 57–60.

33 Locke, "Solidarity," p. 60.

34 *MW*, November 1, 1912.

35 Holdsworth and Roth, "Tom Barker."

36 H. Roth, "Biographical notes—George Phillips," MS-Papers–6164–007, Turnbull Library, Wellington.

37 Erik Olssen, "Tom Barker," in *New Zealand Dictionary of Biography*, online edn., www.dnzb.govt.nz/dnzb.

38 P. Short to N. Kulyabko, March 31, 1935, Percy Short unpublished papers, Short family collection.

39 Holdsworth and Roth, "Tom Barker."

40 *Industrial Unionist* (hereafter *IU*), February 1, 1913.

41 Olssen, *The Red Feds*, pp. 134–5.

42 *IU*, March 1, 1913.

43 *MW*, December 10, 1913.

44 *IU*, July 13, 1913. This and other extracts from Maori-language articles translated by Mark Derby.

45 *IU*, August 1, 1913.

46 *IU*, October 1, 1913.

47 *IU*, August 1, 1913.

48 *IU*, September 1, 1913.

49 *IU*, August 1, 1913.

50 *IU*, August 1, 1913.

51 Holdsworth and Roth, "Tom Barker."

52 Olssen, *The Red Feds*, p. 41. See also Melanie Nolan (ed.), *Revolution: The 1913 Great Strike in New Zealand* (Christchurch, New Zealand: Canterbury University Press, 2006).

53 Eric Fry (ed.), *Tom Barker and the IWW* (Canberra: Australian Society for the Study of Labour History, 1965), p. 13.

54 *IU*, November 13, 1913. This article reappeared unchanged in a later issue (November 20, 1913), suggesting the extreme pressure of work on the editorial team.

55 *IU*, November 13, 1913.

56 *MW*, December 10, 1913.

57 *IU*, November 15, 1913.

58 Burgmann, *Revolutionary Industrial Unionism*, p. 85 *et passim*.

59 Martin, *Tatau Tatau*, p. 49.

60 Jared Davidson, *Sewing Freedom: Philip Josephs, Transnationalism and Early New Zealand Anarchism* (Oakland, Calif.: AK Press, 2011), pp. 126–133.

61 *MW*, September 21, 1921. Former Auckland IWW member Bob Heffron fled to Australia, where he later became Labor Premier of New South Wales.

62 *Direct Action* (Australia), February 15, 1915.

63 "My trip to Paris," Percy Short unpublished papers, Short family collection.

64 "A conversation with a syndicalist from New Zealand," file 3424, Max Nettlau Papers, International Institute of Social History (Amsterdam). Translation by Urs Signer.

65 *Feilding Star*, October 30, 1915.

66 *Feilding Star*, March 13, 1917.

67 Lynley Short, personal communication.

68 Handwritten account of NZSP, Percy Short unpublished papers, Short family collection.

69 Murray et al., "Maori and trade unions," p. 55.

70 Murray et al., "Maori and trade unions," p. 52.

71 Murray et al., "Maori and trade unions," p. 56.

72 Kerry Taylor, "'Potential allies of the working class': the Communist Party of New Zealand and Maori, 1921–1952," in Moloney and Taylor, *On the Left*, p. 108.

73 Taylor, "'Potential allies of the working class'," p. 106.

74 Lynley Short, personal communication.

75 P. Short to N. Kulyabko, March 31, 1935, Percy Short unpublished papers, Short family collection.

76 *Soviet News* (July 1935), p. 19.

77 FSU minutes, Percy Short unpublished papers, Short family collection.

78 P. Short to N. Kulyabko, June 20, 1935, Percy Short unpublished papers, Short family collection.

79 Cole and van der Walt, "Crossing the color lines," p. 7.

12

Patrick Hodgens Hickey and the IWW: A Transnational Relationship

Peter Clayworth

Patrick Hodgens Hickey (1882–1930) was a transnational labor agitator whose relationship with the Industrial Workers of the World (IWW) strongly influenced his development as an activist. His early career as a radical ran parallel to the birth and growth of the IWW. Hickey was a New Zealander who adopted socialism and revolutionary industrial unionism while working as an itinerant miner in the United States. His "conversion" took place in mid-1905, just as the IWW was being founded. Hickey came to prominence from 1907 to 1914 as a militant leader of a major workers' revolt against New Zealand's compulsory arbitration laws. He then worked as a union organizer and anti-conscription campaigner in Australia during the First World War. The IWW became an important force in the New Zealand and Australian labor movements over the same period. This chapter outlines Hickey's changing relationship with the IWW, tracing his evolution from an ally into a bitter opponent of the Wobblies.

The Western Federation of Miners (WFM) was one of the major initiators behind the foundation of the IWW in June 1905. Around the time of the founding conference in Chicago, Pat Hickey arrived at Bingham Canyon, Utah. Finding work as a copper miner, he joined WFM Local 67, beginning a long career as a union activist. Hickey grew up in New Zealand's rural backcountry and first came to the United States in 1900. Traveling as a hobo, he worked in the American West's mines and smelters. Back in New Zealand in 1901, Hickey became a coal miner at Denniston. He returned to the United States in 1903, after visiting Ireland. Working his way across the continent, Hickey ended up in Utah. Up to that time he had shown little interest in unions or socialism.[1]

Hickey joined the WFM immediately after the Colorado "Labor Wars" of 1903–4. The union had been driven out of Colorado after bitter, violent strikes at Cripple Creek and Telluride. Hickey met veterans of these struggles at Bingham Canyon. He wholeheartedly adopted the WFM view that workers must organize along class-conscious lines to win the class war. Defeat in Colorado also compelled the WFM to take a leading role in founding the IWW. On May 20, 1905, Local 67 voted its approval of the upcoming Chicago convention and any new organization formed there. Local 67 supported Bingham Canyon IWW Local 93 from its formation in late 1905, until its disbanding in 1909. Historian Philip Mellinger describes Local 93 as a "dependency" of WFM Local 67. This close relationship may explain why Local 67 ignored the 1907 WFM national conference decision to cut all ties with the IWW.[2]

In September 1905, Hickey left Bingham Canyon to avoid the Utah winter, armed with a new commitment to the class struggle and socialism. He advocated revolutionary industrial unionism and political action through the vehicle of a socialist party. These beliefs have prompted some commentators to suggest Hickey followed the ideas of Daniel De Leon. Most likely, however, Hickey's industrial and political views developed from his experiences living and working in western mining towns rather than from De Leon's theories. Hickey respected De Leon as a socialist but also admired Eugene V. Debs, leader of the Socialist Party of America (SPA). In 1902, the WFM had officially endorsed socialism and the SPA. Hickey followed the WFM policy of combining political and industrial action, and he joined the SPA rather than its rival, De Leon's Socialist Labor Party.[3]

When Hickey returned home in 1906, New Zealand had been under a compulsory arbitration system since 1895, with no major industrial disputes since 1893. Conciliation boards and an arbitration court settled disputes, while lockouts by employers and strikes by registered unions were illegal. Hickey's return coincided with growing worker resentment over the arbitration system's perceived failure to deal with inflation. From February to June 1908, Hickey took a leading role in an illegal strike by the Blackball Miners' Union, directly challenging the arbitration system. After winning the strike, Hickey and fellow socialists Robert Semple and Paddy Webb organized the New Zealand Federation of Miners, an industrial federation modeled on the WFM. Hickey and other militants urged member unions to cancel their registration under the arbitration system and take direct action through the federation. In 1910, the newly renamed New Zealand Federation of Labour (NZFL) expanded to include all unions who wished to join. The NZFL soon became known as the "Red Feds."[4]

Canadian agitator H. M. Fitzgerald first founded a short-lived IWW branch in Wellington in 1907, but the IWW only really became a force in New Zealand after 1911. This followed the arrival in Auckland of a group of Vancouver Wobblies, including labor agitator J. B. (John Benjamin, or "Jack") King. They advocated Chicago IWW principles and opposed those of De Leon's "Detroit IWW." This meant the Vancouver Wobblies rejected electoral politics, arguing instead that workers should concentrate on industrial organization. They recruited local Auckland activists, including former New Zealand Socialist Party (NZSP) member Tom Barker (see de Angelis, Chapter 16), and began spreading industrial unionist propaganda.[5]

The IWW influence on the militant wing of New Zealand's labor movement reached its peak in 1912. A number of Wobblies, including King, attended the 1912 NZFL annual conference. By this time the NZFL included miners, longshore workers, general laborers, tramways workers, shearers, brewery workers, gas stokers, and flax mill workers. The 1912 conference voted unanimously to reorganize as a national industrial union along IWW lines. It also approved Hickey's motion to adopt a version of the IWW preamble. The Red Feds were co-opting IWW organizing principles rather than actively supporting the official IWW. The federation remained open to electoral politics, a position the Wobblies strongly opposed after 1908. Hickey had been an NZSP parliamentary candidate in the 1911 election and supported the NZFL's political stance. The new NZFL constitution was supposed to come into force in January 1913, but its adoption was derailed by events at the gold mining town of Waihi.[6]

The powerful Waihi Miners' Union, an NZFL affiliate, went on strike in May 1912, after the Waihi Gold Mining Company helped establish a breakaway, pro-arbitration Engine Drivers' Union (see Derby, Chapter 11). In July 1912, the Reform Party, strong supporters of farming and business interests, took power in New Zealand. The new prime minister, William Ferguson Massey, authorized mass police intervention in Waihi, while the company recruited "free laborers" who doubled as vigilantes. J. B. King, Waihi's IWW organizer, fled to Australia as repression closed in on the mining town. Hickey traveled around Australia from July to December, touring the mining towns raising funds for the Waihi strikers. By the time he returned to New Zealand, police and vigilante violence had crushed the Waihi strike.[7]

The struggle exacerbated tensions between the NZFL and moderate unions. The moderates refused to support the strike, arguing it was an inter-union dispute. State-sanctioned violence at Waihi shocked moderates and militants, leading both groups to reassess their positions. The NZFL

Miners' Hall, Runanga, circa 1910 (1/2-179351-G). Courtesy of the Alexander Turnbull Library, Wellington, New Zealand.

abandoned its iww-influenced constitution, instead opening unity negotiations with moderate unions. Hickey acted as an organizer for the Unity Campaign, serving as secretary of the Unity Conferences held in January and July 1913.[8]

The iww refused to participate in the Unity Conferences. They believed the proposed new federation structure would be dominated by professional union leaders, watered down by the inclusion of moderate unions, and flawed by promoting political action. The Wobblies particularly objected to federation executive control of the strike weapon, an idea Hickey defended. At the July 1913 Unity Congress, the old NZFL combined with a number of moderate unions, forming the United Federation of Labor (UFL). The UFL dropped the iww preamble and organizational system. Hickey was elected UFL secretary-treasurer, with his old comrade Bob Semple as organizer. A new political organization, the Social Democratic Party (SDP), was also created at the Unity Conference. The iww dismissed the UFL and the SDP as organizations of "professional labor spongers and reactionary craft officials." Hickey, a professional labor organizer, became more ideologically separated from the iww, as he increasingly favored political action. Police violence at Waihi had convinced him workers must gain control of the state's coercive structures through the ballot box.[9]

In October 1913, the Great Strike broke out (see Derby, Chapter 11). A coal miners' strike at Huntly and a longshore workers' strike in Wellington escalated into a nationwide strike of maritime workers, miners, and seamen. For employers, farmers, and Massey's government, the dispute was an opportunity to force unions out of the UFL and back into the arbitration system. Strike supporters and special constables fought armed street battles in Wellington, while Auckland experienced a brief general strike. The Great Strike was broken in December 1913, as first the seamen and then the longshore workers went back to work. The mining unions held out until January 1914. The UFL was weakened by the strike, with many unions leaving the federation. Hickey and Semple lost their UFL organizing jobs and became subject to employers' blacklists. The IWW strongly supported the strike, with Tom Barker among those arrested for sedition. Following the strike's defeat many Wobblies, including Barker, departed for Australia. After war was declared in August 1914, Wobblies still in New Zealand were subjected to surveillance, censorship, and arrest.[10]

Hickey strongly opposed the First World War and became frustrated by the splits it initially created in New Zealand's labor movement. A blacklisted militant with a family to support, he eventually took a job laboring on a backcountry government road gang. In November 1915, Hickey left for Australia with his wife Rose and two-year-old son, Patrick Jr. Hickey feared New Zealand would introduce conscription and believed job prospects would be better across the Tasman. He found work as an organizer for the Victorian Railways Union and joined the Victorian Socialist Party, Australian Labor Party, and One Big Union campaign. From 1919 to 1920 he worked as an organizer and newspaper editor for the Queensland Railways Union. Hickey and Rose both worked as anti-conscription activists during the conscription referenda of 1916 and 1917.[11]

The Australian IWW campaigned against the war and for industrial unionism, with Barker and King as two of its most visible activists. Despite holding similar beliefs on war and industrial organization, Hickey now bitterly opposed the IWW. He took up a successful libel case against the Australian prime minister, W. M. Hughes, who had accused him of being a Wobbly. Yet Hickey defended Tom Barker, imprisoned for printing a seditious cartoon. He described Barker as "too good and too loyal a member of his class to be caged in a Bastille."[12]

Hickey became convinced that IWW attacks on union officials and supporters of political action seriously threatened Australian working-class solidarity. He responded with an anti-IWW pamphlet, *Solidarity or Sectionalism?*, published by the Australian Workers' Union in 1918. Hickey based *Solidarity or Sectionalism?* on material he had received from the United States. He repeated accusations the WFM had made against the

IWW, along with criticisms of the Wobblies from American socialists such as Debs, De Leon, and William Trautmann, who had left the IWW in 1912. Hickey continued to admire the WFM and the American socialists. His attack against a younger generation of militants could be seen as the response of an older generation still claiming the right to define industrial unionism. Hickey refused to acknowledge that IWW ideas and actions were not far removed from his own early militancy. It is not clear what impact *Solidarity or Sectionalism?* had on the labor movement, but labor's opponents seized on it as evidence of disunity in the workers' ranks.[13]

Hickey returned to New Zealand in 1920, renewing his activism in the labor movement and New Zealand Labour Party. He continued to promote industrial unionism but now as a labor journalist, Labour Party activist, and union official rather than a militant agitator. Following a series of setbacks in both the industrial and political fields, Hickey became disillusioned with the New Zealand labor movement. He and his family moved back to Victoria, Australia, in 1926, where he managed hotels and renewed his activities with the ALP. He was selected as an ALP state parliamentary candidate in 1929, but retired from the electoral contest due to a head injury. He died from the resulting brain damage in 1930.[14]

The period of Hickey's militant labor activities, from 1905 through 1920, ran parallel to the birth, growth, and repression of the IWW in the United States, New Zealand, and Australia. Hickey's introduction to revolutionary industrial unionism and socialism came through the WFM, the union that helped found the IWW. His early militancy and general sympathy with the IWW reflected his time as an itinerant miner and convert to revolutionary industrial unionism and socialism. While actively involved in building the NZFL, Hickey became interested in IWW organizational ideas, which apparently showed a way of creating a militant industrial federation from a range of occupational unions. At the same time, Hickey's belief in political action contradicted the Chicago IWW's anti-political principles. Hickey's developing career as a union organizer brought him under attack from the Wobblies, a rift that was deepened by his work in creating the UFL. The defeats of the Waihi Strike and 1913 Great Strike seem to have dampened Hickey's belief in direct action, whereas Tom Barker and J. B. King remained enthusiastic direct action advocates. By the time he first moved to Australia, Hickey was convinced the Wobblies were a disruptive element in the labor movement. He now thought the class war could be won through established union organizations and working-class party politics. This set him completely at odds with the IWW, who still believed in rejecting electoral politics and labor leaders in favor of direct action by workers themselves.

Notes

1   John Weir, "The 'Red' Feds: P. H. Hickey and the Red Federation of Labour," unpublished manuscript, c.1970, pp. 28–50, MS 119, John Weir Papers, Acc 664, Macmillan-Brown Library, University of Canterbury, New Zealand; Erik Olssen, "Hickey, Patrick Hodgens," in *Dictionary of New Zealand Biography*, www.TeAra.govt.nz/en/biographies/3h22/1 (accessed June 30, 2016).

2   Vernon Jensen, *Heritage of Conflict: Labor Relations in the Non-Ferrous Metals Industry Up to 1930* (Ithaca, N.Y.: Cornell University Press, 1950), pp. 118–96; Elizabeth Jameson, *All That Glitters: Class, Conflict and Community in Cripple Creek* (Urbana, Ill.: University of Illinois Press, 1998), pp. 199–225; Melvyn Dubofsky, *We Shall be All: A History of the IWW* (New York: Quadrangle, 1969), pp. 76–87; Francis Shor, "Left labor agitators in the Pacific Rim of the early twentieth century," *International Labor and Working Class History* 67 (April 2005): 152; Philip Mellinger, "How the IWW lost its Western heartland: Western labor history revisited," *Western History Quarterly* 27:3 (1996): 310.

3   Patrick Hodgens Hickey to Mary Jane Hickey, November 20, 1905, Eileen Thawley Collection (hereafter ETC). I must thank Pat Hickey's relatives Eileen Thawley, Noelene McNair, and John Weir for allowing me access to their collections. Norman Jeffrey, "My estimate of Bob Ross and Pat Hickey," in Herbert Roth, Patrick Hodgens Hickey biographical notes, MS-Papers-6164–035, Roth papers, Alexander Turnbull Library (hereafter ATL), National Library of New Zealand; Francis Shor, "Bringing the storm: syndicalist counterpublics and the Industrial Workers of the World in New Zealand, 1908–1914," in Pat Moloney and Kerry Taylor (eds.), *On the Left: Essays on Socialism in New Zealand* (Dunedin, New Zealand: Otago University Press, 2002), pp. 63–4; Patrick Hodgens Hickey, *"Red" Fed Memoirs: Being a Brief Survey of the Birth and Growth of the Federation of Labour from 1908 to 1915* (Wellington: New Zealand Worker Print, 1925), pp. 6, 9; John Enyeart, *The Quest for "Just and Pure Law": Rocky Mountain Workers and American Social Democracy, 1870–1924* (Stanford, Calif.: Stanford University Press, 2009), pp. 138–44; Jameson, *All that Glitters*, pp. 161–3, 194–6.

4   James Holt, *Compulsory Arbitration in New Zealand: The First Forty Years* (Auckland, New Zealand: Auckland University Press, 1986), pp. 33–70; Hickey, *"Red" Fed Memoirs*; E. Olssen, *The Red Feds: Revolutionary Industrial Unionism and the New Zealand Federation of Labour, 1908–1913* (Auckland, New Zealand: Oxford University Press, 1988).

5   Olssen, *Red Feds*, pp. 4, 17; Peter Steiner, *Industrial Unionism: The Industrial Workers of the World in Aotearoa* (Wellington: Rebel Press, 2007), pp. 2–4. Eric Fry (ed.), *Tom Barker and the IWW* (Brisbane, Qld: Industrial Workers of the World, 1999), pp. 12–13; Alec Holdsworth to Herbert Roth, July 18, 1961, in MS-Papers-6164–120, Roth papers, ATL.

6   New Zealand Federation of Labor, *Report of Proceedings, Fourth Conference, 23 May to 6 June 1912* (Wellington: *Maoriland Worker*, 1912), pp. 3–4, 56–58, 75.

7   Philip Rainer, "Company town: an industrial history of the Waihi Gold Mining Company, Ltd, 1887–1912," MA thesis, University of Auckland, 1976; Olssen, *Red Feds*, pp. 132–4, 148–60; Hickey, *"Red" Fed Memoirs*, pp. 53–6.

8   Hickey, *"Red" Fed Memoirs*, pp. 56–74; Olssen, *Red Feds*, pp. 163–79.

9 *Industrial Unionist*, February 1, March 1, April 1, June 1, July 1, August 1, September 1, 1913; *Maoriland Worker*, October 25, December 13, December 20, 1912, March 21, 1913.

10 Melanie Nolan (ed.), *Revolution: The 1913 Great Strike in New Zealand* (Christchurch, New Zealand: Canterbury University Press, 2005); Olssen, *Red Feds*, pp. 180–209; Fry, *Tom Barker*, pp. 13–18. On the repression of the Wobblies, see Jared Davidson, *Remains to Be Seen: Tracing Joe Hill's Ashes in New Zealand* (Wellington: Rebel Press, 2011).

11 Patrick Hodgens Hickey to Mary Jane Hickey, n.d. [1915], November 18, 1915, November 19, 1916, January [?], 1918, ETC; Weir, "Red Feds," pp. 321–40.

12 Verity Burgmann, *Revolutionary Industrial Unionism: The Industrial Workers of the World in Australia* (Cambridge/Melbourne: Cambridge University Press, 1995), pp. 180–245; *Railways Union Gazette*, July 1917, August 1917; Patrick Hodgens Hickey to Mary Jane Hickey, May 12, 1917, ETC; *Labor Call*, May 11, 1916.

13 *The Argus*, July 19, 1917; Patrick Hodgens Hickey, *Solidarity or Sectionalism? A Plea for Unity* (Brisbane, Qld.: Worker Newspaper Proprietary, 1918), pp. 10–20; Leader, April 18, 1919; *Sydney Morning Herald*, March 10, 1919; *Evening Post*, April 14, 1919.

14 Weir, "Red Feds," pp. 348–67.

13

"The Cause of the Workers Who Are Fighting in Spain Is Yours": The Marine Transport Workers and the Spanish Civil War

Matthew C. White

With the precipitous decline of the Industrial Workers of the World (IWW) in the 1920s, many Wobblies looked to Spain, the Confederación Nacional del Trabajo (National Confederation of Labor or CNT), and the international labor organization to which the CNT belonged, the International Working Men's Association (IWA, also sometimes referred to as the IWMA) as models to rebuild around. When the Spanish Civil War began in 1936, IWW members saw not only the workers' revolution they dreamed of but also a battle against the fascism that they saw spreading around the world, including the United States. Not surprisingly, given their preference for direct action and a millenarian view of the revolution and war in Spain, many Wobblies, mainly sailors, volunteered to fight in Spain. Sadly, though, the cream of the new generation of the IWW's Marine Transport Workers Industrial Union No. 510 (MTW) were either killed or wounded there. Furthermore, the experience of Spain exacerbated the already toxic relationship between Wobblies and Communists which pushed Wobbly seamen into the Sailors Union of the Pacific (SUP), which eventually subsumed much of the MTW. For IWW sailors in the 1930s, Spain was the life of the MTW—and, for many, their own grave.

The IWW in Decline

The IWW entered the 1930s in a sharp decline that began in the mid-1920s.

In 1925, emerging from the so-called Emergency Program split, the IWW had at least 16,970 members, but five years later, it had only 2,300.[1] More than any other factor, the 1924 split triggered an exodus from the IWW that deprived the union of resources, which in turn further hastened the departure of members. By 1932, the IWW stood on the precipice of ruin with barely a thousand members and $29 on hand.[2] While MTW 510 also hemorrhaged members, the sailors remained the only element of the IWW with a significant presence in their industry.[3]

The sailors of the Marine Transport Workers had a singular history within the IWW and US sailors' unions in general. The MTW's early base of strength was among Spanish and Latin American sailors who came to the union in 1913 after abandoning the International Seamen's Union (ISU) because of its anti-immigrant, racist policies. These sailors gave the MTW a cross-cultural, evangelical, anarcho-syndicalist cast (see Alonso, Chapter 5) which continued into the 1940s. From the 1910s to the early 1930s, the MTW spread the IWW to Mexico, Chile, Uruguay, and elsewhere in Latin America, as well as Germany and Sweden.[4] By the 1930s, ships' "black gangs"—those who stoked a steamship's boilers and typically were covered in coal dust, oil, or grease—were largely "Americanized," with a resulting drop in Spanish and Latin American sailors. However, their legacy continued to influence a new generation of US-born, typically white sailors. Tommy Ray, a future Communist, joined the IWW after encountering a ship's black gang, characteristically made up of Spanish sailors, singing Wobbly songs, in 1924.[5] Crew lists reveal significant overlap between Spanish sailors of the 1920s and non-Spanish Wobblies of the 1930s.

Like their fellow deep-water sailors, IWW sailors traveled extensively and found themselves in situations few other Americans did. Future Wobbly International Brigades volunteer Robert Charles Watts, for example, served in the Mexican Army during the Cristero War in the late 1920s.[6] The effect of such socialization led sailors like Harry Lundeberg to join anarcho-syndicalist unions abroad, including the Argentine Federación Obrera Marítima and the CNT.[7] By the early 1930s, it also led some IWW members, particularly sailors, to look to Spain and affiliation with the CNT and IWA to reenergize their own moribund organization.

Meanwhile, in 1934, after many attempts to rebuild the union in Philadelphia, Detroit, and elsewhere, IWW organizers finally found a foothold in Cleveland.[8] By the mid-1930s, the sailors and the Cleveland group had become the two most powerful elements of the IWW, but they stood at odds with each other because the anarcho-syndicalists of the MTW typically opposed contracts, while the Cleveland group, led by socialists of various stripes, did not oppose signing agreements with employers.[9] The sailors accused the Clevelanders and national headquarters of unresponsiveness to their needs. When the MTW attempted to organize workers in Puerto Rico in 1934, the slow reaction of the Chicago headquarters stymied their efforts. This and similar incidents convinced sailors of the necessity of affiliation with the IWA to prevent future failures.[10]

The sailors no longer believed the IWW to be a viable international organization.[11] MTW militant and future International Brigades volunteer Harry F. Owens lost patience with those who argued that the IWW could not affiliate with the IWA because the IWW itself organized internationally. Owens, a Philadelphia-born sailor who joined the IWW in 1921 at the age of 18, worked to reinvigorate the IWW's radicalism and organizing attempts. He argued that "just because we take in every nationality does not make us international." Owens reckoned that to help build a truly international organization that could compete against capital and the Communists, the IWW must affiliate with the IWA and the CNT. Owens continued, "we are not dogmatic and are living in a revolutionary age. The IWMA has millions of members [mainly in Spain, as Owens pointed out]. The IWW will get lots of prestige and members from this affiliation. Let's have One Big Union the world over and crush capitalism before it crushes us."[12] Owens articulated an idea that became more powerful in the ensuing years: that the CNT's notoriety and strength would ultimately lead to a rejuvenated IWW. Ultimately, the Cleveland group nullified a successful vote for affiliation with the IWA with another vote, further deepening the enmity between both groups (see Thorpe, Chapter 6).

Wobbly–Communist Acrimony

The animosity between the Clevelanders and sailors, however, paled in comparison to the hatred that developed between Wobblies and the Communist Party of the United States (CPUSA). The toxic relationship stretched back to 1920 and the so-called "Philadelphia controversy," and the IWW's refusal to affiliate with the Profintern. By the middle of the 1920s, evidence emerged of Communists attempting to subvert the IWW, and in 1926 a Communist attempt to take over the MTW failed.[13] When it became apparent that the MTW was not going to become an appendage of the CPUSA, and with international communism entering the so-called Third Period, the Communists founded their own Maritime Workers Industrial Union (MWIU), largely based on Wobbly principles. For the entirety of the 1930s, usually in the pages of the MWIU's newspaper, Communist waterfront organizers and cadres battled MTW members. But while many Communist leaders despised the Wobblies and vice versa, many rank and file Communists remained sympathetic to the IWW.

Most Communist critiques of the MTW had little to do with MTW strategy, and instead mocked IWW pretensions of being a mass union when many Wobblies seemed content to sit in their halls and debate philosophy.[14] Such critiques also rang true for Wobblies like Harry Owens. If only "Hall cats had put their shoulder to the wheel, we would have a parade all by ourselves with millions of members," he charged. Instead, organizations such as the MWIU seemed to thrive.[15] Owens and his circle of Wobbly sailors refused to let the "revolutionary age" pass them and the MTW by.

The MTW in the Mid-1930s

When the West Coast maritime union resurgence began in 1934, the IWW still had a dual card presence in longshore and sailor unions. For example, Wobblies played a crucial role in rebuilding the Sailors Union of the Pacific (SUP). SUP leader Harry Lundeberg, a longtime syndicalist and possibly an IWW member at one time, began tailoring the SUP to the IWW because of the strong Wobbly sentiment among many members. Wobbly sailors, in turn, supported the SUP and Lundeberg, who would eventually call on them in his ideologically tinged turf war against the International Longshore and Warehouse Union (ILWU), National Maritime Union (NMU), and CPUSA, discussed below.[16] During the last years of the 1930s, the SUP newspaper printed both the SUP and IWW card numbers of contributors, and a number of SUP leaders were dual-carders, such as Lloyd "Sam" Usinger, who would run the blockade to deliver materials to Republican Spain during the war.[17] The IWW's relationships with both the SUP and the Communists also spilled over into Spain, and would reverberate back again to the United States.

While West Coast Wobblies seemed content to build up the SUP in lieu of making the MTW a single-card union, East Coast Wobblies pursued a different strategy. In the Gulf Coast ports of Texas, the MTW remained the only viable sailor's union in the first half of the 1930s.[18] On the Atlantic Coast—particularly Philadelphia, Baltimore, New York, and Boston—the MTW still boasted a sizable membership. Because of the corruption of the International Seamen's Union (ISU) and the void created by the Communists after disbanding the MWIU in 1935 in favor of boring from within the ISU, the MTW saw a chance to become a major sailors' union again. MTW members continued "quickie" strikes to better conditions, and in 1934 more ambitiously called port-wide strikes, thereby demonstrating their power on the Gulf.[19] By the middle of 1936, the ISU sat on its deathbed and the MTW seemed poised to fill this vacuum.

Not coincidentally, MTW efforts coincided with the Popular Front. In 1934, with the arrival of the Popular Front, relations softened between Communists and Wobblies on the East Coast. While the organizations' leaders continued hating each other, the waterfront section of the Communist Party earnestly began to recruit ex-Wobblies. Party leaders noted, to their chagrin, that many waterfront members were "anarchists."[20] Incredibly, many long-time Wobblies joined the CPUSA in these years, even as they continued to be loyal members of the IWW. Future Wobbly International Brigades volunteers, including James O. Yates, Bernard Spaulding, and Virgil Morris, all joined the CPUSA at this time.[21] Briefly, at least, East Coast maritime IWW members and Communists shared a common purpose: turning the wreckage of the ISU into a fighting industrial union. After July 19, 1936, waterfront Wobblies and Communists shared another goal, namely supporting the Spanish Popular Front against fascism.

Spain, the Strike of 1936, and the MTW's Resurgence

On the waterfront, the MTW did all it could to support revolutionary Spain. Rank-and-file Communists in Philadelphia in turn supported the MTW's actions. In September 1936, IWW sailors led by Harry F. Owens struck a ship carrying explosives for Fascist Spain. The shipping company and the ISU were taken aback by the strikers' show of solidarity with the Spanish people. According to Owens, "the captain of the ship asked the sailors 'what have you fellows to do with the Spanish workers?' The crew responded, 'they are workers, and we are workers, and an injury to one is an injury to all'."[22] As a strike leaflet informed their fellow workers, "the cause of the workers who are fighting in Spain is yours."[23] Presumably the sailors hoped that some of the CNT's prestige might rub off on the IWW. Eventually the ISU shipped scabs down from New York to break the strike, but unlike in past actions, Communists did not interfere on the ISU's behalf because they likely supported the strikers.

After the West Coast waterfront strike of 1934, East Coast longshore workers and sailors eventually agreed to strike again to boost the sailors' conditions and wages. The International Longshoremen's Association (ILA) and SUP agreed to walk out in late October 1936. Renegade ISU members and the MTW hoped to go out with them in order to tie East Coast wages and conditions to those of the West Coast and, importantly, to challenge the dominance of the floundering ISU and ILA. When the strike began in early November, the heads of the ISU and ILA told the press and government that the strike was illegal and strikers should be arrested by local authorities. These unions' leaders believed this to be a fight to the death, and so took any and all measures to defeat their opponents.[24]

In Philadelphia and several Gulf Coast ports the MTW led the strike. This strike, as sailor Fred Hansen later argued, proved the last chance for the MTW to establish itself as a major sailors' union. Hansen remembered, "I was in Philly and the sentiment for the IWW was great."[25] On November 1, Wobblies started picketing and calling on ships to strike. By the end of the day nearly every ship in Philadelphia was crewless, and Wobblies convinced ILA longshore workers (many of them former IWW members) to walk off as well.[26] On November 2, Mayor Samuel Davis Wilson declared the strike "outlaw and illegal" and ordered the strikers arrested. The police targeted the so-called "ringleader" of the strike and arrested Harry Owens, as well as ten other Wobblies.[27] Owens received 30 days in jail. A day later, three sailors' unions, some affiliated with the AFL, told the mayor that they had authorized the strike, and Mayor Wilson relented. One of the protesting organizations was the Ship Cleaners' Union of Philadelphia, led by Wobbly and Communist Virgil Morris.[28] The Popular Front had actually helped Wobblies.

But with the government, police, shippers, the ISU, and the ILA united against the Wobbly-led strikers, violence soon broke out in Philadelphia. The shippers and spurned unions hired private detective agencies, which worked in tandem with police to break the strike. Hired goons began roughing up strikers. In one instance, Burns Detective agents attempted to kidnap strikers, successfully grabbing one and prodding him into a car with a pistol. IWW onlookers rushed the agents, who shot at the Wobblies. On the scene, IWW member and future International Brigades volunteer Fred Miller asked the police if the Burns shooters were also Philadelphia cops. The cops responded affirmatively, to which Miller replied, "You are liars. This car has New Jersey license plates."[29] When Walter Dickey, an ISU agent in Houston, killed Johnny Kane, a young IWW militant and delegate, Dickey got off with a slap on the wrist.[30] This violence was nothing new to older Wobblies used to this level of collusion between the government, capital, and rival unions, but to younger strikers their concerted action came as a shock. The lack of justice infuriated the strikers and suggested to them that fascism was not merely a European problem.

Eventually, the combined weight of the opposition defeated the strikers. Most supporting unions backed away, sometimes with Communist prodding, but not Virgil Morris's Cleaners' Union.[31] Meanwhile, news from Spain ran side by side with strike news in the left and labor press, striking a deep chord with the sailors. Wobblies and Communists alike, frustrated by what they perceived as the rise of fascism in the United States but heartened by the prospect of a revolution in Spain that could provide an alternative to both fascism and capitalism, began to see the Spanish conflict as the most important of their generation. If they could not win this strike and beat fascism in the United States, they could defeat it in Spain. As Harry Owens wrote, it was "the workers in Spain who are fighting the fight of the world-wide working class! If we don't [win] we will have to fight the same black beast of reaction here."[32]

Wobblies and the Spanish Civil War

In the latter part of 1936, the CPUSA began to recruit volunteers to fight in Spain. The waterfront section of the CPUSA proved particularly successful at recruiting from the ranks of "outlaw" strikers as the strike began to falter. This first group included a number of Wobbly sailors, including Virgil Morris and Ray Steele. Regardless of the political persuasion of individual sailors, they did not lose their group integrity. With their love of direct action and ultra-masculine culture, sailors flocked to fight in Spain. There, they made up the bulk of several companies and influenced the political culture of the predominantly "American" International Brigades units such as the Lincoln Battalion, Washington Battalion, MacKenzie-Papineau Battalion, 2nd Squadron of the 1st Transportation Regiment, John Brown Battery, and an assortment of smaller units.[33] The Popular Front thaw that led Communists to unite with Wobblies in Philadelphia continued in Spain.

When the first contingent of the Lincoln Battalion arrived in Spain in early January 1937, a few Wobbly sailors were already there serving in anarchist militias.[34] Later, several Canadian Wobblies, including one sailor, went to Spain and joined the International Shock Battalion of the Durruti Column, but by far the greatest number of American Wobblies served in the International Brigades.[35] The IWW's presence in a Communist-controlled organization must appear strange given the general toxicity of the Communist–Wobbly relationship and the IWW's affinity for the CNT, but the IWW was not in a position to raise its own unit of volunteers. When the Socialist Party began recruiting its own Eugene V. Debs Column, in competition with the Communists, some Wobblies joined this more ideologically friendly organization, including anarchist and occasional sailor Pat Read and Mike Raddock.[36] When they arrived in Paris in February

American sailors in the Lincoln Battalion, Jamara, Spain, 1937. The man holding the newspaper is IWW member Bernard Spaulding; standing third from the right is fellow Wobbly Virgil Morris. Courtesy of the Abraham Lincoln Brigade Archives, Tamiment Library, New York University.

1937, they found the Debs Column stillborn, so reluctantly they joined the Communist effort. Later, when Wobbly construction worker Ivan A. Silverman was killed in Spain, his obituary noted he joined the International Brigades "with the knowledge that it was Commie dominated but at that time it seemed to be the only way of getting over there fast."[37] Indeed, for many Americans eager to get to Spain, the International Brigades remained their only choice. With few exceptions, the Debs Column volunteers and the sailors were the only Wobblies who went to Spain who did not hide their IWW membership. By contrast, many other Wobblies sensed their politics might not be popular among their Communist comrades.[38] Hiding one's dissenting politics in the American units of the International Brigades initially was unnecessary because of the diverse political culture within them, but still reasonable considering the speed at which tensions between Communists and their opponents on the left heated up in early 1937.

Spain became the latest flashpoint of conflict between the IWW and CPUSA. The IWW supported the CNT and the revolution that the Spanish anarchists were staging there. When the Communist Party's line turned against the CNT's revolution, party members fought a propaganda battle and more than a few physical street battles with CNT supporters in the United States.[39] To win the propaganda battle against the Communists and support the revolution in Spain, various American anarchist and socialist groups founded the United Libertarian Organizations (ULO), which produced the newspaper *Spanish Revolution*.[40] The MTW helped found the ULO, and as one of the major constituents, many MTW members attended ULO conferences and served in its leadership. Fresh from the defeat of the 1936–37 strike, Harry Owens attended one of these founding meetings and was elected recording secretary. In this particular meeting, the organization discussed future International Brigades member Jack Altman's attempts to bring the Socialist Party into the Communist fold. Owens knew of the ongoing battle between Communists and his IWW and anarchist comrades, yet in the two months after this meeting a number of Philadelphia Wobblies, including Owens, James O. Yates, Barney Spaulding, and Fred Miller, joined the International Brigades.[41]

Wobblies and the Popular Front in Spain

What Wobbly volunteers saw in Spain after arriving in the early months of 1937 awed them. Harry Owens wrote that it "will gladden the heart of every Wob to know that the unions in Spain have apparently taken over industries themselves."[42] Numerous Wobblies joined the CNT, including Pat Read and Barney Spaulding. The revolution that they dreamed about was coming to pass and they were participants. However, the political situation in Spain was changing rapidly. The coalition of Communists, socialists, republicans, and anarchists that governed Spain soon fractured and this eventually affected Wobbly volunteers.

As the situation in Spain evolved, so did the American maritime situation. East Coast sailors still wanted to put the final nail in the ISU's coffin and so, in the spring, began talks about forming a new National Maritime Union affiliated with the AFL's new rival, the Congress of Industrial Organizations. Wobblies, who despised the ISU and possibly had different ideas about the future shape of the NMU, supported this new union. The sailors of the Abraham Lincoln Battalion, regardless of politics, heralded this new union's birth. When sailors in training camp elected a representative to send greetings from Spain to the NMU's founding convention, they chose the openly Wobbly James Oscar Yates.[43] While Wobblies and Communists fought each other on the streets of New York and docks of San Francisco, in Spain they remained good comrades—at least for a while—but events in both Spain and the United States threatened to poison their relationship.

The American units of the International Brigades were politically diverse organizations, and in the early part of their existence, occasionally democratic. The wide net the Communists cast recruiting party members during the Popular Front period, as well as for the International Brigades, brought in a cross-section of the early twentieth-century left, including many imbued with republican and revolutionary ideas of military structure and discipline. A number of volunteers, Communist and non-Communist alike, said they would happily fought for bourgeois democracy, but even more so for revolutionary democracy. Many volunteers were revolutionaries grounded in radical traditions which they brought to Spain and which paralleled Spanish anarchist traditions. The volunteers expected an egalitarian army, and briefly had the power to create one. When the first Communist cadres sent to Spain to lead the volunteers did not live up to the troops' expectations, battalion leaders chose new leadership with input from the volunteers, and in some cases volunteers elected their commanders democratically. In the American transportation unit, the 2nd Squadron of the First Transportation Regiment, volunteers elected Wobbly Mike Raddock as adjutant. In the Lincoln Battalion, Wobbly Pat Read virtually created the battalion's transmission section. When the Estado Mayor of the xvth International Brigade (to which the Lincoln Battalion belonged) established a Transmissions Company, it was widely recognized—and accepted by the CPUSA—that Read was the most qualified to command the unit. Democratic and well-functioning units were not contradictory, and well-functioning units not only served the Spanish Republic but also reflected well on the CPUSA.

Eventually these radical traditions and democratic, egalitarian methods of ordering revolutionary militaries butted up against the needs of the Spanish Republican Army and the Communist conception of the Popular Front. The commander of the George Washington Battalion complained that too many revolutionary military ideas existed among the troops, who believed, in his summation, "we're volunteers. If we want to accept orders and discipline, it's OK. But if we do not like an order, we don't have to carry it out. We have the right to decide what to obey and what to reject."[44] Sailors, Wobblies, and "Wobbly traditions" were often blamed for these radical ideas. Edward Cecil-Smith, Washington Battalion company commander and later commander of the American-Canadian MacKenzie-Papineau Battalion, argued that numerous volunteers "retain many traditions which the west has inherited from the Wobblies" when speaking about the unit's lack of discipline.[45] In the Washington Battalion Machine Gun Company, Young Communist Carl Geiser complained that "our present corporal [Harry Owens] is an IWW member, and has Constitutional objections to giving orders, besides drinking a bit heavy."[46] To Geiser, winning the war demanded that participants give and take orders, so revolutionary ideas had to be quashed.

Trouble in Spain and at Home

At the end of 1937, as the Republic's fortunes declined, the Republican Army became a conventional military force on the Soviet model, with a rationalized structure and new disciplinary regime. In the Lincoln Battalion, this coincided with the introduction of a new group of politically intolerant, hands-on Communist leaders as well as rumors of strife both in Spain and the United States between Communists, Wobblies, and "Trotskyites." Similarly, on American waterfronts, Communists and Wobblies returned to a war footing. The West Coast feud between the SUP, ILA, and newly formed NMU became violent and politicized. According to its leader Harry Lundeberg, the SUP was fighting an anti-Communist crusade. The Communists accused Lundeberg and his Wobbly allies of being Trotskyites, mimicking the language used by the Communists against Wobblies and anarchists in Spain. Because of the MTW's connection to the SUP, the East Coast MTW became a de facto SUP auxiliary, placing NMU Wobblies in an awkward position and Wobbly sailors in Spain in a worse one. The comradeship in Spain that insulated American Wobblies from these controversies frayed.

The new acrimony affected even popular Wobblies like Pat Read and Mike Raddock. As Wobbly lumberjack Axel Rheinholm complained, "criticism of the governmental policies were severely discouraged; to criticize was to invite the epithet 'Trotskyite,' the favorite term of abuse by the clique in charge."[47] Raddock was beloved by the 2nd Squadron of the 1st Regiment de Tren, but became hated by Communist functionaries by late 1937. According to one report, Raddock was "very disruptive and destructive politically. Undisciplined, [and] slanderous of leadership."[48] Read, whose bravery earned the respect of his transmissions company and much of the 15th Brigade, was accused of verbally attacking Brigade leadership. Commissar John Gates wrote that Read was an "anti-political-die hard I.W.W." who carried "on a campaign against the leadership."[49] Eventually, as punishment, Read was demoted and expelled from Spain. His Communist comrade and good friend, Harry Fisher, remembered Read declaring, "the head commie told me that I'm a bad boy, doing the fascists' job, by knocking the party."[50] Questioning the International Brigades' leadership, as Read and Raddock did, pushed the boundaries of a democratic army and exceeded the shrinking boundaries of the Popular Front. But while Read was expelled from Spain, his punishment never went further. For some sailors, the story was very different.

Virgil Morris's troubles began well before the decline of Republican fortunes, and were compounded by Wobbly–Communist acrimony in the United States. Communists accused him, like other Wobblies, of "creating a bad relationship between the volunteers and the military and political leadership of the Battalion."[51] His pranks made him well known and initially popular among his fellow volunteers, but after a few months, Morris and many other volunteers believed that they deserved a rest or to possibly go home. When neither came to pass, Morris deserted. He was sentenced to a labor battalion. There, Morris frequently attempted to escape, often using fantastic methods. In one case, his jailer, Lincoln Battalion volunteer Tony DeMaio, accused him of attempting "to leave the camp without permission, attacking the guard, getting [his] rifle and calling on the men to kill the officers."[52] Eventually he found himself in prison, away from his circle of sailors, where the American maritime union situation in the United States made his life more miserable. Suddenly, his IWW membership mattered and was a strike against him. Far from being a Communist hero of the strike of 1936, he was listed as "a labor spy and provocateur in the U.S.A."[53] As with other volunteers, it appears that his punishment included beatings.[54] Later, Morris was released to work on fortifications and then returned home.

A similar case involved Morris's comrade in the 1936 strike, Fred Miller. Miller arrived in March of 1937 with several other Wobblies, including his friend Harry Owens. After the battle of Brunete, where Owens was killed, Miller attempted to desert but was caught and sent to Camp Lukas, a disciplinary and rest center. After his release, he was arrested four more times, possibly for drunkenness, but eventually was investigated for "sabotage and disorganizational agitation."[55] His file hints at what that might mean: like Raddock, Read, and Morris, Miller "was very antagonistic toward the c.p. He is a useless, good for nothing lumpen."[56] A further snippet of his file mentions that Miller was a "wobbly diehard" and an "anarchist element."[57] According to fellow sailor William McQuistion, Miller suffered severe beatings at the hands of his jailers, including Tony DeMaio. In both Morris's and Miller's cases, the moment they deserted they put themselves in increased danger because they no longer remained within the confines of their circle of comrades in the Lincoln Battalion who respected "the 'wobbly' outlook."[58] The jailor who supposedly beat Morris and Miller, DeMaio, knew full well of the struggles between Wobblies and Communists on the waterfront, and believed that Wobblies were "Trotskyites."[59] Miller was released in February 1938, just in time to participate in "the retreats."

The decline of the Republican war situation only heightened the suspicion and contempt that some Communist leaders and functionaries had for Wobblies. On March 7, 1938 the Fascists launched a devastating offensive in Aragon which quickly sent the Republican Army, including the Americans of the XV Brigade, into a chaotic retreat. Fred Miller was one of the lucky volunteers who merely was captured, whereas the Fascists executed Wobblies Ivan Silverman and Robert Charles Watts. Many volunteers, with few places to retreat and assuming the Republic defeated, deserted and attempted to find ways to exit Spain via Barcelona. During the retreats, an American ship with several Wobblies in its crew arrived in Barcelona, including SUP leader and IWW delegate Lloyd "Sam" Usinger.

Usinger, a longtime Wobbly, was one of Lundeberg's lieutenants and likely one of those who argued the SUP was worth rebuilding as a vehicle for Wobbly unionism. Now Usinger was in Spain, attempting to aid "Spanish workers to secure food and ammunition to carry on their war against the Fascist invasion."[60] Instead, he arrived at the exact moment that hundreds of international volunteers converged on Barcelona to leave Spain. Usinger and other Americans, with assistance from the CNT, helped these volunteers to do just that. Many of the demoralized volunteers arrived with stories to tell that rationalized their desertions. While the underlying truth in their tales should not be discounted, much was bogus. A number of the stories fed to Usinger by volunteers including William McQuisition—who later told the same tale to the House Un-American Activities Committee—contained many exaggerations or outright lies. Usinger broadcast their version of events in an article in the SUP newspaper, *West Coast Sailors*, as part of an attack on the Communist Party and NMU. Usinger's piece prompted the SUP to cease supporting the Spanish Republic and expel Communist International Brigades volunteers, which set off a chain reaction eventually leading to Communists expelling Wobblies from the NMU.[61] The cleavage between the two organizations split wide open. The Popular Front that had led Wobblies to go to Spain with their fellow sailors was dead.

Disaster and Decline

The Spanish Civil War ultimately proved a disaster for the IWW. While the casualties in Spain hurt much of the American left, the MTW experienced a death blow. The defeat of Spanish anarchism was also a Wobbly defeat. The ascendency of the Spanish anarchists had given the MTW a much-needed boost, and the MTW tied its fortunes to the CNT, but with the anarchist revolution defeated, the MTW became demoralized. Making matters worse, many of the new generation of MTW leaders were either killed or "broken" in Spain defending what they believed was the revolution that would transform the world. The Philadelphia Branch's leadership was hit particularly hard. Branch secretary Oscar Neef was wounded and fell out of the IWW soon after returning from Spain.[62] Fred Miller stayed in the IWW but never held another leadership position.[63] Nearly two years of war left Barney Spaulding "demoralized" and "cynical" which, along with his CNT membership, precluded him from joining the Spanish Communist Party.[64] Spaulding instead dropped out of both the IWW and the Communist Party. Virgil Morris returned to the West Coast and dropped out of the IWW. However, the branch's worst loss was Harry Owens, a leader who had the ability to articulate the need for an independent, militant maritime union and mobilize people around that idea.

Compounding the loss of IWW members who had fought to build a competitive, independent MTW, events in Spain ensured that Wobblies were merely pawns in the power struggle between the SUP and NMU. When the SUP, with Wobbly support, began to expel Communists, it was only a matter of time until the Communists expelled the Wobblies from the NMU, pushing the IWW sailors deeper into the SUP. After building a substantial dual-card presence within that union, many Wobblies abandoned the IWW altogether, "singing the praises of Harry Lundeberg and giving the blessing to the SUP [to] scab the NMU out of existence," in Fred Hansen's words, and completely undermining any solidarity between the SUP, NMU, and Wobblies in both organizations.[65] Before the war, Wobbly sailors had scrupulously avoided scabbing—even on their Communist enemies—for to scab signaled that their organization was dying. Alas, it had died, in Spain.

Notes

1 Leland Walter Robinson, "Social movement organizations in decline: a case study of the IWW," PhD dissertation, Northwestern University, Evanston, Ill., 1973, p. 79. Robinson's estimates are conservative, to say the least. In 1924 several historians claimed that the IWW had around 100,000 members. Similarly, his estimates going forward into the 1930s don't quite gibe with the record.

2 Fred Thompson and Jon Bekken, *The Industrial Workers of the World: Its First One Hundred Years* (Boston, Mass.: IWW, 2006), p. 149.

3 Thompson and Bekken, *The Industrial Workers of the World*, p. 153; Jon Bekken, "Marine Transport Workers IU 510 (IWW): direct action unionism," *Libertarian Labor Review* 18 (1995): 18–19.

4   Norman Caulfield, *Mexican Workers and the State: From the Porfiriato to* NAFTA (Fort Worth, Tex.: Texas Christian University Press), p. 23.

5   Bruce Nelson, *Workers on the Waterfront: Seamen, Longshoremen, and Unionism in the 1930s* (Urbana, Ill.: University of Illinois Press, 1990), p. 28.

6   Watts, Fond 545, Opis 3, Delo 512, Russian State Archive of Socio-Political History (hereafter RGASPI), Tamiment Library, New York.

7   Stephen Schwartz, *Brotherhood of the Sea: A History of the Sailors' Union of the Pacific 1885–1985* (New Brunswick, N.J.: Transaction, Rutgers, 1986), p. 90.

8   Thompson and Bekken, *The Industrial Workers of the World*, p. 157.

9   Sam Dolgoff, *Fragments: A Memoir* (Cambridge: Refract, 1986), pp. 134–5.

10 *General Organization Bulletin* (hereafter *GOB*), September 1935, p. 7.

11 *GOB*, September 1935, p. 8–9.

12 *GOB*, September 1935, p. 8–9.

13 For a discussion of Communists versus Wobblies see Thompson and Bekken, *The Industrial Workers of the World*, pp. 121–48; Bekken, "Marine Transport Workers," p. 22; Peter Cole, *Wobblies on the Waterfront: Interracial Unionism in Progressive-Era Philadelphia* (Urbana, Ill.: University of Illinois Press, 2007), chap. 7.

14 *GOB*, September 1935, pp. 8–9.

15 *GOB*, May 1935, p. 3.

16 Nelson, *Workers on the Waterfront*, pp. 192–270; Schwartz, *Brotherhood of the Sea*, pp. 117–24.

17 *West Coast Sailors* (hereafter *WCS*), September 16, August 26, 1938.

18 Schwartz, *Brotherhood of the Sea*, p. 92.

19 Schwartz, *Brotherhood of the Sea*, p. 92.

20 Nelson, *Workers on the Waterfront*, p. 183.

21 6/1017 and 6/993, RGASPI; *Industrial Worker* (hereafter *IW*), May 8, 1937.

22 *IW*, September 19, 1936.

23 MTW strike leaflet, September 1936, Box 71, Folder 12, Industrial Workers of the World Collection, Walter P. Reuther Library, Wayne State University, Detroit, Mich.

24 See Nelson, *Workers on the Waterfront*, p. 214.

25 Fred Hansen to Fred Thompson, June 29, 1980, Box 10, Frederick W. Thompson Collection, Walter P. Reuther Library, Wayne State University (hereafter Thompson Collection).

26 *IW*, January 9, 1937.

27 *Philadelphia Record*, November 3, 1936; *IW*, November 14, 1936.

28 *Philadelphia Record*, November 4, 1936; *Pilot*, August 6, 1937.

29 *IW*, November 28, 1936; *Daily Strike Bulletin*, November 22, 1936.

30 *Pilot*, January 6, 1937; *IW*, December 26, 1936.

31 *IW*, January 16, 1937.

32 *IW*, September 19, 1936.

33 Arthur Landis, *The Abraham Lincoln Brigade* (New York: Citadel, 1967), p. 385.

34 *IW*, October 23, 1937; Kenyon Zimmer, "The other volunteers: American anarchists and the Spanish Civil War, 1936–1939," *Journal for the Study of Radicalism* 10:2 (2016): 19–52.

35 The author has documented at least 28 volunteers who were remembered as Wobblies or claimed to be Wobblies at the time. There were Wobblies in the

American units from their beginning to their end. One of the last Americans killed in Spain was Wobbly sailor Herbert Schlessinger.

36 Undated interview, Box 1, Folder 4, Sandor Voros Spanish Civil War Collection, Adelphi University, Long Island, N.Y. (hereafter Voros Collection).

37 *IW*, September 10, 1938.

38 See Gulsted 6/904 RGASPI as an example.

39 For examples see Dolgoff, *Fragments*, p. 19; *Challenge*, June 10, 1939.

40 See Kenyon Zimmer, "Premature anti-communists? American anarchism, the Russian Revolution, and left-wing libertarian anti-communism, 1917–1939," *Labor* 6:2 (2009): 45–71.

41 United Libertarian Organizations, "Organizational Conference of the United Libertarian Organizations –February 21, 1937," RG 1477, Folder 111, Spanish Civil War Collection, YIVO Institute for Jewish Research, New York, Center for Jewish History.

42 *IW*, May 8, 1937.

43 *Pilot*, July 23, 1937.

44 Mirko Markovics interview with Sandor Voros, July 1937, Box 1, Folder 1, Voros Collection.

45 Edward Cecil-Smith, "Statement," undated, 6/569 RGASPI.

46 Peter Carroll and Fraser Ottanelli (ed.), *Letters from the Spanish Civil War* (Kent, Ohio: Kent State University Press, 2013), p. 28.

47 *IW*, December 24, 1938.

48 Raddock, 6/967 RGASPI.

49 Read, 6/969 RGASPI.

50 Harry Fisher, *Comrades: Tales of a Brigadista in the Spanish Civil War* (Lincoln, Neb.: University of Nebraska Press, 1998), p. 119.

51 Morris, May 18, 1937, 3/451 RGASPI.

52 Morris, 6/950 RGASPI.

53 Morris, 6/950 RGASPI.

54 Palega, 6/959 RGASPI; McCuistion Testimony, House Committee on Un-American Activities, *Investigation of Un-American Activities in the United States*, 76th Congress, 3rd Session (1940), vol. 13, p. 7829.

55 Report of February 1938, 3/451 RGASPI.

56 Miller, 6/948 RGASPI.

57 Miller, 6/948 RGASPI.

58 John Cookson interview, September 1937, Box 1, Folder 3, Voros Collection.

59 Corbin, 6/876 RGASPI.

60 *WCS*, August 15, 1938.

61 *WCS*, July 15, 1938.

62 Oscar Neef, File 100-362957, Record Group 65, Records of the Federal Bureau of Investigation, National Archives and Records Administration, Tacoma Park, Md.

63 Ann Allen, "Interview with Sam and Esther Dolgoff," 1972, https://theanarchistlibrary.org/library/ann-allen-sam-dolgoff-esther-dolgoff-interview-with-sam-and-esther-dolgoff

64 Spaulding, 6/993, RGASPI.

65 Fred Hansen to Fred Thompson, June 29, 1980, Box 10, Thompson Collection.

14

Edith Frenette:
A Transnational Radical Life

Heather Mayer

Edith Bonny Frenette was a border-hopping Wobbly. Born in Maine in 1881 to Canadian parents, Frenette worked as a cook in the lumber camps of Port Alberni, British Columbia but also spent time in the United States. She frequently crossed the US–Canadian border during her active years, and fought for and with the Industrial Workers of the World (IWW) in both countries. A true "Rebel Girl," Frenette did not let fear of arrest keep her from fighting for the right to free speech. She roused her fellow workers with her rendition of "The red flag" outside the jailhouse in Spokane, Washington. She struck fear into the heart of the mayor of Everett and was characterized as the mastermind of the Wobbly free speech fight in that city. Though she has not been memorialized as much as other Wobbly heroes, no one can deny Frenette's impact on the union in the region.[1]

In the early twentieth century, the Wobblies of the Pacific Northwest undertook multiple free speech fights. Street speaking was an essential tool of Wobbly organizers. When workers came to town from the lumber camps or agricultural fields, the organizer met them on the street, denouncing the wage system and advocating industrial unionism. Thus, when cities banned street speaking, the Wobblies attempted to force the repeal of such bans by bringing in so many people to speak as to make enforcement impossible.

An early IWW free speech fight occurred in Missoula, Montana in 1908. IWW organizer Elizabeth Gurley Flynn and her husband Jack Jones were organizing there when the city banned street speaking. The police arrested several Wobblies, who were sentenced to 15 days in jail, before the IWW put out the call for more members to come to Missoula. Both Flynn and Frenette were arrested during the fight. The *Industrial Worker*, the official Northwest organ of the IWW, reported that "when Mrs. Frenette was arrested there was an enormous crowd [that] followed her to the jail, and while not riotous, were certainly indignant."[2] An anonymous "Free speech fight diary," published in the *International Socialist Review* in November 1909, noted that Mrs. Charles Frenette was a member of the Spokane local and its advisory board. The diarist also wrote that, when she was arrested, the crowd "threw stones at the police, severely injuring Officer Hoel."[3] Edith had been married for about two years at the time of the Missoula fight. While several husband-and-wife Wobbly teams organized in the region, Charles received no mention as actively participating in the struggle.

In her autobiography, Elizabeth Gurley Flynn recalled that the female Wobblies arrested were "treated with kid gloves by the Sheriff and his wife," though this same sheriff badly beat up her husband a few days earlier.[4] This points to one of the most important contributions IWW women made to free speech fights: they usually gained release earlier and received more lenient treatment than male Wobblies. While most Wobbly women objected to this preferential treatment, it allowed them to go back on the street faster, where they could publicize their experiences and continue the fight.

After a few weeks, the authorities caved in and dropped all charges against those arrested. The *Industrial Worker* declared the Missoula fight over, but October 25 marked the beginning of another fight, in Spokane, Washington. Edith Frenette traveled the 200 miles back to her home base in Spokane to join this struggle.

By November 10, Frenette sat in the Spokane county jail, arrested for street speaking along with Agnes Thecla Fair and Mrs. McDaniels. The *Industrial Worker*, which often exhorted its union readers to "be a man," noted, "it ought to make some of you great, husky, imitations of men ashamed of yourselves when women suffer that you may have your rights."[5] Frenette remained active in the Spokane fight, and was released and arrested twice more within two weeks.[6]

Speaking on the street was not her only "offense." Frenette also was arrested and tried for disorderly conduct after singing "The red flag" in front of the Franklin school, where many of the arrested men were held. During her trial, the chief of police, as well as six other officers, testified that Frenette "acted as if she were drunk, that she had carried on in a disorderly manner on the streets since this trouble started, and one said she acted like 'a lewd woman'." Frenette recited "The red flag" by request of the court, and did so "with such dramatic force that the Judge was horrified at its treasonable and unpatriotic sentiment." He sentenced Frenette to 30 days and fined her $100.[7]

The *Spokane Spokesman-Review* became interested in Frenette and the other Wobbly women arrested. The paper described Agnes Fair as a "slim girl in a black waist with a flaming red scarf" who advocated $8 a day for four hours of work. Ann Arquet, also arrested at the IWW hall, was described as "a tall, masculine woman who had been haranguing the crowd at the hall with much vehemence, and a younger girl who was much excited." Under the subheading "Pretty woman arrested," the paper detailed the case of Frenette, described as "plump and pretty" and "by far the most attractive of the day's batch of guests at the station." During her trial, after a few days in jail, Frenette "seemed as neatly groomed and pink-cheeked as though she had spend the time at home."[8] Although her appearance and apparent femininity made for good copy, the attention they received demonstrated the paper did not take seriously Frenette's and the others' commitment to free speech. Nevertheless, the Wobblies eventually won the right to speak on Spokane's streets.

Subsequently Frenette popped up here and there in IWW newspapers, but it was a relatively quiet period in the region. In May 1910, she served as the literature agent for the Tacoma IWW local. In 1911 she wrote a letter to the *Industrial Worker* about a mass meeting in Port Alberni, British Columbia. There she stepped on to the soapbox after her brother-in-law Henry was heckled: "This was something they hadn't figured on as they were hardly prepared to beat up a woman .... I called them a few choice names and appealed to their manhood, if they had any." Frenette learned that a mob planned to "bind and gag Henry and myself and ship us out of town on the steamer which was to come into port that night. They changed their minds for some reason and we are still here." She then called for more IWW organizers to come to the region.[9]

Tragically, in 1912 the *Industrial Worker* reported that Stella Frenette, the daughter of Edith and Charles, died after a one-week battle with measles followed by pneumonia. She was only 9 months old. At this point the family still lived in Port Alberni.[10] Infant mortality rates were quite high, especially for working-class families, during this period—one of the reasons why many Wobblies supported more access to birth control information.[11] After her loss, Frenette is not mentioned again in the *Industrial Worker* until the 1916 Everett free speech fight, this time without her husband.

Although the Everett Massacre remains one of the most infamous events in the history of the IWW, little investigation has been made into the role women played in the events leading up to the killings and during the trial. Frenette's role in Everett previously has been ignored or downplayed by historians. This dismissal of women contrasts sharply with the contemporary activists and writers who found it important to highlight the involvement of Frenette and other women.

The free speech fight in Everett began in August 1916. Organizer James P. Thompson had arrived with 20 or so Wobblies from Seattle to speak on August 22, but no hall would rent to the IWW, so they decided he would speak on the street. Everett sheriff Don McRae announced he would not allow it and threatened to throw out of town any Wobbly he could find.[12] Thompson commenced speaking on a street regardless. He lasted about 20 minutes before the police arrived to break up the meeting. After Thompson and his wife Florence were arrested, James Rowan, Lorna Mahler, Frenette, and several others all attempted to speak but were also arrested.[13]

The following morning, the police deported James and Florence Thompson, Herbert and Lorna Mahler, and Frenette back to Seattle. Frenette, Lorna Mahler, and James Thompson spoke at a meeting there that same night, raising $50 for the cause.[14] By September 7, the Wobblies resumed speaking in Everett, resulting in Frenette and five male Wobblies being arrested. The *Everett Tribune* noted that Sheriff Luke "encountered considerable trouble in placing Mrs. Frenette under arrest when she displayed indignant resistance."[15] The men were sentenced to 30 days but Frenette was released the next morning.

That night two more Wobblies were arrested, and a "crowd of Everett citizens, in company with the few IWW members present" marched to the jail to demand the prisoners' release. The *Everett Tribune* described the crowd as consisting of "an element of youths and general loiterers, curious pedestrians and a large representation of women."[16] While there, the crowd knocked over a fence, which led to Frenette being arrested and charged with inciting to riot. She was later released on $1,000 bail, a huge amount for a labor activist in this period.[17] The *Tribune* warned its readers that these street meetings were no place for place for children, and that women and girls, "who lately have been in the thick of the excitement," should stay away.[18]

Everett officials checked incoming trains for Wobblies, so on September 9 a few of them—including Frenette—took the train to the nearby town of Mukilteo and boarded the *Wanderer*, a boat which Frenette had arranged to take them to Everett. They were met on their way, however, by another boat carrying Sheriff McRae and 60 deputies, who fired six shots at the *Wanderer*; McRae then boarded the boat and arrested everyone on board, including the captain. In jail, McRae and the other deputies beat the men repeatedly. On September 11, Rowan returned to Everett but was arrested as soon as he stepped off the train. That night McRae took Rowan from the jail and dropped him outside of town on the road leading back to Seattle. After walking a little way down the road, a group of a dozen or so men with guns met Rowan. They threw a cloth over his head, beat him with guns and clubs, tore off his clothes, leaned him over a stump, and whipped him 50 or more times. Rowan returned to Seattle after the beating and had photographs taken of his wounds; these photos were circulated around Seattle, encouraging—rather than deterring—more people to join the Wobblies' free speech fight.[19]

Frenette, meanwhile, went to Police Chief Kelley to complain of the vigilante beatings of Wobblies. She told Kelley:

> It seems that there is an ordinance here against street speaking and we feel that it is unjust. We feel that we have a right to speak here. We are not blocking traffic, and we propose to make a test of the ordinance. Will you have one of your men arrest me or any other speaker who chooses to take the box, personally, and take me to jail and put a charge against me, and protect me from the vigilantes who are beating the men on the street?

Kelley responded noncommittally; he would do what he could but claimed Sheriff McRae really controlled the situation.[20]

The tragedy that followed is one of the most infamous in IWW and Washington State history. On November 5, a group of Wobblies boarded the *Verona* and headed to Everett for a free speech rally. Sheriff McRae tried to stop the boat from docking and exchanged words with the men on board. Then shots were fired, leading to the deaths of at least four Wobblies and two deputies, including Jefferson Beard. Afterwards, everyone aboard the *Verona* was arrested; eventually 74 Wobblies were charged with Beard's death.

Frenette testified during the first trial, of defendant Tom Tracy. Though she had played a large role in the events leading up to the massacre, Frenette had not been on the *Verona* and was thus not on trial for Beard's murder. Instead she had spent the night of November 4 in Everett, which was proven during the trial after one prosecution witness claimed to have seen her in Seattle the morning of November 5 discussing bringing red pepper to Everett to use against the vigilantes.[21] The defense disproved this by submitting as evidence the ledger from the hotel in Everett where Frenette stayed the night before the massacre.[22] Immediately after the shootout, Frenette, along with Lorna Mahler and Joyce Peters, had returned to Seattle, where they were arrested. It was initially reported that all three were arrested for attempting to throw cayenne pepper in the face of

Figures Prominent in Legal Proceedings
Resulting From I. W. W. Riot at Everett

70 MORE I. W. W.
ARE JAILED ON
SAME CHARGE

Held for Unlawful Assembly
in Connection With In-
vasion of Everett
November 5.

—By Staff Photographer.

1—Mrs. Joyce Peters, held on an open charge, released Tuesday after habeas corpus proceedings.
2—Mrs. Edith Frenette, similarly held, and turned over Tuesday to Snohomish county authorities to be prosecuted for assault in first degree.
3—Mrs. Herbert Mahler, wife of I. W. W. secretary, held by authorities and released at same time as Mrs. Peters.
4—Secretary Herbert Mahler, of the local I. W. W., in consultation with (5) Attorney Fred H. Moore, of Los Angeles, who will assist in the defense of members of the organization.

Formal complaints charging seventy more members of the Industrial Workers of the World, who were participants in the fatal attempt to defy the authorities of Everett on November 5, with unlawful assemblage, were filed by Deputy Prosecuting Attorney Heisell before Justice of the Peace Gordon Tuesday morning, and later in the afternoon these men with the excep-

From left to right: (top row) Joyce Peters, Edith Frenette, "Mrs. Herbert Mahler," (bottom row) Herbert Mahler, Fred H. Moore. *Seattle Post-Intelligencer,* November 15, 1916.

Sheriff McRae while being transported to the hospital. Frenette was eventually charged with first-degree assault after witnesses declared she had pointed a gun at McRae after the shooting.[23] She was jailed for three weeks then released on $2,500 bail. The charges were later dropped.[24]

During the Tracy trial, Frenette was portrayed as one of the main organizers of the Everett free speech fights. When Everett Mayor Dennis Merrill testified regarding the confrontation between Wobblies and city officials preceding the massacre, he claimed that the Wobblies, specifically Frenette, tried to intimidate him.[25] In his report for the *Seattle Union Record* on the day's proceedings in the Tracy trial, Albert Brilliant referred to Frenette as "the terror of the prosecution ... who during the entire trial has been pointed to by the state as the center of a conspiracy which had for its object the invasion of the city of Everett, the assassination of city authorities, and the destruction of the city by fire."[26] Although she was not on trial, authorities viewed her as the mastermind behind the Wobblies' presence in Everett.

In legal proceedings, Wobblies were often questioned on moral grounds, whether or not they related to the charges. These questions were asked to demonstrate the defendants' character and insinuate that Wobblies believed in changing not only economic relations but social ones as well. Frenette's testimony in Everett proved no exception. When examining her, after asking about the events on the day of the massacre, defense attorney George Vanderveer asked if she had lived in the same room as Earl Osborne, another IWW member, while residing in a Seattle rooming house during the free speech fight. It is likely that he wanted to address any potentially damaging testimony before the prosecution did. The cross-examination, indeed, pressed the point, interrogating Frenette about her personal life, trying to get information about her relationship with her husband and where exactly she called her home. When asked where Mr. Frenette's home was, Edith replied that he lived on Vancouver Island; when asked when she had last lived there, she replied that she had not been there in a year. Had she been "home" since? She said, "not to that home. Any place one stops is a home. A hotel is a home."[27] The prosecution continued pressing her on whether or not she had ever lived in the same place as Osborne, and she replied that she never had made it her home. Where she had lived and with whom had nothing to do with her actions in Everett, yet a woman who left her husband and lived with another man could be seen as morally suspect and easier for a jury to view as an outsider. Thus, the prosecution implied that her testimony was not trustworthy nor was she entitled to the same protections as "respectable" Everett citizens.

Eventually Tom Tracy was acquitted, and since there was no more evidence against any other arrested Wobblies, all other charges were dropped. This was a high point of support for the organization in the United States, but alas, it was followed closely by US entry into the First World War, which triggered massive, nationwide repression of Wobblies.

Sadly, after playing such a significant role in Spokane and Everett, Edith Frenette disappeared from the headlines. Since it seems that she had left her husband, she possibly remarried and changed her name. James Thompson, a Spokane free speech fight veteran, was one of 100 Wobbly leaders on trial for espionage during the First World War. In June 1918, when examined during the trial in Chicago of the United States vs. William D. Haywood and others, Thompson was asked about Frenette. The prosecution asked whether he knew her and whether or not she had belonged to the IWW in 1917. To this query he replied, "I am not sure. She owns a homestead up in Canada, and that technically might bar her out, but I am not sure whether or not she has a card."[28]

While we do not know where Edith Frenette ended up, her actions clearly demonstrate her dedication to fighting for the working class, regardless of nationality. She did not believe that the interests of workers stopped at a border, just as borders did not stop her from moving for work, family, or activism. She valued belonging to the IWW, an organization that also believed in her.

Notes

1 Heather Mayer, "Beyond the Rebel Girl: women, Wobblies, respectability, and the law in the Pacific Northwest, 1905–1924," PHD dissertation, Simon Fraser University, Burnaby, BC, 2015.

2 *Industrial Worker*, October 20, 1909.

3 Philip Foner (ed.), *Fellow Workers and Friends: IWW Free Speech Fights as Told by Participants* (Westport, Conn: Greenwood Press, 1981), p. 28.

4 Elizabeth Flynn, *The Rebel Girl: An Autobiography, My First Life (1906–1926)* (New York: International Publishers, 1973), p. 104.

5 *Industrial Worker*, November 10, 1909.

6 *Industrial Worker*, November 24, 1909.

7 Elizabeth Gurley Flynn, "The shame of Spokane," *International Socialist Review*, January 1910, reprinted in John Duda, *Wanted: Men to Fill the Jails of Spokane! Fighting for Free Speech with the Hobo Agitators of the Industrial Workers of the World* (Chicago, Ill.: Charles H. Kerr, 2009), p. 62.

8 *Spokane Spokesman-Review*, November 3, 1909, copy found in Frederick W. Thompson Papers, Walter P. Reuther Library, Wayne State University, Detroit, Mich.

9 *Industrial Worker*, May 7, 1910, November 2, 1911.

10 *Industrial Worker*, April 18, 1912; Physician's certificate of death, British Columbia Vital Records, March 26, 1912.

11 In 1912 there were 170 deaths for every 1,000 children under one year old in the United States. In 2016, the death rate is closer to 6 per 1,000. Department of Commerce, Bureau of the Census, Mortality Statistics: 1912, Washington, DC: Government Printing Office, 1913; Centers for Disease Control and Prevention, "National Center for Health Statistics," https://www.cdc.gov/nchs/fastats/infant-health.htm (accessed January 11, 2017).

12 Walker Smith, *The Everett Massacre: A History of the Class Struggle in the Lumber Industry* (Chicago, Ill.: IWW Publishing Bureau, 1918), p. 36.

13 Smith, *The Everett Massacre*, pp. 36–38; *Industrial Worker*, August 26, 1916.

14 Smith, *The Everett Massacre*, pp. 40–41.

15 *Everett Tribune*, September 8, 1916.

16 *Everett Tribune*, September 9, 1916.

17 Smith, *The Everett Massacre*, p. 49; *Industrial Worker*, September 30, 1916.

18 *Everett Tribune*, September 9, 1916.

19 Smith, *The Everett Massacre*, pp. 50–6.

20 Smith, *The Everett Massacre*, p. 61.

21 Smith, *The Everett Massacre*, p. 155.

22 Smith, *The Everett Massacre*, p. 194.

23 *Seattle Post-Intelligencer*, November 6, November 9, 1916.

24 *Industrial Worker*, December 2, 1916. Mahler and Peters were released on November 14.

25 *Seattle Union Record*, November 11, 1916.

26 *Seattle Union Record*, April 14, 1917.

27 *Everett Tribune*, April 13, 1917.

28 Industrial Workers of the World Collection, Box 109, Folder 2, Walter P. Reuther Library, Wayne State University, Detroit, Mich.

Part III

Beyond the Union: The IWW's Influence and Legacies

15

Jim Larkin, James Connolly, and the Dublin Lockout of 1913: The Transnational Path of Global Syndicalism

Marjorie Murphy

The ideas of "One Big Union," or industrial democracy, as espoused by the Industrial Workers of the World (IWW), captured the imagination of a global community of young socialists (broadly defined) who hungered for social justice in their own lives and world. Jim Larkin and James Connolly grew up in two different Irish immigrant communities outside of Ireland. Both traveled to America and participated in all that the IWW had to offer, and then together they launched an aggressive, successful One Big Union drive in Dublin. Even in the most obscure immigrant neighborhoods, the Irish imagined an entirely different way of life and, for a brief moment, took the idea of One Big Union and made it theirs. The explosive nature of the 1913 Dublin lockout and its consequences, however, reverberated throughout the British Empire, leading Larkin and Connolly down the path of Irish republicanism and armed struggle.

These two Irish socialists—Jim Connolly and James Larkin—came to America in 1902 and 1913 respectively, and participated in the IWW at two different and formative moments. Exiles more than immigrants, they were intimates of Elizabeth Gurley Flynn, William Z. Foster, and "Big Bill" Haywood. The cities involved were more disparate: New York, Chicago, Philadelphia, Dublin, Belfast, Liverpool, and Edinburgh. But as Robert M. Fox noted:

In outlook and method both Larkin and Connolly owed a great deal to the

IWW, or rather, one would say, they represented the same kind of movement in Ireland, a movement of unskilled "outcast" workers, believing in sudden strikes, in sympathetic action; a coming together of men who felt they had to rely on their own strength to achieve anything because the law was always weighted against them and their rights as citizens [were] denied.[1]

The methods were often the same; however, it is not always obvious whether the Irish socialists were influencing the IWW or the other way around. Furthermore, some successful tactics in America simply did not work in Ireland. The idea of syndicalism captured the hearts and minds of so many, yet the yoke of colonialism was such that the competing need for self-determination forced these organizers' hands. By the time the First World War offered the Irish the opportunity to rise up against the British, these two men had organized a military extension of the working class; even Lenin admired their panache. Yet at that revolutionary moment, with international socialism failing all around them, they chose the nationalist path—not the narrow vision of republican orthodoxy, but the visionary path that tied the Irish struggle to a global struggle of emancipation.[2]

This chapter focuses on the similarities in content and tactics between the IWW and Irish syndicalists, but it begins with the conditions required for the knitting-together of a global response to the era's extreme exploitation and conditions of the working class. Engels, of course, began his description of the working class in England with the Irish living and working in British textile mills in the 1840s, and by the 1890s these conditions had seriously declined. Connolly and Larkin came from the slums of Edinburgh and Liverpool, and nowhere, in either writings or speeches, did they seem as bitter as when they talked about the condition of working-class housing. The Dublin slums were the worst in Europe—worse, they said, than those of Calcutta. At the height of the 1913 lockout in Dublin a tenement collapsed on Church Street, one of the poorest neighborhoods in Ireland. The building just fell apart, killing seven people instantly. The incident seemed to signify the complete disregard for the city's working poor. Many such eighteenth-century townhouses fell in on themselves while the new Catholic middle class collected rents beyond wages for the little that could be had. The only two leaders who stood openly with the Irish poor were James Connolly and Jim Larkin.[3]

James Connolly's escape from the slums of Scotland came, ironically, via the British Imperial Army. He was assigned to the British military barracks in Dublin where he met and married his wife, only to desert the military and move back into Edinburgh. There he learned the basics of socialism, first from the Socialist League and then from Keir Hardie, the founder of the Independent Labour Party and mentor to both Connolly and Larkin. Connolly returned to Dublin from 1896 to 1903, to write and organize for the new Dublin Socialist Club, where he encountered more poverty and resistance in the slums of the city. Undaunted, he launched the Irish Socialist Republican Party (ISRP) within a month of his 1896 return to Ireland. The ISRP's membership card carried the famous saying later incorporated into the essence of "Larkinism": "The great appear to be great to us because we are on our knees. Let us Arise."[4]

In the late 1890s Connolly and a handful of fellow travelers managed to keep the *Workers' Republic* newspaper afloat, organized outdoor meetings, demonstrated against the Diamond Jubilee of Queen Victoria, celebrated the Paris Commune, and produced a commemoration of the rising of 1798 which Connolly put together with the famous actress Maude Gonne. After a celebration of the British defeat at Dundee in the Boer War in 1899, the club admitted it no longer had funds to pay Connolly as its organizer. By 1901 the ISRP launched municipal election campaigns and the *Workers' Republic* appeared monthly, then bimonthly, while Connolly accepted speaking engagements in England, Scotland, and America. Daniel De Leon and the Socialist Labor Party (SLP) of America invited him in the early spring of 1902. Although he returned to Ireland and Scotland that same year, by the spring of 1903 he had returned to the States for a seven-year, self-imposed exile. He arrived as some American socialists, anarchists, and radical unionists contemplated a new kind of organization, the IWW, then just a glint in their eyes.[5]

Connolly's escape from a hand-to-mouth existence in Dublin led him to a tortuous encounter with SLP politics in the United States. The party literally ran him ragged with speaking engagements in the new country, while he sold subscriptions to the *Workers' Republic*. Yet SLP organizers attacked him for taking off too much time, not appearing at all of the speaking engagements contracted for, and refusing to repudiate a letter published in his Irish paper from Father Thomas Hagerty, a Catholic priest and one of the founders of the IWW. Hagerty was best known for creating an organizational chart, known as Father Hagerty's Wheel, for the newly-formed outfit. Furthermore, Connolly had to contend with De Leon, with whom he immediately entered into a controversy over wages. Doctrinaire, vituperative, and vindictive, De Leon engaged in an open controversy with Connolly about whether wages followed prices. Much to De Leon's chagrin, his fellow IWW members agreed with the Irish newcomer, and moreover kicked De Leon out of the IWW in 1908.[6]

By then Connolly had moved his family to New Jersey, where he worked at the Singer Sewing Machine Company and, for the first time, provided his family with financial stability. The job did not allow Connolly much time to work for the IWW, however, so soon he went on the road again. The IWW hired him as a New York organizer, lining up dock workers, traveling for the IWW, and writing *Socialism Made Easy* for Charles H. Kerr Publishers. He never lost touch with Ireland, and paid attention to Jim Larkin's strikes and lockout in Belfast as well as to the spreading of the idea of One Big Union. His family moved closer to Elizabeth Gurley Flynn in the Bronx and, while not in the suburban, middle-class housing of their old life, they were back among the Irish-Scottish community of socialists where Connolly continued to labor.[7] The temperamental American economy failed in 1907 and subsequently Connolly's family again suffered.[8]

At this time he began a new Irish newspaper, the *Harp*, in which he explained that Irish people had the wrong impression of the prosperity of America. Connolly warned his Irish brethren that America was not the "free" country they might have dreamed of; indeed, he urged them to think twice before leaving Ireland. He pointed to the IWW free speech movement in Spokane, Washington; spoke bitterly of the convict labor system in Galveston, Texas (where 50 convict laborers had been beaten to death); and warned his audience not to take the word "convict" to heart because "it is easy to become a convict in America." To his Irish audience, he warned against the false impression that silent relatives had become too rich to reach back to their Irish peasant past. In fact, he told them those relatives were probably unemployed, unable to reach anything or barely scraping by; that is, they had nothing to write home about. He had no illusions about English capitalism in Ireland, and argued that even if the Irish could overthrow British colonialism, they still would be faced with capitalist oppression. And yet in the end, he joined Tom Clarke and the old Irish Republican Brotherhood (IRB), committing his life to the ill-fated uprising of 1916. When Irish nationalists rose up in armed rebellion at Easter 1916, and declared an Irish Republic, only to be brutally suppressed by the British, Connolly was not surprised. He had long held that the cause of Irish socialism required a national identity. Furthermore, he knew he would be killed by the British. He only worried that his socialist friends might not understand why he was there. His explanation was, "I am an Irishman."[9]

The 1905 Teamsters' strike in Chicago, the IWW's birthplace, also offered potential lessons to Connolly and Larkin. The Teamsters struck in support of the tailors who were then on strike from Montgomery, Ward and Company. The Teamsters' sympathy strike grew into a general strike which threatened to shut down the entire city. The strike operated on the idea of Teamsters' refusal to carry "tainted goods" as well as the most basic principle of the newly-formed IWW: "An injury to one is an injury to all." But Chicago, unlike the British colonial city of Dublin, had just elected a very pro-labor mayor, and the local labor federation just had ousted a corrupt union leadership with the help of the recently organized teachers' union. The potential for greater violence was moved past, as the representatives of labor and capital sought a solution. This incident reveals one of the big differences between the Americans and Irish: violent and clearly partial as the justice system was in the United States, the IWW and other unions sometimes could achieve victories. In contrast, the Irish persistently faced the wall of imperialism. Connolly and Larkin had no illusions about American justice and supported the revolutionary IWW, but the situation in Ireland persistently pulled them back into the nationalist agenda.[10]

The Global Transmission of IWW Ideas

Connolly stayed in America until 1910. His experiences with Irish nationalists in the Clan na Gael (an American organization of Irish republicans) and Irish Americans in the IWW gave him ideas about how to organize workers once back in Ireland. Before then, he had grown very close to Elizabeth Gurley Flynn and her father Tom, in the Bronx. One of her most well-known chapters as a Wobbly organizer occurred in the Lawrence strike of 1912, in a time when the IWW started to line up increasingly radical garment workers. The famous Bread and Roses strike eventually shut down all of the textile shops in Lawrence and engulfed 20,000 strikers between January and March of 1912. The strike escalated quickly and mill owners just as quickly closed the plants. Workers picketed and threw ice at factory windows, the militia was called upon, and "Big Bill" Haywood traveled all over Massachusetts to raise funds for striking families. Finally, in the bitter cold of February and to save them from starvation, the IWW decided to send children to sympathetic working-class families in New York and Philadelphia.[11]

The tactic came from Italy originally and was imported to Lawrence. Perhaps Flynn learned of it from her fellow Wobbly organizer Carlo Tresca, who also helped lead the Lawrence strike. On February 10, 1912, 119 strikers' children traveled to Grand Central Station where working-class families, in solidarity, waited to provide shelter for them until the strike ended. The IWW called on Flynn to popularize the program, which garnered terrific press coverage. The sight of "adopting" parents picking up emaciated children who then, later, appeared for a press review—but now were well-fed with new, warm clothes—made it simple for the media to broadcast the Wobblies' point: the strike was starving the children. The move proved so popular that the IWW planned a second children's crusade, this time for Philadelphia. But this time, Lawrence city officials sent police to the railway station to prevent the children's departure. Images of police with batons charging mothers with children, causing many tears and much pandemonium, resulted in headlines and a congressional hearing in Washington, D.C., which further exposed the horrific conditions in the mills. Flynn's participation in the strike, and in particular in the children's campaign, guaranteed that this tactic later found its way into the Irish Lockout of 1913.

When Connolly and Larkin introduced the children's campaign tactics into Ireland, however, they were stopped by the Irish Catholic hierarchy. In particular, Archbishop William Walsh feared the children would be given to British working-class families, possibly even "socialists and anarchists." To prevent this eventuality, Walsh sent 50 priests to "rescue" the children. The church condemned these striking working-class mothers for threatening the spirituality of their children. Simultaneously, the Dublin Metropolitan Police threatened the escorts for the children and arrested some of them, which also intimidated the children. Apparently, the church and state worried more about the state of these children's souls than their physical well-being. And unlike the Lawrence strike, no congressional investigation occurred.[12]

By the time the Dublin strike began in 1913 James Connolly had returned to Ireland and met Jim Larkin for the first time. Connolly went to Belfast to run the dock workers' union while Larkin began building the organization in Dublin, a very different economy. Dublin, an old imperial city and jewel in the British crown in the 18th century, had been supplanted by Bombay in the 1860s. By then, the great Irish orator Daniel O'Connell had convinced the British Parliament to rescind its severe restrictions on Irish Catholics, and a new Irish Catholic middle class had risen to replace the old Protestant ascendancy. Dublin, however, had not fully recovered from colonial rule. It remained the entrepot for British goods, the finished materials of England's industrial revolution, while the Irish continued to produce beef, butter, and other agricultural products to feed the British Empire. The Irish economy, therefore, stagnated while other European industrial revolutions took off. Workers in Dublin largely worked the docks, though some made biscuits at Jacob's factory, or worked as carters, draymen, and teamsters. One of the largest employers, the Guinness

Brewery, had only a few Catholic employees, in accordance with company policy, and those were on the docks. The dockers were Larkin's favorite union men. Larkin had been so successful in Liverpool as a dockside orator that his British union sent him to Belfast, where he achieved the enormous success in the strike and (earlier) lockout of 1907.[13]

The Protestant and Catholic dockers, living in the poorest sections of Belfast, did not receive the higher wages of their (unionized) counterparts in Liverpool, and so pushed first, for union recognition, in order later, to gain the same wages as were paid in Britain. When Thomas Gallaher, owner of a tobacco factory and chairman of the Belfast Steamship Company, refused, the dockworkers struck—joined by carters, shipyard workers, sailors, firemen, boilermakers, coal heavers, transport workers, and the women who worked in Gallaher's tobacco factory. Larkin helped organize one big industrial organization, bringing in all sympathetic workers who received strike pay from Larkin's own union, the National Union of Dock Labourers (NUDL). After five months, the leadership of the union decided to settle the strike and get the men back to work, thus undermining Larkin's strike leadership. This resulted in his founding the Transport and General Workers Union in 1908. Despite the leadership struggle between Larkin and the NUDL, the strike proved to have an enormous impact on workers in Belfast, Liverpool, and Dublin: bringing in thousands of previously ignored workers, raising pay rates, and including both Catholic and Protestant workers.

The Challenges of Organizing in Dublin

But most importantly, the industrial nature of Larkin's new union spread. In Liverpool the dock workers formed their own industrial union, which led to the 1911 general transport strike, introducing mass organizations and heralding a new era of general labor unrest in England, Scotland, and Wales.[14] Dublin proved more difficult to organize. Connolly and Larkin worked there together between 1911 and 1913, using tactics and methods they had learned in the United States while in the IWW. The Irish Transit and General Workers Union (ITGWU) was Larkin's answer to the trades unions he had belonged to in Liverpool. This new organization included everyone from newsboys to biscuit workers, and eventually brought in tramway workers, one of Dublin's most lucrative industries. When the ITGWU needed financial help for its 1913 strike, Big Bill Haywood toured Dublin, Liverpool, and Manchester on behalf of the hard-hit Irish workers. However, William Martin Murphy, one of Dublin's wealthiest capitalists

Lockout supporters in front of union headquarters with signs "Murphy Must Go!" referring to their nemesis William Murphy. Notice the children without shoes holding the signs, the cold winter of 1913 settling in. Courtesy of the National Library of Ireland.

(owner of a hotel, newspaper, tramways, and much property) and part of the rising Catholic bourgeoisie, was determined not to allow syndicalism to take over his city. He organized 396 employers, nearly all of Dublin's capital class, into an association to keep workers locked out while Larkin brought 20,000 workers into his growing union. The stand-off, which began at the end of July 1913, grew progressively over time and lasted until February 1914.

One incident best illustrates the way in which Larkin's appreciation of the IWW's sense of theatre and defiance marked the strike. At the height of tensions, on August 29, Larkin, who had been jailed but later escaped, and Connolly came down from Belfast to step in, only to be arrested. A big union rally had been set for Sackville Street across from Murphy's aptly named Imperial Hotel, where rumor circulated that Larkin would appear. Workers mingled in the wide streets of this commercial thoroughfare with upper-class shoppers, all wondering about the large contingent of police armed with batons also milling about. A large car pulled up and from it emerged an old gentleman in formal clothes and a beard. He energetically headed straight for a second-story balcony, where he revealed that indeed he was Murphy's nemesis Jim Larkin, and proceeded to bark out his defiance on the doorstep of the capitalists' prize hotel.[15]

A riot ensued, and here is where the IWW tactic—of turning a workplace action in a community strike, as in Lawrence—turned into something far more serious than that of the Bread and Roses strike. Clubbing indiscriminately, police chased the poorest of Larkin's followers into the Northern Corporate dwellings, another of Dublin's slums. The police did not leave a single window intact, and in a neighborhood where few had personal possessions, it was reported not a teacup was left unbroken. Cracked furniture and cracked heads left two dead, others in comas, and between 300 and 400 injured. The police did not just chase the poor to their homes, they invaded them, beat the tenants—including women, children, and the infirm—and smashed what they could. The neighborhood invasion reaffirmed British colonial power over the local population, the very reason why Connolly insisted that the socialists must push for a workers' republic in Ireland; not just socialism but republicanism—a break from the empire.[16]

Though it struggled on, the strike proved a losing proposition. Although 20,000 workers struck or were locked out, the British unions failed to send the food and supplies Irish workers needed. By January 1914 the starving strikers went, hat in hand, to sign anti-union contracts, accept even lower wages, and submit to Murphy's triumph. Larkin's use of IWW direct action or Larkinism, a term for Larkin and his politics derisively used by Murphy and others, had been defeated, but the man remained undaunted. Employers used Larkinism "as a short-hand for militancy, the cult of the agitator and the sympathetic strike." Ultimately, even in the face of defeat, both Larkin and Connolly saw a future for socialism, industrial unionism, and—not least—republicanism.[17]

The Struggle Between Irish Republicanism and Internationalism Comes to a Head

The final difference between Larkinism and the IWW rested on the fact that Larkin and Connolly felt they literally were engaged in class warfare in the summer of 1913. Although the Wobblies had no illusions about the role of the police, militia, and private military forces, in the United States they did not advocate forming a working-class army. But both Larkin and Connolly can take credit for the formation of the Irish Citizen Army (ICA), though the real impetus came from the British Colonial Office. Convinced the Irish were an inferior race and not worthy of the rights of the English, the Royal Irish Constabulary (RIC) operated under the assumption that their job was to respond as they would to any colonial subject: ignore their humanity. On the eve of the 1913 strike, Murphy had notified the police that they would be called upon to protect his property, and the RIC immediately partnered with them. In response, the union created its own army to protect workers, which raised issues of armed struggle, in both Ireland and the United States. Armed with hurling sticks, the ICA appeared as early as November 1913.

Larkin's ties to the creation of the ICA certainly would have brought him into close contact with Tom Clarke, the old Fenian fighter and a leading member of the paramilitary IRB. The secrecy of the IRB indicated that these old republicans hesitated to bring either Connolly or Larkin into the fold, but the very existence of the ICA, parading publicly in Croyden Park, certainly got the Brotherhood interested in the two labor leaders. The exact nature of their relationship may never be known, but Larkin's protests of innocence to the contrary, armed struggle surely was the main topic of discussion within the IRB and in its cousin organization, John DeVoy's Clan na Gael in New York City. The Clan Na Gael and the IRB hoped to turn England's disadvantages during the First World War into Ireland's opportunity.

By July 1914 German guns arrived, via the sailing boat *Asgarth*, and some were dispersed to the ICA. As founders and leaders of the ICA, neither Connolly nor Larkin could have been ignorant of these events. In New York, the republican cause began to rely on Roger Casement, a prominent Irish nationalist with German connections; concurrently in Dublin, the old IRB used Tom Clarke's Tobacco shop on Sackville Street to keep John DeVoy, Clarke's former boss in NYC, well informed. The Clan Na Gael and the IRB both followed the Irish nationalist agenda. For his part, after the guns of August began, DeVoy ran to the German Consulate to negotiate for arms and support for an Irish uprising. His plans included Larkin, who arrived in New York a few months later. The long historical debate over the reasons for Larkin's departure from Ireland remains unresolved. We know that Larkin and Connolly tried to salvage relations with British trade unions. Connolly's bitterness over their failure to aid the striking dockworkers, however, often outweighed his devotion to the idea of international socialism. A second—and far more important—blow to internationalism came, of course, with the support of the continental socialist parties for the war.[18]

Jim Larkin barely had disembarked in New York City before being recruited by the Socialist Party of America and John DeVoy's Clan na Gael and given a scheduled speaking tour. Almost immediately, Larkin went to Madison Square Garden to address 15,000 New York socialists celebrating the election of Meyer London to the US Congress. As Larkin followed a whirlwind of such speaking appointments, it soon became clear that Larkin did not share DeVoy's agenda. How much Larkin knew about the scheme for an armed uprising in Ireland in late 1914 or early 1915 remains unclear, but he lost no time in making contact with Connolly's friends, Tom Flynn and his daughter Elizabeth Gurley Flynn, nicknamed the "Rebel Girl" by Joe Hill (see Halker, Chapter 19).

It may have been Flynn who suggested that Larkin give the keynote speech at the January 1915 memorial service for the IWW poet and troubadour Hill. Though not the main speaker at the memorial, Larkin spoke at the graveside. There, he argued that "Joe Hill was shot to death because he was a member of the fighting section of the American Working Class, the Industrial Workers of the World," though he also made it clear that he did not belong to the IWW. Indeed, he specifically indicated that he refused to belong to any one organization but, rather, would speak freely and set his own schedule.[19]

Larkin was in no hurry to embrace the IWW or other organizations around him. Such reticence might explain why he gained a reputation as a "Catholic communist," who had no problem denouncing the British, supporting the Kaiser, and waving his gold cross to audiences while declaring: "I stand by the Cross and I stand by Karl Marx." But his cross was a Celtic one—that is, not a symbol of the Roman Church, or the Christianity of the largely Protestant socialists in America. Catholicism was a signifier for Irish, and if there was a distinctive Irish race, then Larkin identified with it. He was not an immigrant to America, rather just a visitor. Plus, Larkin and Connolly were about to take a separate path from their Wobbly comrades. They maintained their socialist principles but embraced the anticolonial struggle as they moved into the nationalist camp.[20]

In America, the growing militancy of the working class raised issues of direct action, sabotage, and syndicalism, whereas armed struggle preoccupied the Irish. Big strikes in the clothing industry in Chicago, New York, Boston, Philadelphia, and Baltimore in 1915 led to intense IWW activity. Telephone and telegraph workers unionized, public school teachers in Chicago reaffiliated with the national AFL, and William Z. Foster (having left the IWW to pursue his strategy of boring from within) joined forces with Chicago's labor federation chief and Clan na Gael fellow-traveler John Fitzpatrick. Larkin could not have been better situated to see a grand vision of the IWW and the American labor movement. Foster had just published an influential pamphlet on syndicalism, in which he spoke of the "naked power" of capitalist forces and proposed that to face this challenge syndicalists must even contemplate exterminating the scabs used to undermine the workers' cause. While debate raged within the IWW and socialist press in America, only Foster seemed to want to take direct action to extremes. Foster also urged workers to resist the thought that American democracy held any remedies for the working class, and declared that its republican ideology was just a "pretense" with which to deceive working people.

The Irish possessed no rights so long as the British occupied Dublin Castle—and the Great War presented the Irish with an opportunity to remove them. We do not know exactly what Jim Larkin was up to in 1916, or what happened to James Connolly during a few days in January when he was back in Dublin. But when Connolly returned to Dublin, he embarked on a steady path to join the Irish rising planned for April 1916. Meanwhile, Larkin was being introduced to the German legation in New York City, who subsidized him for two years and, in February 1916, brought him to Hoboken to learn about chemical explosions. On April 18, his German contact was arrested in New York while waiting for Larkin, who disappeared. Larkin's training occurred only six days before Connolly marched the ICA to the General Post Office building in Dublin, beginning the Irish rising of 1916, for which Connolly was executed. When Larkin reemerged in Butte in June, he told the largely Irish miners, "be true to the spirit which inspires the rebellion in Ireland." Larkin remained focused on events in Ireland and longed to return home.[21]

Much has been written about Larkin's jealousy of Connolly for going ahead with the rebellion. Some writers even go so far as to argue that Larkin, selfishly, was angry that the rebellion happened without him. Regardless, Larkin never forgot Connolly or the Easter Rising, and he constantly reminded his Irish-American audiences of his Irishness. He viewed the world through a prism shaped more by the contours of the lockout of 1913 than the Socialist International of 1914. Republicanism was part of his socialism, just as it had been for Connolly. If a Catholic identity and admiration for the republican promises of rejecting privilege were unsightly to the more sophisticated radicals of New York and Chicago, then neither Larkin nor Connolly cared. Their experiences in Ireland had left neither with any illusions about what Irish capitalism looked like to the ordinary Irish working people; yet in their near-simultaneous pursuit of German aid between 1914 and 1916, neither one backed away from the IRB.[22]

In 1923 Jim Larkin returned to Ireland, where he continued his pursuit of radical labor politics. After his death in 1947, he was buried in Glasnevin Cemetery, just outside of the plots reserved for the Easter Rising martyrs. The lockout and the Rising remain the main signposts on the road to Irish independence. Two of the men at the center of both events worked closely with the IWW in the United States, and the influence of the One Big Union idea stuck with them and gained expression in the Dublin lockout of 1913.

Notes

1 Robert M. Fox, *Jim Larkin: The Rise of the Underman* (London: Camelot, 1957), pp. 133–4.

2 Bruce Nelson, *Irish Nationalists and the Making of the Irish Race* (Princeton, N.J.: Princeton University Press, 2012), p. 256.

3 Friedrich Engels, *The Condition of the Working Class in England* (Stanford, Calif.: Stanford University Press, 1958). Compare Gareth Stedmon Jones, *Outcast London: A Study in the Relationship Between Classes in Victorian Society* (New York: Pantheon, 1984), p. 296 to Kevin C. Kearns, *Dublin Tenement Life* (London: Penguin, 1994), pp. 7–17; James Plunkett, *Strumpet City* (Dublin: Gill & Macmillan, 2013), pp. 421–6.

4 Donal Nevin, *James Connolly, A Full Life: A Biography of Ireland's Renowned Trade Unionist and Leader of the 1916 Easter Rising* (Dublin: Gill & Macmillan, 2005), ch. 4; Sean Cronin, *Young Connolly* (Dublin: Repsol, 1978), pp. 15–40; Lorcan Collins, *16 Lives: James Connolly* (Dublin: Dublin Press, 2012), pp. 51–5 (quote from Camille Desmoulins, the French revolutionary).

5 Carl Reeve and Ann Barton Reeve, *James Connolly and the United States* (Atlantic Highlands, N.J.: Humanities Press, 1978), pp. 26–59.

6 Sean O'Callaghan, *James Connolly: My Search for the Man, the Myth and His Legacy* (London: Penguin, 2015), pp. 51–6; Nevin, *Connolly*, p. 23.

7 Elizabeth Gurley Flynn, *The Rebel Girl: An Autobiography* (New York: International Publishers), pp. 73–6. *Socialism Made Easy* was published by Charles H. Kerr.

8 Reeve and Reeve, *James Connolly and the United States*, pp. 158–74; *Harp*, August 1908.

9 *Harp*, August 1908.

10 David Witwer, *Corruption and Reform in the Teamsters Union* (Urbana, Ill.: University of Illinois Press, 2003), pp. 28–37.

11 Flynn, *Rebel Girl*, pp. 135–43; Bruce Watson, *Bread and Roses: Mills, Migrants and the Struggle for the American Dream* (New York: Penguin, 2005), pp. 141–61.

12 Padraig Yeates, *Lockout: Dublin 1913* (Dublin: Gill & Macmillan, 2013), pp. 269–91.

13 David Dickson, *Dublin: The Making of a Capital City* (Cambridge, Mass.: Harvard University Press, 2014); Gary Granville, *Dublin 1913: Lockout and Legacy* (Dublin: O'Brien Press, 2013), pp. 29–67; Yeates, *Lockout*, pp. 105–10.

14 Emmet O'Connor, *Big Jim Larkin: Hero or Wrecker?* (Dublin: University College Dublin Press, 2015), pp. 22–42.

15 William D. Haywood, *Bill Haywood's Book: The Autobiography of William D. Haywood* (New York: International Publishers, 1929), pp. 273–4; O'Connor, *Big Jim Larkin*, pp. 124–5; Yeates, *Lockout*, pp. 68–9.

16 Yeates, *Lockout*, pp. 69–75.

17 Yeates, *Lockout*, pp. 564–5; Diarmaid Ferriter, *A Nation and Not a Rabble: The*

Irish Revolution 1913–1923 (London: Profile, 2015), pp. 140–1; O'Connor, *Big Jim Larkin*, p. 134; W. K. Anderson, *James Connolly and the Irish Left* (Dublin: Irish Academic Press, 1994), pp. 66–71; Owen McGee, *The IRB: The Irish Republican Brotherhood from the Land League to Sinn Fein* (Dublin: Four Court Press, 2005), pp. 354–5; O'Connor, *Big Jim Larkin*, p. 22.

18 Terry Golway, *Irish Rebel: John Devoy and America's fight for Ireland's Freedom* (New York: St. Martin's Griffin, 1998), pp. 202–9; O'Connor, *Big Jim Larkin*, pp. 157–67; David Convery (ed.), *Locked Out: A Century of Irish Working-Class Life* (Dublin: Irish Academic Press, 2013), pp. 20–1, 63, 66–7.

19 Jim Larkin, "Murder most foul," *International Socialist Review*, November 1915.

20 Edward P. Johanningsmeier, *Forging American Communism: The Life of William Z. Foster* (Princeton, N.J.: Princeton University Press, 1994), pp. 56–87; O'Connor, *Big Jim Larkin*, pp. 150–6; Anderson, *James Connolly*, pp. 97–106.

21 O'Connor, *Big Jim Larkin*, pp. 174–83.

22 Nelson, *Irish Nationalists*, pp. 3–29, 229; Anderson, *James Connolly*, pp. 41–8.

16

Tom Barker and Revolutionary Europe

Paula de Angelis

In February of 1920, maritime worker and Industrial Workers of the World (IWW) organizer Tom Barker ended his tenure as general secretary of the Marine Transport Workers Industrial Union (MTW) chapter in Buenos Aires, Argentina. He worked his passage to London aboard a Norwegian steamer with an IWW crew, carrying with him almost a decade's experience as a "globetrotting agitator."[1]

A self-educated worker in a classic socialist tradition, erudite, multilingual, and widely read, Barker wrote vividly and with a masterful grasp of the IWW rhetorical style. His contemporary writing, as well as his autobiography (recorded as an oral history in 1963), tell the story of a fascinating transnational Wobbly activist in an exciting time and place—post-war revolutionary Europe—and provide unique insights from a working-class perspective.

Barker acquired his initial political education and red card in New Zealand, where he had emigrated in 1909. An effective strike organizer and talented soapbox orator, he crossed to Australia in 1914, where he became the business manager of the IWW newspaper *Direct Action*, took care of the workers that came through the IWW Hall in Sydney, and organized anti-war and conscription rallies in the Domain, which became a daily occurrence as the campaign escalated (see also Burgmann, Chapter 10, and Derby, Chapter 11).[2]

Barker landed in Sydney to find a working class wrapped in war fever. The craft unions (generally referred to in Australia as "trades unions") very much supported "the war effort." The Labor Party, established in the 1890s by the trades union movement to represent workers' interests in Parliament, furnished the leaders and Cabinets of the wartime governments. The trades unions entered into no-strike agreements for the duration, and then found themselves hamstrung in the face of growing rank-and-file discontent, unable to deploy their most effective method of redressing grievances and helpless in the face of a Labor government that had turned on the unions despite their support of the war.

Barker and the Australian Wobblies agreed with their Irish fellow worker James Connolly, who stated, "a bayonet is a weapon with a worker on either end." When in a fit of patriotism the waterside workers' union expelled their "enemy" members, Barker wrote impatiently:

> Now that the Empire is in danger the Sydney Wharfies have risen to the occasion. They have determined not to allow Germans, Austrians or Turks, naturalised or unnaturalised, to get a living on the Sydney water-front .... The whole thing is childish in the extreme and unworthy of men who pretend to be unionists.[3]

Convinced that success depended on universal working-class solidarity, the purposes and dangers of "boneheaded patriotism" (a favored phrase amongst Australian Wobblies) were obvious, creating false divisions amongst the working class, and putting workers at a disadvantage in their conflict with employers and the capitalist state.

For the US IWW, the First World War was primarily a political issue, related to state persecution rather than direct industrial conditions. The American IWW press followed the events in Europe closely and discussed the effects of the war on the European working class, but since the US IWW officially chose to not take a stand on the war itself, those Wobblies who actively opposed the war and US participation in it did so through the Socialist Party and similar groups.[4]

By contrast, the First World War had profound socio-economic effects on the Australian working class. Owing to its export-driven economy, the conditions and living standard of the working class in Australia steadily worsened during the war, compounding the effects of a terrible drought in 1914 and 1915. Trade with Germany, Australia's second-biggest export market, ceased overnight. The importation of manufactured goods, coming mostly from Britain, slowed to a trickle. Even a population that unequivocally supported the Allies, as indeed most of the working class in Australia did, soured on the war effort after four years of sharply declining living standards and the real possibility of widespread starvation. Since they were responding to different local forces, the Australian IWW were actively involved in the anti-war and conscription movements. They formed coalitions with socialist parties and peace organizations, and partic-

Tom Barker (1887–1970), circa 1912. Courtesy of the Alexander
Turnbull Library, Wellington, New Zealand.

ipated in campaigns against conscription. Barker himself was jailed twice in
Australia for anti-war propaganda.

His third jail sentence was in preparation for his deportation as a
"foreign radical," a common experience for Wobblies and other radical
itinerant workers in both Australia and the United States. Deported to—
and, shortly afterwards, from—Chile, Barker made his way to the Buenos
Aires docks in Argentina and founded an IWW chapter specifically devoted
to organizing and representing the many foreign seafarers who passed
through this busy international port. Primed by a familiarity with French

grammar, he quickly learned Spanish and immersed himself in the marine transport industry as a worker and job delegate.

Barker admired the syndicalist, highly organized union that represented the local dock workers. "From 1919 when the Marine Transport Workers Union was first established for the foreign-going seamen in Buenos Aires," he wrote in 1922, "the dockworkers systematically gave solidarity to their comrades from over-seas at any time upon demand."[5] He left Buenos Aires convinced that building the One Big Union of the Sea was an urgent necessity, indeed the key to working-class mastery of the international industrial system. When he left for Europe, the national syndicalist Federación Obrera Regional Argentina (Regional Labor Federation, or FORA) gave him delegate credentials, and he attended several transport union and revolutionary congresses on their behalf.[6]

Tom Barker returned to the country of his birth in 1920 with his Wobbly principles firmly intact, his practical experiences having confirmed his commitment to industrial unionism and preference for syndicalist methods. The two years he spent in Europe as an itinerant revolutionary—in particular, his role and choices during his visit to the Soviet Union in 1921—provide remarkable insights into his character and perspective.

He combined his duties as a FORA delegate with his role as an international organizer for the MTW and IWW. Technically based in London, multiple political hats kept him traveling and writing extensively until he arrived in Moscow in June 1921. First, he traipsed the United Kingdom speaking to his countrymen and women to gather support for the campaign to free his Australian fellow workers (later known as the IWW Twelve) who were still political prisoners in Australia's jails.[7] Later in the year he attended transport worker congresses and union meetings in Copenhagen and Berlin, acquiring work on the docks as he went; he fulfilled his delegate role at these meetings while also fostering MTW branches and or local equivalents, and building political connections with syndicalist-oriented unions.

This travel and networking sharpened his fluency in the languages he had been learning, especially Spanish, and established the lifelong multilingual correspondence that Barker maintained with comrades and friends around the world.[8] It also prepared him well for the job that he assumed in New York after visiting the Soviet Union, recruiting volunteers for an "industrial colony" in Russia; an office report noted in 1923 that Barker's tasks included reading and responding to correspondence in every language except Finnish.[9]

Barker's own words provide the best evidence of his choices, analysis, and character during this 18-month period, since he wrote for IWW publications in both the Antipodes and United States. Conference documents provide supporting evidence, particularly those of the Red International of Labor Unions Congress, held in Moscow in July 1921. This meeting, set up under the auspices of the Communist International, gathered together some 300 radical union delegates from 42 different countries in order to establish a revolutionary trade union international, later known as the Profintern.

Two significant arguments emerged amongst delegates at the Congress. First, should the Profintern directly affiliate with the Communist International (or Comintern)—then simultaneously holding its own Congress in Moscow? A second debate erupted over "the policy of working within the (mainstream) Unions versus the destruction of the Unions and the building of new revolutionary organisations."[10] (The US IWW literature described this matter as the "dual unionism versus the boring-from-within" debate). English syndicalist Tom Mann argued both for affiliation with the Comintern and for boring from within, a position diametrically opposed to Barker's.

Mann and Barker had both lived and worked in Australia at different times. Both were familiar with the parliamentary wing of the Australian union movement and possessed syndicalist convictions; yet they drew very different conclusions from their shared experiences. Mann argued that the revolution in Russia had changed the game, and that the Comintern offered the best option for building a real revolutionary International. He also argued that setting up competing unions in Britain was "doomed to failure." Rather, "We must try to force radical changes inside the old organisations."[11]

IWW principles, experiences in the marine transport industry, and exposure to South American syndicalism all resulted in Barker drawing different conclusions. In 1908, the IWW chose "to confine the activities of the organization to economic functions." This did not mean that they ceased the sort of political activity traditional to socialist groups; on the contrary, they continued to produce propaganda and engage in civil disobedience. They simply directed it towards fostering direct action at the point of production. Barker's travels in Europe only confirmed his conviction, formed in Buenos Aires, that industrial unionism was a local form of syndicalism. "I have been in Norway for a month," he wrote to *Solidarity* in June 1920:

and have had the pleasure of meeting most of the active boys of Norway. The Norwegian Syndicalist Federation ... is as near to the ideas and practices of the One Big Union as they can reasonably get, after taking local conditions into consideration.[12]

Whatever the attitude to political action, the IWW and the syndicalists agreed that keeping unions separate from political party affiliations was a question of strategic necessity. Barker and the other syndicalists from Europe and South America cited the French argument that a union "groups together, independently of all political schools, all workers who are conscious of the struggle to be carried on for the abolition of the wage system." Moreover, the IWW Constitution stated: "to the end of promoting industrial unity and of securing necessary discipline within the organization, the I.W.W. refuses all alliances, direct and indirect, with existing political parties or anti-political sects."[13] From this viewpoint, Profintern affiliation with the Comintern seriously compromised an important syndicalist principle (see Thorpe, Chapter 6).

The syndicalist minority published a dissenting statement on this question, and Barker publicly spoke against affiliation. Barker did not respond directly to the question of the appropriate attitude to the craft unions at the congress, or to Mann's opinion that success required working within the mainstream union organization. Barker's writing of the time shows quite clearly what he thought, though, especially in the British case. "Life is too short to bore from within," he once wrote.[14]

> The basis of marine unionism in Great Britain is rotten to the core, and neither fine-sounding names, nor aggressive talk can alter that fact .... The dockworkers are cursed with officials who only regard their jobs as stepping stones to get to Westminster .... Their main joy is to hang around the tradesman's entrance at Buckingham Palace and exhibit their taste in spats as a way to bring about better working class conditions .... The axe has to go to the root; the spirit and structure of craft unionism must be destroyed.[15]

Decades later he commented, more tolerantly:

> To get the best out of the power you have you must be united .... We haven't even got it in Britain yet, we have craft unionism hanging on and no real effort to put an end to it, although there is a good deal of latent solidarity which largely gets over these problems.[16]

When Barker made his way to Moscow, he was fired with enthusiasm for the successful workers' revolution, and eager to contribute, locally and internationally. He remained in the Soviet Union for several months after the Congress, and his visit resulted in radical changes to his personal life—he married a Russian dancer named Bertha while there—and political direction. It is clear that he was a conscientious but not enthusiastic conference delegate. He wrote at the time, "Industrial unionism takes the economics of Marx out of the class-room, popularizes them and applies the lessons .... [A] twenty-minute talk on the job in the vernacular is worth twenty meetings dealing with generalities."[17] Ideologically, Barker's commitment to the One Big Union emerged from his early socialist education, and was confirmed by eight years experience as a working-class militant. Personally, he enjoyed the life of an itinerant revolutionary, and was by nature suited to the direct action approach to organizing embraced by the iww. He had a personal distaste for bureaucracy, a deep distrust of church and state, and a decided preference for on-the-ground organizing and the company of working-class people.

A love of oratory and the soapbox might have directed him towards a politically oriented career, if it were not balanced by a gregarious and informal nature, a distaste for ceremony and meetings, and a lifetime of manual labor. "I didn't have a parliamentary mind and I never have had one," he joked later, when discussing the reasons he first joined the New Zealand iww, and before the Profintern Congress even ended, Barker had found a project much more suited to his nature and preferences, through his new friendship with the legendary iww founder and leader William D. "Big Bill" Haywood, who had fled to the Soviet Union earlier that year.[18] Based in the Siberian basin, Haywood's ambitious brainchild later became known as the Kuzbas Autonomous Industrial Project.

The Kuzbas Project was developed as a joint endeavor between iww members then present in Moscow and the Bolshevik government. The project's New York office, where Barker spent the following five years, recruited American industrial workers and engineers to live on the commune established in the Siberian mining district in the Kuzbas basin, build modern industrial facilities and work systems, and teach those systems to local workers.[19] Yet Barker did not uncritically embrace Soviet communism, later recalling:

> When we had settled the plans for Kuzbass it was decided that I should go the United States with HS Calvert .... Then the question came up of whether I was expected to join the Communist Party. I told them that would go against my grain, because some of the iww ideas did not agree with some of the Communist ideas.[20]

Barker never felt this decision was held against him, nor did it occur to him to question the different decisions of others. The project's Moscow-based planning committee included, at Barker's insistence, Tom Mann, whom he continued to regard with genuine admiration and warmth throughout several decades of association. Always active in his local community and union, Barker maintained lifelong friendships and working relationships with labor politicians, anarchists, and Communist Party organizers alike, judging his fellow revolutionaries on their track record and devotion to the principle of working-class liberation, rather than their organizational affiliations.

Late in 1921, Barker traveled to New York with the Calverts and his new wife. There he deployed his language and literature skills in the US recruiting office of the Kuzbas Project, writing the publicity material and prospectuses, and handling its multilingual correspondence. His connection to the MTW continued; characteristically, he refused to become involved in the sectarian conflict raging between the Communist Party and IWW, which was particularly virulent in New York. He concentrated on his tasks at the office, keeping himself and his new bride fed, and rewriting his serial *The Story of the Sea* for the MTW to distribute in pamphlet form. In 1923, Barker objected vociferously to the Soviet government's decision take over the administration of the Kuzbas Project, but was persuaded to return to his job as a salaried worker; thereafter, he evidently relegated the Soviet Union to the status of another boss.

The political position Tom Barker took at the Profintern congress, and indeed all of his public perceptions and actions in post-war revolutionary Europe, were colored and informed by his own experiences during the previous decade. The First World War, and its economic and cultural effects on the Australian working class in particular, cemented a distaste for parliamentary politics and party-based ideologies, as well as a profound opposition to state-induced racism and patriotism. His work as a maritime union organizer in Buenos Aires proved the soundness of industrial unionism in practice, and supported a lifelong belief in the capabilities and mission of his class. His convictions on "the historic mission of the working class" ran so deep that they informed the very basis of his rhetorical strategy. "We learn by experience," he wrote in 1922:

> Therefore it is our duty and should be our joy to encourage action, to dissipate ignorance and, by working within the field of our experience and with the things and the men with whom we have contact, to make steady progress toward our objective.[21]

Tom Barker retained his indifference to political affiliations and labels throughout his long and active life. Worker solidarity, for him, always went beyond ideologies. He came to industrial unionism by a uniquely transnational route and articulated its principles with passion and skill. He joined a revolutionary union in a time of economic and social turbulence, but the ideas and convictions he embraced in the 1910s and 1920s remained with him. His affiliations and tactics changed with his circumstances, but his internationalism, commitment to solidarity, and interest in his community remained constant throughout his life.

Notes

1 Verity Burgmann, *Revolutionary Industrial Unionism: The Industrial Workers of the World in Australia* (Cambridge/New York: Cambridge University Press, 1995), p. 70.

2 E. C. Fry (ed.), *Tom Barker and the IWW* (Brisbane, Qld.: IWW General Membership Branch, 1999), p. 33.

3 *Direct Action*, January 1, 1915, p. 2.

4 Eric Chester, *The Wobblies in Their Heyday: The Rise and Destruction of the Industrial Workers of the World during the World War I Era* (Santa Barbara, Calif.: Praeger, 2014).

5 Tom Barker, *The Story of the Sea: Marine Transport Workers Handbook* (Chicago, Ill.: IWW, 1922), p. 53.

6 Fry, *Tom Barker and the IWW*, p. 43.

7 *One Big Union Monthly*, January 1920, p. 54.

8 Fry, *Tom Barker and the IWW*.

9 Box 1, Folder 27, Mellie and Herbert S. Calvert Collection, Walter P. Reuther Library, Wayne State University, Detroit, Mich

10 J. T. Murphy, *The "Reds" in Congress: Preliminary Report of the First World Congress of the Red International of Trade and Industrial Unions* (London: British Bureau, Red International of Trade and Industrial Unions, 1921), p. 8.

11 Murphy, *The "Reds" in Congress*.

12 *Solidarity*, May 5, 1920, p. 2.

13 *The IWW Reply to the Red Trade Union International (Moscow) by the General Executive Board of the Industrial Workers of the World* (Chicago, Ill.: IWW, 1922), p. 10.

14 *One Big Union Monthly*, December, 1920.

15 Barker, *The Story of the Sea*, p. 45.

16 Fry, *Tom Barker and the IWW*, pp. 12–13.

17 Barker, *The Story of the Sea*, p. 76.

18 Barker, *The Story of the Sea*, p. 76.

19 J. P. Morray, *Project Kuzbas: American Workers in Siberia (1921–1926)* (New York: International Publishers, 1983).

20 Fry, *Tom Barker and the IWW*, p. 46.

21 Barker, *The Story of the Sea*, p. 73.

17

P. J. Welinder and "American Syndicalism" in Interwar Sweden

Johan Pries

When Pär Jönsson Welinder returned home to Sweden some time in the spring of 1925, he should have been a broken man. Twice he had been part of veritable hurricanes of labor militancy. And twice he had seen them utterly defeated.

In his mid-20s, P. J. Welinder had participated in the cataclysmic Swedish "Great Strike" of 1909. This series of strikes and lockouts was driven by demands from the labor movement's grassroots, forcing the leadership into an all-out battle with employers. The entire country eventually came to a complete standstill for a month, transforming unruly local conflicts into a disciplined war of attrition involving as many as 300,000 workers.[1]

In the end, the 1909 strike was broken. Sweden's social democratic unions almost collapsed in the aftermath, and turned towards extreme gradualism. Out of this cataclysmic event emerged Swedish syndicalism. Labor radicals disappointed with the social democrats' unenthusiastic leadership of the strike formed the syndicalist Sveriges Arbetares Centralorganisation (Swedish Workers Central Organization, or SAC) in 1910.[2]

Welinder, however, followed thousands of blacklisted grassroots unionists who refused the employers' demand to tear up their union cards, and instead boarded a ship bound for America. Within a few years he established himself as an Oregon-based logger, but again found himself in the middle of a massive grassroots struggle. This time it was the 1917 Northwestern lumber strike, one of the key events of the explosion of militancy taking place around the Industrial Workers of the World (IWW) in the late 1910s. At this decisive moment, Welinder joined the rapidly growing IWW.[3]

In the following years, powerful employers and state agencies outma-

P. J. Welinder, circa 1930.
Used with permission from
the Sveriges Arbetares
Centralorganisation.

neuvered and crushed the IWW's momentary strength. Welinder briefly
rose to prominence within the movement, first in the leadership of the
Portland IWW branch in 1921, and then as a 1924 candidate for IWW general secretary. Welinder appears to have been involved in the group of
self-proclaimed IWW traditionalists based in the Pacific Northwest and
their struggle against what they understood as centralists within the union.
After the great schism resulting in two simultaneous 1924 IWW conventions, Welinder served a brief spell as the temporary general secretary of
the smaller of the two IWW fractions battling for control of the organization, the so-called "Emergency Program" group. Just a few months later
he abandoned this remnant of a union and began an arduous voyage back
to Sweden. Interestingly, these experiences of defeat never seem to have
embittered Welinder, but traveled with him and became mythic materials
he used to shape political struggles in new situations.[4]

The SAC: Growing Up and Slowing Down

Early in 1925, Welinder showed up at a syndicalist meeting in Gothenburg.
The SAC had, by the mid-1920s, grown to almost 40,000 members, with

the large port city of Gothenburg one of its crucial urban strongholds. Welinder instantly leveraged his status as a prominent IWW old-timer to gain influence in the SAC and set about implementing what he saw as the crucial lessons of "American syndicalism."[5]

The discussions among the SAC's central figures at this moment largely centered on how syndicalists could draw on the cultural politics and institutional strength that their social democratic competitors so clearly displayed. Gradualist ideas were rapidly winning ground through discussions about syndicalists engaging in non-union organizations like cooperatives to create a wider network of radical allies. The SAC's left-leaning majority blocked some of the most clearly reformist proposals, but the notion of restrained and protracted struggle for local hegemony had nonetheless become a fundamental part of Swedish syndicalism by the early 1920s.[6]

In this battle over the shape of syndicalism to come, Welinder initially sided, as he had in America, with the decentralists who dominated the organization's left. In April 1926 the growing group around Welinder founded a weekly paper, *Arbetare-Kuriren*, which furiously attacked those seeking to bring the SAC closer to social democracy. This Gothenburg-based group seems to have written most of the paper's longer pieces and international coverage, largely focusing on the IWW. Shorter and more mundane reflections appear to have been sent in by a dispersed network of local sympathizers. A remarkable feature of this clearly marginal, workerist paper was how it managed to publish several soon-to-be famous writers, like the 1940s best-selling novelist Folke Fridell, the 1969 Nobel literature laureate Harry Martinson, and very early translations of Langston Hughes's poetry.

It quickly became clear that the people coalescing around *Arbetare-Kuriren* wanted to be more than a counterforce to the SAC's slide towards a more social democratically influenced syndicalism. Their agenda was neither to conserve what the SAC had become by the mid-1920s, nor simply to return to its 1910 program. Rather, they argued for a third kind of syndicalism which, based on the American experience, they claimed as tactically superior to both the SAC's right and left factions.

As the SAC's centralists in the late 1920s began to leave syndicalism and return to the actual social democratic unions, the fault lines of Swedish syndicalism shifted. On the one side was an uneasy truce between some of the old leftist decentralists and the more moderate centralists, agreeing in general terms on long-term tactics focusing on creating durable parallel structures outside the state to fight for hegemony from below. On the other side, Welinder's *Arbetare-Kuriren* group argued that struggles should be disruptive, quick, and unbound from the restraints of allied civil society organizations.[7]

The "American" position increased its influence after Welinder was employed as an agitator by the SAC's Southwestern Regional Committee, spending most of 1926 on a speaking tour visiting countless towns and rural communities during the launch of *Arbetare-Kuriren*. The old Wobbly, who by all accounts was a superb public speaker and regularly drew large crowds, used this opportunity to create a network of supporters, subscribers, sellers, and contributors to his weekly far beyond Gothenburg. By 1927, *Arbetare-Kuriren* had been endorsed by the SAC's four southernmost regional committees. As tensions increased, these four regional districts started to break away from the SAC. In October 1928, a second syndicalist union formed around the *Arbetare-Kuriren* tendency. Interestingly, the new Syndikalistiska Arbetare-federationen (Syndicalist Workers Federation, or SAF) never officially tried to organize within the IWW's structure, yet presented itself as the "interpreter" of Wobbly ideas in Sweden, and even urged sailors in Swedish ports to join the IWW's existing transnational Marine Transport Workers Industrial Union rather than set up SAF locals.[8]

The new organization initially included just over 2,000 members, less than 10 percent of the SAC's total membership before the split. Most of these were based in a dozen locals in the southwestern part of the country, between Gothenburg and Malmö. The largest locals were in Borås, Helsingborg, and Gothenburg, which together initially comprised more than half of the membership. Members overwhelmingly worked in logging, construction, railroads, and the large textile mills of Borås and Mölndal. The SAF grew rapidly, more than doubling its membership in a few short years and reaching its zenith around 1933.[9]

"American" Syndicalism in Sweden

Despite both groups claiming a true syndicalist pedigree, the SAF and SAC had drastically differing strategic visions. The most contentious issue, however, was the spiraling costs associated with the SAC's central administration and two daily newspapers, *Arbetaren* and *Norrlandsfolket*. These disagreements might appear to have little bearing on the contemporary situation, and often have been treated in strictly political and programmatic terms. But neither side in the conflict maps neatly onto the grand narratives of interwar politics, or onto the syndicalists' more narrow centralist-decentralist debates. Several key "centralist" figures in the SAC had strong anarchist leanings, most prominently *Arbetaren*'s editor Albert Jensen. The SAF "decentralists" on the other hand combined unashamed Marxist class analysis and close attention to state regulation of "social issues" with an absolute dismissal of Leninism and a much more radical anti-nationalism than the sac's majority.[10]

Instead of emphasizing different political programs, this debate makes more sense and can be drawn on more fruitfully today, by considering how it reframed the iww experiences of 1917—as Welinder sought to mobilize memories of that historic moment in his alternative to the sac's gradualism. Particularly interesting is the way the saf drew on how the iww had imagined its own social basis, in that it invites a discussion about how social movements make sense of political time. Welinder argued for the remaking of the "overly organized" sac and keeping dues at a bare minimum not only out of decentralist principles, but also in order to become more accessible to "the most destitute" parts of the working class as the iww had. These marginalized workers, key to the saf's strategy, would be attracted by the organization's affordability.[11]

Reining in the costs of a centralized bureaucracy, large strike funds, and cultural projects like daily newspapers went hand in glove with a strategy that had a completely different temporal imagination and understanding of struggle than the sac's gradualism. Welinder and his group saw the slow accumulation of resources, allies, and respectability as futile. The property-owning class never could be defeated "with money," in Welinder's words. All that this institutional build-up of resources was understood to do was block the natural escalation of local conflicts through the working class's internal bonds of solidarity.[12]

To avoid such slow institutional preparation for protracted battles, Welinder's group, like the iww, argued against signing contracts with fixed expiration dates. In this way the employers could not set the stage for struggle and entice workers into isolated and long battles of attrition. Instead, the Welinder group advocated short bursts of disruptive activity. The entire union focused upon one or a few points of brief and intense struggle—and at a time of their own choosing. In this rendering, direct action fixated less on a specific method, such as a strike or sabotage, than a temporal intensity surging through the links of solidarity forged by previous moments of struggle.[13]

Creating a culture of autonomy and instilling "a force of initiative, desire for great deeds and will to struggle" among workers was crucial for this strategy. Only this self-reliance enabled groups of workers to act quickly and with a minimum of central coordination.[14] It was as if this brand of syndicalism understood itself less as a formal organization than a strategic tendency within the working class which had to be nurtured culturally.

The cultural image of workers evoked was far from the respectable union member steadily paying dues in rational apprehension of disciplined battles to come, an image associated with the most skilled sections of the working class and crucial to social democratic claims to hegemony. Welinder's vision of working-class culture highlighted sudden and overwhelming passion erupting in moments of intense struggle, spreading through the emotional ties of solidarity within the working class. This sense of time and tactics clearly bears traces of Welinder's two formative political events.

Both the 1909 Great Strike and the 1917 lumber strike began as unruly moments from below, with official labor leaders only partly controlling them. Only when the insurgency slowed down and ossified into two opposing camps did the superior institutional strength of the employers become decisive. Welinder's view of syndicalism as happening in intense moments of struggle seems to owe more to these experiences where self-activity had been so crucial, and to a weariness over the way they had been defeated, than to simply turning a naïve revolutionary romanticism into a political tactic.

What makes Welinder's strategy different from the IWW's is that it did not address precarious workers in the same direct way. We can find no examples in *Arbetare-Kuriren* of the romanticized "hobo" who played such a crucial role for the IWW. The SAF never directly mimicked the way in which the IWW had drawn strength from the dispersed routines of mobility and struggles of seasonal labor migration. Instead of a mobile working-class subject signifying flexibility, SAF literature evoked a much more general notion of class that gained specificity through the construction of political time. Only by framing action as sudden and outside the slow, disciplined gradualism of the rational and respectable union member was the unruly culture associated with precarious workers evoked.[15]

An Untimely End

The small but extraordinarily active milieu around Welinder did not last. Its success hinged on a strategy of sudden disruptive moments of struggle interlinked across time and space by intensely emotional solidarity. Sweden in the early 1930s did see a series of flashpoints where labor unrest spiraled out of hand—most notably the Ådalen events of 1931 which left four demonstrators dead at the hands of the army—and advances by both the SAC and SAF. But by the middle of the decade, the conflict between broad populist nationalist alliances and Nazism increasingly came to dominate Sweden, as it did the rest of Europe.

This not only made different tactical objectives central to the labor movement, but also introduced a different sense of political time. The Nazis' rapid rise to power in Germany shattered the very notion of the workers' movement operating within a progressive flow of history, whether slow and gradual or fast and disruptive. In the years that followed, time seemed to move backwards, as the left instead became engaged in what Geoff Eley calls "the politics of retreat."[16]

Enduring the unprecedented level of state repression unleashed by Nazi Germany became the key strategic question of they day. Not only did the rhythm and pace of the SAF's "American" syndicalism seem untimely; its sense of direction, the idea of workers' struggles driving history forward towards the inevitable liberation of a socialist future through isolated acts of disruption, suddenly made little sense. No room for such disruptive moments existed in the new paradigm of preventing the collapse of the existing order through cross-class alliances. The careful discipline of slow struggles became a key component of the democratic rearguard actions which replaced the fight for a socialist future.

The SAF had, since its formation, been involved in a series of labor disputes. Most of these were local conflicts on Sweden's west coast, the most infamous being the 1932 protracted battle of 80 striking millworkers in Mölndal which, unsurprisingly, yielded very mixed results for an organization pulled into the kind of battle it sought to avoid. With the death of Pär Jönsson Welinder from tuberculosis between two of his never-ending speaking tours in October 1934, the SAF lost what little momentum it still had. Only a shell of its former self, the SAF reintegrated into the SAC in 1938, bringing with it just over 1,000 members.[17]

Historical judgment has not been kind to Welinder and the SAF. Syndicalism in Sweden's Southwest never recovered from the organizational chaos that followed the SAF's collapse.[18] But the theoretical work that the SAC–SAF debate provoked, and the rich archive it has left for posterity, may provide a less bleak legacy for our present moment. The way that this bitter debate rearticulated the IWW's appeal to precarious workers, by making temporal imagination a crucial terrain for political strategy rather than nomadic mobility, might prove more useful today than in the 1930s.

The two temporalities emerging from the SAC–SAF debates are perhaps best understood when read alongside Antonio Gramsci's discussion of the need for socialists to shift strategies between wars of position and wars of maneuver. Instead of seeing the two senses of time in this bitter debate as mutually exclusive, they can be seen as complementary, as ways to navigate different strategic situations.

Gramsci wanted to transform civil society to indirectly influence the state before a decisive revolutionary push to rapidly seize power.[19] But neither the SAF nor the SAC seemed interested in the state, whether in terms of reforms or revolution. And perhaps it is this syndicalist concern with shaping everyday conduct, rather than Gramsci's attention to how the capitalist state could be repurposed by cultural struggle, that is more relevant in our own neoliberal conjuncture than in Welinder's day. Can the potential of intense moments of struggle to escalate and connect through links of solidarity be a way to understand the flickers of disruption seen today, rather than dismissing them as failed revolutions? And can we think about the tasks of the grindingly slow activism that surrounds these moments as building institutions and nurturing cultures of solidarity and self-activity, thus creating the conditions for disruptive moments to spread, rather than reforms that never seem to add up to real change? Brought to bear on the present in this way, Welinder and the Swedish quasi-Wobblies of SAF provide an example to learn from.

Notes

1   *Arbetare-Kuriren*, no. 41, 1934; Bernt Schiller, *Storstrejken 1909: förhistoria och orsaker* (Gothenburg, Sweden: Elander, 1967).

2   Lennart K. Persson, *Syndikalismen i Sverige 1903–1922* (Stockholm: Federativ, 1993), pp. 110–27.

3   Solon De Leon, *The American Labor Who's Who* (New York: Hanford Press, 1925), pp. 246, 264; Henry Bengtson, *On the Left in America: Memoirs of the Scandinavian-American Labor Movement*, trans. Kermit B. Westerberg (Carbondale, Ill.: Southern Illinois University Press, 1991), pp. 62, 364.

4   De Leon, *The American Labor Who's Who*, p. 264; Ingemar Sjöö, *Fackliga Fribrytare: episoder från hundra år av svensk syndikalism* (Stockholm: Federativ, 2011), pp. 166–7, 191; Eric Chester, *The Wobblies in their Heyday: The Rise and Destruction of the Industrial Workers of the World during the World War I Era* (Santa Barbara, Calif.: Praeger, 2014), ch. 7.

5   Sjöö, *Fackliga Fribrytare*, p. 186; P. J. Welinder, *Den amerikanska syndikalismen* (Stockholm: Stockholms LS, 1977 [1926]).

6   Sjöö, *Fackliga Fribrytare*, pp. 164–5. See also Arwid Lund, *Albert Jensen och revolutionen* (Stockholm: Federativ, 2001), pp. 39–42; Persson, *Syndikalismen i Sverige*, pp. 237–8.

7   Sjöö, *Fackliga Fribrytare*, pp. 186–7.

8   Ingemar Sjöö, *Göteborgs apacher: Syndikalism i Göteborg 1911–1991* (Gothenburg, Sweden: Göteborgs lokala samorganisation, 1991), p. 12; Sjöö, *Fackliga Fribrytare*, p. 165; *Arbetare-Kuriren*, no. 31, 1930.

9   Sjöö, *Fackliga fribrytare*, pp. 168–90, 184; Sjöö, *Göteborgs apacher*, p. 12.

10 Sjöö, *Fackliga fribrytare*, pp. 165–6; Herbert Anckar, "Schiscmen SAC-SAF," in Karl

Bergkvist and Evert Arvidsson (eds.), *SAC 1910–1960: jubileumskrift* (Stockholm: Federativs, 1960), pp. 94–5.

11 Sjöö, *Göteborgs apacher*, pp. 11–12; *Arbetare-Kuriren*, no. 44, 1928. See also *Arbetare-Kuriren*, no. 6, 1928.

12 *Arbetare-Kuriren*, no. 19, 1930; P. J. Welinder, *Medlen och målet: en analys av organisationsformerna* (Gothenburg, Sweden: Arbetare-Kuriren, 1931), pp. 29–30.

13 Welinder, *Medlen och målet*, pp. 31–32; *Arbetare-Kuriren*, no. 19, 1930.

14 P. J. Welinder, *Ett Aktionsprogram: Den Syndikalistiska-Arbetarefederationens grundidé* (Gothenburg, Sweden: Arbetare-Kuriren, 1932), pp. 18–23.

15 See, for example, Matthew S. May, *Soapbox Rebellion: The Hobo Orator Union and the Free Speech Fights of the Industrial Workers of the World, 1909–1916* (Tuscaloosa, Ala.: University of Alabama Press, 2013), pp. 24–34; Don Mitchell, "Controlling space, controlling scale: migratory labour, free speech, and regional development in the American West," *Journal of Historical Geography* 28:1 (2002): 67–8.

16 Geoff Eley, *Forging Democracy: The History of the Left in Europe, 1850–2000* (Oxford: Oxford University Press, 2002), p. 261. Other contributions to this discussion on the left's sense of historical direction include Walter Benjamin, *Illuminations*, trans. Harry Zorn (London: Pimlico, 1999), pp. 248–51; Wendy Brown, *Politics Out of History* (Princeton, N.J.: Princeton University Press, 2001), pp. 160–3.

17 Sjöö, Fackliga *fribrytare*, pp. 196–210.

18 Sjöö, *Göteborgs apacher*, p. 13; Sjöö, *Fackliga fribrytare*, p. 210.

19 Antonio Gramsci, *Selections from the Prison Notebooks*, ed. and trans. Quintin Hoare and Geoffrey Nowell Smith (New York: International Publishers, 1977), pp. 238–9.

18

"All Workers Regardless of Craft, Race or Colour": The First Wave of IWW Activity and Influence in South Africa

Lucien van der Walt

The Industrial Workers of the World (IWW) quickly spread across the globe, its ideas and organizing model having a notable impact in a wide variety of contexts. In South Africa, the IWW had an important influence on sections of the left, labor, and national liberation movements beginning in 1908. By the end of 1910, IWW-style syndicalism was an important influence on local socialist networks, and on the country's main left weekly, the *Voice of Labour*; an active IWW union had waged significant strikes in Johannesburg, and also spread into Durban and Pretoria; and the local IWW and Socialist Labour Party (SLP) actively promoted variants of the IWW approach through written propaganda and public meetings.

By 1913, this early wave of IWW-influenced activity had almost completely faded away. It has since been overshadowed by a second upsurge of syndicalism, starting in 1915, and the founding of the Communist Party of South Africa (CPSA) in 1921. However, it bears closer examination. It helped lay the foundations for later left activism by promoting industrial unionism and syndicalist ideas, pioneering a class-based anti-racist left perspective on South Africa's social and national questions, and forging a layer of militants who would play important roles in subsequent years.

It is also worth revisiting in order to recall, and reflect upon, its limitations. While syndicalist (and communist) organizing from 1915 onward was notable for building a substantial base among black African, Coloured, and Indian workers, the first wave of IWW organizing and influence was not. Instead, it was marked by an inability to break out of a largely immigrant, white, and English-speaking working-class milieu. The reasons for the contrasting situations—which lie largely at the level of politics—are important to understand, and will be considered in the conclusion.

Context: An African Capitalist Revolution

iww ideas and models traveled into South Africa along the rivers of human labor that flowed into the territory to work in large-scale capitalist diamond mining, centered on Kimberley, and gold mining in the Witwatersrand. Prior to the late 1800s the territory was marginal to the world economy, mainly comprising non-capitalist agrarian societies. The new mines, however, rapidly attracted massive amounts of Western foreign direct investment, more than the rest of Africa combined.[1] The Kimberley mines were run by a monopoly and used cheap labor, a pattern of centralization reproduced on the Witwatersrand, where the mines—large, dangerous, deep-level operations—were soon controlled by an oligopoly of giant foreign firms. By 1898, the Witwatersrand was producing 27 percent of the world's gold. Mining towns sprang up along the reef, running east to west, the most of important of which was Johannesburg, which exploded from a population of 3,000 in 1886, to 100,000 in 1896, and then 250,000 in 1913.[2]

The mines spurred a massive expansion in infrastructure, a boom in port towns like Cape Town and Durban, agricultural commercialization, the rise of secondary industries, and the emergence of a southern African regional political economy. They developed in the context of late nineteenth and early twentieth-century globalization, based on unprecedented flows of commodities, capital, and labor, and premised on advances in geography, telecommunications, and transportation which enabled, for the first time, a genuinely global economic system.[3]

This was also the era of the Scramble for Africa. In southern Africa, Britain was the dominant power, waging a series of wars from 1879 to 1902 in which all the remaining independent black African kingdoms, Coloured polities, and Afrikaner republics were conquered or subjugated. (The term "Black Africans" refers to the indigenous, agrarian, Bantu-language-speaking peoples. "Coloureds" in southern Africa means the "brown" people, largely of mixed race, Afrikaans-speaking and Christian, many descended from slaves and servants. "Afrikaners" (or "Boers") are a local white group, largely descended from Dutch, French, and German settlers, and distinct from local "English" whites. "Indians" refers to people of South Asian descent, who lived in South Africa in significant numbers, many arriving as indentured laborers.)

Almost the whole region was carved into British territories, aside from German South West Africa and Portuguese-ruled Angola and Mozambique. The centerpiece was the Union of South Africa, into which the older British Cape and Natal colonies were merged with conquered Afrikaner republics and black African polities by a 1909 Act of the British Parliament. The Union was a racist state: all the formal elements of parliamentary democracy were in place, but almost all voters were white men, no person of color could sit in Parliament, and a battery of laws enforced racial discrimination and subjugation. The Union's total population in 1911 was just short of 6 million: 4 million black Africans (67 percent), 1,276,000 whites (21 percent), 525,000 Coloureds (9 percent), and 150,000 Indians (2.5 percent). The majority of parliamentarians represented Afrikaner landed interests, British and South African "English" capital, and powerful interests like the military. Black Africans were largely governed as subjects, through a system of indirect rule administered by black chiefs in the 10 percent of land set aside as "native reserves."[4]

Subordinate to Britain economically and politically, South Africa had dominion status like Australia, Canada, and New Zealand, entailing substantial autonomy within the imperial framework. Force was central to the formation and consolidation of the new South African state, and every prime minister before the apartheid Parliament of 1948 was a former general. Mining, farming, and manufacturing were largely in (white) private hands, but the state soon dominated communications and transportation, including rail, and played a growing role in electricity, heavy industry, and forestry.

The Working Class: White, Black, and Red

The working class in South Africa was drawn from across the world. White immigration boomed: the white population in the Transvaal republic (later province), site of the gold mines, grew eightfold in this period. White immigrants were largely working class, many (but by no means all) skilled, and came mainly from Britain and Australia. In 1905, 85 percent of white underground gold miners were British-born; in 1921, 59.8 percent of typesetters, 55.8 percent of fitters, and 48.3 percent of carpenters were foreign-born. Large numbers of landless Afrikaners also entered wage labor: often unskilled, they were employed in mines, state industries, and manufacturing, and formed the core of the pool of poor whites.[5]

But cheap Coloured, Indian, and above all black African labor comprised the bulk of the workforce and the bedrock of capitalism. Coloureds, centered in the Cape, were the largest part of Cape Town's proletariat, and included many artisans; they were also important on the Witwatersrand. Indians, concentrated in Natal, were increasingly urbanized, and integral to the Durban economy. A growing population of urbanized and proletarianized black Africans was important across the country.

The biggest battalions of labor were black African migrant men, concentrated in mining, heavy industry, and the docks, in both the private and state sectors. They were cheap and unfree labor, and employed on terms amounting to indenture which made strike action and quitting criminal offences. Subject to an internal passport system (the pass laws), and housed in closed compounds, they returned periodically to rural homesteads, where their families resided, and to which they retired. Imperial war, land dispossession, and colonial taxation generated migrant labor across the region. In 1920, for example, only 51 percent of African miners working in South Africa were locals; the rest were from either Mozambique or British colonies. As in other sectors, divisions between blacks were fostered in the mines, with compounds divided by ethnic group and country of origin, and elements of an ethnic division of labor in place.[6]

The working class in South Africa was, in short, a stratified one, fractured by skill, ethnicity, race, and place of origin, as well as urban versus migrant divisions. Tensions festered within the multi-racial slums that could be found in all the big cities (despite state efforts at creating segregated townships), sometimes flaring into race riots, while ethnic clashes were a recurrent feature of the mines.

The Rise of (White) Labor

By 1913, the Witwatersrand economy employed 195,000 black Africans in mining, 37,000 in domestic service, and 6,000 in factories, workshops, and warehouses; plus 22,000 whites on the mines, 12,000 in industries like building, tramways, printing, and electricity, and 4,500 in rail. Whites, concentrated in urban areas, sometimes reached half of the population of the bigger cities and towns: in 1904, for example, Johannesburg had 155,462 residents, 82,000 of them white.[7]

The urban white working class, concentrated in working-class districts, dominating the skilled trades in the mines, and central to manufacturing and transport, was a potent force. It is hardly surprising, given its large immigrant component, that its politics and traditions were deeply affected by international trends. White workers founded labor unionism in southern Africa. The first two successful unions were formed in 1881 in Cape Town on the British craft model; one, the Amalgamated Society of Carpenters and Joiners, was actually a branch of a British union. American influences were also not unknown—there was, for example, a short-lived effort to form a Knights of Labor branch in Kimberley around 1890—and Australian labor was another important reference.

By the start of the twentieth century, the labor movement's center of gravity had shifted to the Witwatersrand, where the Transvaal Miners' Association (TMA) and the Witwatersrand Trades and Labour Council (WTLC) were formed in 1902. White miners led largely unsuccessful general strikes in 1907, 1913, 1914, and 1922, centered on winning union rights, job security, and wage, health, and other concessions. Steeped in racial prejudice, and fearing replacement by "cheap docile labour," the white unions were isolated from the mass of black workers. There were, however, some efforts to organize the unemployed across racial lines, notably in Cape Town in 1906.[8]

Union weakness, the rise of labor parties in Australia and Britain, and the opening of the electoral road with grants of responsible government and then dominion status to whites, all fostered a turn towards electoral politics. Union-backed candidates ran for office in Johannesburg in 1903 and 1904 and in Cape Town in 1905, and three labor-backed men were elected to the Transvaal parliament in 1907. In October 1909, the South African Labour Party was formed with union backing, winning four seats in the September 1910 South African general elections and capturing the Transvaal provincial government in 1914. It was heavily influenced by the "White Australia" policy, and its program combined social-democratic reforms with demands for race-based job reservation, residential segregation, and Indian repatriation. This "White Labourism" was the main current in South Africa's organized labor movement.

Thunder on the Left

But running against this tide, especially in Cape Town and Johannesburg, was an alternative, revolutionary, socialist current in the white working class. This too was deeply influenced by movements abroad; its founders were mainly Scottish and English immigrants. A notable example was Glasgow-born fitter Archie Crawford, a former British soldier, fired from Pretoria's state-run railway works in 1906 for agitation, central to a 1907 unemployed movement in Johannesburg, and elected to the Johannesburg municipality on a pro-labor ticket, he launched a General

Workers Union (GWU) in 1908.[9] Moving steadily leftwards, Crawford formed the Johannesburg Socialist Society with comrades like Irish-born Mary Fitzgerald of the TMA. The Society campaigned unsuccessfully for the Labour Party to adopt a clear socialist goal, and stress class, not color. Crawford was one of two unsuccessful Socialist Society candidates in the 1910 general elections. His dismal performance (eight votes) was at least partly because of his racial politics. Rather than avoid the color issue, as some historians have charged, he was notorious for opposing segregation in his campaign: "more than one time it looked like he would be torn to pieces by an ignorant mob."[10]

Crawford and Fitzgerald produced the *Voice of Labour* beginning in 1908. Initially a free bulletin for the GWU, it survived that union's 1909 collapse, and was relaunched as a "weekly journal of socialism, trade unionism and politics." Claiming a circulation of 2,000, it reached "the leading Socialists of Durban, Kimberley, Bloemfontein, Pretoria, Cape Town and Johannesburg." The first sustained local socialist paper, it provided a forum for activists dissatisfied with craft unions and the Labour Party.[11]

The content was eclectic, with articles on everything from "Good government: a noble legacy," to pieces by local anarchists such as Henry Glasse and Wilfred Harrison. Correspondents like Glasse promoted syndicalism and "direct action ... over politics—I mean of course Parliamentary politics." The paper carried extracts from publications such as the *Bulletin international du mouvement syndicaliste*. Daniel De Leon and the syndicalism of the American SLP, which had local supporters, was also prominent, articulated by figures like Philip Roux, an unorthodox Afrikaner chemist who fought for the British in the Anglo-Boer War (1899–1902). Roux saw One Big Union as the alternative to craft divisions, colonialism, and militarism. He was close to Jock Campbell, a "Clydeside Irishman, a self-educated working man," who "had long ceased to work at his trade and now lived for and on the movement," and who was reputedly the "first socialist to make propaganda amongst the African workers."[12]

Hostility to craft unionism, the Labour Party, and White Labourism became defining features of the left network that emerged around the *Voice*, and these traits would be integral to the syndicalist current that emerged within it. Crawford, for example, insisted socialist ethics recognized no color bar, and called segregation "foolish in the extreme." "It is useless for the white worker to kick his coloured brother slave." Segregation schemes could never halt the capitalist drive for cheap labor. Glasse similarly argued that white workers, in fighting class battles "independent of the coloured wage slaves—the vast majority," exhibited "idiocy."[13]

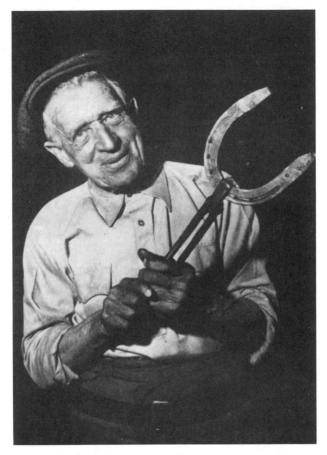

Andrew Dunbar, blacksmithing at 80 years of age, in 1960. From Ivan L. Walker and Ben Weinbren, *2000 Casualties: A History of the Trade Unions and the Labour Movement in the Union of South Africa* (Johannesburg, South Africa: South African Trade Union Council, 1961).

In 1910, South Africa experienced a rise of syndicalist and IWW ideas and a "vigorous reaction" against "parliamentary reform." One spur was British syndicalist Tom Mann's February–March tour of Durban, Cape Town, Johannesburg, and Pretoria. Besides promoting syndicalism, Mann publicly insisted that black and Coloured workers be included in unions, contrary to claims by later writers.[14]

Mann also persuaded the WTLC to set up an Industrial Workers' Union (IWU) in March 1910, for workers outside existing unions. It attracted a few small organizations of bootmakers, bakers, confectioners, and tailors, and held Sunday night meetings at Johannesburg's Market Square. In June,

IWW enthusiasts associated with the *Voice* network "captured the organisation and put it on a proper basis." Tom Glynn, an Irishman and ex-soldier who worked on the Johannesburg tramways, played a key role. An ardent Wobbly who first encountered the IWW in New Zealand, he became IWU general secretary. Glynn worked closely with Andrew Dunbar, a Scottish-born blacksmith who led a large strike on the Natal railways in 1909 before moving to Johannesburg, where he worked at the tramways and joined the Socialist Society.[15]

Glynn and Dunbar helped reposition the IWU as a "class-conscious revolutionary organisation embracing all workers regardless of craft, race or colour," renaming it the Industrial Workers of the World (South African Section). The IWW-SA identified itself with the Chicago wing of the American IWW, but it is not clear when this affiliation was formally recognized on the American end. While some unions like the bootmakers left over these changes, the local IWW-SA union made rapid gains at Johannesburg's City and Suburban Tramways Company.[16]

The tramways had been taken over by the municipality in June 1904, and electrified beginning in February 1906. Trams were housed and re-paired adjacent to the main municipal power station in Newtown. By 1914, they carried 30 million passengers. Like other state operations, trams were segregated. The lines were concentrated in white working-class areas and the multiracial slums of western and central Johannesburg; the tram-yards and adjacent President Street power station were located in the central slums. In January 1911, the trams had 351 white workers: 1 waiting room attendant, 5 pointsmen, 11 inspectors, 150 drivers, and 153 conductors, not counting the workers doing maintenance at the yards, or the employees at the power station, which also employed black migrants.[17]

Meanwhile, the SLP formed in Johannesburg in March 1910. Vaguely described in the historical literature as "Marxist," it was actually a De Leonist grouping, and maintained especially close links to the SLP in Scotland. It ran meetings at Market Square on Sunday mornings, selling a "steady stream of journals and pamphlets" from Glasgow and Chicago, including the *Socialist* (also sold through shops) and the American *Weekly People*. Besides Roux and Jock Campbell, key figures included John Campbell (a Scot), Charlie Tyler (an English immigrant and unionist), and Israel Israelstam (a Lithuanian immigrant with ties to the local General Jewish Labor Bund).[18]

Changes, meanwhile, were afoot at the *Voice*. Crawford left South Africa in late 1910 for a 13-month trip around the world, and was replaced as editor by an unidentified Capetonian syndicate called "Proletarian."

"Proletarian" advocated "an organisation of wage-workers, black and white, male and female, young and old," along with "a universal general strike preparatory to seizing and running the interests of South Africa." Under his editorship, the *Voice* carried extensive IWW material, weekly "IWW notes" by Dunbar and Glynn, and regular SLP contributions. Gone were the pieces on "Good government." Instead, the *Voice* commissioned a series on IWW history, "specially written for *The Voice*" by Chicago IWW general secretary Vincent St John. The Chicago IWW, in turn, carried reports on the IWW-SA, often sourced from the *Voice*, in its *Industrial Solidarity* and *Industrial Worker*. The *Voice* never lost its open character, but its emphasis shifted, as contemporaries noted, "From Trades Unionism and Politics ... to Industrial Unionism and Direct Action."[19]

International divisions between the rival IWW trends represented by St John's "Chicago IWW" and De Leon's "Detroit IWW" played out locally, between local militants embedded in different international networks—the IWW-SA, connected to the Chicago IWW, and the South African SLP, connected to the Glasgow SLP. Criticizing the IWW-SA for "physical force" politics and "Anarchism," SLP members would arrive at the IWW-SA's Sunday night meetings at Market Square armed with party literature and claiming to represent the "true" IWW. Heated exchanges took place, and Dunbar complained that the SLP members, not the employers, had proved the union's "most bitter opponents." However, the divide was not absolute: some SLP members also belonged to the IWW-SA.[20]

On the Left Track: Strikes in Johannesburg

While both the SLP and IWW-SA invested much energy in propaganda, the IWW-SA was qualitatively different from other small leftist groups such as the SLP and the Socialist Society—it was also a functioning union. For Glynn, the "other socialisms" confined their activities to propaganda or elections, but the IWW aimed, "here and now," to forge "the structure of the new society within the shell of the old" through revolutionary unions. Ruling-class power did not lie in the control of ideas or parliament, but in control of capital. Thus, revolution required workplace organizing. "Proletarian" agreed: the "parliamentary gas-house" was the "biggest farce imaginable." This outlook helps explain why a May 1911 effort to unite the IWW-SA, SLP, Socialist Society, and groups in Cape Town and Durban into an "Industrial Freedom League" lasted only a few weeks.[21]

The IWW-SA did not care much about that debacle, as it was preoccupied with the tramways. Workers' earlier efforts to organize had failed. However, they made a breakthrough with the iww-sa. Authoritarian management was a major grievance, and the spark was resentment at the impending return of an unpopular inspector, J. E. Peach. On Monday January 16, 174 conductors and drivers signed a letter of objection: this was rejected by management in a notice on Thursday January 19, stating that Peach was resuming duties immediately. Glynn organized a meeting that day, which sent another protest letter. Then, at a further meeting at 1 a.m. on Saturday, he successfully proposed a strike, despite opposition by Labour Party supporters.[22] When the morning shift started, strikers rallied at the yards, wearing "bits of red ribbon" and listening to speakers standing on a repairing car. The trams sat idle as strikers' representatives negotiated with "emissaries of the municipal authorities" in an empty tram and police watched the scene of "perfect peace." Glynn and others also approached the power station workers, who agreed to shut down the plant in solidarity at 1 p.m.[23]

Management initially promised a commission to look into the complaints, then when this failed, threatened arrests using the 1909 Industrial Disputes Prevention Act, which forbade lockouts and strikes without 30 days' notice and imposed a lengthy conciliation process. Glynn, in typical Wobbly style, retorted: "You can start with me and my place will be filled in regular order until we are all in jail, and who then will run your cars?" And to his fellow strikers, he enthusiastically declared: "For every leader seized there are half a dozen here to take his place."[24]

His confidence was well founded: employers were not obliged to recognize unions, but workers in strategic positions in industries such as transport, mining, and power could defy the law. At eight minutes to 1 pm, the municipality capitulated: the power station was then the only functioning municipal power and gas supplier.

The mayor appeared in person, promised a commission of enquiry, and also that Peach would not be an inspector. Excited workers drove the tramway cars out in a long "triumphant procession," to "a cheering and sympathetic populace." Almost the entire tramway workforce then enrolled in the iww-sa, forming a Municipal Industrial Union presided over by Glynn. Crawford exaggerated slightly by claiming iww-sa membership began to "exceed that of any other working class organisation," but it compared favorably with the 800 members reported by the tma in 1909.[25]

May 1911 saw a second tramway strike, centered on the terms and composition of the municipal commission. Wobblies Glynn and W. P. Glendon organized a boycott of the hearings at the City Hall, fearful of a biased inquiry. The first hearing on April 25 was blockaded by iww-sa pickets, and an employee who arrived to give evidence was assaulted. The inquiry exonerated Peach, but Glynn and Glendon were subsequently summoned by the tramways management and dismissed for their role in the strike and assault.[26]

The night of Thursday May 11 witnessed "reckless speeches" at the tramway sheds. A strike resolution was again passed. Glynn declared that the IWW-SA "recognised no Industrial Disputes Act," but "claimed the right to cease work when they wanted." The dismissals were an attack on "the cause of the working class." The crowd, growing to 500, proceeded to Market Square, where Dunbar stated they must all be willing to go to jail. The SLP's John Campbell also spoke, stressing that "any little differences between the labour organisations" must be "brushed on one side in times of trouble."[27]

At 5 a.m. Friday morning, the IWW-SA struck, demanding that no January strikers be penalized, and that Glynn and Glendon be reinstated. This time, however, the municipality was well prepared: police surrounded the power station, patrolled the streets, and protected scabs. They also arrested Glynn and Glendon. Fitzgerald led a contingent of women with red banners through police lines to physically block the trams, and workers erected barricades in Market Square. On Saturday, the municipality invoked an archaic 1894 Transvaal proclamation banning public meetings of six or more, and mounted police started to clear the Square. Police clashed with demonstrators and arrested speakers, one after the other, including Dunbar, John Campbell, and Glynn (who had just been released on bail).[28]

Public sympathy was high: even the Labour Party rallied behind the strikers. On Sunday, mounted police charged protestors, leading to more injuries and arrests. The police also arrested two IWW-SA members, William Whittaker and T. Morant, for allegedly placing dynamite on the lines. The dynamite story, plus the ongoing disruptions in transport, helped shift public feeling. Within the week, the trams were running. Seventy workers were fired. Glynn got three months hard labor. Blacklisted, he left South Africa in late 1911 and became a leading figure in the Australian IWW.[29]

The IWW-SA remained active, holding successful meetings at Market Square. It gained new notoriety in October 1911 and January 1912 when Dunbar, Glynn, Fitzgerald, Morant, and others formed a "Pickhandle Brigade" which broke up election meetings for councilors blamed for smashing the May strike. The Voice and the IWW meanwhile organized a solidarity campaign for Whittaker and Morant, whose trial dragged on into 1912. The case collapsed when it emerged that a government agent, John Sherman, had laid the dynamite. Whittaker successfully sued for damages. A Whittaker-Morant Fund operated into June 1912 to aid the men.[30]

When the Pretoria railways hired Sherman in late 1911, the IWW organized protest meetings at Pretoria's railway works, addressed by Crawford, Dunbar, Fitzgerald, Glynn, and others, with some support from the Amalgamated Society of Railway and Harbour Servants. An IWW-SA "Pretoria Local" attracted workers, including "some of the Railway Servants Association," and government fears that the tramway strikers' open defiance of labor law might spread onto the railways seemed likely to be confirmed. The IWW also spread to Durban, the country's principal port, where "comrade Webber" from Johannesburg played an active role. A "very forceful and fluent" speaker, specializing in "blood-curdling class war propaganda," he spoke on "Syndicalism versus socialism" at the Town Gardens, championing direct action and presenting the Labour Party as class traitors.[31]

A Party Affair

But the "revolutionary methods" of the Pickhandle Brigade did little to advance on-the-job organizing. The shattered Municipal Industrial Union collapsed by early 1912. A further blow to the IWW-SA came from Crawford. He returned in November 1912, took control of the *Voice*, ousted "Proletarian," and campaigned for a united socialist party. He had long advocated a socialist party for "political action," and its "absolute corollary," parliamentary action, and clearly envisaged the IWW-SA as the proposed party's union wing. An admirer of the Socialist Party of America (SPA), he insisted it was closely allied to the IWW, and that the IWW, in turn, supported parliamentary action. St John fired off an angry letter repudiating Crawford's misrepresentations, but it only appeared in the *Voice* in mid-1912.[32]

Texts favoring elections and party-building flooded the *Voice*. In January 1912, Crawford announced a socialist unity conference set for Easter. The SLP, seeing an opportunity to promote its positions, cautiously expressed support. Dunbar, Morant, and "Proletarian" remained resolutely hostile to elections and parties. But Crawford had supporters in the now-smaller IWW-SA. In September 1911, Dunbar managed to defeat "a certain few" in their "attempt ... to take the IWW management." In early 1912, the union seemed on the verge of splitting. The Crawford faction secured a resolution that "the IWW instruct its speakers not to attack the Socialist Party." It triumphed at the February 7 IWW-SA conference. Dunbar, the best remaining organizer, was expelled for his anti-party positions, and a newly elected committee, headed by Fitzgerald, took over. On April 7, Easter Sunday, the

United Socialist Party (USP) was founded. The IWW-SA attended, but made no substantive contribution. The USP identified with the Socialist Second International, and its rules were "modelled after ... the American S.P."[33]

The short-lived USP was not a success. Webber clashed with others in the USP in Durban. SLP members tried to win over the USP and, failing, withdrew to work within the Labour Party. USP affiliates ignored party work and directives. IWW-SA organizing, beyond Whittaker-Morant solidarity, died off. The USP focused instead on lectures, elections, and international solidarity campaigns. Articles in the *Voice* complained of apathy in the USP and its slow growth, and of growing problems in financing the *Voice*. By the time of the great 1913 general strike on the Witwatersrand, the IWW-SA, the USP, and the *Voice* were dead.[34]

Conclusion

The great majority of local Wobblies and syndicalists before 1915 were radical, English-speaking white immigrants, mostly from Britain. Immigrant radicals like Dunbar, Glasse, Harrison, Israelstam, and John Campbell played a pivotal role in promoting syndicalism locally. Local radical circles were linked into transnational radical networks through the movement of people and the international circulation of the radical press, and developments like the 1908 IWW split into "Chicago" and "Detroit" sections had an important local impact.

This is not to say that developments abroad were simply copied locally. Radicals in South Africa had to grapple with the challenges of a social order substantively different from that of, for example, Australia, Britain, or the United States. They developed innovative tactics, such as the women's contingent in the May 1911 strike, and the subsequent Pickhandle Brigade, as well as innovative analyses, crucially through the critique of White Labourism.

Noting a growing number of strikes by black workers with approval, local Wobblies and syndicalists condemned the "idiocy" of restricting the labor movement to a minority of workers, all white and most of them artisans. The "'aristocrats' of labour" "attitude of superiority" was damned as "grotesque." All workers, the radicals insisted, had a common interest in the abolition of the cheap labor system, its cause, capitalism, and its defender, the state. Either workers of color would secure the same rights and wages as the whites, or the "stress of industrial competition" would compel the whites to "accept the same conditions of labour as their black brethren." Meanwhile, nationalism was rejected as the politics of "small capitalists."[35]

There is certainly no evidence for later claims, pioneered by Communist Party writers but repeated by scholars, that groups like the IWW-SA or SLP capitulated to white racism. What set these radicals apart from the mainstream labor movement was precisely their principled commitment to the formation of an inter-racial labor movement.[36]

This position alienated the majority of the white working class, yet the radicals also proved unable to build a base amongst black African, Coloured, and Indian workers. The obstacles to organizing these workers were, of course, substantial, including racial divisions, language barriers, repressive labor laws, restrictions on free movement, and the closed compound system. But the obstacles were not insurmountable: several craft and general unions in Cape Town had organized skilled Coloured workers by 1910, and in 1917, syndicalists formed the first unions among Indians in Durban (the Indian Workers' Industrial Union) and black Africans in Johannesburg (the Industrial Workers of Africa).

The radicals' failure was a political one, a failure to translate *principled* opposition to racism and national oppression into *mobilizing* African, Coloured, and Indian workers around class *and* national *and* racial demands. Condemning White Labourism and advocating One Big Union across racial barriers were essential, but inadequate, steps. They had to be turned into a specific *strategy* to organize workers of color, who were obviously not being drawn in by the *Voice* or through Sunday meetings on the Market Square, or through speeches at the tramyards or railway works. And organizing had to involve more than abstract denunciations of capitalism: it had to involve addressing the reality of national and racial oppression and grievances, by fighting against racist laws like the pass system, through the One Big Union.

The big syndicalist breakthroughs from 1915 onward happened when organizations like the International Socialist League and the Industrial Workers of Africa built a large base of black, Coloured, and Indian support through precisely these methods. However, the ideas of the *Voice*, IWW, and SLP helped lay the ideological basis for this breakthrough—and veterans like John Campbell, Dunbar, and Tyler all became central players in that second syndicalist wave.[37]

Notes

1   Nancy Clark and William H. Worger, *South Africa: The Rise and Fall of Apartheid*, 3rd edn. (London/New York: Routledge, 2016), p. 14.
2   Riva Krut, "The making of a South African Jewish community," in Belinda Boz-

zoli (ed.), *Class, Community and Conflict: South African Perspectives* (Johannesburg, South Africa: Ravan, 1988), pp. 135–7.

3 Eric Hobsbawm, *The Age of Capital, 1848–1875* (London: Weidenfeld & Nicolson, 1975), p. 66 *et seq.*

4 The Cape retained a qualified franchise system, allowing a minority of black African and Coloured men to vote, while excluding poor whites. Natal had a similar but far more restrictive system. Population data is from Pieter van Duin, "South Africa," in Marcel van der Linden and Jürgen Rojahn (eds.), *The Formation of Labour Movements, 1870–1914* (Leiden, Netherlands: Brill, 1990), p. 640 n. 38.

5 Clark and Worger, *South Africa*, p. 14; Bill Freund, "The social character of secondary industry in South Africa, 1915–1945," in Alan Mabin (ed.), *Organisation and Economic Change* (Johannesburg, South Africa: Ravan, 1989), p. 85; Elaine Katz, *The White Death: Silicosis on the Witwatersrand Gold Mines, 1886–1910* (Johannesburg, South Africa: Witwatersrand University Press, 1994), p. 65; David Ticktin, "The origins of the South African Labour Party, 1888–1910," PhD thesis, University of Cape Town, 1973, pp. 259–60; Wessel Visser, "Die Geskiedenis en Rol van Persorgane in the Politieke en Ekonomiese Mobilisasie van die Georganiseerde Arbeiderbeweging in Suid-Afrika, 1908–1924," PhD thesis, University of Stellenbosch, 2001, p. 2.

6 David Yudelman and Alan Jeeves, "New labour frontiers for old: black migrants to the South African gold mines, 1920–85," *Journal of Southern African Studies* 13:1 (1986): 123–4.

7 D. Hobart-Houghton, *The South African Economy* (Cape Town, South Africa: Oxford University Press, 1964), pp. 106, 116; Lis Lange, *White, Poor and Angry: White Working Class Families in Johannesburg* (Aldershot, UK and Burlington, Vt.: Ashgate, 2003), pp. 12, 39, 84.

8 Darcy Du Toit, *Capital and Labour in South Africa: Class Struggle in the 1970s* (London: Routledge, 2010), pp. 85–94.

9 Jack Simons and Ray Simons, *Class and Colour in South Africa, 1850–1950* (1969; reprint edn. London: IDAF, 1983), p. 150.

10 *Voice of Labour* (hereafter *VOL*), September 11, 1909, September 16, 1910. Claims against Crawford were popularized in Communist Party works like Simons, *Class and Colour*, pp. 141, 154, and repeated in the likes of E. Katz, *A Trade Union Aristocracy: A History of White Workers in the Transvaal and the General Strike of 1913* (Johannesburg, South Africa: Institute for African Studies, 1976), p. 273.

11 *VOL*, August 14, 1909.

12 *VOL*, August 14, 1909, July 1, September 15, 1910, January 26, 1912; Eddie Roux and Win Roux, *Rebel Pity: The Life of Eddie Roux* (London: Rex Collings, 1970), pp. 3–7; *VOL*, December 18, 1909; Robert Cope, *Comrade Bill: The Life and Times of W. H. Andrews, Workers' Leader* (Cape Town, South Africa: Stewart Printing, n.d.), p. 93.

13 *VOL*, December 4, July 31, October 23, 1909, January 26, 1912.

14 Cope, *Comrade Bill*, pp. 108–10; Katz, *Trade Union Aristocracy*, p. 271; van Duin, "South Africa," pp. 648–9.

15 Katz, *Trade Union Aristocracy*, pp. 299–301; Archie Crawford, "The class war in South Africa," *International Socialist Review* (hereafter *ISR*) (August 1911), p. 30.

16 *VOL*, July 22, 1910; Katz, *Trade Union Aristocracy*, p. 301; *Solidarity*, October 1, 1910.

17 Charles van Onselen, *Studies in the Social and Economic History of the Witwatersrand, vol. 1: New Babylon* (Johannesburg, South Africa: Ravan, 1982), p. 183; "The strength of the staff," *The Star*, undated press clipping, in "Tramway strike Johannesburg. Report by Inspector White Labour on above dated 24 January 1911," Mines and Works, SAB89127355, National Archives, Pretoria (hereafter "Tramway strike").

18 "Socialist Labour Party of South Africa—Incorporation," Department of Law, file LD 1806–AG677/10, National Archives, Pretoria; Roux and Roux, *Rebel Pity*, p. 7; *VOL*, November 24, 1911; *The Socialist*, October 1910, January 1912, June 1912; Ivan Walker and Ben Weinbren, *2,000 Casualties: A History of the Trade Unions and the Labour Movement in the History of South Africa* (Johannesburg, South Africa: South African Trade Union Council, 1961), p. 319.

19 *VOL*, October 27, 1911, January 12, 1912; *Industrial Solidarity*, October 1, 1910; *Industrial Worker*, March 7, 1912; *VOL*, August 4, 1911.

20 *The Socialist*, April 1912; *VOL*, July 21, November 24, 1911; Katz, *Trade Union Aristocracy*, p. 301.

21 *Solidarity*, October 1, 1910; *VOL*, February 9, 1912.

22 Crawford, "The class war," p. 81; Inspector of White Labour to Acting Secretary for the Mines, 24 January 1911, in Mines and Works, SAB89127355, National Archives, Pretoria; Katz, *Trade Union Aristocracy*, p. 303.

23 "Tram strike," *The Star*, undated press clipping in "Tramway strike"

24 Crawford, "The class war," p. 82; "Tram strike," *The Star*.

25 "Tram strike," *The Star*; Crawford, "The class war," p. 82; *VOL*, February 9, 1912; Katz, *Trade Union Aristocracy*, pp. 176, 252.

26 Inspector of White Labour (R. Shanks) to Acting Secretary for the Mines, May 12, 1911, in "Johannesburg tramway employees strike. Special report by Inspector of White Labour," MM331/11, National Archives, Pretoria (hereafter "Johannesburg tramway"); *Solidarity*, June 24, 1911; Crawford, "The class war," p. 83; *Transvaal Leader*, May 12, 1911, "Tramway crisis," press clipping in "Johannesburg tramway."

27 Inspector of White Labour (R. Shanks) to Acting Secretary for the Mines, May 12, 1911; "Trams today," *Rand Daily Mail*, May 12, 1911, press clipping, both in "Johannesburg tramway."

28 *Transvaal Leader*, May 12, 1911; Walker and Weinbren, *2,000 Casualties*, p. 30; Appendix in "Johannesburg tramway."

29 Katz, *Trade Union Aristocracy*, p. 307; *VOL*, January 12, 1912.

30 *VOL*, June 16, September 15, 1911; Archie Crawford, "The Pick Handle Brigade," *ISR* (February 1912), pp. 494–5; Katz, *Trade Union Aristocracy*, pp. 301–12.

31 *VOL*, November 24, December 1, 1911; Inspector of White Labour to Acting Secretary for Mines, Department of Mines, SAB89128145, National Archives, Pretoria; Tommy Boydell, "Foreword," in Wilfred Harrison, *Memoirs of a Socialist in South Africa, 1903–47* (Cape Town, South Africa: Stewart, 1948), p. xii; *VOL*, June 14, 1912.

32 *VOL*, October 27, 1911, February 9, 16, March 1, June 21, 1912.

33 For example, *VOL*, September 15, 1911, January 12, 19, February 2, 9, 23, April 12, 1912.

34 *VOL*, June 21, 28, 1912; Archie Crawford, "Socialist Party progress in South Africa," *ISR* (July 1912), p. 50; *VOL*, November 8, 1912; Roux and Roux, *Rebel Pity*, p. 8; *VOL*, May 24, 31, June 7, 21, July 12, 19, September 13, November 1, 1912.

35 For example, *VOL*, October 27, 1911, January 26, 1912.

36 For example, Katz, *Trade Union Aristocracy*, p. 320; van Duin, "South Africa," p. 649.

37 See Lucien van der Walt, "Bakunin's heirs in South Africa: race, class and revolutionary syndicalism from the IWW to the International Socialist League," *Politikon* 30:1 (2004): 67–89; Lucien van der Walt, "Revolutionary syndicalism, communism and the national question in South African socialism, 1886–1928," in Stephen Hirsch and Lucien van der Walt (eds.), *Anarchism and Syndicalism in the Colonial and Postcolonial World, 1870–1940: The Praxis of National Liberation, Internationalism and Social Revolution* (Leiden, Netherlands: Brill, 2010), pp. 33–94; Lucien van der Walt, "Anarchism and syndicalism in an African port city: the revolutionary traditions of Cape Town's multiracial working class, 1904–1931," *Labor History* 52:2 (2011): 137–71.

19

Tramp, Tramp, Tramp:
The Songs of Joe Hill Around the World

Bucky Halker

Of the many people who passed through the Industrial Workers of the World (iww) and achieved some degree of public recognition, only songwriter Joe Hill (1879–1915) realized mythic status and international fame, albeit posthumously. Hill long ago ascended to the upper realm in the pantheon of protest songwriters, and his music continues to be sung and heard in areas far removed from the United States. The legendary Woody Guthrie and Pete Seeger understood Hill's esteemed stature and acknowledged his importance. They included three Hill songs in their collection *Hard Hitting Songs for Hard-Hit People*, and Guthrie wrote a song entitled "Joe Hillstorm."[1] That workers like Joe Hill even wrote songs is testament to the human will to create art under difficult circumstances. Nevertheless, working-class songwriting was an established tradition in the American labor movement decades before Hill arrived in the United States.[2]

The process by which Hill became mythical is well documented.[3] By contrast, the process by which his songs moved beyond the United States to other parts of the world remains largely untold. This essay explores that remarkable story, offering a description and an examination of the international migration and dissemination of Hill's songs.

Joel Emmanuel Hägglund (or Hillström) was born in Gävle, Sweden, to a musical, religiously devout, financially comfortable family. But after his father, a railroad conductor, died from occupational injuries in 1887, the family fell into poverty. Joel and his siblings had to leave school and work. Joel survived severe tuberculosis, and after his mother's death in 1902, he and his brother departed for the United States. Hill spent several years as a migrant laborer, learned English, got involved in labor struggles, joined

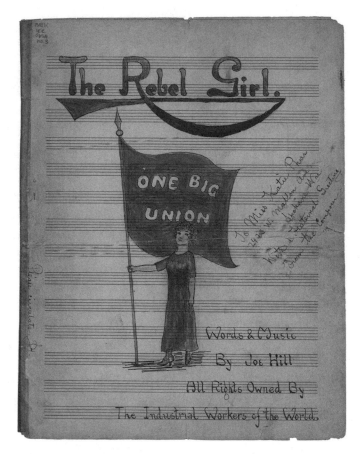

Rebel Girl (1915), Joe Hill's original cover art drawn while in prison in Salt Lake City, Utah, and inscribed to Katie Phar, a 10-year-old Wobbly singer in Spokane

the IWW around 1910, and fought in the Mexican Revolution. He served as an organizer, cartoonist, and journalist for the IWW, but it was his songs that garnered him a real audience. Hill's clever lyrics, often laced with humor, irony, slang, sarcasm, and seriousness of purpose, typically were set to the tunes of hymns and popular melodies of the day. They appeared in Wobbly publications and found use at strikes, demonstrations, and meetings.[4] Unfortunately, Hill traveled to Utah, where the IWW and the Western Federation of Miners had a base. He became an easy mark for the authorities, who charged him with the murder of a grocer and his son. Despite the lack of evidence or motive, a jury found him guilty in a few hours and the state executed Hill by firing squad on November 19, 1915.

Before his death, Hill's songs circulated widely in working-class ranks.

Though he wrote only a few dozen, a handful of which featured original music, pieces like "The preacher and the slave," "Mr. Block," and "Scissor Bill" found regular service in Wobbly battles between 1911 and 1915. Like other IWW songs, workers memorized Hill songs, transported them around the country, and put them to use on street corners and picket lines, passing them along to others. Both sociologist Nels Anderson and poet Carl Sandburg made note of Wobbly and Joe Hill songs in their path-breaking early folksong collections.[5]

As an itinerant himself, Hill played a first-hand role in spreading his music across borders. In 1911, Hill was one of dozens of Wobblies who joined the forces of the Partido Liberal Mexicano in Tijuana, Mexico, where his singing helped boost morale, and that same year he and a fellow Wobbly took passage to Hawai'i, a beehive of Wobbly activity among Chinese, Korean, Filipino, Hawaiian, and other workers. While working in Hilo, Hill composed "A trip to Honolulu," an original instrumental piece, and played his and other Wobbly songs for his fellow workers, though little evidence survives about his time in Hawai'i.[6] A year later, Hill traveled to Canada's Frasier River region during a strike against the Canadian Northern Railroad. Borrowing the tune from the 1905 hit song "Where the River Shannon flows," Hill penned "Where the Fraser River flows" and found an immediate audience with strikers and other Canadian workers. His work continued to resonate with them after his death.[7]

Other factors proved more important in the migration of Hill's songs than his own travels. Wobbly activity around the world, especially the wide distribution of IWW newspapers and the *Little Red Songbook*, proved vital in the transmission process.[8] The persistent efforts of individual artists and activists also proved essential. The spread of technology, from 78 rpm recordings to the internet, cannot be underestimated either.[9] Today, Hill's music has a wider audience and artist base than ever, though this growth rarely has been steady.

Joe Hill's songs in Sweden illustrate the process and factors that influenced the pace of dissemination. During his life, Hill wrote songs only in English, interacted minimally with Swedish-Americans, and made no effort to publish in his homeland, where he remained virtually unknown. A posthumous Swedish pamphlet on his life appeared in 1916, and from 1924 to 1940 articles, pamphlets, and songbooks in Sweden featured his songs.[10] Though a biography by Hill's early translator, Ture Nerman, appeared in 1951, the next flourish of music activity came during the counter-culture years when younger Swedish musicians (re)discovered Hill.[11] Monica Nielsen, Finn Zetterholm, Fred Akerström, Mats Paulson, Oskar

Joe Hills Sånger: The Complete Joe Hill Songbook (Stockholm: Prisma, 1969). Translations from English to Swedish by Jacob Branting.

Norrman, Pierre Ström, Hayati Kafe, Anders Granell, and the group Mora Träsk all recorded Hill songs between 1969 and 1980.[12] Jacob Branting also provided the first nearly complete Swedish collection of Hill's songs in 1969.[13] Ingvar Söderström's biography of Hill, a two-hour TV special in 1970, and a feature film in 1971 further aided the cause. In 1980, Sweden even issued a Joe Hill commemorative postage stamp.[14] The Swedish spotlight shone brightly on Joe Hill.

In Australia and New Zealand, the Joe Hill song tradition preceded Sweden's. From its 1905 beginning, the IWW garnered support on ocean freighters and in international ports. Australia and New Zealand were key points on international shipping lanes and for the migrant labor economy, on and off the seas (see Chapters 10 by Burgmann, 11 by Derby, and 12 by Clayworth). Little wonder that IWW ideas and songs sailed the seas to both countries. Remember, too, that IWW founder and leader William Trautmann was born in New Zealand, and miners from there appeared at the Wobblies' founding convention. Branches appeared as early as 1907 in Sydney, Australia and 1908 in Wellington, New Zealand, and newspapers and songbooks followed. Prior to being repressed for anti-conscription and anti-war efforts during the First World War, the union held considerable influence among labor in the two regions and engaged in a number of key strikes. Participants recalled singing and hearing Joe Hill and Wobbly songs at events.[15] IWW member and editor Tom Barker (see de Angelis, Chapter 16) reported: "We used to have really good singing at our meetings. We usually picked up the Salvation Army crowd when they had finished and marched away."[16] During the prosecution of Wobblies in Perth, Australia, the prosecutor read Hill's "Casey Jones, the union scab" as evidence of conspiracy. Reports in 1926 stated workers sang "The preacher and the slave" during a demonstration in Wooloomooloo Bay, Australia. In 1929, Labor members sang that and other Wobbly songs in Canberra at the Parliament House![17]

Unfortunately, documentation of Hill's musical legacy from 1915 to 1950 in other parts of the world remains less complete than for Sweden, Australia, New Zealand, Canada, and the United States. Wobbly and Hill songs certainly traversed the seas to England, where a songbook appeared in 1917. John Hasted, a physicist, activist, and figure in the British folk revival of the early post-Second World War period, recalls that Wobblies "began to contribute songs that travelled back across the Atlantic and became popular in Britain" in labor circles, and specifically cites the songs of Joe Hill.[18] The widespread distribution and influence of IWW songbooks and newspapers, many in languages other than English, also demands highlighting. Among Finnish Americans, Wobbly songs found a large audience. Various editions of Finnish-language IWW songbooks printed by *Työmies* (*The Worker*) in Superior, Wisconsin made their way to Finland in the First World War era. Well-known Finnish-born tenor Hannes Saari (1886–1967) even recorded Hill's "Workers of the world, awaken!" for Columbia Records in New York City in 1928.[19]

Nevertheless, Hill's musical legacy was anything but solidified outside North America by 1930, until Paul Robeson helped change this situation.[20] From 1949 to the 1960s, Robeson's international music tours regularly featured "I dreamed I saw Joe Hill," unquestionably keeping Hill in the limelight. Robeson sang the song, written in 1936 by Earl Robinson with lyrics from a 1930 Alfred Hayes poem, to great fanfare in 1949 in Edinburgh, Moscow, London, Stockholm, and elsewhere, as well as during his 1960s performances in Australia and New Zealand. Robeson's concerts and recordings released in England after 1952 made the song a "standard" among the left, elevated Hill into the mythical realm, and established Hill songs as "sing-alongs" in the early British folk revival. One scholar argued that the Hayes-Robinson composition "is possibly the best known Labour song in Britain."[21] The story in Scotland and the German Democratic Republic (GDR) followed parallel paths. Subsequently, younger musicians inspired by Robeson felt compelled to locate the songs of Joe Hill and record his work.[22]

Joan Baez inspired audiences and musicians in similar fashion some 20 years later. Her recording of "I dreamed I saw Joe Hill," from the legendary Woodstock music festival in 1969, found its way to literally millions of listeners and viewers, thanks to LPs and a film dedicated to the festival. Some people no doubt asked, "Who the hell is Joe Hill?" The performance inspired musicians like myself to seek out IWW songbooks and learn Hill songs. Of course, one factor in the reception given to Baez and Hill was the thirst for new music by counterculture participants. If 1950s hipsters searched out old blues and jazz recordings, the counterculture put a premium on opening minds to new music and politics. As a result, Hill's international audience picked up in the 1970s and continued unabated thereafter.

In Finland, the Turku Student Theatre group recorded an LP of Hill songs and the Hayes-Robinson piece, released in 1975 as *Joe Hill in Lauluja*. The group included members of the Red Carnation Band, whose repertoire featured Hill songs. Although the LP reportedly sold poorly, the group's version of "Antti Mäntii" ("Casey Jones") received radio play.[23]

Perhaps the most unusual region in Joe Hill's musical journey has been Germany. Germans and German-Americans, including Trautmann (the son of German immigrants to New Zealand) and the United Brewery Workers' Union, played a key role at the IWW's founding. But it was an American NATO soldier named Victor Grossman (originally Stephen Wechsler) who swam the Danube to the German Democratic Republic (GDR) in 1952, and did much to promote Hill's legacy there. After defecting, Grossman helped introduce American folk and protest music to East Germany's discontented youth. From 1958 until 1990, he promoted Hill's music and "I dreamed I saw Joe Hill" in the GDR. He and Canadian folksinger Perry Friedman featured Hill songs in tours in the 1960s, and years later Grossman joined Earl Robinson on tour, highlighting Robinson's famous song. Grossman

Never Forget Joe Hill (Venice: FuoriPosto, 2015), Book and CD project by Rino De Michele and the artist collective ApARTe° in collaboration with the Instituto Ernesto De Martino and Macacorecords.

also often aired Robeson's recording and other Hill songs on his radio program. He acted as Pete Seeger's interpreter during the singer's 1976 and 1986 tours, and wrote articles on Hill for GDR publications. In his books *Von Manhattan bis Kalifornien: Aus oder Geschichte der USA* (1974) and *If I Had a Song: Lieder and Sänger Der USA* (1990), Grossman included Hill's story and music. He recently recalled a largely forgotten opera staged in East Berlin in 1970 entitled "Joe Hill," a work written by leftist British composer Alan Bush which featured Joan Baez in performance. Joe Hill may not have had much traction in the Federal Republic of Germany, but in the GDR he was certainly known.[24]

Not surprisingly, the hundredth anniversary of Hill's execution brought an outpouring of concerts, plays, and recordings around the world. The

Joe Hill, *The Little Red and Black Songbook* (Paris: Éditions CNT-RP, 2015).

IWW and an army of musicians—including Tom Morello, Joan Baez, Ziggy Marley, and myself—organized nationwide tours and other events in the United States.[25] In Germany, musician Elmar Wigand began to play Joe Hill songs in 2006 after joining the IWW in Cologne and performing with the Grand Industrial Band, later reformed as the Overall Brigade. Wigand and his musical mates recorded two Hill songs, including Wigand's German translation of "The tramp."[26] Italian artist Rino de Michele conceived, edited, and published *Never Forget Joe Hill* (2015), a remarkable multi-language graphic history and CD. It features de Michele's artwork and musicians performing Hill and Hill-inspired songs in Swedish, Catalan, traditional Roman dialect, and Italian. The artist also involved himself in Hill tribute performances in Italy and Sweden.[27]

The most unique recent Hill rendering can be found in the Austrian "radical Eurodance" duo Circle A's 2015 version of "The preacher and the slave." More conventional folk and punk rock recordings feature versions of Hill and Hill-inspired material by a range of performers including the Wobbly Brothers, 12 Dead in Everett, and Chumbawamba from England, Fred Alpi in France, and Lucas Stark and Jan Hammarlund of Sweden. Hammarlund, Stark, Alpi, the Overall Brigade, Bethan Wellbrook, Billy Bragg (England), Ewan McVicar (Scotland), Tom Morello (USA), and Stina K (Sweden) all performed Hill concerts, while Hammarlund and American artists David Rovics, George Mann, Sons of Hanzo, Anne Feeney, and myself ventured to foreign lands in 2015–16, spreading his songs.[28]

Today, Joe Hill's musical legacy continues to expand. Workers may no longer carry his songs in their heads, riding the rails and loading ocean freighters, but the IWW songbook remains a strong seller and musicians continue to discover Hill anew. Others learn Hill songs from tracks on the internet. Word of mouth and learning from other musicians, however, remains a critical part of the process, anchoring Hill's music in the folk tradition. Which artists in what countries are performing or recording Joe Hill songs may change, but on any given night someone will surely be singing, "You'll get pie in the sky when you die, that's a lie."

Acknowledgments

The author would like to thank those who contributed comments, advice, and information: Toni Wright Halker, Nathan Moore, Marcus Cederstrom, Lucas Stark, Jan Hammarlund, Fred Alpi, Elmar Wigand, Donald Dalton, Stina K, Billy Bragg, Juha Niemalä, Jim Leary, Mark Gregory, Jared Davidson, Victor Grossman, Derek Schofield, Ron Cohen, Alexis Buss, Jon Bekken, Rino de Michele, Ewan McVicar, Bethan Wellbrook, Pete Pesonen, Hilary Virtanen, Phillip Deery, and Teresa Pitt.

Notes

1   Woody Guthrie, Alan Lomax, and Pete Seeger, *Hard Hitting Songs for Hard Hit People 1967* (New York: Oak Publications, 1967). "Joe Hillstrom" appears in Woody Guthrie, *American Folksong* (New York: Oak Publications, 1961).

2   Philip Foner, *American Labor Songs of the Nineteenth Century* (Urbana, Ill.: University of Illinois Press, 1975); Clark "Bucky" Halker, *For Democracy, Workers and*

God: Labor Song-Poems and Labor Protest, 1865–1895 (Urbana, Ill.: University of Illinois Press, 1991).

3 William M. Adler, The Man Who Never Died: The Life, Times, and Legacy of Joe Hill, American Labor Icon (New York: Bloomsbury, 2011); Franklin Rosemont, Joe Hill: The IWW and the Making of a Revolutionary Workingclass Counterculture (Chicago, Ill.: Charles H. Kerr, 2003).

4 Joyce Kornbluh, Rebel Voices: An IWW Anthology (Chicago, Ill.: Charles H. Kerr, 1998); IWW, I.W.W. Songs, Joe Hill Memorial Edition (1917; reprint Chicago, Ill.: IWW, 2015).

5 Nels Anderson, The Hobo: The Sociology of the Homeless Man (Chicago, Ill.: University of Chicago Press, 1923); Carl Sandburg, The American Songbag (New York: Harcourt, Brace 1927).

6 Rosemont, Joe Hill, pp. 82–3, 94–9.

7 Rosemont, Joe Hill, pp. 89–93; Kornbluh, Rebel Voices, pp. 134–5; Edith Fowke, "Labor and industrial protest songs in Canada," Journal of American Folklore 82 (January 1969): 34–50; Archie Green, David Roediger, Franklin Rosemont, and Salvatore Salerno (eds.), The Big Red Songbook (Chicago, Ill.: Charles H. Kerr, 2007).

8 Green et al., The Big Red Songbook.

9 Archie Green, Only A Miner (Urbana, Ill.: University of Illinois Press, 1972).

10 Rosemont, Joe Hill, pp. 73–6. Songbooks include Sånger av Joe Hill (Stockholm: IWW #510, 1924), Sånger av Joe Hill, 3rd edn. (Stockholm: IWW #510, 1924), Socialistiska Kampsånger (Stockholm: Bokförlaget Brand, 1925), I.W.W.'s Sångbook (Stockholm: IWW #510, 1928 [and 1929]), Frihetssånger (Stockholm: Storms Förlag, 1940).

11 Ture Nerman, Arbetarsångaren Joe Hill: Mördare Eller Martyr? (Stockholm: Federativ, 1951).

12 Rosemont, Joe Hill, p. 76.

13 Jacob Branting, Joe Hills Sånger: The Complete Joe Hill Song Book (Stockholm: Prisma/FIBS Lyrikklubb, 1969). See also the 1973 edition by politician-writer Enn Kokk.

14 Rosemont, Joe Hill, p. 76.

15 Verity Burgmann, Revolutionary Industrial Unionism: The Industrial Workers of the World in Australia (Melbourne, Vic.: Cambridge University Press, 1995); Peter Steiner, Industrial Unionism: The History of the Industrial Workers of the World in Aotearoa (Wellington: Rebel Press, 2007); Jared Davidson, Remains To Be Seen: Tracing Joe Hill's Ashes in New Zealand (Wellington: Rebel Press, 2011); and Davidson's interview, "Wobblies Down Under," www.radionz.co.nz/national/programmes/wobbliesdownunder/audio/2500435/wobblies-down-under (accessed January 24, 2017).

16 Davidson, Remains To Be Seen, p. 27.

17 Mark Gregory, "Joe Hill centenary and IWW songs in Australia," Labour History 109 (2015): 169–74; Gregory, "Sixty years of Australian labor union songs: the Australian folk revival and the Australian labour movement since the Second World War," MA thesis, Macquarie University, Sydney, NSW, 2003, http://unionsong.com/ebooks/thesismg.pdf (accessed January 24, 2017).

18 John Hasted, *Alternative Memoirs* (Shiptongreen, Itchenor, UK: Greengates Press, 1992), p. 41.

19 Email correspondence with Pete Pesonen, Finnish Labor Archive; Työväen Arkisto in Helsinki; Juha Niemalä in Turku; and Hilary Virtanen at Finlandia University, Hancock, Michigan.

20 Martin Duberman, *Paul Robeson: A Biography* (New York: New Press, 1995).

21 Samuel Richards, "Joe Hill: a labour legend in song," *Folk Music Journal* 4 (1983): 367–84.

22 Duberman, *Paul Robeson*; Gregory, "Joe Hill," 174; email correspondences with Jared Davidson on Robeson in Wellington and Walter Grossman on the GDR.

23 Information on Turku Student Theatre and 1975 LP *Joe Hill in Lauluja* in possession of author. Their version of "Casey Jones" is at https://www.youtube.com/watch?v=kRpAHbg6PBo (accessed January 24, 2017).

24 Victor Grossman, *Crossing the Water: A Memoir of the American Left, the Cold War, and Life in East Germany* (Amherst, Mass.: University of Massachusetts Press, 2003); Grossman, *Von Manhattan bis Kalifornien: Aus oder Geschichte der USA* (Berlin: Kinderverlag, 1974); Grossman, *If I Had a Song: Lieder and Sänger der USA* (Berlin: Lied der Zeit Musikverlag, 1990). Grossman provided this author with information on American folk music in the GDR.

25 Joe Hill Roadshow, https://joehill100.com/ (accessed January 24, 2017); Tom Morello and Friends, Joe Hill Centenary Concert, www.troubadour.com/event/988019-tom-morello-friends-los-angeles/ (accessed January 24, 2017).

26 Email correspondence with Elmar Wigand.

27 Email correspondence with Rino de Michele, book/CD project in possession of author.

28 Email correspondence with Lucas Stark and Jan Hammarlund (Sweden), Fred Alpi (France), the Overall Brigade/Elmar Wigand (Germany), Bethan Wellbrook (England), Ewan McVicar (Scotland), Sons of Hanzo/Donald Dalton (USA), Stina K (Sweden) and Billy Bragg (England). Information on additional artists garnered from the author's involvement in Joe Hill concert tours marking the hundredth anniversary of his execution.

Index

12 Dead in Everett (band), 296

A
Abad de Santillán, Diego, 122n36
Abraham Lincoln Battalion *see*
    International Brigades
AFL, 3, 4, 6, 7, 39, 76, 91, 93, 105–6;
    and 1936 maritime workers' strike,
    217; in Canada, 146, 148, 151; and
    International Secretariat of National
    Trade Union Centers, 106–7;
    membership of, 46, 107; in Mexico,
    116, 130; and WFM, 144
African Americans, 76, 96; in IWW, 6,
    7, 95
agricultural workers, 5, 7, 53, 61, 75–6,
    77–8, 174, 228
Agricultural Workers Organization *see*
    AWO
Ahlqvist, J. W., 150
Akerström, Fred, 290
Algoma Central Railway, 145, 146, 148,
    149
Allen, José, 135
Almereyda, Miguel, 46
Alonen, Gust (or Gus), 35
Alpi, Fred, 296
Altman, Jack, 220
ALU, 32
American Federation of Labor *see* AFL
American Labor Union *see* ALU
Amsterdam (Netherlands), 70, 113
anarchism, 29–40; of Har Dayal, 64–65;
    "opacity" of, 29, 39; in Sweden, 31,
    265; of Leo Tolstoy, 35; transnation-
    alism of, 29; *see also*
    anarcho-syndicalism, anarchists
anarchist newspapers, 32; *Agitator*, 39;
    Blast, 35; *Cultura Obrera*, 38; *Cultura
    Proletaria*, 92, 100; *Demonstrator*,
    39; *Emancipator*, 39; *Free Lance*, 39;
    Free Society, 32; *Freedom* (England),
64; *Fuerza Consciente*, 96; *Germinal*
    (Mexico), 133; *Germinal* (USA),
    33; *Kakumei*, 37; *Mother Earth*, 39;
    Questione Sociale, 30, 32, 33, 90;
    Regeneración, 38, 65, 78, 82, 126, 134;
    Revolución, 78; *Rodo*, 37; *Spanish
    Revolution*, 220; *Temps Nouveaux*
    (France), 39; *Tribuna Roja* (Mexico),
    127; *Voz de la Mujer*, 78
anarchists: French, 33, 52, 66; German,
    32; and Ghadr movement, 69, 70–1;
    Italian, 30–1, 83, 90, 91, 135–136;
    in IWW, 29–40, 95–96; Japanese, 75;
    Mexican, 77–8, 80–4, 86, 124–37;
    Spanish, 89–100, 127; US, 75; *see also*
    anarchism, anarcho-syndicalism
anarcho-syndicalism: in IWW, 32, 93–4,
    213; of MTW, 213; of Syndicalist
    League of North America, 34; of
    Thomas J. Hagerty, 33; of UORW,
    37; *see also* anarchism, anarchists,
    syndicalism
Anderson, Ed, 93
Anderson, Nels, 290
Andrà, Antonio, 32
Andreytchine, George, 35–6, 37
anti-racism, 4, 6–7, 186–7, 271–2, 276,
    283–4
Arab Spring, 13
Aragon (Spain), 224
Argentina, 37, 110; *see also* IWW foreign
    administrations and branches
Arnesen, Eric, 97
Astoria (Wash.), IWW in, 63
Atlantic Coast Marine Firemen, 92, 93,
    94
Auckland (New Zealand), 187, 191–2,
    194–6, 206, 208
Australia, 291–2; demographics of IWW
    members, 173–4; *see also* IWW foreign
    administrations and branches
AWO, 7

Azuara, Aurelio V., 71, 84

B
Baez, Joan, 293, 294, 295
Baja California (Mexico), 38, 39
Baker, James, 157
Bakunin Institute, 65–6
Baltimore (Md.), iww in, 36, 215
Barker, Tom, 170, 173, 180, 192, 194–7,
    208–9, 254–61, 292
Baron, Aron, 37
Baron, Fanya, 37
Baronio, Ninfa, 30
Barry, Jack, 144
Batchewanna River (Canada), 149
Bazora, Florencio, 3, 32
Belinsky, S., 110–11
Bengali revolutionaries, 60
Berenguer, José, 92
Bergman, Gustav, 35
Berkeley (Calif.), 37, 65, 71
Berkman, Alexander, 35, 70
Berlin (Germany), 63, 69, 110, 118
Bisbee (Arizona), 9, 76, 84, 127
Black Tom Island (New Jersey), 53
Bodine, George, 93
Boer War, 173, 241, 276
Bolsheviki (newspaper), 135
Borås (Sweden), 265
Borghi, Armando, 108, 109
"boring from within," 34, 39, 151
Borrán, Jorge D., 127
Boston (Mass.), iww in, 215
Boston Creek (Ont.), 143
Boyd, Frederick Sumner, 50
Brage, Secundino, 92
Branting, Jacob, 291
Brazier, Richard, 143
Bridgeport (Conn.), iww in, 4
Brissenden, Paul F., 10, 15
British Columbia, 151, 156–65
British Empire, 60–2, 66–9, 71
Bronx (N.Y.), 242, 243; iww in, 35
Brooklyn (N.Y): iww in, 38, 92; Port, 95
Brotherhood of Timber Workers (btw),
    6

Browder, Earl, 115
Bruno, Giordano, 148
Buccafori, Vincent, 55 n7
Budapest (Hungary), 107
Buddhism, 65
Buenos Aires (Argentina), 255–7
Buhle, Paul, 13, 17
Bush, Alan, 294
Butte (Mont.), 8, 250

C
Cabrera, Vicenta, 127, 132
California, iww in, 52–3; Commission
    of Immigration and Housing, 52, 53
Calles, Plutarco, Elías, 136
Cama, Bhikaiji, 68–9
Caminita, Ludovico, 30–31, 33–4, 38
Canada see iww foreign administrations
    and branches
Canadian Copper Company, 144, 145
Canadian Northern Railroad, 290
Canadian Pacific Railroad, 140
Canberra (Australia), 292
Cannon, James P., 115
Cárdenas, Lázaro, 136
Carmona, Rafael, 77
Casa del Obrero Mundial see com
Casas, Laurent, 39
Casement, Roger, 248
Castilla Morales, José, 38
Cecil-Smith, Edward, 221
Cedervall, Frank, 119
Centro Femenil de Estudios Sociales, 127
cgt (France), 41–6, 197; anti-militarism,
    47–8, 51, 52 106, 109; and First World
    War, 52–3; membership, 46, 107, 258;
    Second International, 106; Toulouse
    Congress of, 44, 50
cgt (Mexico), 116, 129
Chandra, Ram, 60
Chang, Kornel, 59, 62, 71
Chaplin, Ralph, 35, 44, 50, 71, 78
Chester, Eric, 11
Chicago (Ill.), 242–3; anarchists in,
    32, 36, 37–8; iww in, 37; Chicago
    Debater's Club, 32

Chile *see* IWW foreign administrations and branches
Chinese revolutionaries, 63
Chumbawamba (band), 296
cigar workers, 38
CIO, 220
Circle A (band), 296
Clan na Gael, 243, 248, 249
Clarke, Tom, 242, 248
Cleveland (Ohio), IWW in, 213–4
CNT, 98, 107, 109; and IWA, 114; and IWW, 90, 212, 213–14, 216, 219, 224
Cobalt (Ontario), 140; IWW in, 143–4
Cobalt Miners' Union Local 146 (WFM), 143
collective bargaining, 151–2
Colorado labor wars, 47
COM, 124, 127, 128
Comintern, 10, 109, 110, 111, 120, 121, 130, 131, 257–8
Communist International *see* Comintern
Communist Party of Canada, 151
Communist Party of Mexico (Partido Comunista Mexicano) *see* PCM
Communist Party USA *see* CPUSA
Confederación General de Trabajadores *see* CGT (Mexico)
Confédération Générale du Travail *see* CGT (France)
Confederación Nacional del Trabajo *see* CNT
Confederación Regional Obrera Mexicana *see* CROM
Congress of Industrial Organizations *see* CIO
Congress of South African Trade Unions, 18
Conlin, Joseph R., 11, 15
Connolly, James, 239–51
construction workers, 5, 128, 163, 171, 174–5, 265
Copper Cliff (Ont.), IWW in, 144, 145, 147, 149
Coria, Pedro, 78, 84, 127, 133, 134
Corna, Joseph, 32, 39
Cornelissen, Christiaan, 108

Cornell Dramatic Club, 53
Corvallis State Agricultural College, 63
CPUSA, 10, 11, 34, 35, 85, 115, 212, 214–16, 218–22, 225
Crawford, Archie, 275–6, 278, 280, 282
criminal anarchy law (N.Y.), 35
criminal syndicalism laws, 8, 53, 85
CROM, 131, 132
Cuba, 95, 97; anarchists in, 38, 90
Cultura Proletaria collective, 92; *see also* anarchist newspapers

D

Das, Taraknath, 71
Dayal, Har, 38, 63, 64–7, 69–71
Debs, Eugene V., 3, 205
De Leon, Daniel, 3, 4–5, 8, 77; at 2nd IWW convention, 33–4; expelled from IWW, 34; influence in Australia, 168; influence in Canada, 159; influence in Ireland, 241; influence in New Zealand, 190; in South Africa, 276, 278–9; *see also* SLP, WIIU
DeMaio, Tony, 222
Denjiro, Kotoku (Shusui Kotoku), 37, 75
Department of Justice (USA), 70
DeShazo, Peter, 12
Detroit (Michigan), IWW in, 213
"Detroit" IWW *see* WIIU
DeVoy, John, 248, 249
Díaz, Porfirio, 133
Dickey, Walter, 217
Diogones, 66
direct action, 4, 33, 46, 48, 49, 54, 67, 68, 80, 93, 106, 108, 114, 117, 120, 151, 205, 209, 247, 249, 250, 257, 259, 266, 276, 279, 282
Direct Action and Sabotage (Trautmann), 49
Doña Cecilia (Mexico), 126
Dorame, Rosendo, 77
Downing, Mortimer, 75, 85, 164
dual-card union members, 179–80, 215, 225
dual unionism, 107, 110, 111
Dublin lockout, 239–51

Dublin Socialist Club, 241
Dubofsky, Melvyn, 11, 12, 14
Duluth (Minn.), iww in, 142
Dumas, Michel, 33
Dunbar, Andrew, 277–9, 281–4
Duncan, James, 107
Durruti Column, 218

E
Edwards, A. S., 16
Eley, Geoff, 268
Elk Lake (Ont.), wfm in, 143
Emerson, Laura Payne, 81
Engels, Friedrich, 240
England, 111, 257–8
Ernesto, Frank, 92
Espionage Act (usa), 8, 9, 36, 53, 60, 71,
   96, 133
Esteve, Pedro, 3, 33, 90–91, 93, 95
Ettor, Joseph, 6, 48, 77–8, 160
Eugene V. Debs Column, 218–19
Everett (Wash.): iww in, 228, 230–5;
   Massacre, 8, 230–5

F
fascism, 118, 212, 217–18, 224
Federación Obrera Marítima
   (Argentina), 213
Federación de los Obreros del
   Transporte de América see fota
Feeney, Anne, 296
feminism see women's emancipation
Ferrer i Guardia, Francisco, 65, 67, 81,
   92, 128
Figueroa, Anselmo, 77
Filguerira, José, 94
Finnish Organization of Canada see foc
Finnish Socialist Federation (usa) see
   fsf
Finnish socialist newspapers: Raivaaja,
   146; Sosialisti, 142, 147, 148, 153n10;
   Toveri, 146; Työkansa (Canada), 142,
   144, 145, 146, 147; Työmies, 146;
   Vapaus (Canada), 147
Finnish Socialist Organization of
   Canada see fsoc

First World War, 16, 124; Australia,
   180–2, 208, 254–5; European syndi-
   calism, 108–9; France, 52–3; Ireland,
   240, 248, 250; New Zealand, 292;
   United States, 8, 53, 71, 75, 235
Fisher, Harry, 222
Fisher, Joe, 122n36
Fitzpatrick, John, 249
Fletcher, Ben, 7, 71, 97, 186
Flores Magón, Enrique, 65, 71, 126,
   134
Flores Magón, Ricardo, 65, 78, 82, 99,
   126, 134
Flynn, Elizabeth Gurley, 160, 239, 242,
   243, 249; and Lawrence strike, 48; and
   Paterson silk strike, 30; and sabotage,
   50
foc, 151
Foner, Philip, 11
Ford, Dick, 52
Fort William (Ont.), fsoc in, 146
Foster, William Z., 34, 107, 239, 249
fota, 95
Fox, Jay, 32, 34, 39
Francisco Ferrer School, 50
Franco, Francisco, 120
Fraser River railway strike (1912), 146
Fraternity of the Red Flag, 65
Freijomil, Dionsio, 95
French railroad strike (1910), 45–6, 48,
   49
French syndicalism, 10, 16, 34, 45, 54,
   107–8; see also cgt (France)
Frenette, Edith, 160, 228–35
Fresno (Calif.), 79, 80, 82, 83
Fresno Labor League, 37
Fridell, Folke, 264
Friedman, Perry, 293
Friends of the Soviet Union, 199
fsf, 35, 142
fsoc, 142, 144–50
Furuseth, Andrew, 92

G
Gale, Linn A., 130, 131
Gale's Magazine, 130

Gallaher, Thomas, 245
Gallo, Firmino, 30
Gambs, John S., 10
Gammons, Ed, 69
garment workers, 36, 45, 243
Gates, John, 222
Gävle (Sweden), 288
GDR, 292, 293, 294
Geiser, Carl, 221–2
General Recruiting Union (IWW), 148
general strike, 4, 33, 106, 144, 159–60
George, Harrison, 112, 115
George Washington Battalion *see* International Brigades
German Democratic Republic see GDR
German Revolution (1918–19), 150
Germany: alleged support of US radicals, 53–4, 70; and France, 48; Ghadr movement in, 60; and sabotage, 54, 58n73; syndicalism in, 107, 109, 110; trade unions in, 106; *see also* GDR, IWW foreign administrations and branches
Germinal group, 127, 132
Ghadar-di-Gunj (songbook), 69
Ghadr (newspaper), 68
Ghadr movement, 38, 59–71
Giovannitti, Arturo, 6, 48, 50, 78
Glasgow dock workers' strike (1889), 49
Glasse, Henry, 276, 283
Globe (Ariz.), 76, 78
Glynn, Tom, 173, 278–82
Goldfield (Nev.), 4, 76
Goldman, Emma, 35, 38, 39, 70–1, 134
Golin, Steve, 30
Gompers, Samuel, 106–7, 130, 156
Gonne, Maude, 241
González, Herminio, 38
Goodwin, Robert C., 33
Gorelik, Anatolii, 36, 37
Gosden, Robert, 159–60
Gothenburg (Sweden), 263–4
Gowganda (Ont.), WFM in, 143
Gramsci, Antonio, 268–9
Granell, Anders, 291
Grant, Donald, 171–2

Grays Harbor (Wash.), IWW in, 146
Great Railroad Strike of 1877, 47
Green, Archie, 164
Gregory, Thomas Watt (US Attorney General), 70
Grossman, Victor (Stephen Wechsler), 293, 294
Grupo Hermanos Rojos, 135
Gruppo Diritto all'Esistenza, 30
Guabello, Alberto, 30
Guabello, Paolo, 30
Gulf Coast, IWW on, 215–6
Guthrie, Woody, 288
Gutiérrez de Lara, Lázaro, 77, 81

H
Hagerty, Thomas J., 32, 33, 241
Halsted, Robert J., 12
Hammarlund, Jan, 296
Hansen, Fred, 119, 217, 225
Hanson, Albert, 117
Hardie, Keir, 241
Hardy, George, 109–11
Harp (newspaper), 242
Harvard University, 65
Hasted, John, 292
Hawai'i, 32, 65
Hayes, Alfred, 293
Haymarket riot, 32
Haywood, William D. "Big Bill", 133, 239; in Canada, 143; Charles Moyer on, 143; in Chicago IWW trial, 54; Founding Convention, 3; in Lawrence strike, 48, 243; in Leavenworth Penitentiary, 71; Murder trial, 5; and Paterson silk strike, 30; and Russian Revolution, 109; on sabotage, 45–7; in Southern California, 79; in Soviet Union, 36; and SPA, 5, 49; visits Europe, 45–6, 245; visits Vancouver, 160
Heatherton, Christina, 71
Hegel, Georg Wilhelm Friedrich, 65
Helsingborg (Sweden), 265
Hervé, Gustave, 46, 47, 52
Heslewood, Fred, 106

Hibbing (Minn.), 142
Hickey, Patrick Hodgens, 204–9
Hill, Joe (Joel Emmanuel Hägglund
   or Hillström), 13, 148, 160–1, 249,
   288–96
"Hindoos," 61
Hinduism, 65
"Hindu–German conspiracy" trial, 60
Hindustan, 59, 60, 66
Hitler, Adolf, 118
"Hoboes," 75, 174–7, 267
Hollinger Mining Company, 144
Holtville (California), 76, 78, 82, 83
Home (Wash.), 39
Hopkinson, William C., 66
House Un-American Activities
   Committee (USA), 224
Hughes, Langston, 264
Huppunen, John, 148
Hussey Hall (Sault Ste. Marie), 148

I
ICA, 247, 250
Immigration Act of 1903 (USA), 70–1
Independent Labor Party (Ireland), 241
India, 63; see also Hindustan
India House, 64
Industrial Disputes Investigation Act
   (Canada), 144
industrial unionism, 4, 113, 117, 144, 157
Industrial Workers Club of Chicago, 33
Industrial Workers of the World see IWW
ILA, 216–17, 222
insurrectionary politics, 60–1
International Brigades, 218–24
International Federation of Trade
   Unions, 109
International Longshore and Warehouse
   Union, 215
International Longshoremen's
   Association (AFL) see ILA
International Seamen's Union (AFL) see
   ISU
International Secretariat of National
   Trade Union Centers, 106–9, 121; see

also International Federation of Trade
   Unions
International Socialist Review, 45, 144
international syndicalist congresses,
   107–8, 110, 113
International Working Men's
   Association see IWA
IRB, 242, 248, 250
Irish Citizen Army see ICA
Irish Republican Brotherhood see IRB
Irish republicans, 71
Irish Socialist Republican Party see ISRP
Irish Transit and General Workers
   Union see ITGWU
ISRP, 241
ISU, 89, 91, 92, 93, 94, 95, 96, 213,
   215–17, 220
Italian anarchists, 6, 17, 30, 32, 38,
   135–6
Italy, 114
ITGWU, 245
IWA, 35, 112, 113–20, 212, 213–14
IWW: anarchists in, 29–40, 216; anti-
   colonialism, 66–71, anti-militarism,
   53, 67–8; centralization vs.
   decentralization in, 34, 115, 119, 263;
   and communists, 126, 129–31, 136–7;
   conception of sabotage, 44–55; constitution, 3–4, 31, 33–4, 119, 168–9,
   190–1, 206; conventions see entry
   below; and CPUSA, 34, 35, 112, 115,
   214–16, 218–22, 225; decline, 212–14;
   "Emergency Program" faction, 10,
   16, 34, 85, 263; federal trial (Chicago),
   9, 36, 39, 44, 54; and First World War,
   36, 53–4; foreign administrations and
   branches see entry below; free speech
   fights, 5, 75, 79, 80, 82, 83, 242;
   General Defense Committee, 99, 133,
   134; General Executive Board, 33,
   158; and Ghadr movement, 59, 62–70;
   immigrant members see entry below;
   inclusivity and anti-racism, 162–5;
   industrial unionism, 113, 117, 162;
   and international affiliation, 105–21,
   214; internationalism, 33, 66, 67–8,

71, 74, 105–21, 148; membership, 46,
114, 171, 173–4, 213; name, 33, 105,
157–8; newspapers *see* entry below;
nickname, 164, 166; prisoners, 34,
119; relationship to electoral politics
(in Australia), 168–71; repression of,
(in Canada) 150–1, (in USA) 53–4, 71,
84–6, 96–7, 98; scholarship on, 29; *see
also* MTW
IWW conventions: 1905 founding, 3,
32–3, 75, 105; 1906 (2nd), 33–4;
1908 (3rd), 34, 46; 1916 (10th), 36;
1922 (14th), 113–14; 1924 (16th), 34,
115, 213, 263; 1925 (17th), 117; 1932
(20th), 117–18; 1934 (21st), 118–19
IWW foreign administrations and
branches, 3, 8, 12, 14, 105, 115, 116,
117, 119; Australia, 12, 14; Canada, 8,
11, 105, 120, 140–52, 156–65; Chile,
8, 11, 14, 114, 116, 119, 120, 213;
Germany, 213; Mexico, 8, 11, 14, 105,
115, 116, 124–37, 213; New Zealand,
12 ; Russia, 37; Sweden, 8, 14, 116,
213
IWW, immigrant members of (in USA),
6, 29, 32, 74–86, 89–100; Asian, 35,
160; Chinese, 163–4; Finnish, 29, 35,
140–52, 292; French, 39; Hungarian,
4; Italian, 4, 6, 29, 39, 150; Japanese,
37–8; Lithuanian, 36; Mexican, 29, 38;
Russian, 29, 150; South Asian, 62–3,
69–70; Spanish, 29, 213
IWW newspapers, 31, 34–9, 131; circulation, 34; *Cultura Obrera*, 38, 93–94,
95, 96, 97, 99, 100; *Darbiniku Balsas*,
36; *Direct Action* (Australia), 170,
172–3; *General Organization Bulletin*,
119; *Germinal*, 125; *Golos Truzhenika*,
36, 37; *Huelga General*, 84; *Industri–
Arbetaren*, 35; *Industrial Solidarity*,
111, 112, 115; *Industrial Union
Bulletin*, 16, 77, 79; *Industrial Unionist*,
16, 186–7, 193, 195–6, 199; *Industrial
Worker*, 34, 39, 49, 79, 80, 115, 108,
144, 161, 164; *Industrialisti*, 16, 35,
142, 149, 150, 151; *Libertad y Trabajo*,

77, 78; *Liberator*, 38–9; *Luokkataistelu*,
35; *Maoriland Worker*, 189–90, 192–3;
Marine-Arbeiter, 16; *Marinarbetaren*,
16; *New Solidarity*, 36; *Nouseva
Voima*, 148; *Nueva Solidaridad*, 127;
Nya Världen, 35; *Obrera Industrial, El*,
38; *One Big Union Monthly*, 31, 35, 36,
99, 110; *Probuda*, 36; *Proletaras*, 36;
Proletarian, 37–8; *Rabochaia Rech'*, 36;
Rabotnicheska Misul, 36; *Rabotnicheska
Probuda*, 36; *Rabotnik*, 36; *Rebelde*,
84, 96; *Solidaridad*, 38; *Solidarity*, 36,
45, 107, 110; *Sosialisti*, 142, 147, 148,
153n10; Spanish-language, 38, 77;
Työmies, 292; *Union Industrial, La*, 77,
78, 79, 84

J
Japan, 38, 68; Japanese IWW Propaganda
League, 37–8; Japanese Workers'
Union, 37
Jensen, Albert, 265
Jesus Christ, 119
Johannesburg (South Africa), 271–2,
274–82
Johannsen, Anton, 69
Jones, Mary Harris "Mother," 3, 160
Journeymen Tailor's Union (AFL), 32

K
Kafe, Hayati, 291
Kamloops (B.C.) strike (1912), 161–3
Kane, Johnny, 217
Kanellos, Nicolás, 38
Kannasto, Sanna, 148
Kant, Immanuel, 65
Kaur, Gulab, 68–9
Khankhoje, Pandurang, 62–3, 66, 68
King, John (Jack) Benjamin "J.B.," 172,
191–2, 206
Kingsland (N.J.), 53
Kingston Penitentiary (Canada), 150
Klemencic, Andrew "Al," 32, 33, 38,
39
Knights of Labor, 75
Kornbluh, Joyce, 11

Kotoku, Shusui *see* Denjiro, Kotoku
Kropotkin, Peter, 35, 64
Ku Klux Klan, 85
Kuzbas Project (Russia), 259–60

L
Laborers' Protective Union of Ontario, 146
Lahore (India), 62, 69
Lahore conspiracy case, 60
Larkin, Jim, 239–25
Laukys, Juozas, 36
Lawrence "Bread and Roses" strike (1912), 5, 39, 48, 78, 146, 243, 244, 247
Leavenworth Federal Penitentiary, 60, 71, 99, 134
Legien, Carl, 106, 107
Leier, Mark, 151
Lenin, Vladimir, 111, 130, 240
Lessig, Adolf, 30
Levine, Louis, 10, 34
Lewis, Austin, 45, 51
Lindström, Varpu, 141
Little, Frank, 8, 78–79, 80
Little Lady of the Big House (London), 70
Little Red Song Book, 69, 143, 148, 290
London (England), 64, 92
London, Charles, 70
Los Angeles (Calif.), 47, 74–78, 81, 82, 84, 85, 96, 127, 128, 164
Los Angeles Times bombing, 47, 69
Löwy, Michael, 15
Lozovsky, Alexander, 111
Lumber and Saw Mill Workers Union (AFL), 151
lumber workers, 63, 140, 145–6, 149, 151, 164, 174, 265
Lumber Workers Industrial Union (OBU), 151
Lumber Workers Industrial Union of Canada *see* LWIUC
Lumber Workers Industrial Union No. 120 (IWW), 141
Lumbermen and Laborers' Union (AFL), 148

Lundenberg, Harry, 213, 215, 222, 224, 225
LWIUC, 141, 151

M
MacKenzie–Papineau Battalion *see* International Brigades
McGuckin, Henry, 161–2
McNamara brothers, 47
McQuistion, William, 223, 224
Mahler, Herbert, 118
Malatesta, Errico, 90
Malmö (Sweden), 265
Malvido, Gerardo, 97
Mancini, Giuseppe, 148
Mann, George, 296
Mann, Tom, 257–8, 277
Mansonen, Dave, 148
Maori, 186–200; culture, 187, 193–4, 199; language, 186–9, 198; relations with IWW, 193–4; workers, 189–92, 195–8
Marine Firemen, Oilers, and Water-Tenders Union *see* MFOW
Marine Transport Workers Industrial Union (IWW) *see* MTW
maritime workers, 38, 116, 194–8, 212–25, 253–6, 260, 265
Maritime Workers Industrial Union *see* MWIU
Marley, Ziggy, 295
Márquez, Maria, 127
Martignago, Umberto, 148
Martínez, Juan, 92, 93, 96
Martínez, Santiago, 133
Martínez, Tomás, 84
Martinson, Harry, 264
Marx, Karl, 65, 112, 249
masculinity, 177–8, 218
Maximoff, G. P., 37
Mayor, Estado, 221
Mechanic, Julia, 32
Mellinger, Philip J., 76
Merle, Eugène, 46
Mesabi Iron Range (Minn.), IWW in, 35–6, 148

Mexico: Ghadr movement in, 60, 63; Mexico City, 63, 129 Revolution, 38, 63, 75, 83–4, 125, 126, 159, 289; *see also* IWW foreign administrations and branches
MFOW, 91
Michele, Rino de, 295
migratory workers, 3, 5, 7, 61, 75, 174–5, 267
Miller, Fred, 217, 220, 223, 224, 225
miners, 4, 8–9, 37, 76, 79, 90–1, 143–5, 156–7, 159, 168–9, 175–6, 179, 190–2, 206–8, 273–5
Minneapolis (Minn.), 39
Mixed Claims Commission, 54
Mixed Workers' Union (IWW), 145, 146–7
Modern Schools, 65
Mohegan (N.Y.), 35
Mölndal (Sweden), 265; 1932 mill-workers' strike, 268
Mora Träsk, 291
Morello, Tom, 295
Morgan, James, 189
Morris, Virgil, 216, 217, 218, 223, 225
Morrison, Jean, 140
Moscow (Russia), 110, 111, 113
Mosquito (newspaper), 78
Moya, Jose, 29
Moyer, Charles, 144–5
MTW, 7, 95, 97, 98; in 1936 maritime workers' strike, 217; and CPUSA, 214–6, 218–22; global spread of, 213; and IWA, 116–17, 118; in Mexico, 127; and Spanish Civil War, 212–25; in Sweden, 265; and ULO, 220
Muslims, 62
Mussolini, Benito, 135
MWIU, 214–5

N
Narain, Shanti, 64
National Civic Federation, 54
National Industrial Union of Forest and Lumber Workers (IWW), 146
National Maritime Union *see* NMU

National Union of Dock Labourers *see* NUDL
Naval (union), 97
Nazism, 120, 267–8
Neef, Oscar, 225
Nelson, Bruce, 95
Nerman, Ture, 290
Netherlands, 107, 109, 110
New Left, 13
New Orleans (La.), 97–8
New York City, 45, 69; MTW in, 215, 220; port of, 90
New Zealand, 186–200, 204–9, 291–2; Federation of Labor ("Red Fed"), 190–1, 193, 205–7; Socialist Party, 189–90, 192; *see also* IWW foreign administrations and branches
Nielen, Monica, 290
NMU, 215, 220, 222, 225
Norrman, Oskar, 291
Northwestern lumber strike of 1917, 262, 267
Norwood, E., 65
NUDL, 245

O
O'Connell, Daniel, 244
Oakland (Calif.), IWW in, 65, 66
OBU, 133, 134, 151, 239, 242, 251
Occupy Wall Street, 13, 17
Ojeda, Armando M., 84
One Big Union *see* OBU
Ontario (B.C.), IWW in, 140–52
Ontario Provincial Police, 149
Order of the Red Flag, 65
Orders-in-Council (Canada): PC 1003, 151; PC 2381, 150; PC 2384, 150
"Overalls Brigade," 160
Owens, Harry F.: and 1936 maritime workers' strike, 217; on IWA, 119–20, 214–15; and Spanish Civil War, 216, 218, 221–2, 223, 225; and ULO, 220

P
Pacific Connections (Chang), 62
Paivio, Carl, 35

Palokangas, John, 148
Palomares, Fernando, 77–8, 79, 80–1, 82
Panama Canal, 89
Parenti, Luigi, 39
Paris (France), 108, 218; bakers' strike (1906), 49; Commune, 241
parliamentary politics *see* political action
parrhesia, 66–7
Parsons, Lucy, 3, 32, 34, 38, 105, 160
Partido Laborista Mexicano, 132
Partido Liberal Mexicano *see* PLM
Paterson (N.J.), IWW in, 4, 6, 29–31, 33, 90, 92; silk strike (1913), 29–30, 50
Paulson, Mats, 290
Payne, C. E., 115
Pazos, Genaro, 97
PCM, 130, 136, 137
Pequeño Grande (newspaper), 135
Pestaña, Angel, 110
Peukert, Josef, 32
Philadelphia (Penn.), IWW in, 7, 9, 95–8, 213, 215, 225
"Philadelphia controversy," 214, 217
Philippines, 68–9
Phillips, Utah, 164
Phoenix (Ariz.), 74, 75, 77, 82, 83
Phoenix (B.C.), 32, 159
Pinkerton National Detective Agency, 6, 52
Plato, 66
PLM, 15, 77, 78, 80, 126, 134; and Ghadr movement, 63, 65–6; and IWW, 38, 80, 86, 127, 133; in Mexican Revolution, 38, 82, 290; repression of (in USA), 71, 84
political action, 67, 106, 110, 114, 168–71, 208–9, 257–8
Popular Front, 120, 151, 216, 217, 218, 220–4
Port Arthur (Ont.), 146, 148–9
Portland (Ore.), IWW in, 263
Portugal, 118
Pouget, Emile, 44, 49
prefigurative politics, 60–1
Prego, Frank, 98
Prego, José, 98

Prensa (newspaper), 134, 135
private detectives, 144, 217; *see also* Pinkerton National Detective Agency
Profintern, 35, 36, 110–13, 114, 115, 117, 120, 121, 151, 214, 257
Pueblo (Colo.), 32
Puerto Rico, IWW in, 214
Pullman strike (1894), 47
Punjabis, 61, 65

R

race, 11, 13, 18, 62, 75, 80, 156, 160, 162, 163, 165, 187, 189, 196, 198, 247, 249, 272, 274, 275, 278
racism, 4, 6, 76, 164, 260, 284; of AFL, 76, 90; anti-Asian, 4, 61–2, 63, 65, 71, 164, 166n15; anti-black, 6, 97; anti-Maori, 186, 187; of ISU, 96, 213; in South Africa, 273–4, 284
Raddock, Mike, 218, 221, 222, 223
railway workers, 45, 145, 146, 160–3, 174, 265, 281–2
Ramnath, Maia, 62, 69
Rani, Sundar, 64
Ray, Tommy, 213
Raymond, Louis G. *see* Manuel Rey
Read, Pat, 218, 220, 221, 222, 223
Red Carnation Band, 293
Red International Affiliation Committee (IWW), 112
Red International of Labor Unions *see* Profintern
Red November, Black November (Salerno), 12, 29
Red Scare (USA), 71, 98, 134, 161
Redlands (Calif.), 76, 78, 79
Reeve, Charlie, 172–3
Renshaw, Patrick, 11, 12
respectability politics, 67
revolutionary syndicalism *see* anarcho-syndicalism, syndicalism
Rey, Manuel, 95, 96, 97, 99, 100
Rheinholm, Axel, 222
RIC, 247–8
Richards, Hugh R., 110
Riley, Charles, 69

Riordan, John, 32, 33, 157–9
Risto, William, 35, 153n10
Rivera, Diego, 63
Rivera, Librado, 82, 134
Roadhouse, Robert, 143
Robeson, Paul, 292, 293, 294
Robinson, Earl, 292, 293
Rocker, Rudolf, 114, 115, 120
Rosemont, Franklin, 10, 13
Rosenthal, Anton, 85
Rossi, Victor, 148
Rovics, David, 296
Roy, Manabendra Nath, 131
Royal Irish Constabulary see RIC
Russia, 36, 54; IWW members in, 37, 256–9; Revolution (1905), 3, 36; Revolution (1917), 37, 71, 109, 113, 130, 136, 150
Russian anarchists, 36–7; see also Union of Russian Workers of the United States and Canada
Ryan, Albert, 32, 33, 38

S
Saari, Hannes, 292
Saarinen, Oiva W., 141
sabotage, 44–55, 60, 159, 266
Sabotage (play), 53
Sabotage (Pouget), 49, 50
Sabotage Act (USA), 53
SAC, 107, 109, 110, 116, 262, 263–6, 267–9
Sacco, Nicola, 135–6
SAF, 265–9
sailors see maritime workers
Sailors Union of the Pacific (AFL) see SUP
Salerno, Salvatore, 12, 14, 29
Salo, Arthur, 148
San Diego (Calif.), 76, 78, 79, 80; free speech fight, 82, 83, 159
San Francisco (Calif.), 32, 37, 74, 75; Ghadr Party in, 60, 69; IWW in, 39, 220
San Pedro (Calif.), 78, 85
Sandburg, Carl, 290

Sandgren, John (Johan), 31, 35, 36, 110
Sanger, Margaret, 30
Santiago, Myrna, 126
Sanzhur, Yakov, 36
Sarnoff, Lilly (Ellen White), 99
Sault Ste. Marie (Ont.), IWW in, 144, 145, 146, 148, 150
Saxton, Alexander, 76
Schwartz, Stephen, 93
SDPC, 142, 146
Seattle (Wash.), IWW in, 35, 115
Second International, 46; and First World War, 109; and IWW, 105–6; Stuttgart Congress (1907), 69, 106
Sedition Act (USA), 8, 9, 53, 60, 133
Seeger, Pete, 288, 294
Selective Service Act (USA), 96
Shatoff, Vladimir "Bill," 37
Sherman, Charles O., 33, 158
Ship Cleaners' Union (AFL), 217
Shop Stewards movement (UK), 110
Short, Percy, 187–200
Sikhs, 62, 65
silk workers, 30, 33
Silver Centre (Ont.), WFM in, 143–4
Silverman, Ivan A., 219, 224
Singh, Arur, 60
Singh, Balwant, 60
Singh, Ram, 60
SLP: in USA, 3, 4, 15, 33, 76, 77, 78, 241
Smedley, Agnes, 68–9
Smith, Britt, 119
Smith, C. N., 148
Smith, Vern, 112, 115, 122n36
Smith, Walker C., 49–50
Smithville (Minn.), 142
Snellman, Frank, 144
Social Democratic Party of Canada see SDPC
Social Revolutionary Party (USA), 37
Socialist Labor Party see SLP
Socialist League (Ireland), 241
Socialist Party of America, 282 see SPA
Sociedad Pro-Prensa, 95
Söderström, Ingvar, 291

songs, 69, 143, 148, 213; *see also Little Red Songbook*
Sons of Hanzo, 296
Souchy, Augustin, 115
South Africa *see* IWW foreign administrations and branches
South Asian diaspora, 30, 61–6, 68; *see also* Ghadr movement
South Porcupine (Ont.), WFM in, 143–4, 145
South Porcupine miners' strike (1912–13), 144
Soviet Union *see* Russia
SPA, 5, 15, 33, 46, 76, 77, 79, 82, 248; and CPUSA, 220; and sabotage, 48–9, 50; and Spanish Civil War, 218; *see also* Finnish Socialist Federation (USA), socialists
Spanish anarchists: and IWW newspapers, 38; and MTW, 224; *see also* CNT
Spanish Civil War, 120; anarchist militias in, 218; IWW views of, 212, 218, 219–22; *see also* CNT, International Brigades
Spaulding, Bernard "Barney," 216, 220, 225
Speed, George, 75
Spielman, Jean E., 32, 39
Spokane (Wash.), IWW in, 5, 80, 143, 242
Spring-Rice, Cecil, 69
Spring Valley (Ill.), 32
St John, Vincent, 32, 108, 143
St John's College, Oxford, 64
Stanford University, 61, 65
Stark, Lucas, 296
Steele, Ray, 218
Stelton anarchist colony (N.J.), 100
Steunenberg, Frank, 47
Streisant, H., 120
Ström, Pierre, 291
Sudbury (Ont.), 140; IWW in, 144, 145
Suhr, Herman, 52
Sun Yat-sen, 63, 65, 68
Sundstedt, May, 85
SUP, 212, 215, 222, 224, 225

Sveriges Arbetares Centralorganisation *see* SAC
Swasey, George, 121–2n11
Swastika (Ont.), WFM in, 143
Sweden: general strike (1909), 262, 267; syndicalism in, 31, 35, 262–9; *see also* IWW foreign administrations and branches, SAC
Switzerland, 70
Sydney (NSW), 169–70, 172–6, 180, 182, 253–4
syndicalism: "American" (in Sweden) 265–9; anti-militarism of, 108–9; of Ghadr movement, 68; gradualist vs. immediate, 265–9; and IWW, 1–2, 90, 93–95, 108, 113–15, 118, 121; in Paterson, N.J., 30; in South Africa, 271, 276, 284; and the state, 269; *see also* anarcho-syndicalism, syndicalist newspapers
Syndicalist League of North America, 34, 107
syndicalist newspapers: *Arbetare-Kuriren* (Sweden), 264–5, 267; *Arbetaren* (Sweden), 265; *Bataille syndicaliste* (France), 10; *Bulletin international du mouvement syndicaliste* (Netherlands), 108; *Guerre Sociale* (France), 46, 47–8; *Norrlandsfolket* (Sweden), 255; *Vie Ouvrière* (France), 36, 115; *see also* IWW newspapers
Syndikalistiska Arbetare-federationen (Sweden) *see* SAF

T
Taipele, Jaakob, 144
Takahashi, T., 38
Tampa (Fla), IWW in, 38, 89
Tampico (Mexico), IWW in, 84–5, 124–37
Temiskaming and Northern Ontario Railway, 143
temporality of struggle, 266–7, 268–9
Texas, IWW in, 215
textile workers, 5–6, 243, 265, 268
Third International *see* Comintern

Third Period, 151, 214
Thompson, Edward P., 165
Thompson, Fred, 10, 12, 119, 162–3
Thunder Bay (Ont.), IWW in, 141
Tolstoy, Leo, 35
Topp, Michael Miller, 14
Toronto (Ont.), 140
Torttila, August, 148
transnational history, 1–2, 12–14, 18, 29
transnationalism: of IWW, 14, 16–17, 39,
    129, 133, 156–7, 160–3, 165, 171, 197
Transport and General Workers Union,
    245
Trautmann, William, 49, 158, 292, 293
Traven, B. (Ret Marut), 128
Tresca, Carlo, 243
Treviño, Ricardo, 127, 132
Tridon, André, 10
Trotsky, Leon, 37
"Trotskyites," 222, 223
Turcato, Davide, 29, 85
Turku Student Theatre Group, 293

U
Ucha, Antonio, 93
UFCEA, 89, 90
Ukraine, IWW in, 37
ULO, 220
UMW, 3, 32, 91
union contracts, 151, 213–14, 266
Unión de Fogoneros, Cabos, y
    Engrasadores del Atlántico see UFCEA
union dues, 266
Union of Russian Workers of the
    United States and Canada see UORW
Unione Sindacale Italiana, 107–8, 118
United Brewery Workers' Union, 293
United Brotherhood of Carpenters and
    Joiners (AFL), 151
United Fruit Company, 97, 98
United Kingdom see British Empire,
    England
United Laborers (AFL), 76
United Libertarian Organizations see
    ULO
United Mine Workers see UMW

University of California (Berkeley), 61
UORW, 36–7
Uruguay, IWW in, 213
US–Philippines war, 48
Usinger, Lloyd "Sam," 215, 224
USSR see Russia

V
Valadés, José, 129
Välimäki, John, 144
Vancouver (B.C.), IWW in, 66, 160–1
Venhola, Verner, 145, 146–7
Vanzetti, Bartolomeo, 135–6
Velarde, Fernando, 77, 78, 79, 84
Vidal, Jaime, 92–3, 94, 96, 100
vigilantes, 8, 61, 83–5, 156, 206
Vigo, port (Spain), 100
Viita, Nick, 149, 150
Vilariño, José, 96
Villa, Francisco "Pancho," 124
Villareal, Antonio, 82
Vladivostok (Russia), IWW in, 37
Voice of Labour (newspaper), 276, 281–4

W
Wabos (Ont.), IWW in, 145
Wagner, Joseph, 116, 117–18, 119
Waihi Strike (New Zealand), 191–2, 206
Walsh, John H., 97, 160, 164
Walsh, William, 244
Washington state, 61
Watts, Robert Charles, 213, 224
Weber, Devra, 11, 77, 78, 82
Weinberger, Harry, 99
Welinder, Pär Jönsson, 262–9
Wellington (New Zealand), 207–8
Wermich, A. see Wrink, A.
West Coast Sailors (newspaper), 224
West Coast waterfront strike (1934), 216
Western Federation of Miners see WFM
WFM, 3, 4, 5, 32, 47, 76, 77, 79, 91,
    143–5, 157, 159, 169, 204–5, 289
Wheatland hop riot (1913), 7, 51, 83
White, M. E., 32, 33
White labourism, 275–6, 283
Whitehead, Tommy, 161–2

Wigand, Elmar, 295
Wilhelm II, 48
WIIU, 5, 8, 206, 279, 283
Williams, George, 110
Wilson, Fanny, 148, 150
Wilson, John J. (Johan Filsson), 148,
  150
Wilson, Samuel Davis, 217
Wilson, Woodrow, 8, 53
women, 136, 157, 162, 256; emancipa-
  tion, 65, 68; in Ghadr movement,
  68–9; in IWW, 6, 12, 76, 81, 127–8,
  132, 177, 178, 192, 229–31, 245, 247,
  281
Woodbey, George Washington, 76
Wooloomooloo Bay (Australia), 292
Work People's College, 142–3, 145, 147
Workers Defense Union, 99
Workers' International Industrial Union
see WIIU

Workers Prison Relief Committee, 99
Workers' Republic (newspaper), 241
"Wobblies," origin of nickname, 164,
  166; *see also* IWW
Wobbly Brothers (band), 296
World War I *see* First World War
Wrink, A., 32

Y
Yates, James O., 216, 220
Yugantar Ashram, 60

Z
Zafirov, Georgi, 36
Zapata, Emiliano, 63
Zapatistas (Mexican Revolution), 63, 66
Zetterholm, Finn, 290